Examinations are formidable even to the best prepared, for the greatest fool may ask more than the wisest man can answer."

-Charles Caleb Colton

"Put your confidence in us. Give us your faith and your blessing, and under providence all will be well. We shall not fail or falter; we shall not weaken or tire. Neither the sudden shock of battle nor the long-drawn trials of vigilance and exertion will wear us down.

"Give us the tools and we will finish the job."

-W. Churchill 1941 to Roosevelt

This book is dedicated to my husband and children Shreeya, Aryan and Sitara.
To our families and friends in South Africa and United Kingdom
Our Gratitude and thanks to all those who contributed in compiling this book.
A special thanks to my dear friend Gosia Demetriou.
And last but not the least this book is dedicated to our patients, their families, carers and mental health professionals.

CONTENTS

CONTRIBUTORS

Dr Nilofar Ahmed, MBBS, Staff Grade Learning Disability, Milton Keynes, UK

Dr Regi Alexander, MBBS, MRCPsych, Consultant Learning Disability Psychiatrist, MRCPsych, UK

Dr Manjula Atmakur MBBS, MRCPsych, ST5 in Old Age Psychiatry, Cambridgeshire and Peterborough NHS Foundation Trust, UK

Dr Rajnish Attavar MBBS, MRCPsych Consultant Learning disability Psychiatrist, Oxfordshire ,UK

Dr Champa Ballale, MBBS, MRCPsych, Consultant Old Age Psychiatrist, Kettering, UK

Dr Saravanan Balasubramanian MBBS DPM DNB MD Phd Consultant General Adult Psychiatrist, Cambridgeshire and Peterborough NHS Foundation Trust, UK

Dr Paul Bradley, MBBS BSc MRCPsych, ST6 in Learning Disability Psychiatry, Cambridgeshire and Peterborough NHS Foundation Trust, UK

Gosia Demetriou, Social Worker, Luton, UK

Dr Tom Dening MBBS, MRCPsych, Consultant Old age psychiatrist , Cambridgeshire and Peterborough NHS Foundation Trust, UK

Dr Simon Edgar, MB ChB MRCPsych Consultant General Adult Psychiatrist and Clinical Director, Milton Keynes, UK

Dr Sepehr Hafizi, MBBS, MRCPsych, Consultant General Adult Psychiatrist, Cambridgeshire and Peterborough NHS Foundation Trust, UK

Dr Essam Hassan, MBBS, MRCPsych, Consultant General Adult Psychiatrist, Milton Keynes, UK

Dr Ehab Hegazi, MBBS, MRCPsych, MSc Consultant Old Age Psychiatrists, Cambridgeshire and Peterborough NHS Foundation Trust, UK

Dr Furhan Iqbal MBBS, MRCPsych, Consultant Psychotherapist Cambridgeshire and Peterborough NHS Foundation Trust, UK

Dr Tony Jaffa, MBBS, MRCPsych Consultant Child and Adolescent Psychiatrist, Cambridgeshire and Peterborough NHS Foundation Trust, UK

Dr Amit Jain MBBS, MRCPsych Staff Grade Herefordshire

Dr Arun Jha, Consultant Old Age Psychiatrist, Hertfordshire, UK

Dr Manaan Kar-Ray MBBS, MRCPsych, MSc, MS Consultant General Adult Psychiatrist, Clinical director, Cambridgeshire and Peterborough NHS Foundation Trust, UK

Dr Nauman Khalil, MBBS, MRCPsych, Consultant Learning Disability Psychiatrist, Cambridgeshire and Peterborough NHS Foundation Trust, UK

Dr Christos Koumistidis, MBBS, MSc, MRCPsych, PhD, Consultant Addictions Psychiatrist, Hertfordshire, UK

Dr Ashaye Kunle, MBBS, MRCPsych Consultant Old Age Psychiatrist, Hertfordshire, UK

Dr Ken Ma, MBBS, MRCPsych Consultant Child and Adolescent Psychiatrist, Coventry and Warwickshire, UK

Dr Nigel Lester, MBBS, MRCPsych Consultant Psychiatrist, Associate Clinical Director Camden and Islington NHS Foundation Trust

Dr Franco Orsucci MBBS, DPsych MD Consultant Psychiatrist in Rehabilitation & Recovery Cambridgeshire and Peterborough NHS Foundation Trust, UK ,(Visiting Professor, Research Department of Psychology and Linguistics, University College London)

Dr Denzil Mitchell, MBBS, MRCPsych Consultant General Adult Psychiatrist,

Southampton, UK
Dr Swali Malanda BSc MB ChB MSc MA MRCPsych Consultant General Adult
33Psychiatrist, Milton Keynes, UK
Dr Jothi Naidoo, MBBS, MRCPsych ST5 in General Adult Psychiatry,
Southampton, UK
Dr Rajeeve Parkianathan BSc MBBS MSc CT3 Psychiatry, Cambridge and
Peterborough NHS Foundation Trust.
Dr Ravi Prakash, CT3 in General Adult Psychiatry, Peterborough and
Cambridge, UK
Dr Raghavakurup Radhakrisknan DPM(NIMHANS), DNB(Psychiatry),
MRCPsych Cambridgeshire and Peterborough NHS Foundation Trust, UK
Dr Rajini Rajeswaran, MBBS, MRCPsych London, UK
Dr Nisha Rani MBBS, MRCPsych ST4 General Adult Psychiatry
Cambridgeshire and Peterborough NHS Foundation Trust, UK
Ferdinand Rensburg, BOJ, London, UK
Dr Chris Robak, MBBS MRCGP, Cambridgeshire and Peterborough NHS
Foundation Trust, UK
Dr Ashok Roy, MBBS, MRCPsych Consultant Learning Disability Psychiatrist,
Birmingham, UK
Dr Meera Roy, Consultant Learning Disability Psychiatrist, Birmingham, UK
Miss Mary P Ryan Bsc (hons), Consultant Medical Devices & Healthcare,
London, UK.
Professor Fabrizio Schifano, Consultant Addictions Psychiatrist, MD,
MRCPsych, Dip Psychiatry, Dip Clin Pharmacology Hertfordshire, UK
Dr Piyal Sen., MBBS, DPM, FRCPsych, DFP Consultant Forensic Psychiatrist,
Northampton, UK
Dr Dinesh Sinha, MBBS MRCPsych MSc MBA, Consultant Psychotherapy
Psychiatrist, Cambridgeshire and Peterborough NHS Foundation Trust, UK
Dr Nicholas Stafford, MBBS, MRCPsych Consultant General Adult
Psychiatrist, London, UK
Dr Zahoor Syed, MBBS, MRCPsych Consultant General Adult and Substance
misuse Psychiatrist, Cambridgeshire and Peterborough NHS Foundation
Trust, UK
Dr MS Thambirajah, MBBS, MRCPsych Consultant Child and Adolescent
Psychiatrist, Birmingham, UK
Dr Jay Thamizhirai Staff Grade, Cambridgeshire and Peterborough NHS
Foundation Trust, UK
Dr Animesh Tripathi, MBBS, MRCPsych ST5 in General Adult Psychiatry,
Hertfordshire, UK
Dr Mike Walker, MBBS, MRCPsych Consultant Old Age Psychiatrist,
Hertfordshire, UK
Dr Theresa Xeurub, MBBS, MRCPsych Consultant Perinatal Psychiatrist,
Coventry and Warwickshire, UK
Dr Rugia Zafar GP ST2 Cambridgeshire and Peterborough NHS Foundation
Trust, UK
Dr Asif Zia, MBBS, Mrcpsych, MD Consultant Learning Disability Psychiatrist,
Peterborough and Cambridge, UK

ACKNOWLEDGEMENTS

A Special thanks to these people I have listed below some of who assisted me during the preparation for my CASC examination.

Dr Subimal Banerjee *Consultant Learning Disability Psychiatrist, Amersham, Oxfordshire, UK*
Dr Raju Banisetti, *MBBS Associate Specialist in Eating Disorders, Reading*
Dr Dulith de Silva, *MBBS MRCPsych, ST5, Old age psychiatry London, UK*
Dr Lalana Desinyake, *MBBS MRCPsych, ST5 General adult Psychiatrist, Bedford and Luton, UK*
Dr Humphrey Enow, *CT2, Cambridgeshire and Peterborough NHS Foundation Trust, UK*
Dr Sanjith Kammath, *MBBS MRCPsych Consultant General Adult Psychiatrist*
Dr Thilak Ratynake, MBBS, *MRCPsych Consultant General Adult psychiatrist, Bedfordshire and Luton, UK*
Dr Ashok Patel, *MBBS MRCPsych Consultant General Adult psychiatrist, Bedfordshire and Luton, UK*
Dr Farah Nasir, *MBBS, Consultant Old age psychiatrist, Milton Keynes, UK*
Dr Raja Natarajan, *MBBS, Specialisist Registrar, Oxfordshire, UK (also organiser of the Oxford Course)*
Dr Vishelle Ramkisson, *MBBS, MRCPsych, Consultant Old age psychiatry, Bedford and Luton*
Dr Roshelle Ramkisson, *MBBS MRCPsych, ST5 Child and Adolescent psychiatry, Manchester, UK*
Dr Samir Shah, *MBBS, MRCPsych, ST5 General Adult psychiatry Manchester, UK*
Dr Kenneth Singh, *MBCHB Consultant Learning Disability Psychiatrist, Milton Keynes, UK*
Dr Paul St John Smith, *Consultant General Adult Psychiatrist, Hertfordshire, UK*
Dr Akeem Sule, *Consultant Psychiatrist General Adult Psychiatrist*

OTHER
Dr Mark Davies, *BA (Hons), MB.BS, MRCPsych, MBA Consultant General Adult Psychiatrist, RES Consortium, UK*
Dr Albert Michael, *MRCPsych MD, Consultant General Adult Psychiatrist, Bury St Edmunds, UK*
Dr Arun Jha and IOT, *Harperbury, UK*
CDAT, *Stevenage, UK*
Hollies, *Cavell Centre, Peterborough, UK*
Barbra Brook, Stuart Hunt and Roesmarie Neville for assisting with some editing

FOREWORDS

By Dr Dinesh Sinha, Dr MS Thambirajah, Professor Fabrizio Schifano and Dr Asif Zia

Dr Dinesh Sinha

The series of hoops to jump through on the way to the coveted membership of The Royal College of Psychiatrists has grown in the past few years. The process has also seen significant change and in my role as a tutor I hear trainees feeling perplexed and confused about the requirements that they often feel have been foisted upon them. Time and again they go for examinations of various hues and come back feeling censured if unsuccessful, often not even knowing what went wrong! This is also a time when the pressure of service versus training commitments has increased, imposing further restrictions on the availability of space to prepare for the membership examinations.

Psychiatry is prone to becoming a rather formulaic and descriptive discipline and its academic teachings mirror this tendency. Additionally in the CASC examination trainees need to hold onto the great range of theory that the training encompasses while being able to display particular clinical skills that can only come from years of practical experience. The requirement to evidence all of this in a matter of minutes can feel daunting and provoke panic. The need then is for a succinct and reassuring internal dialogue that helps keep frayed nerves at bay.

For these reasons I was pleased to become familiar with this book, as unlike many others in the market it was written by a current senior Specialty Trainee. This brought with it a great benefit, as it specifically sought to address the trainee's dilemma when approaching this key qualification examination. I was reminded while reading it of having started off in Psychiatry and being on call. At that time each case was exotic and potentially full of hidden pitfalls! It was only the eventual development of a mental framework to think about clinical situations that brought understanding and calm.

I found the clearly laid out format of the individual CASC's similarly helpful in guiding the candidate not just in the individual scenarios but in the primary task of developing a mental framework that would allow them to calmly approach hitherto unfamiliar situations.

The absence of unhelpful terminology and excess verbosity was also striking when compared with other choices in this genre. The last thing needed in a time limited examination of 8 odd minutes is the requirement to recall the verbal ramblings of an over enthusiastic author. Thus it is clearly an advantage and no mean achievement that this book is slim enough to carry around when on call in the weeks leading up to the CASC!

Hence I have no hesitation in recommending this book by its enterprising author, as a useful text for success in the CASC.

Dr Dinesh Sinha
MBBS MRCPsych MSc Dual CCT MBA
Consultant Psychiatrist in Psychotherapy
Cambridgeshire and Peterborough NHS Foundation Trust

FOREWORDS

Dr MS Thambirajah

I am pleased to write a foreword for this book on CASC by Seshni Moodliar. The CASC is mainly a test of skills and attitude (by the time they get to take the CASC most trainees have sufficient knowledge of the subject). Although it is difficult to learn these competencies by reading a book, candidates can prepare themselves for the CASC by thinking about typical case scenarios similar to CASC stations. This slim book provides brief glimpses of such cases and compels the reader to reflect on them.

For the trainee psychiatrist, all that stands between him or her and the membership of the College is the CASC examination. While for a few it may be no more that brief clinical encounter, for most it proves to be a challenge and, for a few, an almost insurmountable hurdle. Given that the candidate is given only 'one minute to think' and seven minutes to conduct the interview (in the presence of a mute examiner!) it is all the more important that candidates mentally prepare themselves sufficiently before facing the examination. This book, aimed at those who find the CASC daunting, provides pre examination exercises that most candidates will find useful. The cases are those given in previous examinations or closely simulate them. The discussions are brief and in 'point form' so that the trainee is able to go through them in a short time.

I feel that the reflective element built into the each case in the book to be the most useful. In the CASC, it is the strategy rather than the tactics that matters most. In order to conduct a meaningful interview, one has first to decipher the examiner's aims for the CASC. Do you focus on risks associated with a lethal overdose or do you concentrate on child protection issues for scenario on page 388. How confident are you in insisting on inpatient treatment for a man with morbid jealousy on page 475. In all the cases what matters is the direction in which the candidate chooses to travel, i.e., the strategy. I am sure readers would find the section allocated to 'thinking time' in each CASC extremely useful. Similarly, the section on variation of the theme goes to show how small changes to the station can make a big difference to the aims of the case. This is a warning to candidates by the author not to expect the CASC to be identical to those given in the book.

I would urge the reader not to rush through the cases in the book but to read them one by one taking time to think about and mentally work on each case. Candidates would benefit by using the format given in the book to analyse every case they see in their day to day work, whether it be in outpatients, wards, crisis situations, A&E, as if they were CASC stations. This book highlights the issues that need to be addressed before the candidate encounters CASC stations.

DR. M. S. Thambirajah FRCPsych.
Consultant Child and Adolescent Psychiatrist
Dudley and Walsall Mental Health Partnership Trust

FOREWORDS

Professor Fabrizio Schifano

I am pleased to write the foreword for the book PASS THE CASC for the MRCPsych by Seshni Moodliar.

With the introduction of the CASC exam in spring 2008 the Royal College of Psychiatrists has again taken measures to ensure a high standard of attaining the MRCPsych and gaining membership to the College. The CASC examination is not only a test of their candidate's knowledge but also a test of their clinical and communication skills. It further illustrates the emphasis on the ultimate goal of being able to provide best clinical care and putting our patients at the heart of everything we do.

The author has skilfully written this exam focussed book which comprises of CASC stations that have been encountered by candidates in the MRCPsych CASC examination since spring 2008. The structure of each scenario enables the candidate to identify the salient aspects that need to be focussed on when approaching each station.

As well as providing a structure for preparing for the exams, these guides of interviewing skills in the various psychiatric subspecialties would be beneficial for any aspiring psychiatry core trainee to utilise in their everyday clinical practice with their real patients. All the scenarios have been peer reviewed by consultants and specialist registrars.

They have all been chosen as they are experts in their field, and some of who are experienced CASC examiners.

I would recommend this excellent book to prospective candidates preparing for the MRCPsych examinations, as well as their clinical tutors, trainers and examiners.

Professor Fabrizio Schifano
Chair in Clinical Pharmacology and Therapeutics
Associate Dean, Postgraduate Medical School
Consultant Psychiatrist (Addictions)
University of Hertfordshire, School of Pharmacy,
College Lane Campus, Hatfield, Herts, AL10 9AB (UK)

FOREWORDS

Dr Asif Zia

There are a number of books covering various aspects of the membership examination. This book also covers CASC examination technique and helps trainees to answer questions in a consistent way. It is important to practice regularly a particular technique which will help in answering questions during examination. The questions discussed are also similar to those that come up in the examination.

Books currently available are either written by people just after passing their exams, or people who are involved with the college examinations, past and present. Both have their value. Dr Moodliar has written this book after passing her examination and is well aware of the type of CASC questions and how the techniques need to be used. She has tried to put all this together.

Trainees need to learn the biopsychosocial model of psychiatric practice. This is especially important in psychiatry of learning disability due to heterogeneous and complex population which requires a comprehensive model of understanding the person presenting with a disorder or disability. The author is currently specialising in psychiatry of learning disability and has used the biopsychosocial model to answer the scenarios leading to a biopsychosocial formulation.
She also with skill guides the reader to using this holistic approach in information gathering and assessments.

It is important that trainees have the knowledge and ability to communicate effectively with patients. This requires understanding and experience of the speciality, which is not always available to the trainees. Trainees are also spending less time seeing patients during their training. Hence having experience of standardising the assessment is crucial, and is also quite difficult for people writing examination CASC questions. There is also an element of learning that needs to take place.

Dr Moodliar seems to have grasped the concept of a comprehensive care and has captured these skills in her book. She needs to be congratulated for doing this. I hope trainees appearing for CASC examinations will find this helpful, not only during their examinations but also when carrying out assessments after passing their examinations.

Dr Asif Zia, MRCPsych, M.D.
Consultant Psychiatrist and Clinical Director
Specialist Services Division
Cambridge and Peterborough NHS Foundation Trust
Edith Cavell Health Care Campus
Bretton Gate
Peterborough
PE3 9GZ

INTRODUCTION

Background to the CASC examination
The CASC (Clinical assessment of skills and competencies) examination was introduced in spring 2008 by the Royal College of Psychiatrists. It is based on a previous format used, the OSCEs (Observed structured clinical examinations).

The CASC examination is not only a test of candidate's knowledge but also an assessment of their clinical and communication skills. Whilst this knowledge is imperative, it is the ability and skilfulness to incorporate this awareness into a clinical setting when assessing patients.

Throughout these CASC stations there is an admixture of skills being tested which range from history taking, aspects of mental state examination, communication of diagnoses, management plans conducting thorough risk assessments and clinical examinations.

About this book
Pass the CASC is exclusive in that it integrates everything that you will need in order to tackle and master the array of techniques required for your success in the CASC examinations.

My ultimate goal whilst writing this book was to incorporate both the knowledge and strategies needed for candidates to be successful in the CASC examination. This is something which I found deficient in the texts I perused in preparation for my examination.

This book encompasses common CASC scenarios in psychiatry simulated in an exam focused way. The greatest achievement and asset of these CASC stations is that they all have been peer reviewed by an expert team of about 50 psychiatrists and trainees, some of whom are Royal College examiners. Thus you can be guaranteed that you will be imparted their expertise and knowledge of the 'bread and butter' of psychiatric skills which they are affluent in.

It is fair to say that this is the most up to date book on the CASC examination. Candidates will appreciate the first chapter, found exclusively in this text, as the ultimate revision tool, as it is a summary of the collection of the past CASC examination stations since spring 2008 to date.

The additional distinctive features which make this book, **Pass the CASC** unique and exam focused is the 150 meticulously worked out scenarios which have a clearly laid out format. Each begins with a construct, instruction to the candidate, a mental checklist, communication skills and a suggested approach to the scenario.
I will elaborate further below on each of these distinctive features.

The **mental checklist** is a practical guide on the strategy of how you would need to approach the task; the rationale of that CASC station; the key skills which are being tested by the college and the salient aspects which you would

INTRODUCTION

need to concentrate on. The intention here is for candidates to synchronize this mental framework with their 'preparation time' before each station.

The **communication skills** guide is there to give you an idea of the possible scenario to anticipate and in some cases the 'ice breaker' needed to be surpassed in those 'first 2 minutes', which most examiners consider as one of the crucial factors in determining a pass in the station.
'Develop rapport and show empathy' is one of the communication skills I have repetitively used, and with the intention for this to be one of those take home messages. I will illustrate this using 2 references.

Empathy is defined as: 'We call empathy (from the Greek word 'feeling with') or atunement to express a way a person can be in tune with the internal world of another, and is also connected to what has been called emotional intelligence.' (Orsucci, Mind Force on Human attractions, 2009, p.23)

And following that a description of showing empathy: 'If you believe that the patient is as important as you are, you are mistaken. The patient is more important than you are. Your career depends on how well you can get on with patients, and make them feel good about you. Hence be sensitive and show warmth, empathy, concern and consideration for the patient's feelings. Try to see how you would have felt if you were in the patient's shoes. '(Michael, A OSCE's in Psychiatry, 2004, p. 3)

I believe these both are excellent summations of the components of empathy and as we know it is perhaps one of the most important essential skills required as a psychiatrist.
I believe, if you are able to master this, then I can assure you, you would have won half the battle needed to overcome any given CASC scenario.

The scenario then develops into a **suggested approach** or dialogues which vary from a structured format of questions which need to be probed; to discussing management of the various psychiatric conditions.

These dialogues should not be repeated verbatim, and the skill candidates should aspire to, is to integrate these dialogues to create a balanced mixture of open and closed questions. I would like to further emphasise that these should be used as a mere guide, and tailored according to the given scenario and given task.

In order to succeed in the CASC, I would recommend you to use the format given in the book to analyse every case that you see in your day to day work And needless to say 'practice makes perfect'. So practice these in your examination groups, with consultants, registrars and other colleagues under the timed examination conditions.

I hope trainees preparing for the CASC examinations will find this beneficial,

INTRODUCTION

not only for their examinations but also when carrying out assessments once they have successfully completed their examinations. This would also be an essential read for those core trainees only just starting afresh in their careers in psychiatry to equip them with the fundamental psychiatric interviewing skills.

As psychiatry does not come without its fair share of setbacks, I know from my personal experience the impact that these exams have not only on our family lives and work, but also the financial and emotional implications. Colleagues, the key ingredient are perseverance. If at first you don't succeed, try and try again.

And finally my outlook on psychiatry training whilst incorporating my philosophical view on life, is that whilst it is important for us as psychiatrists to have the knowledge, and continually strive for learning, I believe that it boils down to this, which is the ability to communicate effectively with our patients, families, carers and colleagues, and to put our patients at the heart of everything we do to promote their 'wellbeing and recovery'. I wish you all the best in your career and all the success in this CASC examination. My sincere gratitude goes out to you for reading my book.

Good luck!!

Seshni Moodliar
MBChB, MRCPsych

PAST CASC STATIONS

SUMMARY OF PAST CASC EXAMINATION STATIONS

In this chapter I have summarized the past CASC examination stations since the introduction of the CASC examination in spring 2008 by the Royal College of psychiatrists, with initial advice on the format from Dr Albert Michael.

These themes of the scenarios have been obtained from various sources including candidates that have participated in the examination.

Personally, in preparation for the CASC examination, the invaluable advice I was given was to go through the past examination stations, and I found this as a useful tool for revision and also as a guide upon which areas needed to be focussed upon.

Reading this chapter will help you identify the common themes that appear regularly in the examinations and thus highlight the importance of the task in each and every CASC station.

The scenario summaries for each examination station should be used merely as a guide in preparation of the CASC examination as we know that the MRCPsych examination format is constantly being updated and evolving.

Good luck!!   **Seshni Moodliar**

PAST CASC STATIONS

CASC PAST EXAMINATION STATIONS

A June 2008

B November 2008

C March 2008

D October 2009

E March 2010

F October 2010

G January 2011

H June 2011

Format compiled with advice from Dr Albert Michael

PAST CASC STATIONS

June 2008
Day 1-linked
1-1A Overdose - suicide risk assessment (rape)
1-1B Overdose - discuss management with the consultant
1-2A Conversion disorder - assessment of sudden onset of blindness
1-2B Conversion disorder - discuss management with mother
1-3A Elderly psychoses - assess psychopathology and perform cognitive examination
1-3B Elderly Psychosis - discuss management with daughter
1-3A Antidepressants - sexual side effects -history taking
1-4B Antidepressants - sexual side effects - discuss management with wife
1-5A Morbid Jealousy - history taking and assess delusional beliefs
1-5B Morbid Jealousy - discuss management with wife
1-6A Head injury - collateral history from mother
1-6B Head injury - perform a cognitive examination including frontal lobe tests

June 2008
Day 2-linked
2-1A Head injury - collateral history from mother
2-1B Head injury - perform a cognitive examination including frontal lobe tests
2-2A ADHD (Attention Deficit Hyperactivity Disorder) - collateral history from mother
2-2B ADHD (Attention Deficit Hyperactivity Disorder) - explain management to father
2-3A Overdose - suicide risk assessment with teacher
2-3B Overdose - discuss management with her friend
2-4A Capacity assessment - for endoscopy due to haematemesis
2-4B Capacity assessment - discuss management with on call consultant
2-5A Puerperal illness - history taking and mental state examination
2-5B Puerperal illness - discuss management with husband
2-6A Panic Attacks - history taking
2-6B Panic Attacks - discuss management with mother

June 2008
Day 3-linked
3-1A ADHD (Attention Deficit Hyperactivity Disorder) - collateral history from mother
3-1B ADHD (Attention Deficit Hyperactivity Disorder) - discuss management with father
3-2A Overdose - suicide risk assessment-teacher
3-2B Overdose - discuss management with her friend
3-3A Capacity assessment - for endoscopy due to haematemesis
3-3B Capacity assessment - discuss management with on call consultant
3-4A Puerperal illness - history taking and mental state examination
3-4B Puerperal illness - discuss management with husband
3-5A Panic Attacks - history taking
3-5B Panic Attacks - discuss management with mother

PAST CASC STATIONS

3-6A Head injury - collateral history from mother
3-6B Head injury -conduct a cognitive examination

June 2008
Day 4-linked
4-1A Erotomania - conduct a mental state examination
4-1B Erotomania - discuss management with consultant
4-2A Delirium Tremens -assess psychopathology
4-2B Delirium Tremens - discuss management with orthopaedic nurse
4-3A Dementia - collateral history from care home
4-3B Dementia - discuss management of BPSD with son
4-4A Overdose assessment - suicide risk assessment rape
4-4B Overdose - discuss management with medical nurse
4-5A Antidepressants - sexual side effects - elicit a history
4-5B Antidepressants - sexual side effects - discuss with management with
wife
4-6A Anorexia nervosa - elicit a personal and family history
4-6B Anorexia nervosa - discuss management with nurse on medical ward

November 2008
Day 1- linked
1-1A Footballer- cognitive distortions - demonstrate selective abstraction,
maximization and minimization
1-1B Footballer - cognitive distortions- discuss management with
the coach
1-2A ADHD (Attention Deficit Hyperactivity Disorder) - collateral history from
mother
1-2B ADHD (Attention Deficit Hyperactivity Disorder) - discuss management
with father
1-3A Anorexia nervosa - elicit a personal and family history
1-3B Anorexia nervosa - discuss management with nurse on medical ward
1-4A Elderly man- Indecent exposure -assess history of presenting complaint
1-4B Elderly man- Indecent exposure -discuss management with wife

Day 1 - Single
1-1A Overdose assessment - suicide risk assessment - rape
1-2A Schizophrenia - explain management to mother
1-3A Psychosis - perform a mental state examination
1-4A Cognitive examination - perform a mini mental state examination
(MMSE)
1-5A Antidepressants - sexual side effects - assess history of presenting
complaint
1-6A Explain systematic desensitization
1-7A Psychosis - assess delusional beliefs
1-8A Overdose - suicide risk assessment-teacher

November 2008
Day 2 - linked
 2-1A Post Myocardial Infarct (MI) Depression -Assess social history and do a

PAST CASC STATIONS

capacity assessment
2-1B Post Myocardial Infarct (MI) Depression - discuss management with consultant
2-2A Early onset Schizophrenia - assess history of presenting complaint
2-2B Early onset Schizophrenia-Discuss management with mother
2-3A Overdose- suicide risk assessment (Rape)
2-3B Overdose -discuss management with the consultant
2-4A Footballer- Cognitive distortions-demonstrate selective abstraction, maximization and minimization
2-4B Footballer -Cognitive distortions- discuss management with the coach

Day 2 - Single
2-1A Antidepressant - Sexual side effects-assess
2-2A Polysubstance misuse - history taking
2-3A Grief reaction – history taking
2-4A Temporal lobe epilepsy - elicit history
2-5A Head injury - obtain collateral history from mother
2-6A Anxious woman - history taking with a view of a diagnosis
2-7A Paedophile - conduct a risk assessment

November 2008
Day 3- linked
3-1A Learning disability - Indecent exposure - assess
3-1B Learning disability - Indecent exposure - discuss management with mother
3-2A Elderly Psychosis- assess psychopathology and perform a cognitive examination
3-2B Elderly Psychosis - discuss management with his wife
3-3A Agoraphobia - history taking
3-3B Agoraphobia - discuss management with his wife
3-4A Overdose Assessment - suicide risk assessment- bullying
3-4B Overdose Assessment - talk to consultant about management

Single
3-1A PTSD – obtain history and assess mental state
3-2A Conversion disorder - assess upper and lower limb paralysis
3-4A Violent Risk Assessment – conduct risk assessment
3-5A Explain rationale and process of desensitisation therapy for Agoraphobia
3-6A Alcohol dependence - establish history of alcohol dependence
3-7A Anxious woman - history taking
3-8A Deliberate self-harm – perform risk assessment

November 2008
Day 4-Linked
4-1A Hypochondriasis - assess history of presenting complaint and obtain medical history
4-1B Hypochondriasis - discuss management with girlfriend

PAST CASC STATIONS

4-2A Overdose Assessment - suicide risk assessment- bullying
4-2B Overdose Assessment – discuss with consultant about management
4-3A Elderly Psychosis- assess psychopathology and perform a cognitive examination
4-3B Elderly Psychosis - discuss management with her brother
4-4A Methadone in Pregnancy - elicit a drug and alcohol history and social history
4-4B Methadone in pregnancy - discuss management with her partner

Single
4-1A Anorexia Nervosa-Discuss with mother
4-2A Elderly Psychosis- elderly lady assess psychopathology and perform cognitive examination
4-3A Wandering – elderly man found wandering the streets. Perform a cognitive exam
4-4A Schizophrenia – perform a mental state examination
4-5A Social phobia - assess bride who is worried about her reception
4-6A Agoraphobia - explain management
4-7A Erotomania - conduct a mental state examination
4-8A Somatoform pain disorder – assess history of presenting complaint

March 2009
Day 1-Linked
1-1A Elderly man- Indecent exposure - assess history of presenting complaint
1-1B Elderly man - Indecent exposure - discuss management with wife
1-2A Early onset Schizophrenia - assess history of presenting complaint
1-2B Early onset Schizophrenia - discuss management with consultant
1-3A Antidepressants - sexual side effects - assess history of presenting complaint
1-3B Antidepressants - sexual side effects - discuss management with wife
1-4A Morbid Jealousy - assess his delusional beliefs
1-4B Morbid Jealousy - discuss management with wife

Day 1 - Single
1-1A Refractory Depression - assess weight gain with Venlafaxine and Fluoxetine.
1-2A Bulimia Nervosa - assess for prognostic factors
1-3A Psychosis - Schizophrenia - inpatient wants to go on leave –conduct a risk assessment
1-4A ECT - explain and obtain consent
1-5A Generalised Anxiety - assess women stressed at work
1-6A Psychosis - assess mental state examination
1-7A Cognitive examination - perform on an elderly lady who has visual loss
1-8A Schizophrenia - explain diagnosis and management to mother

March 2009
Day 2-Linked
2-1A Antidepressants - sexual side effects - assess history of presenting complaint

PAST CASC STATIONS

2-1B Antidepressants - sexual side effects - discuss with wife
2-2A Morbid Jealousy - assess history of presenting complaint and delusional beliefs
2-2B Morbid Jealousy - discuss with management with wife
2-3A Early onset Schizophrenia - assess history of presenting complaint
2-3B Early onset Schizophrenia - discuss management with consultant
2-4A Head injury - obtain collateral history from mother
2-4B Head injury - perform a cognitive examination with focus on frontal lobe tests

Day 2 - Single
2-1A ECT - explain and obtain consent
2-2A Schizophrenia - explain management to mother
2-3A OCD - history taking
2-4A Psychosis - assess delusional beliefs
2-5A Cognitive examination- perform a mini mental state examination (MMSE)
2-6A Bulimia Nervosa - assess for prognostic factors
2-7A Refractory Depression - discuss management
2-8A Schizophrenia - assess inpatient who wants to go on leave

March 2009
Day 3-Linked
3-1A Morbid Jealousy - assess mental state and delusional beliefs
3-1B Morbid Jealousy - discuss with management wife
3-2A Puerperal illness -assessment of history and mental state
3-2B Puerperal illness - discuss management with husband
3-3A Post MI Depression - assess social history and do a capacity assessment
3-3B Post MI Depression - discuss management with consultant
3-4A Elderly man confused - assess mental state examination
3-4B Elderly man confusion - discuss management with consultant

Day 3 - Single
3-1A Paedophile -conduct a risk assessment
3-2A Polysubstance misuse - history taking
3-3A Frontal lobe examination - perform
3-4A ECT - explain and obtain consent
3-5A Schizophrenia - on the ward - assess reason for distress
3-6A Bulimia Nervosa - assess for prognostic factors
3-7A Physical Examination - thyroid examination
3-8A Deliberate self-harm-suicide risk assessment

March 2009
Day 4 - Linked
4-1A Overdose Assessment - suicide risk assessment- bullying
4-1B Overdose Assessment - talk to consultant about management
4-2A Erotomania - assess mental state and establish delusional beliefs
4-2B Erotomania - discuss management with consultant
4-1A Dementia – collateral history from carer

PAST CASC STATIONS

4-3B Dementia - discuss management of BPSD with son
4-4A Hypochondriasis - assess history of presenting complaint and obtain medical history
4-4B Hypochondriasis - discuss management with girlfriend

Day 4 - Single
4-1A Psychosis - assess delusional beliefs
4-2A Alzheimer's Dementia - discuss diagnosis and management with her daughter
4-3A Hypomania - conduct a mental state examination
4-4A Cognitive examination - perform frontal lobe tests
4-5A Psychosis - perform a mental state examination
4-6A Overdose assessment - suicide risk assessment
4-7A Agoraphobia - Explain management

October 2009
Day 1-Linked
1-1A Puerperal illness - obtain history and conduct a risk assessment
1-1B Puerperal illness - discuss management with husband
1-2A Lewy Body Dementia - discuss management with the carer
1-2B Lewy Body Dementia - discuss management with son
1-3A Footballer - cognitive distortions - demonstrate selective abstraction, maximization and minimization
1-3B Footballer - cognitive distortions- discuss management with
The coach
1-4A Conversion disorder - assess upper limb paralysis
1-4B Conversion disorder - discuss management with her husband

Day 1 - Single
1-1A Panic Attacks - explain systematic desensitization
1-2A Clozapine - rehabilitation - discuss with mother
1-3A Arson - conduct a risk assessment
1-4A Overdose Assessment - suicide risk assessment rape
1-5A Psychosis - assess for first rank symptoms
1-6A Alcohol dependence - establish history of alcohol dependence
1-7A Treatment resistant Depression - weight gain with Mirtazapine and Venlafaxine
1-8A Downs Syndrome- collateral history to differentiate dementia and Depression

October 2009
Day 2 - Linked
2-1A Head injury - collateral history from mother
2-1B Head injury - perform cognitive examination with focus on frontal lobe tests
2-2A Morbid Jealousy - assess history of presenting complaint and delusional beliefs
2-2B Morbid Jealousy - discuss with management with wife
2-3A Post MI Depression - assess social history and do capacity assessment

PAST CASC STATIONS

2-3B Post MI Depression - discuss management with consultant
2-4A Assertive Outreach Team (AOT) - collateral history from nurse
2-4B Assertive Outreach Team (AOT) - discuss with management with father

October 2009
Day 2 - Single
2-1A Lithium Augmentation-explain
2-2A Anorexia nervosa-explain diagnosis and management
2-3A Breaking bad news - discuss with relative about relative with brain tumour
2-4A Elderly Psychosis- elderly lady assess psychopathology
2-5A Cognitive examination - perform frontal lobe tests
2-6A Alcohol dependence-history taking
2-7A Interpersonal therapies (IPT) - assess suitability for IPT
2-8A Violent Risk Assessment – conduct risk assessment
2-9A OCD-history taking

October 2009
Day 3 - Linked
3-1A Elderly man - collateral history
3-1B Elderly man - cognitive examination with focus on frontal lobe examination
3-2A Footballer - cognitive distortions - demonstrate selective abstraction, maximization and minimization
3-2B Footballer - cognitive distortions - discuss management with the coach
3-3A Delirium Tremens - assess psychopathology
3-3B Delirium Tremens - discuss management with orthopaedic nurse
3-4A Early onset Schizophrenia - assess history of presenting complaint
3-4B Early onset Schizophrenia - Discuss management with mother

Day 3 - Single
3-1A Panic attacks - explain systematic desensitization
3-2A Rehabilitation - discuss with mother
3-3A Arson - conduct a risk assessment
3-4A Overdose - suicide risk assessment and, need for compulsory detention
3-5A Alcohol Examination - conduct a neurological examination
3-6A Psychosis - elicit first rank symptoms
3-7A Panic Attacks - history taking
3-8A Alcohol Dependence - history taking

October 2009
Day 4 – Linked
4-1A ADHD (Attention Deficit Hyperactivity Disorder) - collateral history from mother
4-1B ADHD (Attention Deficit Hyperactivity Disorder) - discuss management with father
4-2A Vascular Dementia - collateral history
4-2B Vascular Dementia-explain management to wife

PAST CASC STATIONS

4-3A Assertive Outreach Team (AOT) - collateral history from nurse
4-3B Assertive Outreach Team (AOT) - discuss with management with father
4-4A Morbid Jealousy - assess history of presenting complaint and delusional beliefs
4-4B Morbid Jealousy - discuss with management with wife

Day 4 – Single
4-1A Explain Schizophrenia
4-2A Cognitive examination - perform frontal lobe tests
4-3A Depression in elderly-weight loss
4-4A Interpersonal therapy (IPT) - assess suitability for IPT
4-5A Postman Psychosis
4-6A Breaking bad news - discuss with relative about relative with brain tumour
4-7A Depression and alcohol
4-8A Bulimia and prognostic factors

March 2010
Day 1- Linked
1-1A Lewy Body Dementia - discuss management and diagnosis with carer
1-1B Lewy Body Dementia - discuss management with grandson
1-2A Panic Attacks - history taking
1-2B Panic Attacks - discuss management with mother
1-3A Dissociative motor - assess upper limb paralysis
1-3B Dissociative motor disorder discuss with husband

1-4A Delirium - obtain collateral history from son
1-4B Delirium - discuss management with student nurse

Single
1-1A Cognitive examination - perform a mini mental state examination MMSE
1-2A Schizophrenia - discuss management with mother
1-3A Rehabilitation - discuss with mother
1-4A Psychosis - assess mental state examination
1-5A Overdose - suicide risk assessment
1-6A Alcohol dependence - establish alcohol dependence
1-7A Temporal lobe epilepsy - elicit history

March 2010
Day 2-Linked
2-1A Anorexia Nervosa - elicit personal and family history
2-1B Anorexia Nervosa - discuss aetiological factors and psychological management with the nurse
2-2A Morbid Jealousy - displacement man- anxious at work
2-2B Morbid Jealousy - displacement - discuss management with his wife
2-3A Elderly Psychosis- assess psychopathology and perform a cognitive examination
2-3B Elderly Psychosis - discuss management with daughter

PAST CASC STATIONS

2-4A Methadone in Pregnancy - elicit a drug and alcohol history and social history
2-4B Methadone in pregnancy - discuss management with her partner

Day 2 - Single
2-1A Arson - conduct a risk assessment
2-2A Overdose - suicide risk assessment rape
2-3A Cognitive examination - perform a mini mental state examination (MMSE)
2-4A Schizophrenia - discuss management with mother
2-5A ECT - Explain and obtain consent
2-6A Alcohol and Depression - establish the link
2-7A Wandering - conduct a risk assessment and assess suitability for residential care
2-8A Psychosis - perform a mental state examination

March 2010
Day 3-Linked
3-1A Overdose Assessment - suicide risk assessment- bullying
3-1B Overdose Assessment – discuss with consultant about management
3-2A Anorexia Nervosa - elicit personal and family history
3-2B Anorexia Nervosa - discuss aetiological factors and psychological management with the nurse
3-3A Conversion disorder - assess upper limb paralysis
3-3B Conversion disorder - discuss management with her husband
3-4A AOT - collateral history from nurse
3-4B AOT - discuss with management with father

Day 3 - Single
3-1A Opiate Dependence - elicit history of drug and alcohol use
3-2A Interpersonal psychotherapy - assess suitability for IPT
3-3A Temporal Lobe Epilepsy - elicit history
3-4A Dementia - explain diagnosis and management to carer
3-5A Psychosis - elicit mental state examination
3-6A Capacity assessment - haematemesis
3-7A Schizophrenia - detained inpatient who wants to go on leave

March 2010
Day 4-Linked
4-1A Conversion disorder - assessment of sudden onset of blindness
4-1B Conversion disorder- discuss management with mother
4-2A Recurrent Depression - history of treatment resistant Depression
4-2B Recurrent Depression - discuss management of wife about Lithium
4-3A Delirium - obtain collateral history from son
4-3B Delirium - discuss management with student nurse
4-4A Agoraphobia - history taking

PAST CASC STATIONS

4-4B Agoraphobia - discuss management with her husband

Day 4 - Single
4-1A Antidepressants - sexual side effects - elicit a history
4-2A Anorexia Nervosa - refeeding syndrome
4-3A Paedophile - conduct a risk assessment
4-4A Erotomania - assess mental state and establish delusional beliefs
4-5A Cognitive examination - perform a mini mental state examination (MMSE)
4-6A Opiate Dependence - elicit history of drug and alcohol use
4-7A Psychosis - elicit first rank symptoms
4-8A Downs's syndrome - collateral history to differentiate Depression from dementia

September 2010
Day 1- Linked
1-1A Anorexia nervosa - elicit a personal and family history
1-1B Anorexia nervosa - discuss management with nurse on medical ward
1-2A Puerperal illness - history taking and mental state examination
1-2B Puerperal illness - discuss management with husband
1-3A Overdose - suicide risk assessment - teacher
1-3B Overdose - discuss management with her friend
1-4A Capacity assessment - for endoscopy due to hematemesis
1-4B Capacity assessment - discuss management with on call consultant

Day 1 - Single
1-1A Temporal Lobe epilepsy - elicit history
1-2A Learning disability - assess change in behaviour - epilepsy, bruises
1-3A Explain systematic desensitization
1-4A Breaking bad news - discuss with relative about relative with brain tumour
1-5A Social phobia - assess bride who is worried about her reception
1-6A Schizophrenia - outpatient review
1-7A Cognitive examination - perform a mini mental state examination (MMSE)
1-8A Opiate dependence - person in A+E -elicit history

September 2010
Day 2-Linked
2-1A Footballer - cognitive distortions - assess to demonstrate maximization, minimization and selective abstraction
2-1B Footballer - cognitive distortions - discuss management with the coach
2-2A Erotomania - assess mental state and establish delusional beliefs
2-2B Erotomania - discuss management with consultant
2-3A Head injury - collateral history from mother
2-3B Head injury - cognitive examination
2-4A Delirium - collateral history form daughter
2-4B Nurse - discuss management with nurse

PAST CASC STATIONS

Day 2 - Single
2-1A Social phobia - assess bride who is worried about her reception
2-2A Body dysmorphic disorder – history taking
2-3A Autism – explain diagnosis and management
2-4A Capacity Assessment for Gastroscopy
2-5A Overdose Assessment – suicide risk assessment
2-6A Lithium Augmentation – explain management
2-7A Mania – perform mental state examination
2-8A Psychosis – perform mental state examination

September 2010
Day 3-Linked
3-1A Puerperal illness - history taking and mental state examination
3-1B Puerperal illness - discuss management with husband
3-2A Overdose – suicide risk assessment (rape)
3-2B Overdose - discuss management with nurse
3-3A Dementia - collateral history from carer
3-3B Dementia - discuss management of BPSD with son
3-4A Hypochondriasis - assess history of presenting complaint and obtain medical history
3-4B Hypochondriasis - discuss management with girlfriend

Day 3 - Single
3-1A Breaking bad news - discuss with relative about relative with brain tumour
3-2A Lower limb – perform physical examination
3-3A Vascular Dementia – perform cognitive examination
3-4A ECT – explains procedure and obtain consent
3-5A Psychotherapy – transference and assess reasons for discontinuation of therapy
3-6A Psychosis – perform mental state examination - First Rank Symptoms (FRS)
3-7A Opiate dependence - assess for harmful effects of substance misuse
3-8A Polysubstance misuse – assess history of substance misuse

September 2010
Day 4 - Linked
4-1A Dementia - collateral history from care home
4-1B Dementia - discuss management of BPSD with son
4-2A Early onset Schizophrenia – history taking
4-2B Early onset Schizophrenia - discuss management with mother
4-3A Erotomania - assess mental state and establish delusional beliefs
4-3B Erotomania - discuss management with consultant

Day 4 - Single
4-1A Vascular Dementia – perform cognitive examination
4-2A Psychosis – assess male patient suspects nurses and doctors poisoning him
4-3A Depression - history taking

PAST CASC STATIONS

4-4A Psychotic Depression – mental state examinations (nihilistic delusions)
4-5A Alcohol dependence – elicit history of alcohol dependence
4-6A Wandering - conduct risk assessment
4-7A Autism – obtain collateral history
4-8A Morbid Jealousy – displacement - assess man- anxious at work

January 2011
Day 1-Linked
1-1A Erotomania – assess mental state and establish delusional beliefs
1-1B Erotomania - discuss management with consultant
1-2A Delirium Tremens - assess psychopathology
1-2B Delirium Tremens - discuss management with orthopaedic nurse
1-3A Capacity assessment - haematemesis
1-3B Capacity assessment - discuss with key-worker
1-4A Elderly man - Indecent exposure – obtain history
1-4B Elderly man - Indecent exposure - discuss management with wife

Day 1 - Single
1-1A Treatment Resistant Depression - history taking
1-2A Cardiovascular System (CVS) – perform physical examination
1-3A Vascular Dementia - collateral history
1-4A OCD - discussion about psychological therapies
1-5A Delirium Tremens - assess psychopathology
1-6A Schizophrenia – perform mental state examination
1-7A Elderly psychoses – assess delusional beliefs
1-8A Mania – perform mental state examination

January 2011
Day 2-Linked
2-1A Lewy Body Dementia - speak to the carer
2-1B Lewy Body Dementia - discuss management with son/daughter
2-2A Capacity assessment of LD - haematemesis for endoscopy
2-2B Capacity assessment of LD - discuss management with key-worker
2-3A Puerperal illness - history taking and mental state examination
2-3B Puerperal illness - discuss management with husband
2-4A Psychotic – detained by police for breach of restraining order -assess
2-4B Psychotic - discuss management with Crisis Resolution Team (CRT) nurse

Day 2 - Single
2-1A Vascular Dementia – perform cognitive examination
2-2A Refeeding syndrome - discuss with key-worker of anorexic patient
2-3A Heroin addict in A+E- assess poly-substance misuse and impact
2-4A PTSD – obtain history and assess mental state
2-5A Refractory Depression - discuss management
2-6A Deliberate self-harm - suicidal risk assessment
2-7A Psychosis - assess mental state
2-8A Somatoform pain disorder – assess history of presenting complaint

January 2011

PAST CASC STATIONS

Day 3 - Linked
3-1A Footballer - cognitive distortions - demonstrate selective abstraction, maximization and minimization
3-1B Footballer - cognitive distortions - discuss management with the coach
3-2A Morbid Jealousy - assess history of presenting complaint and delusional beliefs
3-2B Morbid Jealousy - discuss management with his partner
3-3A Psychotic - detained by police for breach of restraining order-assess
3-3B Psychotic- discuss management with the social worker
3-4A Post MI Depression - assess social history and capacity
3-4B Post MI Depression - discuss management with consultant

Day 3 - Single
3-1A Extra-Pyramidal Side Effects (EPSE) – perform physical examination
3-2A Anxious woman - history taking
3-3A Vascular Dementia – perform cognitive examination
3-4A Autism – obtain collateral history from mother
3-5A Deliberate self-harm – perform risk assessment
3-6A Mania - perform mental state examination
3-7A Obsessive Compulsive Disorder (OCD) - discuss pharmacological management
3-8A Psychosis – perform mental state examination – assess delusional beliefs of guilt

January 2011
Day 4-Linked
1-1A Morbid Jealousy - assess mental state and delusional beliefs
1-1B Morbid Jealousy- discuss management with his partner
2-2A Treatment resistant Schizophrenia - discuss with AOT nurse
2-2B Treatment Resistant Schizophrenia - discuss management with father
3-3A Agoraphobia – history taking
3-3B Agoraphobia - discuss management with husband
4-4A Head injury – obtain collateral history from mother
4-4B Head injury – perform cognitive examination

Day 4 - Single
1A Alcohol withdrawal – assess mental state examination
2A OCD - discuss rationale for psychological treatment
3A Mania assessment - assess elderly man
4A Schizophrenia – explain management to mother
5A Attention Deficit Hyperactivity Disorder (ADHD) – obtain collateral history from mother
6A Violent Risk Assessment – conduct risk assessment
7A Antidepressant - sexual side effects - assess
8A Psychotherapy – transference - explore options for discontinuation of therapy

June 2011
Day 1-Linked

PAST CASC STATIONS

1-1A Antidepressants - sexual side effects - assess
1-1B Antidepressants - sexual side effects - discuss with wife
1-2A Recurrent Depression - assess elderly man on Lithium and Mirtazapine
1-2B Recurrent Depression - discuss management with wife
1-3A Early onset Schizophrenia – assess mental state
1-3B Early onset Schizophrenia - discuss management with mother
1-4A Psychosis - perform mental state examination – assess delusional beliefs
1-4B Psychosis - discuss with social worker

Day 1 - Single
1-1A Bulimia Nervosa – assess for prognostic factors
1-2A Schizophrenia - explain management to mother
1-3A Interpersonal therapy (IPT) - assess suitability for IPT
1-4A ECG - interpretation of patient on high dose of Quetiapine (additional information - QTC was calculated on the ECG)
1-5A Deliberate Self Harm - perform mental state examination
1-6A Overdose assessment – suicide risk assessment (bullying)
1-7A Alcoholic Hallucinosis- perform mental state examination

June 2011
Day 2-Linked
2-1A Conversion disorder – assess sudden onset of blindness
2-1B Conversion disorder - discuss diagnosis and management with mother
2-2A Recurrent Depression - assess elderly man on Lithium and Mirtazapine
2-2B Recurrent Depression - discuss management with wife
2-3A Elderly man - Indecent exposure – history taking
2-3B Elderly man - Indecent exposure - discuss management with wife
2-4A Mild Cognitive Impairment – history taking
2-4B-Mild cognitive impairment - discuss management with the wife

Day2-Single
2-1A Lithium Augmentation – explain
2-2A Bulimia Nervosa – assess for prognostic factors
2-3A OCD - explain psychological management – exposure and response prevention (ERP)
2-4A Elderly Depression – assess elderly with acopia
2-5A Paedophile – conduct risk assessment
2-6A Psychotic – perform mental state examination (First rank symptoms)
2-7A Schizophrenia - explain management to mother

June 2011
Day 3-Single
3-1A Bereavement – differentiate abnormal vs normal grief
3-2A Paedophile – conduct risk assessment
3-3A Lithium augmentation - explain
3-4A Mania with psychotic symptoms – perform mental state examination
3-5A Morbid Jealousy – displacement – assess man with Anxiety at work
3-6A Cognitive Examination – perform frontal lobe tests
3-7A EPSE - history taking and physical examination

PAST CASC STATIONS

3-8A ADHD (Attention Deficit Hyperactivity Disorder) - collateral history from mother

June 2011
Day 4-Linked
4-1A Overdose – suicide risk assessment (teacher)
4-1B Overdose - discuss management with her friend
4-2A Learning disability - indecent exposure - assess
4-2B Learning disability - indecent exposure - discuss management with mother
4-3A Panic Attacks – history taking
4-3B Panic Attacks - discuss management with mother
4-4A Frontal lobe – obtain collateral history
4-4B Frontal lobe – perform frontal lobe assessment

Day 4 - Single
4-1A Interpersonal therapies (IPT) - assess suitability for IPT
4-2A PTSD - history taking
4-3A Mania – perform mental state examination
4-4A Schizophrenia – outpatient appointment review
4-5A Wandering – conduct risk assessment
4-6A Grief reaction – history taking
4-7A Opioid - take history and assess impact on life
4-8A Schizophrenia - explain management to mother

GENERAL ADULT PSYCHIATRY

GENERAL ADULT

1. Depression-History
2. Depression Diagnosis and management
3. Overdose risk assessment
4. Deliberate Self-Harm
5. Post MI Depression –Assess social History and capacity
6. Post MI Depression –discuss management with consultant
7. Antidepressants-Sexual side effects-history
8. Antidepressants-Sexual side effects-management
9. Lithium Augmentation
10. Treatment resistant depression(TRD)
11. Electroconvulsive Therapy(ECT)
12. Grief
13. Breaking bad news
14. Bipolar Affective disorder
15. Bipolar Affective disorder
16. Psychosis Assess-Delusions and first rank symptoms
17. Psychosis-Delusional disorder
18. Hallucinations
19. Schizophrenia
20. Clozapine Rehabilitation
21. Clozapine
22. AOT-Speak to care coordinator
23. AOT-Discuss management with the father
24. Depot
25. NMS-Neuroleptic Malignant Syndrome
26. Generalised anxiety disorder
27. Panic attacks Assess
28. Panic Attacks Discuss management with mother
29. Conversion Disorder-Blindness PTSD-History
30. Conversion Disorder-Management
31. Social phobia
32. Obsessive compulsive disorder (OCD)-History
33. Obsessive compulsive disorder (OCD)-Management
34. Body dysmorphic disorder
35. Post-traumatic stress disorder (PTSD)
36. Somatoform pain disorder
37. Hypochondriasis
38. Hypochondriasis
39. Dissociative Motor Disorder
40. Dissociative motor disorder
41. Head injury
42. Head injury
43. Haematemesis
44. Haematemesis-Management
45. Temporal lobe epilepsy (TLE)
46. Borderline personality disorder (BLPD)

GENERAL ADULT PSYCHIATRY

1. DEPRESSION

INSTRUCTIONS TO CANDIDATE
You have been asked to see this 45 yr old man Eduardo Constatine who has seen his GP as he is depressed.

TASK FOR THE CANDIDATE
- Elicit a history of Depression.

PAY PARTICULAR ATTENTION TO THE FOLLOWING (MENTAL CHECKLIST)
- Establish core symptoms of Depression.
- Establish the biological symptoms.
- Establish the cognitive symptoms.
- Establish the presence of negative cognitions.
- Conduct a risk assessment including suicidal ideation.
- Establish the presence of psychotic symptoms.
- Exclude co-morbid conditions – i.e. Anxiety, Obsessive Compulsive Disorder (OCD).

COMMUNICATION SKILLS
- Start the interview by developing rapport and showing empathy.
- Show sensitivity.
- Seek to understand the subjective experience of the individual.
- Anticipate that there could be evidence of psychomotor retardation.

Suggested approach
Introduction
C: Hello, I'm Dr... a psychiatrists working in this hospital. I have been asked to see you by your GP. I understand that you have not been feeling well. Can you tell me more about this?

A. Establish Core features of Depression
- How have you been feeling in yourself? (Low mood)
- How are you feeling in your spirits?
- Does that vary at any time of the day? (Diurnal variation)
- Is there any particular time of the day your mood is worst?
- On a scale of 0 to 10 where would you say your mood is on most days?
- How has your energy levels been? (Energy)
- Are you able to enjoy things you usually do? (Anhedonia).
- What are these things? (For example find out about hobbies like going out, etc.)
- How do you spend your day?

B. Biological symptoms

GENERAL ADULT PSYCHIATRY

- How have you been sleeping? (insomnia or hypersomnia)
- Do you ever have any difficulty falling off to sleep?
- Do you get up earlier than usual?
- Do you need more sleep these days?
- How has your appetite been? (Appetite)
- Have there been any changes in your weight? (Weight)
- Has your interest in sex changed? (Libido)

C. Cognitive symptoms
- How has your concentration been? (Concentration)
- Are you able to read a book, newspaper or watch the television?
- How is your memory? (Memory)

D. Emotional symptoms
- How would you rate your self-esteem? (Self-esteem)
- How confident do you feel in yourself?
- Have you cried at all?
- How do you feel like about being with other people? (Isolating themselves)

E. Feelings of hopelessness, worthlessness and helplessness
- How do you see the future now?
- Do you feel hopeless, helpless or worthless in any way?
- (Hopelessness, helplessness and worthlessness)

F. Suicidal ideation, intent and plans
- Have you ever felt like life was not worth living?
- Have you had thoughts of wanting to end it all? (Suicidal ideation)
- What have you done? Or how close have you come to it?
- What plans have you thought about doing?
- Do you think you would harm or hurt yourself?
- Have you at any time mentally rehearsed what you would do? Have you told anyone?

Protective factors
- What would prevent you from doing this? (I.e. family, friends, pets)

G. Establish presence of psychotic symptoms-(Mood congruent delusions and hallucinations)
1. Delusions of Guilt
- Have you been feeling guilty about anything?
- Do you think you might have done something wrong or may have committed a crime or a sin?
- Do you think that you have you might have harmed your family or anyone else? Do you think that you deserve to be punished?

GENERAL ADULT PSYCHIATRY

2. Delusions of Poverty
- Do you have any concerns for your finances?

3. Nihilistic delusions
- Are you concerned about any parts of your body?
- Do you think you are suffering from any serious disease or are there any part of your body unhealthy?
- Have you ever felt that you do not exist?
  Do you think that something terrible is about to happen?

4. Hypochondriacal delusions
- Are you concerned that you might have a serious illness?
- for example cancer, AIDS (Acquired Immune deficiency syndrome)

H. Establish History of Presenting Complaint (HOPC) - onset, duration, progression and severity
- How long have you been feeling like this?
- What do you think may have caused you to feel like this?
- Do you have any particular worries?

I. Impact on biopsychosocial functioning
- How has this affected your family life?
- Do you work? Has your work suffered because of this?

J. Coping and supports
- How have you been coping?
- Some people drink or take street drugs, how about you?

K. Insight
- What do you think is wrong?

Summarise
Thank you for talking to me. To summarise what you have said is that you have been feeling low in mood and you have been experiencing difficulty sleeping. You are unable to enjoy the things you usually would do. You feel tired, and tend to isolate yourself. I think that you might be depressed. We have medication and talking therapies that would be beneficial for you. What do you think? (Insight)

DEPRESSION-HISTORY TAKING

Core features
- Low mood, diurnal variation, energy, anhedonia

Biological symptoms
- Sleep, appetite, weight, decreased libido

Cognitive symptoms
- Concentration, memory

Emotional symptoms
- Self-esteem, confidence, motivation
- Feelings of hopelessness, worthlessness and helplessness
- Suicidal ideation, intent and plans
- Protective factors

Establish presence of psychotic symptoms-Mood congruent
- Delusions and hallucinations delusions-Guilt, Poverty, Nihilistic, Hypochondriacal

Establish History of Presenting Complaint (HOPC) (onset, duration, progression, severity)

Impact on biopsychosocial functioning

Coping and support-drug and alcohol

Insight

Summarise

© Smartsesh

Diagnostic Criteria for Depression F32

(Adapted from ICD-10)

(a) Depression is classified as mild, moderate or severe. The cardinal symptoms are low mood, anhedonia and reduced energy levels of which at least two are required, along with two other symptoms from the lists below, for a period of more than 2 weeks, to make a diagnosis.

(b) Other common symptoms include: fatigability, reduced concentration, reduced attention, low self-esteem, reduced confidence, guilt, ideas of unworthiness, irritability, hopelessness., pessimistic views of the future, disturbed sleep, diminished appetite, and ideas or acts of self-harm or suicide.

(c) Somatic symptoms include; loss of interest in pleasurable activities, early morning waking, Depression worse in the mornings, objective psychomotor retardation or agitation, marked loss of appetite, weight loss, marked loss of libido. If 4 or more symptoms present, 'somatic syndrome 'can be added to the diagnosis.

(d) For moderate Depression two cardinal symptoms and 3 or 4 others are required. Similarly for severe Depression all three cardinal symptoms are present plus 4 other symptoms. Severe Depression is usually characterised by considerable distress, agitation or retardation and can be coded with or without psychotic symptoms.

GENERAL ADULT PSYCHIATRY

2. DEPRESSION

INSTRUCTIONS TO CANDIDATE
You have been asked to see the wife, Marissa Constantine, of the man you assessed.

TASK FOR THE CANDIDATE
- Explain his diagnosis and management of Depression.

PAY PARTICULAR ATTENTION TO THE FOLLOWING (MENTAL CHECKLIST)
- Explain the diagnosis of Depression.
- Explain the epidemiology, aetiology and prognosis.
- Explain the management using a biopsychosocial approach.

COMMUNICATION SKILLS
- Start the interview by developing rapport and showing empathy.
- Show sensitivity.

Suggested approach
Introduction
C: Hello, I'm Dr...I am a psychiatrists working in this hospital. I have seen your husband, and I understand that you wanted to find out more about his condition and how we will be able to treat him.
Before we begin, can you tell me what your understanding of his condition.

W: He is not interested in doing anything anymore, and prefers to keep to himself.

C: From my assessment with him, it appears that he has the core features of Depression. We all get sad or feel miserable in life from time to time. This usually doesn't last for more than a few days. Depression occurs if someone continues to remain sad or unhappy for longer than 2 weeks and it then eventually starts to affect our lives.

W: What are the symptoms and signs of Depression?

C: People who are depressed may feel unhappy, anxious or irritable. They lose interest in activities that were once pleasurable and find it hard to concentrate. They experience problems with sleep leaving them feeling exhausted and fatigued. They lose their appetite leading to weight loss. Depressed people can also have feelings of being inadequate, useless and hopeless. They start to avoid other people and isolate themselves. In severe cases they start to have distressing thoughts of wanting to harm themselves.

GENERAL ADULT PSYCHIATRY

W: How common is Depression?

C: Depression affects 1 in 5 people, and is equally common in both men and women.

W: What causes Depression?

C: There is no one particular cause for Depression. It can be caused by a number of different factors. It can run in families due to a genetic component. From the evidence we have, it is thought to be caused by an imbalance of chemicals in the brain, which act on the areas of the brain that control mood and thinking. [Serotonin]
It can also be triggered by stressful life events, like financial problems, death of a loved one or relationship break down.

W: What are the treatments available to treat his Depression?

C: We have a range of treatment available which includes medication, psychological or talking therapy and the social aspects of care.

W: I have heard about antidepressants, can you tell me about that?

C: Antidepressants are a group of the medication we use to treat Depression.

W: How does it work?

C: Antidepressant act on areas of the brain associated with mood and thinking and correct the imbalance of chemical messengers in the brain. [Serotonin]. Depression is thought to occur because of low levels of these chemicals or neurotransmitters.

W: How long does it take to have effect?

C: Most antidepressants take two to four weeks to build up in our body and have an effect. Our plan would be to start him on the lowest effective dose of the antidepressant. We usually start an antidepressant from the group called the SSRI or selective serotonin reuptake inhibitors [SSRI). We would then review him in 1-2 weeks after commencing the treatment. The dose can then be gradually increased.

W: What are the side effects?

C: Like all other medication, antidepressants also have some side effects. They are usually mild and not everyone experiences these side effects. It is important that he is aware of the side effects. If he does experience any of them then he would need to contact me or his family doctor (GP).

The possible side effects include nausea, vomiting, diarrhoea, sleep problems, loss of appetite and restlessness or Anxiety. Most of the side effects occur in *the early part of the treatment and it is usually because the body becomes is becoming used to the medicine. It should gradually ease away.*

W: What happens if he stops taking the medication?

C: It is important for him to take the antidepressant regularly. It is not advisable to stop them suddenly even if he does feel better. This can cause his Depression to come back and he might experience mild discontinuation symptoms, which can include Anxiety, agitation, headache, dizziness, electric shock sensations in the head and abdominal cramps.

W: Are antidepressants addictive?

C: Antidepressants are not addictive as they are not known to cause any cravings.

W: I have heard that Prozac® can cause people to be suicidal?

C: There has been a lot of publicity in the media about the link between suicidal thoughts and Prozac® (Fluoxetine). The Committee for the Safety of Medicines (CSM) has thoroughly investigated the evidence and did not find a link. Suicidal thoughts commonly occur also as part of the depressive symptoms.

W: Would he be able to take his other medication with these antidepressants?

C: He would need to be cautious and aware of the drug interactions that these medication can have. For example there are some over the counter medicines like painkillers, antihistamines and St John's wart, which can interact with antidepressants so it is best to discuss with the pharmacist or GP doctor, if there are any concerns.

W: How long will he need to take treatment?

C: The first episode of Depression should be treated for 4-6 months after resolution of his symptoms. Patients with two previous episodes should be treated for at least 2 years. In Recurrent Depressive Disorder treatment may be required for many years.

W: What is the prognosis?

C: The outcome is very promising. Nearly 80% of the people benefit from treatment and can lead a normal life. About 4-5 people get better even without treatment.

W: What can I do to help him?
Your support and understanding of his condition is important in his recovery and wellbeing. We will also endeavour to keep you informed at all stages of

GENERAL ADULT PSYCHIATRY

his treatment in order to make decisions about this.

Summarize
Thank you for talking to me. I have told you more about your husband's condition Depression, and the possible treatment options like antidepressant medication. We also have psychological treatment called CBT or Cognitive behavioural therapy which is also recommended. I can arrange to discuss that with you both.

I have some leaflets for you to read. The useful organisations to contact are the National Depression campaign and Depression alliance.

Support groups and websites
Depression Alliance:
Information, support and understanding for people who suffer with Depression, and for relatives who want to help. Self-help groups, information, and raising awareness for Depression.

Depression UK:
It is a national mutual support group for people suffering from Depression.

Royal college of psychiatrist's health information leaflets for patient's www.rcpsych.ac.uk

NATURE -TREATMENT/INTERVENTION TRICYCLIC ANTIDEPRESSANTS (TCA's)

Purpose: *Depression, Anxiety, Eating disorders, Panic, OCD (obsessive Compulsive disorder), Neuropathic pain*

Medication
- *Amitryptilline*
- *Clomipramine*
- *Dosulepin*
- *Doxepin*
- *Imipramine*
- *Lofempramine*
- *Nortriptyline*
- *Trimipramine*
- *Effects/benefits*

Adverse/side effects
- *Common*
- *Anticholinergic side effects: dry mouth, constipation, drowsiness, blurred vision, weight gain, difficulty in micturition*
- *Uncommon*
- *Headache, nausea, palpitations, postural hypotension, sexual dysfunction, sweating*
- *Rare: tremor*

Precautions
- *Discontinuation symptoms if you stop: Anxiety, dizziness, feeling sick, insomnia*
- *Epilepsy, Phaechromocytoma, diabetes, phaechromocytoma, glaucoma, heart, kidney, liver, thyroid or prostate trouble*

Alternatives SSRI's

© Smartsesh

NICE guidelines for Depression
(Adapted from NICE guidance)
- ➤ *Screening high risk primary care attendees (past history, physically ill, demented, etc.) is necessary.*
- ➤ *If co-morbid Depression and Anxiety present, treat Depression first.*
- ➤ *Depression should be classified as per severity for proper management.*
- ➤ *Watchful waiting with no active intervention for mild Depression is an advocated strategy if agreeable; review must be in 2 weeks.*
- ➤ *Antidepressants have poor risk benefit ratio for mild Depression- so not advocated. CBT based guided self-help can be advised.*
- ➤ *For mild/moderate Depression CBT, counselling or problem solving therapy can be advised.*
- ➤ *SSRIs to be used first line as antidepressants.*
- ➤ *With severe Depression, a combination of antidepressants and CBT should be considered as the combination is more cost effective than either treatment on its own.*
- ➤ *For patients with a moderate or severe depressive episode, continue antidepressants for at least 6 months after remission.*
- ➤ *Patients with >2 episodes in the past, or with residual impairment should continue antidepressants at least for two years.*
- ➤ *SSRIs to be used first in atypical Depression before referral to specialist. In women with atypical features, specialists may consider phenelzine if no response to SSRIs.*
- ➤ *Patients who have had multiple episodes but with good response to lithium augmentation of antidepressants, should remain on the combination for at least 6 months.*
- ➤ *Electroconvulsive therapy (ECT) should only be used to achieve rapid and short-term improvement of severe symptoms after an adequate trial of other treatments has proven ineffective, and/or when the condition is considered to be potentially life-threatening, in a severe depressive illness.*
- ➤ *ECT maintenance is not recommended.*

GENERAL ADULT PSYCHIATRY

3. OVERDOSE

Suggested approach
Introduction
C: Hello, I'm Dr ....I am the on call psychiatrist. Thank you for agreeing to see me. I understand from the doctor in the Accident and Emergency department (A+E) that you had been brought here as you had taken an overdose. I am sorry to hear that. Are you able to tell me what happened? [Reassure regarding confidentiality]

A. History of Presenting Complaint (HOPC) (onset, duration, progression and severity)

P: Hello

C: I know this may be difficult for you. However because of what happened I do need to ask you some questions.

Further enquiry about overdose

GENERAL ADULT PSYCHIATRY

Para suicide
- Where were you at the time when you took the overdose?
- What did you do?
- What tablets did you take? How many tablets were there? [Calculate dosage]
- Did you take anything else with them? Did you perhaps take any alcohol?

Degree of Preparation
Planning
- Did you have a plan to end it all and for how long?
- Has it been a spur of the moment decision? (Impulsive)
- How did you get the tablets?

Suicide note
- Did you write a note, send text messages, email, Facebook, or call anyone?

Last acts
- What preparation did you do?
- Did you bid farewell to anyone? Have you told anyone?

Circumstances of overdose
- When did you take the tablets?
- Were you been alone? What did you do to prevent someone finding you?

Post suicidal attempt (after the act)
- How did you feel after taking the tablets?
- What did you do next?
- Did you make yourself sick?
- Did you seek help?
- How were you discovered? How did you get to the hospital?
- Do you regret that your overdose did not succeed in killing you?
- Do you still think about killing yourself? (Suicidal ideation)
- Is it possible you might plan to end it all again? (Suicidal intent)

Suicidal ideation and intent
- What was your intention? What were you thinking at the time?
- Did you have thoughts of wanting to end it all? Did you believe that that amount would kill you? (lethality)

Current suicide risk
- How do you see the future now?
- Do you still have thoughts of wanting to end it all?
- What do you think you might do?

Precipitating factors

GENERAL ADULT PSYCHIATRY

- *Why did you take the overdose?*
- *What sorts of things have been troubling you?*
- *What do you think was the final straw?*
- *How are things at home, school, work, college?*
- *Are you in any relationship?*

Recent history of Depression
- *How have you been feeling in yourself? (Mood)*
- *How has your energy levels been? (Energy)*
- *Have you been able to enjoy things you usually would do? (Anhedonia)*
- *How have you been eating? (Biological symptoms)*
- *How have you been sleeping?*
- *Have you lost or gained any weight?*

Screen for psychotic symptoms if necessary
- *I should like to ask you routine questions which we ask of everybody. Have you had any strange experiences?*
- *Do you ever seem to hear noises or voices when there is no one about, and nothing else to explain it?*

Hopelessness
- *Do you ever feel hopeless?*
- *Do you ever feel that things will not or cannot get better?*
- *Are there times when you cannot see beyond your suffering?*
- *Do you ever wish your life would end?*

Relevant past psychiatric history
B. Past Deliberate self-harm attempts (DSH)
- *Can you tell me how you usually cope?*
- *Have you self-harmed in the past? If so, how serious was it*
- *Other means of self-harm (cutting, jumping in front of a car or a train, bridge, carbon monoxide poisoning, tying ligatures, attempted hanging)*

C. Past psychiatric history
- *Have you ever seen a psychiatrist in the past?*

D. Personal and family history
- *Is there anyone in the family that has any similar problems?*

E. Medical History
- *How is your physical health?*

F. Medication
- *Are you on any regular medication?*

G. Social history (establish social support network)

GENERAL ADULT PSYCHIATRY

- *With whom do you live?*
- *Is there anyone you can confide in? Is there anyone you feel comfortable to share your problems with?*
- *Who is the one person that you are able to trust?*

H. Drug and alcohol history

I. Risk Assessment
Summarise according to severity of risk
To assess for further management plan of inpatient treatment or community treatment dependent on the severity of the risk assessment.

Risk assessment according to severity
a) Mild Risk
Thank you for talking and opening up to me. I know that this must not have been easy. To summarise, you have taken an overdose and it was due to certain personal difficulties. You now regret taking the overdose and have good support at home. What would you like to happen?

b) Moderate risk
Thank you for talking to me. I know this must not have been easy. To summarise you have taken an overdose and this is related to some difficulties you are experiencing. You now regret the overdose, however you have expressed that you are continue to have on-going thoughts of self-harm. I would like to refer you to the crisis team for an assessment. This is a 24hour team that plays an important role in
supporting people, like you in crisis. They would visit you at home, assist with dispensing medication and support you through this.
What do you think?

c. High risk
Thank you for talking to me. I know this must not have been easy. To summarise, you have taken a serious overdose with the intention of wanting to die and that it appears you are experiencing some depressive symptoms. I would like you to stay in hospital so that we can see how best we can get you better. We have treatment options of medication, psychological or talking therapy and the social aspects of care to promote your recovery.
Thank you

If possible you can mention methods to prevent future overdoses, i.e. using blister packs and keeping medication locked away.

Support groups and websites
Samaritans: Telephone and email support for anyone who is worried, upset, or suicidal
NHS direct: a helpline with health advice provided by NHS nurses

The Silent Cry: a charity to help people to deal with self-harm whether a sufferer, relative or partner.

GENERAL ADULT PSYCHIATRY

Possible variations of theme
1. 23 yr old who has taken an overdose of 40 paracetamol following an argument with her boyfriend.
2. 26 yr old lady who has cut herself following argument with her girlfriend.

OVERDOSE –SUICIDE RISK ASSESSMENT
HOPC (onset, duration, progression and severity)
- *Para suicide*
- *Preparation*
- *Preparation*
- *Planning*
- *Suicidal ideation and intent*
- *Precautions*
- *Preparatory acts*
- *Post suicidal attempt*
- *Precipitating factors*
- *Regrets*

Establish presence of underlying mental illness
Past Deliberate self-harm (DSH)-*other methods i.e. cutting, jumping in front of cars etc, carbon monoxide poisoning, tying ligatures)*
Past psychiatric history-*Depression*
Personal and family history-*suicide*
Medical History
Medication
Social history and support network *–confidant*
Drug and alcohol history
Risk Assessment-*tailor management according to severity of risk*
Mild *– discharge home*
Moderate *–referral to crisis team*
Severe- *admission either informal/detained under MHA*

© *Smartsesh*

GENERAL ADULT PSYCHIATRY

4. DELIBERATE SELF- HARM

Suggested approach
Introduction
C: Hello, I'm Dr ....I am the on call psychiatrists. Thank you for agreeing to see me. I understand from the doctor in the Accident and Emergency department (A+E) that you came here because you cut your wrists. Are you able to tell me more about what happened?

P: I'm not sure what got over me. It felt like a release of the tension at the time.

A. History of Presenting Complaint (HOPC) (severity, onset, duration, progression)
Deliberate self-harm attempt
- *Can you tell me what happened?*
- *How did you self-harm? What did you use? (For example glass, razor, knife, broken sharp object)*
- *How were you feeling at the time? (Mood)*
- *What did you do next? Can you describe exactly what you did?*
- *How deep were the cuts? May I have a look please (examine areas of lacerations for depth i.e. superficial or deep)*
- *How did you get to the hospital?*

Precautions

53

GENERAL ADULT PSYCHIATRY

- *Did you take any precautions while you were doing this?*

Planning
- *Was it planned or impulsive?*

Lethality
- *What was your intention at the time of doing this?*

Suicidal thoughts
- *Have you been having thoughts of wanting to end it all?*

B. Past history of Deliberate Self-Harm (DSH)
- *How do you usually cope?*
- *Have you self-harmed in the past? If so, how serious was it*
- *Other means of self-harm (cutting, jumping in front of a car or a train, bridge, carbon monoxide poisoning, tying ligatures, attempted hanging)*

C. Past psychiatric history
- *Have you ever seen a psychiatrist in the past?*

D. Identify Precipitating factors
Biological
- *What do you think could have triggered this? Why do you think you self-harmed?*

Medication
- *Are you on any regular medication?*

Psychological
Contributing underlying mental illness [Depression, Anxiety}
Establish presence of Borderline personality traits
[Emotional stability, tolerance of frustration, risk behaviours, fluctuating mood, empty feeling]
- *How have your relationships worked out?*
- *How has your mood been? Does it fluctuate?*
- *How do you cope if someone annoys you?*
- *How do you react if you lose your temper? Do you ever feel like you have an empty feeling?*

Social history
- *Is there anything that has been troubling you in any way?*
- *How have things been at home, college, work, or with your relationships?*
- *With whom do you live?*
- *Are you in any relationship?*
- *Do you work?*

GENERAL ADULT PSYCHIATRY

Coping
E. Drug and alcohol history
- *Do you drink or take any street drugs?*

F. Suicide Risk Assessment
- *Do you have thoughts now of wanting to end it all?*
- *How do you feel now about what you have done? (Suicidal thoughts) Do you have any regrets?*
- *Do you think you will do this again?*
- *What would prevent you from doing this? (Protective factors)*

G. Personal and family history
- *Is there anyone in the family that has any similar problems?*

H. Medical History
- *How is your physical health?*

I. Social history (establish social support network)
- *With whom do you live?*
- *Is there anyone you can confide in? Is there anyone you feel comfortable to share your problems with?*
- *Who is the one person that you are able to trust?*

J. Insight
- *What would you do the next time you have these thoughts?*
- *What help would you like?*

Summarise
Thank you for talking to me. To summarise, you have been self-harming and this usually occurs when you feel stressed. You find that this helps relieve the tension that you are feeling and that you had no intention of killing yourself. You do want to get the appropriate help for this. We have some talking therapies and medication for you to consider.

I will give you the Crisis team (or the acute home treatment team) helpline number. Some people find it helpful to contact someone when they start to get those distressing thoughts.

Support groups and websites

Samaritans: *Telephone and email support for anyone who is worried, upset, or suicidal*
NHS Direct: *a helpline with health advice provided by NHS nurses*

GENERAL ADULT PSYCHIATRY

The Silent Cry: *a charity to help people to deal with self-harm whether a sufferer, relative or partner*

DELIBERATE SELF HARM (DSH)-SUICIDE RISK ASSESSMENT
History of presenting complaint (HOPC)-*severity, onset, duration, progression*
Deliberate self-harm attempt
- *Precautions*
- *Planning*
- *Lethality*
- *Precipitating factors*
- *Regrets*

Past history of Deliberate Self-harm (DSH) - *other methods i.e. cutting, jumping in front of cars etc, carbon monoxide poisoning, tying ligatures)*
Exclude presence of underlying mental illness- *Depression, Anxiety*
Elicit borderline personality traits-*[Emotional stability, tolerance of frustration, risk behaviours, frustration, fluctuating mood, empty feeling]*
Past psychiatric history
Personal and family history-*suicide, self-harm*
Drug and alcohol history
Social history-*establish support network, confidant*
Suicide risk assessment

©Smartsesh

Possible variation of theme
1.20 yr. old man, known with Asperger's, self-harmed by cutting with a broken glass by his neck
2.18 yr old lady who has come to A+E on a section 136 with cutting herself. She has had numerous presentations for this in the past.

GENERAL ADULT PSYCHIATRY

Borderline or Emotionally Unstable Personality disorder

- *impulsive*
- *find it hard to control emotions*
- *feeling bad about yourself*
- *often self-harm by cutting yourself or making suicide attempts*
- *feel 'empty'*
- *make relationships quickly, but easily lose them*
- *can feel paranoid or depressed*
- *when stressed, may hear noises or voices*

GENERAL ADULT PSYCHIATRY

5. POST MYOCARDIAL INFARCT DEPRESSION

INSTRUCTIONS TO CANDIDATE
You have been asked by the cardiologist to assess this gentleman Nicholas Pritchard who is suspected to be suffering with a Moderate Depressive Disorder.

TASK FOR THE CANDIDATE
- Establish the diagnosis of Depression and attitude to illness.

PAY PARTICULAR ATTENTION TO THE FOLLOWING (MENTAL CHECKLIST)
- Establish his depressive symptoms.
- Establish his social history.
- Enquire about his understanding of MI and his attitude to treatment.
- Establish his insight and motivation.
- Conduct a risk assessment.

COMMUNICATION SKILLS
- Start the interview by developing rapport and showing empathy.
- Anticipate difficulty in engagement.
- Seek to understand the impact of this Myocardial Infarct (MI) on his life.
- Discuss these issues with sensitivity.
- Use motivational interviewing style.

Suggested approach
Introduction
C: Hello, I'm Dr ....I am a psychiatrist working in this hospital. The cardiologists have asked me to come and see you. I gather that you are recovering from a heart attack. I know it has been a difficult time for you but if it is ok with you, I would like to find out how you are feeling and how the heart attack has affected you.
P: Pretty rough!!

C: It would be helpful for me if you could tell me about the heart attack. When did this happen?

A. History of Presenting Complaint (HOPC) (onset, duration, progression and severity)
- Can you describe to me what happened?
- What treatment have you received thus far?
- Have you had a past history of chest pain or angina?
- Do you have family history of cardiovascular disease? I.e. high blood pressure, diabetes, strokes

GENERAL ADULT PSYCHIATRY

What do you understand about your chances of full recovery?

B. Elicit Depressive symptoms
Core features
- *How have you been feeling in yourself since then? (Mood)*
- *If low in mood, for how long?*
- *How's your energy levels been? (Energy). Do you find it easy to perform ordinary daily tasks?*
- *Are you able to enjoy things you usually would do? What is that? (Anhedonia)*

Biological symptoms
- *How have you been sleeping? (Sleep). (Establish if there is a pattern of hypersomnia or insomnia)*
- *How have you been eating? (Appetite)*
- *Have you lost any weight? (Weight)*

Cognitive and emotional
- *How has your attention and concentration been? (Concentration)*
- *How is your memory? (Memory)*
- *How do you feel about yourself? How is your self-esteem? (Self-esteem)*
- *Do you have any guilt feelings? (Guilt)*
- *Establish presence of negative cognitions*

C. Risk assessment
- *It seems like you have gone through a difficult time.*
- *How do you see the future now? Do you think you can get better? (Feelings of worthlessness, helplessness and hopelessness)*
- *Have you had thoughts that life is not worth living at all? (Suicidal thoughts). How might you do it if you thought of ending it all?*

D. Cardiac Rehabilitation
- *Can you tell me more about the cardiac rehabilitation programme*
- *What have they told you about the healthy lifestyle changes? Are you able to identify which lifestyle risk factor affects you?*

Tease out tactfully each of the risk factors and his attitude towards compliance with the rehabilitation programme

E. Risk factors
- *Stress, Alcohol, Work, Diet ,Exercise ,Family, Smoking*
F. Assess level of motivation
- *How motivated are you to engage in this rehabilitation programme? Is it something you are looking forward to?*
- *Have you been taking the medication?*
- *How do you feel about attending the appointments?*
- *What do you think will happen if you don't engage in this? What about your family?*

GENERAL ADULT PSYCHIATRY

- *How do you see the future if you are not able to do this?*

G. Past psychiatric history
- *Have you seen a psychiatrist in the past?*

H. Personal and family history
- *Is there anyone in the family that has any similar problems?*

Summarize
Thank you for talking to me. I know that you have been through a difficult time. The heart attack has resulted in a significant adjustment to your life. I hope you will continue to engage you're your rehabilitation. From what you have told me, I believe that you are now depressed. This is a common occurrence in people after they have had a heart attack.

Insight
We have medication and psychotherapy or talking therapy which will be beneficial for you.
What do you think? (Insight)
I would like to meet with you again.

POST MYOCARDIAL INFARCT DEPRESSION
History of presenting complaint HOPC (onset, duration, progression, severity)
Elicit Depressive symptoms
Risk assessment-*suicidal ideation*
Cardiac rehabilitation-*healthy lifestyle changes,*
- *medication, physiotherapy, appointments*

Assess his attitude towards compliance with the rehabilitation programme
Risk factors
- *Stress, alcohol, Work, Diet, Exercise, Family, Smoking*

Assess level of motivation
Past psychiatric history
Personal and family history
Summary
Insight

© *Smartsesh*

POSSIBLE VARIATIONS OF THEME
1. 34 yr. old man who suffered a heart attack and is refusing to consent to an angiogram. Do a capacity assessment.
2. 64 yr. old lady had a heart attack and depressed and suicidal.

GENERAL ADULT PSYCHIATRY

6. POST MYOCARDIAL INFARCT DEPRESSION

INSTRUCTIONS TO CANDIDATE
You are asked to see discuss the management of the gentleman you saw in the previous station with the psychiatry consultant.

TASK FOR THE CANDIDATE
- Discuss management of Post Myocardial Infarct Depression.

PAY PARTICULAR ATTENTION TO THE FOLLOWING (MENTAL CHECKLIST)
- Give a psychiatric formulation of your assessment.
- Highlight the capacity issues.
- Establish possible differential diagnoses.
- Formulate management plan using a holistic or biopsychosocial approach.
- Highlight risk issues related to Depression and Myocardial infarct (MI).

COMMUNICATION SKILLS
- Explain in a clear and concise manner.
- Adopt a collegiate approach

Suggested approach
Introduction
C: Hello, I'm Dr ..... I am the on call psychiatrist. The cardiologists referred this gentleman who was admitted with a Myocardial Infarct. He is thought to have a diagnosis of Moderate Depressive Disorder. I have come to discuss with you more about my assessment, diagnosis and management.

Psychiatric formulation
A. Give a Brief synopsis including Summary of demographic data
An example would be:
45 yr. old gentleman married, employed, with 2 children. He is presenting with features of a Moderate Depressive Disorder secondary to Myocardial Infarct (MI) (and underlying physical illness).
He is now presenting with decreased motivation, poor compliance and poor engagement with cardiac rehabilitation. This is possibly due to the adverse influence of his Depressive illness.

B. Psychiatric assessment
He has the following relevant history [include the following from your assessment]
- Past psychiatric history
- Personal and family history
- Medical History
- Medication
- Drug and alcohol history
- Forensic, Psychosexual, Social history

- *Risk Assessment*

Comment on evidence of suicidal ideation, intent or plans.

Highlight Risk factors *for cardiac disease: alcohol, smoking, sedentary lifestyle, exercise, diet, stress*

C. Mental state examination [comment on findings]
The following Depressive symptoms were present:
-Core features: low mood, decreased energy, anhedonia.
-In addition to the following biological symptoms (poor sleep, decreased appetite and decreased libido).
-He has feelings of hopelessness, helplessness and worthlessness.
-He has also has ongoing suicidal ideation, intent and plans.

My capacity assessment was to ascertain whether he was able to:
-understand his current medical condition
-retain that information of cardiac rehabilitation
-weigh the risks and benefits of continuing with cardiac rehabilitation
-communicate his decision about this proposed treatment

In terms of capacity, I think his current understanding and judgement of engaging in this cardiac rehabilitation is being affected by his underlying mental illness of a Moderate Depressive disorder, as he lacks motivation and insight to engage in this therapeutic treatment.

My differential diagnoses are
1. Adjustment disorder
2. Moderate -Severe Depressive disorders

Current risks are
- *Increased mortality if myocardial infarct is not treated*
- *3 times increased risk of death also if not treated.*

D. *My* **management plan** *using a holistic or biopsychosocial approach in the immediate, medium and longer term is:*

Biological interventions
Investigations
- *Collateral history and further information from GP, family and other professionals*
- *Check blood investigations – Full blood count (FBC), Urea and electrolytes (U+E) Liver function tests (LFT), Thyroid function tests (TFT) and glucose.*
- *Rating scales- MADRS: to assess changes, HAM-D (Hamilton Rating scale for Depression-severe with somatic), BDI-Becks Depression inventory.*
- *Healthy living advice on general wellbeing and to promote recovery*
- *Address the underlying risk factors*
  - *Diet-promote healthy eating*
  - *Exercise-increase physical activity*
  - *Smoking cessation*
  - *Alcohol*

Medication-my choice of medication would be guided by
- According to the SADHART trial, and NICE(National institute of clinical excellence) guidelines the choice of antidepressant for a person following Myocardial infarct is Sertraline
- I would avoid using other SSRI'S due to the enzyme induction effect on CYP2DT(enzyme)
- I would also avoid using Tri-cyclic antidepressants(TCA's)-due to its known arrythmogenic effect

Psychological interventions
The psychological therapy is Cognitive Behavioural Therapy (CBT). This will help to promote recovery, reduce symptoms and prevent worsening. It can also help to improve motivation, compliance and reduce stress.

Social interventions
I would involve the Multi-Disciplinary Team (MDT) in order to facilitate collaborative multi-agency working with the cardiac rehabilitation. (Psychiatry Liaison service if available).
Social worker:
To assist with gradual reintroduction back to work
To assist with any other social supports

Part of the rehabilitation programme would be to continue with occupational therapy and physiotherapy. They would also advice on any ambulatory aids if necessary.

Longer term
The aim would be to improve the therapeutic alliance and provide regular outpatients with effective community support to promote his wellbeing and recovery

POST MYOCARDIAL INFARCT DEPRESSION-MANAGEMENT
Summary of demographic data
Psychiatric formulation
Psychiatric assessment
- Past psychiatric history, Personal and family history, Medical
- History, Medication, Drug and alcohol, Forensic,
- Psychosexual, Social,

Risk Assessment-If evidence of suicidal ideation, intent or plans
- Risk factors for cardiac disease-alcohol, smoking, sedentary
- lifestyle, exercise, diet, stress

Mental state examination
- Assess for depressive symptoms

My differential diagnoses are
- Adjustment disorder
- Moderate –Severe depressive disorder

Risks: post MI Depression carries a 3 fold risk of mortality if untreated
My management plan using a holistic or bio-psychosocial approach in the immediate, medium and longer term is
Biological interventions
- Investigations
- Collateral history and further information from GP
- Check blood investigations –FBC(Full blood count), U+E(Urea and electrolyte), LFT(Liver function tests), TFT, glucose
- Rating scales- MADRS, HAM-D
- Healthy living advice on general wellbeing

Address the underlying risk factors: Diet, Exercise, Smoking cessation
Alcohol

©Smartsesh

GENERAL ADULT PSYCHIATRY

7. ANTIDEPRESSANTS -SEXUAL SIDE EFFECTS

INSTRUCTIONS TO THE CANDIDATE
You have been asked to see this 35 yr. old, John Blake, who is currently on Fluoxetine for his Depression for the past 4 months. He has been referred to you by his GP as he says he wants to stop his antidepressant medication.

TASK FOR THE CANDIDATE
- *Assess for sexual side effects.*

PAY PARTICULAR ATTENTION TO THE FOLLOWING (MENTAL CHECKLIST)
- *Acknowledge sensitive nature of complaint and importance to client.*
- *Ascertain current depressive features.*
- *Ascertain possible aetiological factors for sexual side effects.*
- *Ascertain the chronology of whether sexual dysfunction was present prior to commencing antidepressant or after.*
- *Discuss possible treatment options available in a collaborative approach.*
- *Consent to speak to partner.*

COMMUNICATION SKILLS
- *Anticipate that the client will be reluctant to discuss his sexual functioning.*
- *Establish rapport by reassuring that this is something psychiatrists commonly see.*
- *Preface personal questions.*
- *Seek to understand the subjective feelings of the individual.*

Suggested approach
Introduction
C: *Hello, I'm Dr ... I am a psychiatrist working in this community mental health team. Thank you for coming to see me. I understand that you want to stop your current antidepressant medication. Would you like to tell me more about this?*

A. History of Presenting Complaint (HOPC) (onset, duration, progression and severity)
Establish current antidepressant treatment
- *Can you tell me when you first started the antidepressant medication?*
- *How were you feeling at the time?*
- *Do you think there have been any changes since then?*
- *In what way do you think the medication has helped, if any?*
- *So what are your concerns now? Why would you like to stop the medication now?*

GENERAL ADULT PSYCHIATRY

B. Explore possible reasons for wanting to stop medication
Are you experiencing any side effects? Some people do experience some stomach upsets, sleep disturbance and sexual side effects. How about you?

P: I have been experiencing some sexual difficulties.

C: I can assure you that this is something I deal with on a regular basis and that you can feel comfortable to be open with me. Because of the nature of what you are describing I am going to have to ask you some personal questions. Is that all right with you?

C. Explore nature of sexual difficulties
- *Can you tell me what the current difficulties you are experiencing are?*
- *How is your desire or interest in sex? (libido)*
- *Do you get aroused? (arousal)*
- *Are you able to get an erection? (erection)*
- *Are you able to ejaculate? How about reach an orgasm? (ejaculation)*
- *Do you have any early morning erections?*
- *Do you experience any performance Anxiety? (performance Anxiety)*
- *How were things before the medication?*
- *What makes you think that this is now due to the medication?*

D. Psychosexual history
- *Can you tell me about your current relationship? (relationships)*
- *Have you discussed this with your partner?*
- *Can you tell me about your previous relationships?*
- *Have you had any such difficulties in the past?*
- *Have you ever been unfaithful? (infidelity)*
- *Do you have any fantasies?*

E. Elicit possible aetiological factors using a bio-psychosocial approach
1. Biological
- *Do you have any physical health problems?*
- *Do you have any history of diabetes mellitus (DM (Diabetes Mellitus)), hypertension (HPT (Hypertension)), injuries, and epilepsy or cardiac problems?*
- *Have you had any STIs? (sexually transmitted infection)*
- *How do you usually cope?*
- *Do you drink or take street drugs? (drug and alcohol history)*

2. Psychological
- *Is there anything that is troubling you? (stressors)*

3. Social
- *Are you working?*

F. Recapitulation

Thank you for talking to me. From what you have told me it appears that the antidepressants have helped to improve your mood and some of the other depressive symptoms. We commonly find in Depression, that it also affects a person's interest in sex. If the Depression is treated, we usually find that this also results in improved sexual desire and function.

I know this is important to you. I would therefore like to work collaboratively with you to discuss the treatment options we have available.

Elaborate further on the management tailored to given scenario.
G. Biopsychosocial approach to management
Biological interventions

- *It is good practice for us to exclude a possible physical cause for this by doing some blood investigations like full blood count, glucose level and thyroid function tests.*

Medication

In terms of antidepressant medication we have the following options:

- *Drug free holidays - meaning that we can consider stopping treatment over weekends.*
- *You can continue the current antidepressant as this has resulted in some symptom improvement. According to the guidelines (NICE National institute of clinical excellence) we follow for Depression, you would need to continue for at least 3-6 months. Hopefully, if symptoms do get better, we will see an improvement in sexual function.*
- *We can consider an alternative antidepressant which has a lesser propensity to cause sexual side effects, like Mirtazapine.*
- *Some people do ask about Viagra; however this is an option at a later stage once we have considered all the possible options. Like all medications; these too have their own side effects.*
- *If however you feel strongly and do decide to stop treatment I have to inform you there is a risk of relapse and you getting unwell. There is also the risk of withdrawal symptoms and what we call discontinuation symptoms.*

Psychological interventions

- *The psychological or talking therapy we can consider is Counselling, Couple Therapy, Sex Therapy or Other Talking Therapy, like Cognitive Behavioural Therapy (CBT). CBT is known to help cope with the sexual dysfunction and reduce the symptoms.*

Advice to promote wellbeing and recovery

- *Advice on healthy eating and lifestyle, exercise, smoking cessation, moderation of alcohol consumption.*

Summarise

GENERAL ADULT PSYCHIATRY

Thank you for talking to me. I would like to see you once we have the blood results back. I would also like to speak to your partner to find out more about this, is that all right with you? (Consent)

Thank you

SEXUAL SIDE EFFECTS- HISTORY
HOPC (ONSET, DURATION, PROGRESSION, SEVERITY)
Establish current antidepressant treatment
Explore possible reasons for wanting to stop medication. Possible Scenario:
- Due Side Effects - Stomach Upsets, Sleep Disturbance and Sexual Side Effect.

Explore nature of sexual difficulties
- Libido, arousal, erection, ejaculate, early morning erections, performance Anxiety.

Psychosexual history
- Current Relationship.
- Partner.
- Previous Relationships.
- Past Sexual Difficulties.
- Infidelity.
- Fantasies.

Elicit possible aetiological factors using a biopsychosocial approach
Biological interventions
- Physical health problems.
- History of DM(Diabetes Mellitus), HPT(Hypertension), Injuries, Epilepsy, Cardiac problems like MI.
- Drugs and alcohol history

Psychological interventions
- Performance Anxiety.

Social interventions
- Relationships.

Recapitulation

©Smartsesh

GENERAL ADULT PSYCHIATRY

POSSIBLE VARIATIONS OF THEME
1. 35 yr. old banker wants to stop anti-depressants due to sexual side effects.
2. 40yr. old man who has a history of alcohol dependence wants to stop medication.

SEXUAL SIDE EFFECTS: MANAGEMENT
Biopsychosocial approach to management
Biological interventions
- Exclude a possible physical cause for this by doing some blood investigations like Full Blood Count(FBC(Full blood count)), glucose level and Thyroid Function Tests(TFT)
- Selective Serotonin Reuptake Inhibitors(SSRI's) can affect the sex cycle- SSRI'S –cause reduced libido, impaired arousal, erectile dysfunction and absent or delayed orgasm, delayed ejaculation.

Options of treatment
- Drug free holidays if due to SSRI'S.
- Continue the current antidepressant as this has resulted in some symptom improvement.
- NICE guidelines-need to continue for at least 3-6 months.
- Alternative antidepressant which has less potential to cause sexual side effects, like Mirtazapine(15mg-45mg)
- Viagra®, (Sildenafil)-phosphodiesterase 5 inhibitor-side effects – headache, facial flushing, upset stomach, bluish and blurred vision, decreased hearing, sensitivity to light.
- Stop Treatment if risk of relapse, withdrawal symptoms and discontinuation syndrome.

Psychological intervention or talking therapy
- Counselling, couple therapy, sex therapy – Masters and Johnsons sensate focus or other talking therapy like CBT.

Social interventions
- **Promote wellbeing and recovery**- healthy eating and lifestyle changes, exercise, smoking sensation, moderation of alcohol consumption.

©Smartsesh

GENERAL ADULT PSYCHIATRY

8. ANTIDEPRESSANTS -SEXUAL SIDE EFFECTS

INSTRUCTIONS TO THE CANDIDATE
You have been asked to see Mrs Linda Blake. She is concerned about her husband and wants to discuss more about this. Address her concerns.

TASK FOR THE CANDIDATE
- *Discuss management of sexual side effects.*

PAY PARITCULAR ATTENTION TO THE FOLLOWING (MENTAL CHECKLIST)
- *Acknowledge sensitive nature of complaint and importance to partner.*
- *Ascertain possible aetiological factors for sexual side effects.*
- *Ascertain the impact of this on their relationship.*
- *Discuss possible treatment options available in a collaborative approach.*

COMMUNICATION SKILLS
- *Anticipate that the partner will be reluctant to discuss this issue.*
- *Establish rapport by reassuring that this is something psychiatrists commonly deal with.*
- *Preface sensitive questions.*
- *Establish common ground in acting in her partner's best interest.*

Suggested approach
Introduction
C: Hello, I am Dr....I a psychiatrists. I have seen your husband and he has given his consent for me to talk to you. Before we begin, can you tell me what your concerns are?

W: Things are not the same since he has been on this medication. I think he should stop this.

C: I can see this is clearly distressing to you as well. Can you tell me more about why you feel this way?

A. Establish husband's premorbid functioning
- *How would you describe your husband before he started the treatment?*

B. Establish Depressive symptoms
- *Can you tell me how he was just before starting the antidepressant medication?*
- *Can you tell me how he has been since starting the antidepressant medication?*
- *What are the changes you have noticed?*

GENERAL ADULT PSYCHIATRY

C. Explore reasons for wanting to stop antidepressant medication
*C: He tells me that he wants to stop the antidepressant; do you have
An idea why this would be?*
- *Do you share his concerns?*

D. Psychosexual history
*C: Because of the nature of the complaints I do need to ask you some
personal questions.*
- *Can you tell me how has the sexual or physical side of your
relationship been? (sexual relationship)*
- *How has his desire been? (desire)*
- *Is he able to get and maintain an erection? (erection)*
- *Is he able to ejaculate? (ejaculation)*

E. Establish impact of this on their relationship
So how has this affected your relationship?

Further response will be tailored to the scenario.

*Thank you for talking to me. I can imagine this must be difficult for you. I
understand this is something important to both of you. You have said that he
wants to stop the medication now. I want to discuss with you the possible
options we have available.*

F. Explain possible reasons for sexual side effects
There are two ways of looking at this:-
- *As we know, with Depression, it can sometimes affect the sexual side
of a relationship. We have found that with treatment this usually
gets better. On the other hand, we know that the Selective Serotonin
Re-uptake Inhibitors (SSRI's) like fluoxetine (e.g. Prozac®) can cause
sexual side effects.*

G. Biopsychosocial approach to management
Biological interventions
*It is good practice for us to exclude a possible physical cause for this by doing
some blood investigations like Full Blood Count (FBC (Full blood count)),
glucose level and Thyroid Function Tests (TFT).*

In terms of antidepressant medication the options are:
- *Drug free holidays is where he can stop medication over weekends.*
- *He can continue the current antidepressant as this has resulted in
some symptom improvement. According to the guidelines we follow
for Depression (NICE-National institute of clinical excellence), he
would need to continue for at least 3-6 months. Hopefully if
symptoms do get better, we will see an improvement in his sexual
function.*
- *We can also consider an alternative antidepressant which has lesser
propensity to cause sexual side effects, like Mirtazapine.*

- *Some people do ask about Viagra. ® This is an option at a later stage once we have considered all the possible options. Like all medication, they also have their own side effects.*
- *If however he feels strongly and does decide to stop treatment I have to inform you there is a risk of relapse in him getting unwell and he can get withdrawal symptoms as part of the discontinuation syndrome.*

Psychological interventions

- *The psychological or talking therapy we can consider counselling, couple therapy, sex therapy or other talking therapy like Cognitive Behavioural Therapy (CBT). CBT is known to help cope with the sexual dysfunction and reduce the symptoms.*

Advice to promote wellbeing and recovery

- *Advice on healthy eating and lifestyle, exercise, smoking cessation and moderation of alcohol consumption.*

Summarise

Thank you. I would like to see the both of you to consider the options available, and we can discuss this at the next appointment. Is that all right?

Support groups and websites

These are some useful website addresses:

www.clinical-Depression.co.uk/.../side-effects-of-antidepressants
www.relate.org.uk- offers relationship counselling, family counselling and sex therapy

SEXUAL SIDE EFFECTS: MANAGEMENT
Establish husbands pre morbid functioning
Establish current Depressive symptoms
Explore reasons for wanting to stop antidepressant
medication
Sexual history
- *Desire (libido) , erection , ejaculate*

Explain possible reasons for sexual side effects
- *Depression,*
- *SSRI's like Fluoxetine can cause sexual side effects- cause reduced libido, impaired arousal, erectile dysfunction and absent or delayed orgasm, delayed ejaculation*

Biopsychosocial approach to management
Biological intervention
- *Exclude a possible physical cause for this by doing some blood investigations like full blood count(FBC(Full blood count)), glucose level and thyroid function tests(TFT).*
- *Antidepressant medication*
- *Drug free holidays*
- *Continue the current antidepressant as this has resulted in some symptom improvement.*
- *NICE guidelines, you would need to continue for at least 3-6 months.*
- *Alternative antidepressant which has less potential to cause sexual side effects, like Mirtazapine*
- *Viagra®- once other options considered,(Sildenafil)-phosphodiesterase 5 inhibitor-side effects –headache, facial flushing, upset stomach, bluish and blurred vision, decreased hearing , sensitivity to light*
- *Stop treatment risk of relapse, withdrawal symptoms and discontinuation syndrome*

Psychological intervention
- *Counselling, couple therapy, sex therapy-Master and Johnson's sensate focus or other talking therapy like CBT.*

Social interventions
- *Support.*
- ***Promote wellbeing and recovery***
- *Healthy eating and lifestyle changes, exercise, smoking sensation, moderation of alcohol consumption.*

©Smartsesh

MEDICATION: SSRI'S
- Acronym for Selective Serotonin reuptake inhibitor
- Citalopram (Cipramil®), Ecitalopram (Cipralex®), Fluoxetine (Prozac®), Fluvoxamine (Faverin®) Paroxetine (Seroxat®), Sertaline (Lustral®)

Effects selectively increase the amount of serotonin (5HT) in the brain
- Usually seen in 2-3 weeks of treatment

Indications: Depression, Anxiety disorders, OCD

Contra-indications
- Caution in pregnancy and breast feeding
- Caution in epilepsy, diabetes, heart or kidney problems
- Drug interactions
- St Johns Wort
- Theophylline

Side effects
- Common: Anxiety, restless, diarrhoea, insomnia, loss of appetite, nausea and vomiting
- Fairly common: sexual dysfunction: difficulty with orgasm. Men: decreased desire and impotence
- Uncommon: dizziness, drowsiness and headache
- **SSRI discontinuation symptoms:** Anxiety, dizziness, sickness, confused, electric shock feelings in the body

Duration of treatment
- 1ST episode: continue for 6 months after you have recovered
- 2nd episode: continue taking for 1-2yrs after you have recovered
- Recurrent Depression: continue treatment for at least 5 years

©Smartsesh

MEDICATION	SIDE EFFECTS
SSRI'S	**Common:** Anxiety, restless, diarrhoea, insomnia, loss of appetite, nausea and vomiting
Selective Serotonin reuptake inhibitor	**Fairly common:** sexual **dysfunction:** difficulty with orgasm. Men: decreased desire and impotence
Citalopram (Cipramil®) Lundbeck 20mg to maximum 60mg	**Uncommon:** dizziness, drowsiness and headache
Ecitalopram (Cipralex®) Lundbeck 10mg to maximum 20mg	
Fluoxetine (Prozac®) Lilly 20mg to maximum 60mg	
Fluvoxamine (Faverin®) Abott Healthcare 50mg to maximum 300mg	
Paroxetine (Seroxat®)GSK 20mg to maximum 60mg	
Sertaline (Lustral®)Pfizer 50mg to maximum 200mg	

TCA'S **Tricyclic antidepressants** *Amitryptilline Triptafen® Goldshiled 75mg up to maximum 200mg* *Clomipramine Anafranil®Novartis 10mg increased to maximum 250mg* *Dosulepin Prothiaden®Teofarma 75mg to maximum 225mg* *Doxepin Sinepin®Marlborough 75mg to maximum 300mg* *Imipramine 75mg to maximum 300mg* *Lofempramine 140-210mg* *Nortriptyline Allegron® 75mg to maximum 100mg* *Trimipramine Surmontil® Sanofi-Aventis*	**Common:** *Anticholinergic side* **Effects:** *dry mouth, constipation, drowsiness, blurred vision, weight gain, difficulty in micturition* **Uncommon:** *Headache, nausea, palpitations, postural hypotension, sexual dysfunction, sweating* **Rare:** *tremor*
MAOI'S **Monoamine-oxidase inhibitors** *Phenelzine Nardil® (Archimedes)* *Isocarboxacid* *Tranylcypromine* *Moclobemide Manerix® (Meda)*	**Common**: *Sleep disturbance, dizziness,* **Less common:** *headache, restlessness, agitation, dry mouth, visual disturbance, oedema* **Rare:** *Raised liver enzymes, hyponatraemia*

9. LITHIUM AUGMENTATION

INSTRUCTIONS TO CANDIDATE
You have been asked to see a 34 yr old lady Mrs Norma Watson who has been tried on a few antidepressants with no improvement. She has come to talk to you about starting Lithium.

TASK FOR THE CANDIDATE
- *Discuss Lithium augmentation.*

PAY PARTICULAR ATTENTION TO THE FOLLOWING (MENTAL CHECKLIST)
- *Establish refractory or Treatment resistant Depression.*
- *Explain rationale for Lithium according to National institute of Clinical Excellence (NICE) guidelines.*
- *Advice on the effects, benefits, side effects, toxicity and precautions of Lithium blood level monitoring.*
- *Inform her of alternative treatment options.*

COMMUNICATION SKILLS
- *Start the interview by developing rapport and showing empathy.*
- *Anticipate that the patient will be concerned due to side effects of medication.*

Suggested approach
Introduction
C: *Hello, I'm Dr.....I understand that you have been tried on a few antidepressants, and that we were considering commencing you on Lithium as the next line of treatment. I would like to tell you a more about this. Is that all right with you? Before we begin, would you be able to tell me what your understanding of Lithium is?*

P: I know one of my friends is on it and it seems to have helped her.

C: *Lithium is known as a mood stabiliser and it has been shown to be effective in the treatment of mania to prevent further mood swings for Bipolar Affective Disorder (BPAD).*
Lithium can also be used in Treatment Resistant Depressive Disorder to enhance the effects of the antidepressant. That is when the antidepressants alone have not been effective in treating Depression

P: What are the side effects?

Shorter term
C: *Like all medication, Lithium does have side effects which are variable, dose related, mild and self-limiting. Many people don't get side effects.*

Some of the common side effects include slight stomach upset, feeling a sick, metallic taste and it can cause dry mouth. It can also cause you to drink more and pass more urine.

Longer term
The longer term effects include tremor, weight gain, acne or skin rash, it can cause under activity of the thyroid gland and affect the kidney function.

P: What do we do prior to starting treatment?

C: Before you start Lithium you will need to have a blood test to check your thyroid function and renal function to ensure that it is safe for you to have Lithium. Lithium can cause the thyroid gland to be underactive. Lithium is also passed in the urine, so we check your kidney function to ensure there is no problem with your kidney function. We will check these bloods every 3 months. [according to NICE and NPSA)

We usually monitor the level of Lithium in the body to make sure you are on the right dose. Your Lithium level will be done initially weekly and then repeated every 3 months once stabilized. We usually take the bloods 12 hours after the last dose.

P: What happens if the Lithium level becomes high?

C: The normal therapeutic range of the Lithium level that we aim for is 0, 6-1mmol/L. If the level goes above this, you might have diarrhoea; feel sick, slurred speech, tremor, unsteady gait and confusion. If this occurs, we usually advise that you have to stop your medication immediately and contact your doctor. We also advise that you drink plenty of fluids. We would need to repeat your bloods to check your level.

P: What skin conditions does Lithium cause?

C: Lithium can cause acne, psoriasis and eczema.

P: what happens if I fall pregnant or want to start a family?

C: Lithium is known to cause some concerns in pregnancy. It can cause foetal heart abnormalities, called Epstein anomaly. This is usually a concern during the first 3 months of pregnancy. The risk is less than 1 in 100. The risk appears low, and we weigh the risks and benefits at the time if you do become pregnant. We do advise discontinuing lithium during the early stages of pregnancy.

We also advise against breastfeeding as Lithium passes through the breast milk. You will need to contact me or your GP to discuss this.

P: Is Lithium addictive?

C: No. There is no evidence to suggest that Lithium causes craving and people to become physically dependent on the medication.

P: Can I take Lithium with the other medication I am on?

C: There are some medications that can interact with Lithium like blood pressure and diuretics or water tablets. Over the counter pain killers like ibuprofen and Aspirin can also increase its level, so do consult your pharmacist or doctor.
This will vary from person to person and also will depend on the indication of use of lithium.

P: Can I have alcohol with Lithium?

C: There is no known interaction of lithium with alcohol; however we do advise that you drink moderately if you are taking medication.

P: Can I drive if I am taking Lithium?

C: This will vary from person to person as a result of the Lithium on your level of alertness. You can discuss this with your doctor if you are experiencing any problems. Caution should also be taken if you are operating machinery.

Other practical tips to highlight:
- If you are taking Lithium we advise the following because Lithium is affected by fluid in the body and salt.
- Drink plenty of water
- If you go on holiday, to a warm climate ,ensure you drink plenty of water
- Avoid a low salt diet
- Avoid the sauna
- Exercise

P: How long will I need to take treatment for?

C: We usually recommend that you continue with treatment for a longer period of time and that it will need to be reviewed by your psychiatrist in outpatient appointments.

Summarize
To summarize, we have discussed more about Lithium, the benefits, side effects and the blood monitoring. I would like you to think about this, and I will arrange to see you again. I have some leaflets for you to read and would like to arrange to see you again to discuss your decision.

Information and leaflets

GENERAL ADULT PSYCHIATRY

If you do decide to start the Lithium, then we have the Lithium treatment pack (purple in colour), which consists of an information booklet, Lithium Alert card and a record for the monitoring of the Lithium level.

Lithium (Camcolit® and Priadel ® Liskonum® Li-liquid®)
Starting dose 200-400mg a day up to maximum 1200mg/day.

LITHIUM
Nature -Treatment/intervention - *Mood stabiliser, Augmentation for Refractory Depression or treatment resistant Depression (TRD)*
Indications:
- *Effective in the treatment and prophylaxis of mania in Bipolar Affective Disorder, Augmentation for treatment resistant depressive disorder or refractory Depression, Adjunct to antipsychotics in treatment of Schizoaffective disorder*

Route: Oral *tablet, dosage*
- *Camcolit 300mg-400mg, 1-1,5g daily*
- *Priadel 0, 4 to 1, 2 g*

Effects/benefits:
- *Treat mania, prevent relapse*

Adverse/side effects
- **Common:** *slight stomach upset, feeling a sick, metallic taste, dry mouth, polyuria, weight gain*
- **Longer term effects:** *include tremor, acne, under activity of the thyroid gland.*
- *Skin conditions: acne, psoriasis and eczema.*
- **Precautions in pregnancy**
- *Lithium is associated with foetal heart abnormalities, called Epstein anomaly. The risk is 1 in 100. It is usually safe after 26 weeks. We advise against breastfeeding as Lithium passes through the breast milk.*

Alternatives
- *Consider psychological treatment*
- *Consider alternative medication*

©Smartsesh

GENERAL ADULT PSYCHIATRY

Precautions
- Pre checks blood test to check your thyroid function TFT and renal function to ensure that it is safe for you to have Lithium.
- Repeat TFT and U+E(Urea and electrolyte) bloods every 6 months.
- Lithium level will be repeated every 3 months and is usually done 12 hours after the last dose.
- We start Lithium treatment we start with a low dose and check the level after a week, and make adjustments if necessary.

Lithium Toxicity
- Lithium level 0.8-1, if higher diarrhoea, feel sick, slurred speech, tremor, unsteady gait and confusion.

Practical Tips
- If you are taking Lithium we advise the following because Lithium is affected by fluid in the body and salt.
- Drink plenty of water
- If you go on holiday, to warm climate, ensure you drink plenty of water
- Avoid a low salt diet
- Avoid the sauna
- Exercise
- Lithium treatment pack, which consists of an information booklet, Lithium Alert card and a record for the monitoring of the Lithium level.

©Smartsesh

LITHIUM	SIDE EFFECTS
Lithium carbonate **Lithium citrate** Camcolit® (Norgine)300mg-400mg, 1-1,5g daily Liskonum ®(GSK) Li-Liquid(Rosemount) Priadel®(Sanofi-Aventis) 0, 4 to 1, 2 g Packs: nhsforms@spsl.uk.com	**Common:** slight stomach upset, feeling a sick, metallic taste, dry mouth, polyuria, weight gain **Long term effects:** include tremor, acne, under activity of the thyroid gland. Skin conditions: acne, psoriasis and eczema. **Precautions in pregnancy** Lithium is associated with foetal heart abnormalities, called Epstein anomaly. The risk is 1 in 100.

GENERAL ADULT PSYCHIATRY

10. TREATMENT RESISTANT DEPRESSION (TRD)

INSTRUCTIONS TO CANDIDATE
You have been asked to see Janet Fowler who is a 34 yr. old lady who has been on Mirtazapine and Citalopram with no improvement.

TASK FOR THE CANDIDATE
- Elicit a history to establish treatment resistant Depression (TRD).
- Explain the treatment options available.

PAY PARTICULAR ATTENTION TO THE FOLLOWING (MENTAL CHECKLIST)
- Establish Treatment Resistant Depression.
- Exclude any physical causes that could be contributing to this.
- Explain rationale and treatment options for Treatment Resistant Depression using a biopsychosocial approach.

COMMUNICATION SKILLS
- Start the interview by developing rapport and showing empathy.
- Seek to understand the subjective feeling of the individual.

Suggested approach
Introduction
C: Hello, I'm Dr....I am one of the psychiatrists. I gather that you have been on 2 different treatments for your Depression; however this has not helped for all your symptoms. I'm here to talk to you about the possible treatment options available. Is that all right with you?

P: Yes Doc, this medication doesn't seem to help. I am feeling the same since I started the treatment.

A. Establish History of presenting complaint (HOPC) onset, duration, frequency and severity)
C: It would be helpful if you could tell me more about when you first started treatment? (Onset)
- May I ask what your concerns are at present?
- Have you been regularly taking the tablets? (Compliance)
- Have you noticed any improvements or changes since commencing treatment?

Explore possible reasons for treatment resistance
- Have you had any worries recently? (Psychosocial stressors)
- Has there been anything at home, work, financial?

B. Establish possible biological causes for Treatment Resistant Depression
Elicit symptoms of Hypothyroidism, Cardiac, Hypertension, and Diabetes
Exclude Co-morbid Substance Misuse

- *How has your physical health been?*
- *Have you had any recent bloods, for example bloods for thyroid?*
- *Explore for symptoms of Hypothyroidism*
- *I would like to ask you some questions related to under functioning of the thyroid gland?*
- *How have you been eating?*
- *Do you have any sensitivity to cold weather?*
- *How has your energy levels been?*
- *This is a rather personal question, but any changes in your periods?*

C. Explain the need for further investigations to exclude underlying medical condition that could be a contributory factor
C: I would like to arrange that we need to do further investigations like blood tests for thyroid to exclude a physical cause.

Explain the treatment options available using a biopsychosocial approach
There are treatment options available like considering alternative medication, psychological treatments and the social aspects of care

*We have the following options in terms of your **medication:***
- *We can optimize your current antidepressant medication. We can Increase Venlafaxine to 225mg(maximum dose)*
- *We could consider changing this to Mirtazapine -commence at 15mg*
- *We could also use a Combination Venlafaxine and an SSRI's (Selective Serotonin Reuptake Inhibitor)*
- *We have options of Augmentation or using another medication to boost or enhance the effects of your current treatment. The medication we use is Lithium [others are Buspirone, Thyroxine and recently Quetiapine]*

{However in severe cases we do consider ECT]

*We can also consider **Psychological** or talking therapies that are available like CBT or cognitive behavioural therapy.*

*The **social** aspects of care could entail you attending day services and looking at support if necessary.*

Summarise
Thank you for talking to me. From what you have told me, you have been taking antidepressants regularly for 3 months and you have not noticed any improvement. I would like to do some blood tests and then we could consider the medical and talking treatments we have discussed.
I have some leaflets for you.

GENERAL ADULT PSYCHIATRY

MIRTAZEPINE
Nature -Treatment/intervention Mirtazapine (Zispin® SolTab- Organon
Purpose Antidepressant
Dosage start 15-30 mg up to maximum 45 mg
Effects/benefits
Antidepressants
Improvement in depressive symptoms
Adverse/side effect
Common increased appetite, weight gain, dry mouth, postural
hypotension, peripheral oedema, drowsiness, fatigue, tremor, dizziness,
abnormal dreams, confusion, Anxiety, insomnia, arthralgia, myalgia,
Less common syncope, hypotension, mania, hallucinations, movement
disorders
Alternatives

©Smartsesh

TREATMENT RESISTANT DEPRESSION (TRD)
Establish reasons for non-response to treatment
- Diagnosis- establish if correct
- Assess duration of treatment (2 or more Antidepressants for 6 weeks)
- Compliance
- Underlying External factors- family, work, finances
- Medical history
- Elicit symptoms of hypothyroidism, cardiac, hypertension, diabetes
- Co-morbid substance misuse

Arrange for further investigations
Management using biopsychosocial approach
Treatment of Refractory Depression.
Biological interventions
- Increase Venlafaxine 225mg
- Change to Mirtazapine –commence 15mg
- Combination Venlafaxine and (Selective Serotonin Reuptake inhibitor) SSRI
- Augmentation-boost/enhance: Lithium, Buspirone, Thyroxine
- ECT for severe cases

Psychological interventions
- CBT

Social interventions
- Support
- Attend day services
- Financial support

©Smartsesh

VENLAFAXINE
Nature -Treatment/intervention: Venlafaxine (Efexor®)
Purpose Antidepressant
Dosage
Venlafaxine (Efexor®) start at 75mg a day. Usually 75 mg-150mg per day
Maximum dose is 375 mg per day
Effects/benefits
Improvement in depressive symptoms
Adverse/side effects
Common Anxiety, constipation, diarrhoea, dizziness, drowsiness, headache, insomnia, nausea, sweating
Fairly common: sexual dysfunction
Uncommon: blurred vision, hypertension, hypotension, rash, urticaria, tremor and vomiting
Alternatives: Augmentation
©Smartsesh

MEDICATION	SIDE EFFECTS
MIRTAZEPINE Mirtazapine (Zispin® SolTab-Organon) **Dosage** start 15-30 mg up to maximum 45 mg	**Common:** increased appetite, weight gain, dry mouth, postural hypotension, peripheral oedema, drowsiness, fatigue, tremor, dizziness, abnormal dreams, confusion, Anxiety, insomnia, arthralgia, myalgia, **Less common:** syncope, hypotension, mania, hallucinations, movement disorders
VENLAFAXINE Venlafaxine (Efexor®) Venlafaxine XL (Efexor®) Start at 75mg a day. Usually 75 mg-150mg per day Maximum dose is 375 mg per day	**Common:** Anxiety, constipation, diarrhoea, dizziness, drowsiness, headache, insomnia, nausea, sweating **Fairly common:** sexual dysfunction **Uncommon:** blurred vision, hypertension, hypotension, rash, urticaria, tremor and vomiting

Possible variation of theme
1. 45 yr old lady with a history of hypothyroidism and treatment resistant Depression.
2. 36 yr old lady on Mirtazepine and is concerned about her recent weight gain.

GENERAL ADULT PSYCHIATRY

11. ELECTROCONVULSIVE THERAPY (ECT)

INSTRUCTIONS TO CANDIDATE
You have been asked to see this 64 yr old gentleman Errol Brown, who has been treated for Depression and he has not responded to treatment. You have been asked to explain to him about ECT.

TASK FOR THE CANDIDATE
- *Explain ECT.*

PAY PARTICULAR ATTENTION TO THE FOLLOWING (MENTAL CHECKLIST)
- *Explain rationale for Electroconvulsive Therapy (ECT).*
- *Explain ECT process, indications, benefits and adverse effects.*
- *Explain consent issues.*
- *Obtain informed consent.*

COMMUNICATION SKILLS
- *Start the interview by developing rapport and showing empathy.*
- *Anticipate an individual who would be concerned about ECT per se and side effects.*

Suggested approach
Introduction
C: Hello, I'm Dr .....I am a psychiatrist working on this ward. I understand you have been treated with two antidepressants and we think it would be best for you to consider ECT. I would like to talk to you about that. Is that all right with you?

P: I don't want that. That's that shock therapy isn't it?

C: It has been known as that. I will explain this a bit more.

P: What is ECT?

C: ECT stands for Electroconvulsive therapy. This means that when a person is asleep under general anaesthetic, a small current is sent to the brain to cause a fit.

P: Why do you use ECT?

GENERAL ADULT PSYCHIATRY

C: It is helpful in people who suffer from severe Depression, and in whom medication has not proved effective. It is also useful in people where there are concerns of physical health because of poor dietary intake.

P: **How does it work?**

C: During ECT, a small electric current is passed across your brain. This current causes a fit which is thought to affect the parts of the brain responsible for our mood, sleep, appetite and your thinking. As a result it is thought to affect the chemical imbalance found in Depression, and normalises them.

P: **How effective is it?**

C: At least 7 out of 10 people respond well to ECT. People who have been severely depressed and respond to ECT, find they look forward to the future, and find themselves able to make a good recovery.

P: **What are the side effects?**

C: The side effects are usually mild and short lasting. Some people experience nausea, headache and muscle pains. Some feel a bit confused for a short while, however this usually wears off.

P: **What is the risk of dying?**

C: There is a very small risk of dying which is less than if you are having a tooth extraction under general anaesthetic. This risk is 1 in 50 000. Prior to you having the procedure, we will do a detailed physical examination, blood tests and a heart tracing to assess the safety for you to undergo this procedure.

P: **Will it affect my memory?**

C: The memory problems related to side effects are mostly mild and transient or short lived. You might have difficulty with memory in recognising familiar people. This is usually temporary and most people report this clearing up. There is insufficient evidence to say the longer term effects of memory problems.

P: **What happens prior to ECT?**

C: You will be seen by an anaesthetist prior to the procedure. You will have to fast overnight. On the morning of the ECT you will be taken to the ECT suite. You will be seen by an anaesthetist, psychiatrist and a nurse.

P: **What happens on the day?**
C: The anaesthetist will give you an injection to make you sleep and a muscle relaxant. You will be asked to breathe oxygen while some equipment is

attached to monitor your blood pressure, heart tracing and brain waves. Once you are asleep 2 electrodes will be placed on your head. A small current will be passed across your head using a machine. This will cause you to have a fit for less that a minute, which, because you are asleep, you will not remember.

Once the anaesthetic wears off, you will regain consciousness and begin to feel a bit drowsy. You will be taken to the recovery area, and one of the staff will accompany you back to the ward.

P: What if I don't want to have ECT?

C: We will ask you to give your informed consent for the procedure, by providing you with the information on the procedure, the benefits, side effects and risks.

You can withdraw your consent at any time. We can also suggest alternative treatments such as the psychological or talking treatments and the option of reviewing your medication.
In life threatening conditions we would have to seek the advice from a (SOAD) Second Opinion Doctor and use the Mental Health Act (MHA 1983).

Summarise
Thank you for talking to me. I know I've given you a lot of information. I have some leaflets. I would like you to think about this and discuss this with your relatives.
I will come and see you when you have made your decision.

GENERAL ADULT PSYCHIATRY

ECT-ELECTROCONVULSIVE THERAPY
Treatment/intervention: ECT
Purpose
- *NICE recommendations for severe depressive disorder with life threatening consequences and psychomotor retardation.*

How it is administered:
- *ECT given unilateral/bilateral*
- *6-12 treatments twice a week*

Effects/benefits:
- *70-75% treatment response*
- *Improvement in depressive symptoms*

Adverse/side effects
- *Confusion, headaches,*
- *Temporary retrograde and anterograde amnesia, more with bilateral*

Precautions
- *Mortality risk is 1 in 50 000 due to general anaesthetic, same as if getting tooth extraction under general anaesthetic*

Alternatives
- *Psychological treatment with alternative antidepressant*

©Smartsesh

GENERAL ADULT PSYCHIATRY

12. GRIEF

INSTRUCTIONS TO CANDIDATE
You have been asked to see Mrs Catherine Barker, who is a
65 yr. old lady, whose husband has died 9 months ago. Her GP was
concerned that she was depressed.

TASK FOR THE CANDIDATE
- Elicit a history to differentiate normal bereavement from pathological bereavement.

PAY PARTICULAR ATTENTION TO THE FOLLOWING (MENTAL CHECKLIST)
- Establish her husband's death.
- Explore the nature of their relationship.
- Establish the presence of normal bereavement process.
- Establish the presence of pathological bereavement.
- Elicit the stages in Kubler Ross model (DABDA).
- Conduct a risk assessment.
- Establish her coping skills and social support.

COMMUNICATION SKILLS
- Start the interview by developing rapport and showing empathy.
- Show sensitivity when discussing her husband's death.
- Anticipate a strong emotional response.

Suggested approach
Introduction
C: Hello, I'm Dr ...I am a psychiatrist working in this Community Mental Health Team (CMHT). I understand that this is a difficult time for you I would however appreciate if you could tell me more about your recent loss.

W: My husband died (patient could be tearful)

C: I'm sorry to hear this. I can see you are clearly upset. It will be helpful if you could tell me more about your husband and how he passed away? What was his name [thereafter personalise the interview by using husbands name]

A. History of Preventing Complaint (HOPC) (onset, duration, progression, severity)

Circumstances of bereavement
- Can you tell me what happened?
- Where were you at the time?
- How long ago was this? (Onset)
- Was his [name] death sudden or expected?
- Can you tell me more about your husband? What type of

a person was he? How was your relationship with him?
- *(Establish nature and impact of death and if any ambivalence present)*
- *Were you able to say goodbye?*
- *How has his death left you feeling?*
- *Have you been to visit the graveyard? If so, how often do you go?*

Establish the Kubler Ross stages of grief
1. Denial
- *Have you cried at all?*

2. Anger
- *Do you feel angry? Do you blame anyone for his death?*

3. Bargaining
- *Do you sometimes wish it was you?*

4. Depression
- *How have you been feeling in yourself? (Mood)*
- *How has your energy levels been? (Decreased energy)*
- *Have you been able to do things you usually would do? (Anhedonia)*
- *How have you been sleeping? (Biological symptoms)*
- *How have you been eating?*
- *Have you lost any weight?*

5. Acceptance
- *Do you think you have come to terms with your loss?*

B. Pathological grief/Atypical
- *Sometimes when someone loses a loved one, they can leave their belongings as if they are still living in their house, how about you? (Mummification)*
- *Do you ever hear or see him or her?*
- *(Pseudohallucinations)*
- *Do you feel guilty? (Guilt feelings)*
- *Do you pine for him/her?*
- *Do you find yourself searching for him/her?*
- *How have you been coping?*
- *How have you been taking care of yourself?*

C. Risk Assessment
- *Do you sometimes feel you were with him?*
- *Have you ever come to the point that you felt like life was not worth living without him? (Suicidal thoughts)*
- *Have you made attempts to end your life? How close have you come to this?*

Protective factor
- *What would prevent you from doing this?*

D. Coping and support
- *How have you been coping?*
- *Sometimes people might drink or take drugs? How about you? (Drug and alcohol history)*
- *How has your husband's death left your family feeling?*
- *How has your family been coping with this?*

E. Possible outcomes of assessment

a. Normal bereavement
Thank you for talking to me. I can imagine how difficult it must be for you. From what you have told me, it appears that you are understandably going through the normal process when we lose a loved one.

b. Pathological Bereavement
Thank you for talking to me. I can imagine how difficult it must be for you. I think it is understandable that you have had difficulty coming to terms with your loss. I think that you might benefit from bereavement counselling. You can think about this and if you agree I can make arrangements for the referral for this.

c. Depression
Thank you for talking to me. I can imagine how difficult it must be for you. I think it is understandable that you have had difficulty coming to terms with your loss and you are now feeling depressed as a consequence.

We do have the options of psychological or talking therapy, medication and social aspects to help you.

I will give you some information about CRUSE which is a charity organisation which helps people like you to come to terms with their loss.
Support groups and websites
Bereavement Advice Centre
Supports bereaved people on a range of practical issues via a single free phone number. It offers advice on all aspects of bereavement from registering the death and finding a funeral director through to probate, tax and benefit queries.
CRUSE bereavement care
This is charity organisation supporting people with bereavement and counselling.

Possible variation of theme
1. 65 yr. old man whose wife died 1 yr. ago under tragic circumstances. He continues to keep the articles of her death and her belongings as if she was still living.
2. 45 yr. old lady whose husband died of a heart attack and she is depressed and suicidal.

BEREAVEMENT
KUBLER ROSS STAGES OF GRIEF (DABDA)
- Denial
- Anger
- Bargaining
- Depression
- Acceptance

Pathological/Atypical grief reaction
- Pining
- Searching
- Preoccupation
- Guilt
- Pseudo hallucinations
- Prolonged mourning
- Mummification
- Self-harm
- Suicide
- Can't function
- Ambivalent relationship
- Mood cognitive
- Biological

© *Smartsesh*

---

13. BREAKING BAD NEWS

INSTRUCTIONS TO CANDIDATE
You have been asked to see the daughter Caroline Smith of the 67yr. old lady Ingrid who had a MRI scan of her brain. The scan results are as follows: frontal lobe meningioma.

TASK FOR THE CANDIDATE
- *Inform the daughter about the results of the scan.*

PAY PARTICULAR ATTENTION TO THE FOLLOWING (MENTAL CHECKLIST)
- *Gauge current understanding of her mother's condition.*
- *Assess the amount of information that needs to be conveyed.*
- *Summarize her mother's condition.*
- *Convey the information in meaningful and manageable chunks.*
- *Discuss diagnosis, management, treatment options available and likely prognosis.*

COMMUNICATION SKILLS
- *Start the interview by developing rapport and showing empathy.*
- *Don't give information all in one go.*
- *Avoid jargon.*
- *Anticipate an extreme emotional response.*

Suggested approach
Introduction
Hello I'm Dr...I am psychiatrists working in this ward. I understand you have come to talk to me more about your mother and the results of her scan she had.

D: Yes Doctor, I came here today to find out more about this from you.

Share this information by giving chunks of Information
Give a brief summary of admission circumstances:
C: As you aware your mother came in with a history of confusion and wandering. We have done a physical examination, memory assessments and we have also completed some blood investigations and a brain scan.

These were done to exclude any other causes which could have resulted in your mother's condition.

I would like to discuss the brain scan results with you:
I'm afraid it looks more serious than we hoped. From the brain scan that we have done it shows that your mother has a tumour in her brain.

Allow for silence and shut down (pause if necessary)

GENERAL ADULT PSYCHIATRY

C: I'm sorry I know this must be difficult for you. You seem upset. (Expect some emotional response)

D: I did not expect this. How long does she have to live?

C: I'm afraid that's a difficult question to answer satisfactorily. But what I can assure you is that we would try to make her life as most comfortable as possible. Later on, if she is experiencing pain, the pain specialists can see her and prescribe some pain relief.

D: What treatment is available?

C: My understanding is that the cancer is advanced and it is unlikely that it can be treated through surgery. I will get the surgical team and cancer specialists to see her and give their expert opinion and management.

Other options are radiotherapy and chemotherapy which the cancer specialists will be able to give more information on. The cancer specialists also have a team of experienced nurses called the Macmillan nurses who are specially skilled and trained in providing support to both patients and family. They would also be able to give you more information for future about the services that hospice offer.
I would like to arrange to see you and your family with some of our multi-disciplinary team to discuss this further.

D: Can I take her home?

C: At present as we have only just made this diagnosis it is best to keep her in hospital. This will ensure that she has easier access to the specialist care that she requires. I know this is a lot of information that I am giving you. Would you like us to call anyone in your family for you?

Summarise
To summarise, we will continue to treat your mother on this ward and I will be referring her to the cancer specialists and the surgical team to give their expert opinion on how to manage this further. I will arrange a meeting with you and the rest of you family if you wish to discuss this.

Support groups and websites
http://www.macmillan.org.uk: provide practical, medical and financial support and push for better cancer care.
Macmillan Cancer Support; McMillan support line: 08088080000

http://www.breakingbadnews.co.uk/

BREAKING BAD NEWS
Preparation
- *Set the scene-summarise*
- *Share information*
- *Silence and sensitivity*
- *Allow for shut down*
- *Pause*
- *Treatment options*

Biological interventions
- *Analgesia-long term*
- *Macmillan nurses-Palliative care*

Chemotherapy
- *Radiotherapy*
- *Multi agency referral*
- *Surgical , medical*
- *Oncology*

Psychological interventions
- *Counselling*

Social interventions
  Hospice

©Smartsesh

GENERAL ADULT PSYCHIATRY

14. BIPOLAR AFFECTIVE DISORDER: MANIA ASSESSMENT

INSTRUCTIONS TO CANDIDATE
You have been asked to see this 34 yr. old man, Nero Brent, who has been brought to A+E. He was found on top of the bridge by police, attempting to fly.

TASK FOR THE CANDIDATE
- Elicit a mental state examination.

PAY PARTICULAR ATTENTION TO THE FOLLOWING (MENTAL CHECKLIST)
- Establish the core features of mania.
- Establish grandiose beliefs.
- Screen for first rank symptoms.
- Conduct a risk assessment.
- Establish his level of insight and the need to be admitted.
- Exclude possible differential diagnoses.

COMMUNICATION SKILLS
- Start the interview by developing rapport and showing empathy.
- Candidate should gently take control of the interview.
- Avoid premature interruption

Suggested approach
Introduction
C: Hello, I'm Dr....I am of the psychiatrists on call. I have been asked by the doctors to see you. I understand that the police brought you in as you were found on top of the bridge attempting to jump. Can you tell me more about why you were doing this?

P: I was trying to fly. Can't you see I can fly?

C: I would like to ask you a few routine questions first.

A. Establish core features of mania
Mood
- How has your mood been?
- Have you been feeling on top of the world?
- Have you been feeling more irritable than usual?

Energy
- How have your energy levels been?

Sleep
- How have you been sleeping?
- How has your interest in sex been?

GENERAL ADULT PSYCHIATRY

Appetite
- *How has your appetite been?*

Thoughts
- *Have you notice your thoughts racing? (Racing)*
- *Have you noticed a change in your speech?*

B. Elicit first rank symptoms (FRS)
Grandiose
- *How do you compare yourself to others?*
- *Have you been having any unusual experiences like seeing things when no one is around?*
- *Are you on any special plans or important missions?*

C. Impulsive
- *Have you been buying things more than usual?*
- *Have you been spending more than usual?*

D. Insight
- *Has your family been concerned at all?*

E. Driving
- *Have you been in trouble with the police recently?*

F. Drug and alcohol history
- *Have you been drinking or taking street drugs?*

G. In taking history screen for differential diagnoses
- *Schizophrenia, Schizoaffective Disorder, Drug Induced Psychosis, Borderline Personality Disorder.*

Insight
What do you think is wrong with you?

Summarise
I think what you have described is that you have been excitable recently, not sleeping, have been feeling like you have a lot of energy and plans. Your family have been concerned about you. I think you need to stay in hospital.

What do you think?

Possible variations of theme
- *34 yr. old nurse presenting with Mania and OCD symptoms*
- *36 yr. old man known with BPAD. Brought in by police as he was found speeding on the motorway.*

Mania
- *Mood*
- *Energy*
- *Sleep*
- *Appetite*
- *Thoughts*
- *Racing*
- *Grandiose*
- *Impulsive*
- *Insight*
- *Driving*
- *Drug and alcohol history*
  ©Smartsesh

GENERAL ADULT PSYCHIATRY

15. BIPOLAR AFFECTIVE DISORDER

INSTRUCTIONS TO CANDIDATE
You have been asked to see the mother of the man in the previous station,
Mrs Carol Brent. She is concerned about her son Nero and wants to know
about his diagnosis and treatment.

TASK FOR THE CANDIDATE
- Explain his diagnosis and management.
- Address her concerns.

**PAY PARTICULAR ATTENTION TO THE FOLLOWING (MENTAL
CHECKLIST)**
- Explain the diagnosis of Bipolar Affective Disorder(BPAD)
- Explain the symptoms and signs.
- Explain the management in terms of biopsychosocial interventions.
- Emphasis the need for compliance.

COMMUNICATION SKILLS
- Start the interview by developing rapport and showing empathy.
- Show sensitivity.

Suggested approach
Introduction
C: Hello, I'm Dr ...I am one of the psychiatrists. I understand this must be a
difficult time for you and you wanted to discuss more about your son's
illness, Bipolar Affective Disorder (BPAD)
Before we begin it would be helpful if you can tell me what your
understanding is of BPAD.

**P: I have heard people say it's when someone gets high! What is bipolar
affective disorder?**

C: Bipolar affective disorder or BPAD is also known as manic Depression. As
the name suggests, these are the 2 poles to this illness. On the one hand a
person will present with symptoms of mania, and on the other symptoms of
Depression. These severe mood swings can last for days, weeks or months.

P: Who usually gets it?

C: It is relatively common mental illness and affects 5 in 100 people. It is
equally common in men and women. It usually starts before the age of 30,
but can occur at any time.

P: What are the causes for this?

C: The exact cause is not known for why people develop this disorder and it is
difficult to pinpoint this in yours son's case. There are due to several factors

---

101

usually working together. It is a genetic disorder, and this means that if someone in the family has it, then there is a 50/50 chance of developing this illness. It is also due to a chemical imbalance and can be caused by stress and disturbance in our sleep wake cycle.

To mention there are different types i.e. Bipolar i, Bipolar ii, rapid cycling and cyclothymia.

P: What are the symptoms?

C: The symptoms of mania are when someone usually feels very happy, full of energy and can get annoyed easily. They have a decreased need for sleep, may find their thinking and speech is a lot faster than normal. They may make impulsive decisions with bad consequences, spend more money and be over familiar with people.

The symptoms of Depression are feelings of being extremely unhappy, tearful, being unable to enjoy things you usually would do and feeling tired. You may have difficulty in sleeping, or waking earlier than usual. It can affect your thinking in feeling negative and have difficulty in concentrating. People also can start feeling hopeless, useless and worthless and start having thoughts of wanting to end their life.

Sometimes it can present with more severe symptoms such as people start believing they have special powers and abilities if they are manic. They may have extreme guilt feelings if they are depressed.

P: How do we make a diagnosis?

C: We usually get a history from the family and observe someone's behaviour. Usually the person themselves might not notice anything is wrong, and it may be that your family will be concerned. .

P: What are the treatments available?

C: The treatment is usually a combination of medication and psychosocial treatment. The medication used is known as mood stabilisers. We can also use antipsychotic medication. There are various types of medication and the treatment will depend on the nature of the illness at the time if urgent treatment is required in an acute situation. We also then consider the options for treatment in long term to prevent someone becoming ill and we call that the maintenance treatment.

To mention if necessary tailored to the scenario
The anti-epilepsy/anticonvulsant medication
- Sodium Valproate and Carbamazepine
- Lithium is also known as a mood stabiliser.
- Antipsychotics: Olanzapine

GENERAL ADULT PSYCHIATRY

P: What are the psychological or talking treatments available?

C: The psychological treatment is the following:
 Psych education.
That is educating your son about his illness, his relapse signs and treatment. We also have a family focussed psychoeducation for you and the rest of the family. We find that if family are able to understand and support him through his illness this will help to promote recovery and his wellbeing. [Family focussed psychoeducation-Miklovitz et al).
We also advise on mood monitoring and mood strategies.
Cognitive behavioural therapy or CBT is also a form of talking therapy which looks at the links between our thinking and feeling and how we can change these into a more helpful way of thinking
Other talking therapy for which there is good evidence for is social rhythm therapy and interpersonal therapy

P: Is there any other form of support that he will receive?

C: Getting support from your family and friends who can recognise when he is getting unwell.

P: Is there anything else we should know?

C: We suggest that he monitor his mood swings are learning more about when your mood is out of control. Keeping a mood diary is beneficial. We advise to avoiding stress, maintaining a balance with life, work, exercise and a healthy diet. It is important for him to continue to take medication. If he does stop his medication, it can lead to another mood swing.
In the long term we can involve the community mental health team to support him in the community. [Elaborate on the multi-disciplinary team (MDT)]

P: How long will he need to continue with medication?

C: In order to prevent any further episodes, he will need to continue medication at least for 5 yrs. or longer.

P: What is the prognosis?

C: The outcome of this illness is difficult to predict and varies from person to person. It is usually a short lived illness and our aim is with the right treatment, we are able to control the symptoms and prevent further episodes.
We know that 16% of affected people do recover with treatment and the outcome is better in bipolar 2 types.

Summarise

GENERAL ADULT PSYCHIATRY

Thank you for talking to me. To summarise I have explained more about your son's illness and about the treatment options available in terms of medical , psychological therapy and the social support.

I know I have given you a lot of information. I can suggest some useful organisations and support group like MDF.

Some useful websites and organisations:
MDF The Bipolar Organisation: *A user-led charity working to enable people affected by bipolar disorder (manic Depression) to take control of their lives.*

Books
*Bipolar information series a guide for patients and carers by Dr **Nicholas Stafford "Lithium for Bipolar Disorder"-** http://mymindbooks.com/*

BPAD –Bipolar affective disorder
Nature -Treatment/intervention: *Sodium Valproate- Depakote®*
Epilim®, Convulex®, Episenta®
Purpose: *mood stabiliser for BPAD and anticonvulsant*
Dosage: *starting 400mg-600mg per day*
Maintenance: 400mg -2500 mg per day
Semi sodium valproate starting dose 250mg tds for acute mania
Effects/benefits
- *Reduces seizures*
- *Mood stabiliser for high and low moods*

Adverse/side effects
- *Common: gastric irritation and*
- *Uncommon: increased appetite and weight gain*
- *Rare: ataxia, confusion, drowsiness, hair loss(alopecia), impaired liver function , tremor*
- *Very rare: rash (Steven Johnsons syndrome, thrombocytopenia/impaired platelet function*
- *Metabollic syndrome and polycystic ovarian syndrome*

Precautions
- *Liver impairment and blood dyscrasia*
- *Teratogenic: neural tube defects (give folic acid in pregnancy)*
    ©smartsesh

F31 Bipolar Affective Disorder

Characterised by at least two episodes of disturbed mood and activity levels. These disturbances can be occasions of elevation in mood with increased energy and activity (either mania or hypomania) or on other occasion's low mood and decreased energy levels or activity (Depression). Recovery is usually complete between episodes and the sex distribution is equal. Manic episodes often begin abruptly and last 2 weeks to 4 months. Depressive episodes tend to last longer usually 6 months. Episodes of either pole are often triggered by stressful life events or mental trauma. The patterns of remissions and relapses are highly variable but with time remissions tend to shorten and depressive episodes are commoner and longer after middle age.

Incl.:
Manic-depressive illness, Psychosis or reaction

Exclude.
Bipolar disorder,
single manic episode (F30.-)
cyclothymia (F34)

GENERAL ADULT PSYCHIATRY

ANTICONVULSANT MEDICATION Indication : MOOD STABILISERS	SIDE EFFECTS
SODIUM VALPROATE Depakote® Epilim®, Convulex® ,Episenta® Dosage: starting 400mg-600mg per day Maintenance: 400mg -2500 mg per day Semi sodium valproate starting dose 250mg tds for acute mania.	Common: gastric irritation and Uncommon: increased appetite and weight gain Rare: ataxia, confusion, drowsiness, hair loss(alopecia), impaired liver function , tremor Very rare: rash (Steven Johnsons syndrome, thrombocytopenia/impaired platelet function Metabolic syndrome and polycystic ovarian syndrome Precautions Liver impairment and blood dyscrasia Teratogenic: neural tube defects (give folic acid in pregnancy)
CARBAMAZEPINE Tigerton ®(Novartis) Carbagen ®SR (Generics) 400mg daily in divided doses Maintenance 400-600mg daily Maximum 1.6g daily	Common: Dry mouth, nausea, vomiting, oedema, ataxia, dizziness, drowsiness, fatigue, headache, Less common: hyponatraemia, blood disorders-thrombocytopenia Dermatitis, urticaria, diarrhoea, constipation, hepatitis, jaundice Rare: pancreatitis, stomatitis, hepatic failure, AV block with syncope

16. PSYCHOSIS-DELUSIONS AND FIRST RANK SYMPTOMS

INSTRUCTIONS TO CANDIDATE
You have been asked to assess this 45 yr old postman Andrew Gates who was brought by police as he was worried for his safety, as he believes that the police are after him. Assess his psychopathology.

TASK FOR THE CANDIDATE
- *Assess his mental state.*

PAY PARTICULAR ATTENTION TO THE FOLLOWING (MENTAL CHECKLIST)
- *Establish history of presenting complaint.*
- *Elicit delusions according to theme relevant to the scenario-paranoid, persecutory, reference, grandiose.*
- *Other delusions to consider are religious, nihilistic, guilt, hypochondriacal, jealousy/infidelity, erotomania and infestation.*
- *Establish degree of conviction.*
- *Elicit passivity phenomena.*
- *Establish if it is a primary or secondary delusion.*
- *Establish if it is a partial or systematised delusion.*
- *Conduct a risk assessment.*

COMMUNICATION SKILLS
- *Start the interview by developing rapport and showing empathy.*
- *Seek to understand the subjective experience of the individual.*

Suggested approach
Introduction
C: Hello, I'm Dr ....I am a psychiatrists working in this ward. Thank you for seeing me. I understand that the police have brought you to hospital.

P: Are you one of them?

C: I can assure you that I am a doctor and I am here to see how best I can help you. What do you mean by one of them?

A. History of Presenting Complaint (HOPC) (onset, duration, progression and severity)
Use a clustering approach to elicit delusional beliefs

C: I can see that you are clearly distressed. I can assure you that you are safe in this hospital. It would be helpful if you could tell me more about what you are concerned about?

GENERAL ADULT PSYCHIATRY

I would like to ask you some routine questions that I ask everyone who comes to see me. They may appear strange to you.

Elicit relevant delusion tailored to the scenario [other types of delusions included for completeness]

Paranoid
- Do you feel that people are out to harm you?
- Who are they? Why do you think that? What do you think they might do?

Persecutory
- Do you feel that there is a specific group of people or agents trying to harm you in any way?
- Do you think there is a conspiracy or a plot against you?
- Do you feel that people are spying on you or following you?
- Do you think they are using any specific equipment?

Reference
- Do you feel people are dropping hints about you?
- Do you feel they say things with a special meaning?
- Do you feel people are gossiping about you? What do they say?
- Has there been any reference to you recently in the newspapers, on the radio or television?

Grandiosity
- How do you compare yourself to others?
- Are you special in any way?
  Do you have any special talents or powers?
  Are you a famous person or are you related to a famous person?

Religious
- Are you especially holy? Are you especially close to God?
- Does God communicate with you in any special way?

Guilt
- Do you feel guilty?
- Do you feel that you have done something wrong?
- Do you feel as if you have committed a crime or a sin?
  Have you harmed your family or anyone else?
  Do you deserve to be punished?

Poverty
- Do you have any concerns for your finances?

Nihilistic
- Are you concerned about any parts of your body?

GENERAL ADULT PSYCHIATRY

- *Do you feel you are suffering from any serious disease or that any part of your body is unhealthy?*
- *Have you ever felt that you do not exist?*
  Do you think that something terrible is about to happen?

Hypochondriacal
- *Are you concerned that you might have a serious illness?*
  for example cancer or AIDS

Jealousy/Infidelity
- *Are you particularly jealous of anyone?*
- *Are you worried that your partner is unfaithful?*
- *Have you experienced any unusual sexual feelings recently?*

Love (Erotomania)
- *Are you in any relationship?*
- *Have you been in love?*
- *Does this person reciprocate your feelings?*

Delusions of infestation
- *Do you think that your body is infested with insects?*

Delusional mood
- *Have you had the feeling that something is going on that you can't explain? What is it like?*
- *Do you feel puzzled by strange happenings that are difficult to account for?*

Control and passivity experiences
- *Do you feel that there is anyone trying to control you?*
- *Do you feel under the control of some force or power other than yourself?*
  As though you were a robot or zombie without a will of your own?
- *As though you were possessed by someone or something else?*
- *What is that like?? What is the explanation?*
- *Do they force you think, say or do things?*
- *Do they cause you to make movements against your will?*
- *Do they change the way you feel?*

Thought alienation
- *Are you able to think quite clearly?*
- *Is there any interference in your thoughts?*
- *Can people read your mind?*
- *Is there anything like hypnotism, or telepathy going on?*

Thought insertion

- *Do you ever feel that there are thoughts put into your head?*
- *How do you know they are not your own?*
- *Where do they come from?*

Thought echo
- *Do you ever seem to hear your own thoughts spoken aloud in your head, so that someone standing near might be able to hear them?*

Thought broadcast
- *Are your thoughts broadcast, so that other people know what you are thinking?*
- *How do you explain it?*
- *Do you ever seem to hear your own thoughts echoed or repeated?*
- *What is it like? Where do they come from?*

Thought block
- *Do you ever experience your thoughts stopping quite suddenly so that there are none left in your mind, even when your thoughts were flowing freely before?*
- *What is that like?*
- *How often does it occur? What is it due to?*

Thought withdrawal
- *Do your thoughts even seem to be taken out of your head, as though some external person or force were removing them?*
- *Can you give me an example? How do you explain it?*

Degree of conviction
- *Even you seem to be most convinced, do you really feel in the back of your mind that it might not well be true?*
- *How convinced are you that this is truly happening to you?*
- *Do you think that there could be another explanation for this?*
- *What have your friends and family said?*
- ***[Establish also if partial or complete delusion]***

Assess impact
- *How does it make you feel?*
- *How do you usually cope?*

Risk assessment
- *What do you think you might do?*
- *What have you done so far?*

Summarize and Insight
Thank you for sharing this with me. Sometimes when people are under stress they can start to believe things that are not real, and I am wondering whether this could be happening to you? What do you think?
I would like to see how we can help you. What help do you think you need?

Possible variations of theme
1. 30 yr. old man who believes he is responsible for the war.
2. 40 yr. old man believes the Al-Qaida is after him.

PSYCHOSIS
History of presenting complaint HOPC (onset, duration, progression and severity)
- *Use a clustering approach to elicit delusional beliefs*
- *Establish whether delusion is primary or secondary*
- *Types :*
- *Paranoid*
- *Persecutory*
- *Reference*
- *Grandiosity*
- *Religious*
- *Guilt*
- *Poverty*
- *Nihilistic*
- *Hypochondriacal*
- *Jealousy*
- *Love erotomania*
- *Infestation*
- *Delusional mood*

Control and passivity experiences
Thought alienation
- *Thought insertion/withdrawal/broadcast*
- *Thought block and withdrawal*

Establish degree of conviction
Establish if Partial or complete delusion
Assess impact
Risk assessment
Summarize and insight

©Smartsesh

17. PSYCHOSIS- DELUSIONAL DISORDER

INSTRUCTIONS TO CANDIDATE
You have been asked to seen Mr Brian Fox who is a 45 yr. old fire fighter. He went to the police station as he wanted to hand himself in for the war he 'allegedly' caused.

TASK FOR THE CANDIDATE
- Explore his delusional beliefs and experiences.
- Perform a mental state examination.

PAY PARTICULAR ATTENTION TO THE FOLLOWING (MENTAL CHECKLIST)
- Explore his delusional beliefs and experiences.
- Do a mental state examination.
- Conduct a risk assessment.

COMMUNICATION SKILLS
- Start the interview by developing rapport and showing empathy.
- Seek to understand the subjective feeling of the individual.

Suggested approach
Introduction
C: Hello, I'm Dr....I 'm one of the psychiatrists. I've been asked to come and see you. The information I have been given is that you have been brought in by the police.

P: Are you one of them? Why don't you take me and lock me up, I am guilty?

C: Mr Fox, I'm a doctor. Can you tell me more about what you are you talking about?

A. Explore history of presenting complaint (HOPC)
Why do you think they would want to do that?
How do you know this?
What else are they doing?

B. Systematically explore his delusional beliefs
[Explore also for presence for first rank symptoms]
- Do you feel that they are out to harm you? (Persecutory delusion)
- Do you feel that they are following you?
- Do they spy on you?
- Do you think there is a conspiracy against you?
- Do you see reference to yourself on the TV/radio?(Delusions of reference)
- Do you have any special powers or abilities? (Grandiose)

- *Do you have any concerns for your physical health? (Hypochondriacal)*

C. Establish the degree of conviction
- *Can you describe this?*
- *How do you know this?*
- *Could there be another explanation?*
- *How convinced are you of this?*
- *Have you told any of your friends and family?*

D. Hallucinations
- *Have you been hearing any voices when there is no one around? (Auditory hallucinations)*
- *How about seeing things that others can't see? (Visual hallucinations)*

E. Thought alienation
- *Do you think there is any interference in your thinking?*
- *Have you felt that thoughts are being put into your head? (Thought insertion)*
- *How about thoughts being taken out? (Thought withdrawal)*
- *How about your thoughts being broadcast or other people can read your thoughts? (Thought broadcast)*

- ### F. Passivity phenomena

- *Do you think that someone is controlling you?*
- *Controlling your movement? (Made act)*
- *Controlling the way you feel? (Made volition)*
- *Controlling your impulses?*

G. History of Presenting Complaint (HOPC) -onset, duration, progression, severity
- *Can you tell me when did this all start? (Onset, duration)*
- *How has this progressed?*
- *How does it make you feel? (Mood)*

H. Recapitulation
Mr Fox, you have told me that you have been working at the post office and that you have this fixed belief that you are the cause of the war. You have also been suspicious about the people you work with and believe that there is a conspiracy against you.

Insight
Sometimes when people are under stress they can have strange experiences like what you have described. What do you think could be wrong?

GENERAL ADULT PSYCHIATRY

Risk assessment
- What are you planning to do?
- Have you confronted any of these people you are concerned about?
- Have you had thoughts of harming anyone else? (Homicidal thoughts)
- Has it ever come to the point that you had thoughts of wanting to end it all? (Suicidal thoughts)
- Can you describe this please?

Summarise
Thank you for talking to me. I know that it appears you are distressed by what you are experiencing. I have explained, from my experience, when someone is under stress they can have strange experiences and I think that you will benefit with medication.

What help would you like?

GENERAL ADULT PSYCHIATRY

18. HALLUCINATIONS

INSTRUCTIONS TO CANDIDATE
You have been asked to see this 34 yr. old man, Simon Raymond, who has been in the medical ward. He has been distressed by the gunmen who he says are after him.

TASK FOR THE CANDIDATE
- Assess his psychopathology.

PAY APRTICULAR ATTENTION TO THE FOLLOWING (MENTAL CHECKLIST)
- Elicit hallucinations in all modalities (auditory, visual, gustatory, and tactile).
- Establish if complex or elementary type.
- Establish if any extracampine hallucinations.
- Establish if hypnopompic or hypnogogic hallucinations.
- Differentiate hallucination from an illusion.

COMMUNICATION SKILLS
- Start the interview by developing rapport and showing empathy.
- Seek to understand the subjective experience of the individual.
- Anticipate a distressed man who is responding to internal stimuli.

Suggested approach
Introduction
C: Hello, I'm Dr ....Thank you for seeing me. I understand that you have been distressed while you have been on this ward. I have come to talk to you more about this. Is that all right?

P: Shh....
Patient could be distressed and responding to external stimuli

C: Would you like sit down and tell me more about it?

A. History of Presenting Complaint (HOPC) -onset, duration, progression and severity
Elicit hallucinations in all sensory modalities

C: I would like to ask you a routine question which we ask of everybody. Do you ever seem to hear noises or voices when there is no one about and nothing else to explain it?

B. Auditory hallucinations
Complex
What does the voice say?

- *Do you hear your name being called?*
  Do they speak directly to you? (Second person)
- *Do they speak amongst themselves about you? (Third person)*
  Do they seem to comment on what you are thinking or doing?
  (Running commentary)
- *Do they discuss you? Do they argue amongst themselves?*
  Do they call you names? (Derogatory)
  Do they command you or give you orders? Do you obey? (Command)
- *Do the voices repeat your thoughts? (Thought echo)*
- *How many voices do you hear?*
- *Do you recognize the voice?*

Differentiate true hallucination from pseudo-hallucinations
- *Where do they come from?*
- *Where do you hear them?*
- *Are these voices in your mind or can you hear them through your ears?*
- *How clear is this voice?*
- *Is it as clear as I am talking to you?*

Auditory hallucinations
Elementary
- *Do you hear noises like tapping or music?*
- *What is it like? (Musical hallucination)*
- *Does it sound like muttering or whispering?*
- *Can you make out the words?*

When eliciting for auditory hallucination, use a clustering approach to elicit hallucinations in other sensory modalities
For example-Do you see anything or smell anything at the same time as you hear voices?

Explanation, effects and coping
What is the explanation?
Do you know anyone else who has this kind of experience?

C. Visual hallucinations
- *Have you had seen things other people couldn't see?*
- *Do you see this with your eyes or in your mind?*
- *What did you see? Can you describe this to me?*
- *How clear is it?*

Lilliputian hallucinations

- *Do you see insects, animals or tiny people? Can you describe them to me?*
- *How many do you see?*

Elementary type
- *Do you see any bright colors, flashes of light or any patterns?*
- *Do you see spots or floaters?*

Complex visual hallucinations or phantom visual experiences
- *Do you see landscapes or scenery?*
- *Do you see small figures with costumes and hats?*
- *Do you see any distorted faces?*

Differentiate an illusion from hallucination
- *Did the vision seem to arise out of a pattern on the wallpaper or a shadow?*
- *How do you explain it?*

Hallucinations in other sensory modalities
Explore if necessary tailored to the scenario. Inclusive list for completeness

Gustatory, olfactory
- *Is there anything unusual about the way things taste or smell?*

D. Olfactory
- *Do you sometime notice strange smells that other people don't notice? What sort of things?*
  How do you explain it?
- *Do you seem to think that you yourself give off a smell which is noticed?*
- *How do you explain that?*

E. Gustatory
- *Have you noticed that food and drink seems to have an unusual taste recently?*

F. Tactile
Haptic
- *Do you ever feel that someone is touching you, but when you look there's nobody there?*
Fornication
- *Do you ever have strange sensations on your skin, for example insects crawling or electricity passing?*
Hyric
- *Do feel like there is fluid in your body?*
Kinesthetic
- *Do you sometimes feel that your muscles are stretched or squeezed?*

Vestibular
- Did you ever feel like you were floating or rotating?

Other
G. Autoscopy
- Did you ever see yourself or your body walking around and doing things while you were observing?

H. Extracampine hallucination
- Have you ever heard people talking to you from miles away?

I. Hypnogogic and hypnopompic hallucinations
- Were you half asleep at the time?
- Has it occurred when you were fully awake?
- Did you realize you were seeing things?

J. Reflex
- Sometimes someone might hear a voice and have another sensation like have a pain in the head?

K. Functional
- Have you ever heard a sound for example the tap running and at the same time heard voices?

Summarize
Thank you for talking to me. From what we have discussed you appear to be clearly distressed by what you are experiencing. You are concerned about he gunmen that are following you, and you have been seeing and hearing them shooting at you.

What do you think could be wrong? (Insight)

Possible variations of theme
1. 60 yr. old man in the medical ward that is frightened and threatening to leave.
2. 45 yr. old lady who is hearing voices telling her to jump into the river.

Auditory hallucinations

Complex
- *second person*
- *third person*
  running commentary
- *derogatory command*
- *thought echo*

Differentiate true hallucination from pseudo-hallucinations
- *Auditory hallucinations*
- *Elementary*
- *Musical hallucination*
  Visual hallucinations
  Lilliputian hallucinations
- *Elementary type*
- *Complex visual hallucinations or phantom visual experiences*

Differentiate an illusion from hallucination

Hallucinations in other sensory modalities
- *Gustatory, olfactory*
  Olfactory
  Gustatory
- *Tactile -Haptic, Fornication, Hyric, Kinaesthetic, Vestibular, Autoscopy*

Extracampine hallucination
Hypnogogic and hypnopompic hallucinations
Reflex hallucination
Functional hallucination

©Smartsesh

GENERAL ADULT PSYCHIATRY

19. Schizophrenia

Suggested approach
Introduction
C: Hello, I'm Dr ..... I am one of the psychiatrists. I have seen your son and I
know you are concerned about him. I am here to talk to you more about his
diagnosis and management. Before I begin, can you tell me what your
understanding is of his condition is.

M: **I know he is just not the same. He has been staying at home and he
has said his mates are after him. One of the nurses said he has
Schizophrenia.**

C: Schizophrenia is a relatively common mental illness. It is when someone's
thinking, feeling and behaviour is affected and they lose touch of reality.

For example:
Your son has become suspicious about people and has strong beliefs that
they are poisoning him despite no evidence of this. This type of thinking is
one of the positive symptoms called a delusion. The other positive symptom is
hallucinations, when someone hears or sees things when there is no one else
around.

Other symptoms are the negative symptoms where they lose they lack motivation to do activities of daily living and in some cases isolate themselves.

M: Who usually gets this?

C: It is serious mental illness that occurs 1 in 100 people. It can develop in the late teens from 15-35 yrs.

M: What are the causes?

C: It is difficult to pinpoint one particular cause. The causes are multifactorial. From the literature available is it is due to a few associated factors. It has a genetic component and can run in families. That means if someone in the family has it, there is a 10 times increased risk of getting this.

It is also due to a chemical imbalance of dopamine, noradrenalin (NA) and serotonin. It can be caused by birth infections, season of birth. We know also that using street drugs like cannabis can also trigger an episode.

M: Is it my fault?

C: No, it is not your fault. A lot of people in your situation do feel responsible. It's important that you understand his illness and therefore your support and understanding plays an important role in his recovery.

M: Will he get better?

C: Our aim is to get him to lead a normal life as possible. This however is not always possible. After one relapse the risk is reduced. The general rule of thumb is that 1/3 will recover, 1/3 will remain chronic and 1/3 another episode. It's difficult to say which category he will be in.

We work in a multidisciplinary team approach (MDT). The team consists of the psychiatrists that will look at the medication. The community psychiatric nurse that will support him at home, the psychologist for psychology or talking therapy, the occupational therapist for vocational training and social worker to assist him with the social aspects like housing, benefits, arranging activities.

M: What is the medication available for him?

C: The medications used to treat Schizophrenia are a group called antipsychotic medication. It works to normalise the chemical imbalance. It helps to make a person think more clearly, weaken the delusions and hallucinations and increase the motivation so that they will be able to take care of themselves.

Like all medication they have side effects. Would you like to know about that?

The typical or older generation of medication can cause stiffness, shakiness and restlessness. [Known as EPSE's or extra-pyramidal side effects]

The atypical or newer generation of medication for example: [elaborate further depending on the antipsychotic medication being prescribed] Olanzapine can cause drowsiness and weight gain. It can also cause constipation, dry mouth, peripheral oedema and postural hypotension. In the longer term it can cause metabolic syndrome where there is raised blood pressure glucose and cholesterol, diabetes and weight gain.

We will monitor him for these side effects and as you know not everyone will develop these side effects. We usually start on a low dose and gradually increase this.

M: How long will he need to continue with this medication?

C: There is a chance if he doesn't take medication that he will relapse. We usually advise that he would need to continue with it for 1-2 years to prevent getting unwell.

I know I am giving you a lot of information. Have you understood me thus far? Please do feel free to interrupt me at any time if you do not understand.

M: What are the Psychological treatments that are available?

C: In the longer term other treatment options available are the psychological or talking therapies called CBT (cognitive behavioural therapy) for the fixed beliefs (delusions) and family therapy. This is usually done at the later stage of treatment.

Another vitally important part is education about his illness, because if people understand the illness, then this would improve their insight and engagement with their treatment. It is also important that you and the rest of the family learn more about his illness to promote his wellbeing and recovery. We could also provide you some support and a carers assessment if you need. Relaxation therapy is also important to minimise the stress. [Elaborate on High Expressed Emotion if relevant]

M: What support will he get?

C: The social aspects involve that of getting him to a functional level. The Occupational therapist (OT) will maximise his potential to ensure he could possibly return to education and vocational training. We have day centres and activities, and encourage people to volunteer at MIND.

M: Does he need to be in hospital?

GENERAL ADULT PSYCHIATRY

C: We usually assess the risk and consider either admission in hospital either voluntary or by means of the Mental Health Act (MHA 1983) (MHA). In cases where a person doesn't voluntarily consent to admission to hospital, and if we feel it is in their best interest and to ensure their safety or the safety of others, we will have to use the Mental Health Act (MHA 1983). [MHA-explain legal caveats accordingly]

Towards the later stages of care we usually involve the EIS or Early Intervention Services, which would provide the community support.

Summarise
Thank you for seeing me today. I know you are concerned about your son. I have told you more about his illness and the treatment options available like medication, psychological and social aspects of care.

I have some leaflets for you to read. I am happy to see you again to discuss this further. Do you have any other questions?
I can suggest some useful organisations and support group like Mind.

Support groups and websites
There are also these useful organisations and charities like MIND, SANELINE and RETHINK.
<u>Mind</u>: Publishes a wide range of literature on all aspects of mental health.

<u>Sane line</u>: A national mental health helpline offering emotional support and practical information for people with mental illness, families, carers and professionals.

<u>Rethink</u> : National voluntary organisation that helps people with any severe mental illness, their families and care

Thank you

Possible variations of theme
Speak to the mother of an 18 yr. old who has been smoking cannabis. She is upset that her son has been given the diagnosis of Schizophrenia as she is certain that it is due to the cannabis.

SCHIZOPHRENIA: Management

Schizophrenia-*common mental illness*
Epidemiology: *1/100, M=F*
Aetiology- *genetic, environmental, viral infections, street drugs,*
Management using biopsychosocial approach
Biological interventions
Rating scales: SANS, PANS
Medication
- *Antipsychotic according to NICE guidelines*
- *Atypical-Risperidone, Olanzapine, Aripiprazole, Quetiapine side effects metabolic syndrome, weight gain, DM(Diabetes Mellitus)*
- *Typical Haloperidol side effects stiffness, shakiness, restlessness*

Psychological interventions
- *CBT/FT-delusion, high expressed emotion*
- *Psychoeducation*
- *Relaxation therapy*

Social interventions
- *Finances*
- *Day centre , activities*
- *MIND volunteer*
- *Vocational services –occupational therapy*

Long term
- *EIS-Early intervention service*

©Smartsesh

Antipsychotics

Antipsychotics are drugs, which are used to treat Psychosis/schizophrenia. Some are also licensed to be used as mood stabilisers. They act on brain chemicals involved with perception, thinking and emotions and correct their imbalance. Medicines do not cure the illness but treat the symptoms and prevent relapses in a large number of people.

Dosage and side effects

Individuals respond differently to medication so finding the right dose might take a little time. Patients are started on the lowest possible dose to avoid side effects. Side effects occur because these medicines not only act on the parts of brain where we want them to act but also affect some other parts of the brain. Fortunately the newer drugs have mostly mild side effects, which usually disappear after being on the treatment for some time.

Common side effects include drowsiness, weight gain, altered bowel movements, low blood pressure and increase in salivation. Weight gain generally occurs in the first 6-12 months of the treatment. If this is something that concerns you, it can be arranged for a dietician to see you and give you advice about diet. Since these tablets cause sedation it is advisable not to drive in the initial part of the treatment.

Available in different forms

Antipsychotics are available in tablet and injection form. Patients at times do not take their tablets regularly. Because of their disorganized thinking they might find it hard to remember to take it or they may feel that they do not need to be on medicines. In such cases injectable form of antipsychotics called depots can be tried. They come in slow release form and can be given every 2-4 weeks.

Antipsychotics should not be stopped suddenly. If you are worried about any of the side effects, discuss it with your doctor and a different drug can be tried as different drugs have different side effect profile.

Aids to facilitate compliance

Medication calendar, dossette boxes, blister packs and pairing medicines with routine activities like meals.

Duration of treatment

After the first episode it is advisable to continue with the medication for 1-2 years. Patients are regularly reviewed and if there are no concerns then initially the dose is decreased. The decision to come off medicines, if the mental state remains stable, is made jointly with the patient.

If there have been more than one episode of Psychosis/schizophrenia, it is advisable to continue with the lowest effective dose.

©Smartsesh

ANTIPSYCHOTICS –TYPICAL, FIRST GENERATION

Nature –Treatment
- Chlorpromazine (Largactil®)-
- Haloperidol (Serenace®, Haldol®
- Pericyazine(Neulactil®)
- Promazine
- Trifluperazine(Stelazine®)
- Purpose: Schizophrenia or Psychosis

Administration: tablet or depot injections

Effects/benefits: treat positive and negative symptoms, and agitation, Anxiety

Adverse/side effects
- Common: Extra pyramidal side effects:
- Akathisia, dystonia, tardive dyskinesia and parkinsonism symptoms
- Anticholinergic side effects: dry mouth, blurred vision, constipation drowsiness
- Raised prolactin:irregular periods, impotence and galactorrhoea in men and women
- Uncommon: hypotension, palpitations, sexual dysfunction: difficulty with orgasm and decreased desire for sex

Precautions
- Epilepsy, Diabetes, Depression, Myasthenia gravis, phaeochromocytoma, Parkinson's disease, glaucoma, heart, liver, breathing, kidney or prostrate trouble
- Caution in pregnancy and breastfeeding
- Rare: photosensitivity, skin rashes
- Very rare: NMS Neuroleptic   Malignant syndrome,
- Agranulocytosis

Alternatives: atypical or second generation antipsychotics

Duration: may need to continue for a long period after remission, symptoms may return within 3-6 months cessation of treatment

©Smartsesh

Atypical Antipsychotics or second generation antipsychotics
Nature -Treatment/intervention
- Risperidone (Risperdal®)

Purpose
- Schizophrenia or Psychosis

Dosage
- Starting dose 0,5 mg-2mg to 4mg-6mg daily

Effects/benefits
- Treat positive and negative symptoms. No effect on prolactin levels

Adverse/side effects
- Common
- Headache, hypotension, restless or agitated
- Raised prolactin
- Uncommon
- Akathisia, constipation, drowsiness, insomnia, movement disorders, weight gain
- Rare :blurred vision, NMS, skin rashes

Precautions
- Parkinsons disease, heart, liver, or kidney problems
- Caution in pregnancy or breast feeding

Alternatives: other atypical medication

Atypical Antipsychotics or second generation antipsychotics
Nature -Treatment/intervention
- Olanzapine(Zyprexa®)

Purpose
- Schizophrenia or Psychosis

Dosage
- Starting dose 5mg up to maximum 20mg per day

Effects/benefits
- Treat positive and negative symptoms, less extra pyramidal side effects

Adverse/side effects
- Common:
- Drowsiness, weight gain, metabolic syndrome
- Uncommon
- Constipation, dry mouth, peripheral oedema, postural hypotension
- Rare altered liver function
- photosensitivity

Precautions
- Parkinson's disease, heart, liver, or kidney problems
- Caution in pregnancy or breast feeding

Alternatives

© **Smartsesh**

F20 Schizophrenia

The schizophrenic disorders are characterized in general by fundamental and characteristic distortions of thinking and perception, and affects that are inappropriate or blunted. Clear consciousness and intellectual capacity are usually maintained although certain cognitive deficits may evolve in the course of time. The most important psychopathological phenomena include thought echo; thought insertion or withdrawal; thought broadcasting; delusional perception and delusions of control; influence or passivity; hallucinatory voices commenting or discussing the patient in the third person; thought disorders and negative symptoms.

The course of schizophrenic disorders can be either continuous, or episodic with progressive or stable deficit, or there can be one or more episodes with complete or incomplete remission. The diagnosis of schizophrenia should not be made in the presence of extensive depressive or manic symptoms unless it is clear that schizophrenic symptoms antedate the affective disturbance. Nor should schizophrenia be diagnosed in the presence of overt brain disease or during states of drug intoxication or withdrawal. Similar disorders developing in the presence of epilepsy or other brain disease should be classified under F06.2, and those induced by psychoactive substances under F10-F19 with common fourth character.

Excl.:
Schizophrenia:
    Acute (undifferentiated) (F23.2)
    Cyclic (F25.2)

Schizophrenic reaction (F23.2)
Schizotypal disorder (F21)

GENERAL ADULT PSYCHIATRY

NICE guidelines for Schizophrenia
(Adapted from NICE guidance)

> Emphasis on recognising and accounting for ethnic, cultural and minority group factors in comphrensive multidisciplinary assessment, treatment and management.

> Facilitate early access to assessment and treatment.

> Ensure access to education and employment opportunities

> Offer carer's assessments, take into account needs of children and families and ensure relatives are kept informed.

> Advocates use of a lead healthcare profession, i.e. care co-ordinator.

> General practitioners to monitor physical health annually.

> CBT and family therapy should be offered to patients in the acute or chronic phases of illness can be offered even as an inpatient.

> Oral antipsychotic medication should be offered after discussion of side effect profiles, intended benefits and ideally in collaboration with the patient.

> Avoid use of regular combined antipsychotic treatments.

> For those who have not responded adequately to treatments above: review the diagnosis, establish adherence to medication, ensure adequate medication trial, review psychological interventions used and explore reason for non-response, i.e. co morbid mental or physical illness.

> Offer clozapine to those who have not responded to the sequential use of adequate doses of at least two different antipsychotic drugs. One of the drugs should be another second generation antipsychotic.

> Consider rapid tranquillisation for people who pose an immediate threat to themselves or others during an acute episode if de-escalation techniques fail.

> Withdraw antipsychotic medication gradually. Regularly monitor for signs and symptoms of relapse for at least 2 years after withdrawal.

> Consider re-referral to secondary care if there is: poor treatment response, non-adherence to medication, intolerable side effects from medication, co morbid substance misuse or risk to the patient or others.

> Assertive outreach should be provided for those: who frequently use inpatient services, have a history of poor engagement with services and those with inadequate accommodation or who are homeless.

GENERAL ADULT PSYCHIATRY

MEDICATION	SIDE EFFECTS
Risperidone (Risperdal®)(Janssen) 4-6mg max oral/IM	**Common:** headaches, hypotension, restless or agitated and raised prolactin. **Uncommon:** Akathisia, constipation, drowsiness, insomnia, movement disorders, weight gain. **Rare:** blurred vision, NMS, Skin rashes
Olanzapine (Zyprexa®) (Lilly) 20mg od at night	**Common:** drowsiness, weight gain. **Uncommon:** constipation, dry mouth, peripheral oedema, postural hypotension. **Rare:** altered liver function, photosensitivity, and metabolic syndrome.
Aripiprazole (Abilify®)(Bristol-Myers-Squibb) 15-30mg	**Common:** Light-headedness, insomnia, Akathisia, somnolence, tremor, blurred vision, nausea and vomiting, dyspepsia, constipation, headache, asthenia. **Uncommon:** tachycardia, orthostatic hypotension.

MEDICATION	SIDE EFFECTS
Quetiapine Seroquel®(Astra Zeneca) Seroquel XL ®(Astra Zeneca) Day 1 25mg bd Day 2 50mg bd Day 3 100mg bd Day 4 150mg bd max 750 mg in divided doses Schizophrenia and 800mg in Bipolar Affective disorder	**Common:** dry mouth, constipation dyspepsia, tachycardia, hypertension, peripheral oedema, elevated triglyceride and cholesterol **Less common:** dysphagia, seizures, restless leg syndrome, eosinophilia **Rare:** jaundice, priapism, hepatitis, Steven Johnson syndrome
Amisulpiride Solian® (Sanofi-Aventis) 400mg-800mg daily in 2 divided doses Maximum 1.2 g daily	**Common:** Insomnia, Anxiety, agitation, drowsiness, gastro intestinal disorders-constipation, nausea, vomiting, dry mouth, hyperprolactinaemia, **Less common:** bradycardia **Rare:** seizures

GENERAL ADULT PSYCHIATRY

20. CLOZAPINE -REHABILITATION

INSTRUCTIONS TO CANDIDATE
You are about to see the mother of Mr Sam Frederick who is known with Schizophrenia and has been admitted under section 2 of the Mental Health Act (MHA 1983).The decision of the multi-disciplinary team is that he would require supported living. He has also had liver function tests which reveal elevated GGT (Gamma-glutamyltransferase) levels.

TASK FOR THE CANDIDATE
- Address her concerns about her son

PAY PARTICULAR ATTENTION TO THE FOLLOWING (MENTAL CHECKLIST)
- Explain reasons for his admission
- Highlight the risk issues present
- Explain team's decision for rehabilitation and supported living
- Explain CPA (Care programme approach)
- Highlight importance of joint working with family to promote his recovery and wellbeing.

COMMUNICATION SKILLS
- Develop rapport and empathy
- Show sensitivity and acknowledge her distress
- Allow her to ventilate her feelings
- Suggest a collaborative approach and keeping her sons best interests at heart to promote his recovery and wellbeing

---

Suggested approach
Introduction
C: Hello, I'm Dr...I'm a psychiatrist working on this ward. I understand you have come to see me about your son. I know this must be a difficult time for you. Before we begin, can I ask what you understand of how he came into hospital?

M: He shouldn't have been admitted [allow her space to ventilate her feelings]

C: I can see this is clearly upsetting you. I can assure you that I and the team have his best interests at heart. We have discussed this at our recent team meeting, and I would like to discuss this with you.

[Below are possible caveats which need to be addressed. It should be a dialogue and would be dependent on addressing his mother's concerns and her responses.]

A. Explain the current admission circumstances and Diagnosis of Treatment resistant Schizophrenia

GENERAL ADULT PSYCHIATRY

From the information I have available to me, I understand that the AOT (Assertive outreach team had been supporting him in the community, but despite their level of support, his mental state deteriorated and he was admitted to hospital under the Mental Health Act (MHA 1983).

He has been on tried on several antipsychotic medications with minimal improvement. In his case it appears that he therefore has Treatment resistant Schizophrenia. The next treatment option available would be Clozapine, however with this medication he would need to have regular blood tests. [Elaborate on Clozapine if necessary]

B. Explain the abnormal liver function tests
We have done his bloods and some of his liver function tests are abnormal. One of the levels is increased and this is usually if a person is drinking alcohol. [Raised GGT]

C. Explain the MDT review
At the multidisciplinary meeting we had the occupational therapist (OT) do activities of daily living (ADL assessment). The assessment indicated that he needs supervision with his daily self-care for example feeding, washing and cooking and would therefore not be able to live independently.

We also take the view of the carers so your input in this decision making is vital. You are probably the best person who knows him. What do you think would be the most suitable placement for him?

D. Discuss the possible options available
-If he goes and lives at home with family, need to ascertain the level of support
-possibility of rehabilitation and supportive living

E. Enquiry about leave
He is currently detained under section 2 of the Mental Health Act (MHA 1983). When he is more settled and he has responded to treatment we can allow him section 17 leave to go home. We can gradually assess his leave and at a later stage consider overnight leave home if that is something you would like.

F. Explain the CPA [care programme approach]
We will keep you informed at all stages of his progress and treatment. In 3-4 months we will invite you for his CPA which will be a meeting with all the people that are involved in his care. Together we will discuss what sort of care package would be appropriate for him in the community and what level of support he will require.

Summarise
Thank you for talking with me. We have discussed the options for your son when he will be discharged. We usually have a weekly multi-disciplinary team meeting weekly; you are most welcome to attend and I have given you some

GENERAL ADULT PSYCHIATRY

information. Here are some leaflets for you. There are also some useful websites and support groups available. I am happy to meet again with you if have any further questions and to discuss your sons progress.

Leaflets / Website
Support and website addresses
Mind www.mind.co.uk

GENERAL ADULT PSYCHIATRY

21. CLOZAPINE

INSTRUCTIONS TO CANDIDATE
You are asked to see this 35 year old man Adam Saunders who has been on 2 different antipsychotics and has been told about Clozapine as the next line of treatment.

TASK FOR THE CANDIDATE
- *Explain about Clozapine.*

PAY PARTICULAR ATTENTION TO THE FOLLOWING (MENTAL CHECKLIST)
- *Explain rationale for Clozapine treatment.*
- *Explain the benefits of Clozapine for treatment resistant Schizophrenia.*
- *Explain the side effects, precautions and need for blood monitoring.*
- *Explain the alternatives available.*

COMMUNICATION SKILLS
- *Start the interview by developing rapport and showing empathy.*
- *Anticipate reluctance with wanting to have regular blood monitoring.*
- *Emphasise the positives and gently impart the side effects.*

Suggested approach
Introduction
C: Hello, I'm Dr...I'm a psychiatrist. I have been asked to come and discuss about Clozapine with you. It would be helpful if you could tell me what your understanding of this is?

P: I know one of my friends is on it and he has to have blood tests every 2 weeks.

C: Yes, that is so. If someone is on Clozapine, they will need to have blood tests. I will explain that more in detail but before that I would like to tell you more about Clozapine, and the benefits of taking this treatment. Is that all right?

P: Ok Doc, what is this Clozapine?

C: Clozapine is a medicine used to treat people with Schizophrenia. It is used when 2 or more medication have not worked.[Treatment Resistant Schizophrenia] It belongs to the group of antipsychotics called the atypical antipsychotics, which do not cause the unpleasant side effects like the older medication [i.e. Extra pyramidal side effects (EPSE'S) rigidity and shakiness]

P: How will this help me?

GENERAL ADULT PSYCHIATRY

C: [Emphasise the positive effects- beneficial for Negative & Positive symptoms]
Clozapine not only helps with the common symptoms of the illness like hearing voices, odd beliefs and paranoia (positive symptoms) but may also help with the lack of motivation, poor communication and poor social interaction (negative symptoms). It has a 1 in 6 chance of a 20 % improvement.

P: What do I need to know before starting Clozapine?
Monitoring

C: Before starting Clozapine patients undergoes routine blood tests and is registered with monitoring services (Clozapine Patient Monitoring Service-ZTAS). This is the company which markets Clozapine. This is because very rarely Clozapine can lower the number of white blood cells or can cause malfunction of these cells. White cells are important because they fight infections.

The risk of dropping the white cell count is 3 in 100 and of severe malfunctioning is 1 in 5000. In order to monitor for these side effects patients taking Clozapine have weekly blood tests for the first 18 weeks of treatment, then fortnightly for the first year of treatment. Thereafter blood tests are done on a monthly basis.

It is important to tell you that if you develop a sore throat or fever, you would need to inform your doctor.

P: What investigations would I need to have apart from the blood tests?

C: Before starting Clozapine, we would need to also do a tracing of the heart called ECG and also EEG tracing of electrical activity of the brain.

P: What are the side effects?

C: Although it has many good effects, it does have some side effects. Common side effects are sedation, increase in salivation, and fluctuation in blood pressure, increased heart rate and increase in body temperature. These side effects normally settle within the first 4 weeks

Some people also experience constipation and weight gain. These can be managed by high fibre diet and advice from dietician. On higher doses it can also cause fits which can be managed with other medication.

P: What is the Dosage?

C: The normal starting dose of Clozapine is 12.5 mg and it is gradually increased over a period of weeks to a daily dose between 300 and 450 mg. It *is usually given in a twice daily dose. At times higher dose is needed. Maximum daily dose is 900 mg/day.*

If you miss your dose for more than two days, Clozapine will have to be restarted at 12.5 mg and will again need to be built up to dose which was found to be helpful.

P: What are the therapeutic Levels?

C: Therapeutic Clozapine level is between 350-420 micrograms. In terms of dose, it is best to be guided by the mental state.
[Norclozapine levels can be done to check compliance. Lower doses are required in non-smokers and elderly females. Levels can be increased by enzyme inhibitors like Fluvoxamine.]

P: What are the serious complications?

C: Fast heart rate (tachycardia) can be because of myocarditis or cardiomyopathy. Myocarditis is usually an early complication and cardiomyopathy a late one but this is not a hard and fast rule. [Other serious side effects are pulmonary embolus and sudden death.]

P: Is it addictive?

C: No

P: How long would I need to take clozapine?

C: Most people need to take Clozapine for a long time, sometimes years. You and your doctor will decide when you would be able to stop this. If you do stop taking Clozapine, there is the risk that your original symptoms will return, but this may not be for 3 to 6 months after you stop the drug.

P: What happens if I miss a dose?

C: If you do miss a dose, take dose as soon as you remember this. Never take double the dose. If it is longer than 24 hours then you need to contact your doctor or CMHT (community mental health team)

P: Can I have alcohol?

C: Officially people taking Clozapine should not take alcohol. This is because both Clozapine and alcohol can cause drowsiness

Summarize
Thank you for talking to me. To summarize, I have told you about Clozapine, and the benefits of taking this medication. I have also told you about the

GENERAL ADULT PSYCHIATRY

regular blood monitoring and the reasons for this. I have some leaflets for you to read. I would like you to think about it and I will come and see you later to see if you have come to a decision. You can also speak to some of your family and staff here to discuss this as well.

MEDICATION	SIDE EFFECTS
Clozapine Clozaril®(Novartis) Denzapine®(Merz) Zaponex®(Teva UK) Day 1 12.5 mg bd Day 2 25-50mg Gradually increased in steps of 25-50mg over 14-21 days up to 300mg in divided doses **Alternatives** Augmentation with: Sulpride/Amisulpride peridone Lamotrigine Omega 3 triglycerides Haloperidol	**Common:**sedation, hypersalivation increase in body temperature Constipation, weight gain, dry mouth, nausea, anorexia, tachycardia , ECG changes, hypertension, drowsiness Blurred vision **Less common:** Myocarditis, cardiomyopathy **Rare:** dysphagia, hepatitis, cardiomyopathy, myocardial infarct, respiratory suppression, priapism, intestinal nephritis, hypercholesteraemia, hypertriglyceridaemia, skin reactions **Caution:** Agranulocytosis Neutropenia and potentially fatal agranulocytosis

GENERAL ADULT PSYCHIATRY

22. AOT-SPEAK TO CARE COORDINATOR

INSTRUCTIONS TO CANDIDATE
You have been asked to see Moira White who is the care coordinator for James Brook. He has been supported by the AOT (Assertive outreach team) and has now been admitted informally to hospital due to deterioration in his mental state.

TASK FOR THE CANDIDATE
- *Elicit a collateral history*

PAY PARTICULAR ATTENTION TO THE FOLLOWING (MENTAL CHECKLIST)
- *Establish the current HOPC (onset, duration, frequency and duration)*
- *Establish psychiatric history in terms of current diagnosis and treatment*
- *Conduct a thorough risk assessment*
- *Assess his current level of functioning and social supports*

COMMUNICATION SKILLS
- *Start the interview by developing rapport and showing empathy*
- *Adopt a collegiate approach*

Suggested approach
Introduction
C: Hello, I'M Dr ...I'm a psychiatrist working on this ward. I understand you are the care coordinator for this gentleman who has been under the AOT and now admitted as an inpatient. I would appreciate if you could give me more information about him and the circumstances leading up to admission?

N: Hello doctor. The AOT (assertive outreach team) have been supporting James

A. History of Presenting Complaint (HOPC) (severity, onset, duration, progression)
C: Can you tell me what led up to his current admission?

Explore more about events that led to admission
- *Do you know about the possible reasons for his admission?*
- *What medication is he currently on?*

B. Past psychiatric history
- *Can you tell me about his past psychiatric history? (Diagnosis)*
- *Do you know whether he had any previous admissions? Were they informal or formal? (Previous admissions and detentions under the Mental Health*

Act (MHA 1983))
- What were the circumstances that resulted in his previous admissions? (Triggers)
- Do you know what medication he has been on previously? (Medication history)
- Do you know if there were any compliance issues? (Compliance and insight)
- Can you tell me more about his CPA (Care Programme Approach) and discharge plans?
- Are you aware if he has support or family involvement? (Social support)

C. Risk assessment
- Has he had any risky behaviour; for example?
- Has he ever attempted to self-harm? (Deliberate self-harm)
- Has he ever taken any overdoses? (Para suicide)
- Has he ever attempted to harm anyone else?
- Has he ever been aggressive?
- Explore other risks: Self neglect, Exploitation, Danger to children

D. Forensic history
- Has he been involved with the police?
- Does he have any convictions or charges?

E. Drug and alcohol history
- Do you know whether he drinks or takes any street drugs?

F. AOT (assertive outreach team)
- How long has he been under the care of the Assertive
- Outreach Team (AOT)?
- Can you tell me more about the level of support he requires?
- How does he spend his time? (ADL functioning)
- Does he do any activities?
- Is he on any benefits? (Finances)
- Has he attempted vocational training?

Summarise
Thank you for talking to me. It has been helpful. To summarise, James has been under the care of the Assertive Outreach Team (AOT) and recently he has been reluctant to engage with the treatment programme. He has presented now with a relapse and from the history it appears that he could be suffering with Treatment Resistant Schizophrenia. We would therefore need to look at the possibility of commencing him on medication like Clozapine.

GENERAL ADULT PSYCHIATRY

I understand his father is keen to discuss his sons care. Is there anything else you would like to add to this?

Thank you

AOT –COLLATERAL HISTORY

History of Presenting Complaint (HOPC) (severity, onset, duration, progression)
- Current admission

Explore more about events that led to admission
- Reasons for his admission
- Medication

Past psychiatric history
- Past psychiatric history (diagnosis)
- Previous admissions informal or formal (previous admissions)
- Circumstances that resulted in his previous admissions (triggers) medication he has been on previously (medication history)
- Compliance issues (compliance and insight)
- Details of his CPA and discharge plans (CPA)
- Support or family involvement (Social support)

Risk assessment
- Overdoses, DSH deliberate self-harm
- Harm to others, history of aggression
- Explore other risks: Self neglect, Exploitation, Danger to children

Forensic history
- Police, convictions or charges

Drug and alcohol history
- Do you know whether he drinks and takes street drugs?

AOT (assertive outreach team)
- AOT, level of support he requires, ADL functioning, activities, finances vocational training

Summarise

©Smartsesh

GENERAL ADULT PSYCHIATRY

23. AOT-DISCUSS MANAGEMENT WITH HIS FATHER

INSTRUCTIONS TO CANDIDATE
You have been asked to see Mr Brook who is the father of James Brook.
He is upset about his son being admitted into hospital and wants to
discuss this with you.

TASK FOR THE CANDIDATE
- Address his father's concern.

PAY PARTICULAR ATTENTION TO THE FOLLOWING (MENTAL CHECKLIST)
- Address fathers concerns.
- Explain diagnosis of Treatment Resistant Schizophrenia.
- Explain management using a biopsychosocial approach.
- Explain longer term management which would include involvement of Community Mental Health Team (CMHT) and Community treatment order (CTO) if necessary.

COMMUNICATION SKILLS
- Start the interview by developing rapport and showing empathy.
- Anticipate a strong emotional reaction and possibly angry father who is concerned about his son.

Suggested approach
Introduction
C: Hello, I'm Dr...I'm a psychiatrists involved in your sons care. Thank you
for coming to speak to me. I have spoken to one of the nurses about your
son. I gather you would like to know more about his treatment.
Can you tell me what your concerns are?

**Reponses should be tailored according to fathers concerns. I have
highlighted possible issues which he would raise. Please use this merely
as a guide.**

F: I wanted to know more about what happened that he came into
hospital?

A. History of Presenting Complaint (HOPC) (severity, onset, duration,
progression)
Summarise your findings from the information given by the nurse

Elaborate further depending on concerns raised:

C: I think you have risen are important and valid points. I would like to
address each one individually

GENERAL ADULT PSYCHIATRY

F: How did he end up coming into hospital?

C: I understand that the AOT has been supporting him since discharge. The level of support I'm told is that they have been visiting him regularly, monitoring his medication and wellbeing. They have also been helping him with his benefits and encouraging him to attend activities. However, he did not take his medication regularly and thus this resulted in him becoming unwell again.

F: How are you treating him?
[Elaborate further on his diagnosis and treatment]

C: As you are aware, he has been diagnosed with Schizophrenia. Not everyone whom we treat respond to treatment. This could be due to associated factors of not taking medication regularly, drinking and taking street drugs, and if there is any other underlying conditions

It would appear that he has not responded to treatment, and that he has Treatment Resistant Schizophrenia. That is when someone has not responded to 2 or more different antipsychotics.

We would therefore need to consider the options of starting him on **Clozapine.**

Have you heard about this treatment? [Tailor answer according to the information required]
It has been found to be beneficial and is the recommended treatment for Treatment Resistant Schizophrenia.
With this type of medication however, one needs to have regular blood tests. As it can cause the white cells or fighter cells in the body to go less, and therefore once started, he would need to have weekly blood tests in the first instance and thereafter fortnightly tests. This is usually done while he is an inpatient.

F: Will he ever get better?

C: Our aim is for him to have a normal life as possible and to live independently. For the rehabilitation process, we use a Multidisciplinary Team Approach (MDT). The team usually consists of different professionals which will contribute to assisting him to ensure that he engages with the team.

The Multidisciplinary Team (MDT) consists of the psychiatrist, the community psychiatric nurse, the occupational therapists, the psychologist, the social worker and vocational worker.

F: When will he be discharged?

C: We will keep you informed at all stages of his progress and treatment. In 3-4 months we will invite you for his CPA which will be a meeting with all the people that are involved in his care. Together we will discuss what sort of care package would be appropriate for him in the community and what level of support he will require.

F: Is there any way of ensuring this doesn't happen in the future?

C: We have a CTO or community treatment order which can safeguard against admissions. It is part of the Mental Health Act (MHA 1983)) which is when someone is on a section 2 or section 3 and is discharged; they would be placed on a CTO with stipulated conditions. This would ensure that if he does relapse and breached his conditions, he would be recalled to hospital.

This would ensure his engagement with his rehabilitation, reduce admission and improve compliance.

Summarize
Thank you for talking to me. I will give you some information and leaflets for you to read. I am happy to meet again with you to discuss your son's progress and treatment.

Section2 MHA (Mental Health Act 1983): *Admission for assessment.*	*__Grounds:__ Mental disorder.* *__An application under s2:__ must be made by an Approved Mental Health Professional (AMHP) or nearest relative.* *__Maximum duration:__ You can be detained for up to 28 days. S2 cannot be renewed but you may be transferred onto a s3.* *__Medical recommendations:__ Two doctors (one approved under section12).* *__Eligibility for appeal to Mental Health Review Tribunal:__ You have the right to appeal against detention to a tribunal during the first 14 days that you are detained.* *__Discharge:__ RMO, Hospital managers, Nearest relatives can be overridden by doctors if necessary.*
Section 3: *Admission for treatment.*	*__Grounds:__ Mental illness, psychopathic disorder, mental impairment, severe mental impairment.* *__An application under S3:__ must be made by an Approved Mental Health Professional (AMHP) or nearest relative.* *__Maximum duration:__ You can be detained for up to 6 months. Detention under S3 can be renewed for further period of 6 months, and then for further periods of one year at a time.* *__Medical recommendations:__ Two medical doctors (one approved under section12).* *__Eligibility for appeal to Mental Health Review Tribunal:__ You have right to appeal against detention to a Tribunal once during the first 6 months of detention, once during the second 6 months and then once during each period of one year.* *__Discharge:__ RMO, Hospital managers, Nearest relatives can be overridden by doctors if necessary.*

Section 4: Emergency admission for assessment.	**_Grounds:_** Mental disorder (urgent necessity). **_An application under S4:_** must be made by an Approved Mental Health Professional (AMHP) or nearest relative. In addition you must be seen by a doctor (preferably one that knows you or one that has been approved under the Mental Health Act (MHA 1983)). **_Maximum duration:_** You can be detained for up to 72 hours. **_Medical recommendations:_** At least one doctor. **_Eligibility for appeal to Mental Health Review Tribunal:_** You have the right to appeal against detention to a Tribunal. You also have the right to appeal to the Hospital Managers. **_Discharge:_** After 72 hours unless section 2 applies.
Section 5(2): Urgent detention of voluntary in-patient.	**_Grounds:_** Danger to self or to others. **_Section 5 (2):_** Is used by a doctor or nurse to prevent someone leaving hospital who is a voluntary patient. **_Maximum duration:_** You can be held for up to 72 hours. This is not renewable. You must be assessed as quickly as possible by an Approved Mental Health Professional (AMHP) and doctors for possible admission under the Mental Health Act (MHA 1983). **_Medical recommendations:_** Doctor in charge of patient's care, or nominated deputy. **_Discharge:_** After 72 hours unless section applies.
Section 5(4): Nurses holding power of voluntary in-patient.	**_Grounds:_** Mental disorder (danger to self or others). **_Application by:_** Registered mental nurse or registered nurse for mental handicap. **_Maximum duration:_** You can be detained for up to 72 hours. **_Medical recommendations:_** None **_Discharge:_** Cases on approval of section3.

Section 135:	Grounds: Mental disorder.
	Application by: Magistrates.
	Maximum duration: You can be detained for up to 72 hours.
	Medical recommendations: Allows power of entry to home and removal of patient to 'place of safety'.
Section 136: Admission by police.	Grounds: Mental disorder.
	Application by: Police officer.
	Maximum duration: You can be detained for up to 72 hours.
	Medical recommendations: Allows patient in public place to be removed to 'place of safety'.
	Discharge: Cases after applied on non-application of other section max 72 hours.

GENERAL ADULT PSYCHIATRY

24. DEPOT

INSTRUCTIONS TO CANDIDATE
You are asked to see Mr Thomas Tinker. He is a 20 year old known with Schizophrenia and he has come to talk to you about depot medication.

TASK FOR THE CANDIDATE
- *Discuss the option of depot medication.*

PAY PARTICULAR ATTENTION TO THE FOLLOWING (MENTAL CHECKLIST)
- *Establish history of compliance.*
- *Establish the benefits of being on treatment.*
- *Explain the rationale for depot.*
- *Explain follow up arrangements.*
- *Explain alternative treatment options available.*

COMMUNICATION SKILLS
- *Start the interview by developing rapport and showing empathy.*
- *Establish common ground for collaborative working.*
- *Anticipate some reluctance with depot*

Suggested approach
Introduction
C: Hello, I'm Dr...I'm one of the psychiatrists. Thank you for coming to see me. I understand you have been on medication for your illness and you are thinking of the option of an injection, which might be better for you.

P: I don't like taking medication.

Establish symptom severity
C: Can you take me to the beginning when you started treatment?

P: I was hearing voices and became paranoid about the people around me.

A. Establish compliance
C: Have you been taking your medication regularly?
- *How many different medications have you been on?*
- *For how long have you been on each medication?*
- *Have you had any side effects?*
- *If so, what have you been taking for that?*

Relapse due to non-compliance
- *Have there been times when you have forgotten your medication?*
- *What happened?*

Drug and alcohol
- Sometimes, my patients tell me they cope with drinking or taking street drugs, how about you?

Insight
- What do you think about taking medication?

B. Elaborate on Depot medication.

P: What is this depot medication?

C: The depot is the antipsychotic medication in an injection form. It is usually given every week, every 2weeks, or 4 weeks depending on the type of depot.

This would mean that you wouldn't have to remember taking tablets. It also will help for your symptoms and you stand a better chance of being well.

P: How is it given?

C: It is usually given at your CMHT (Community Mental Health Team) or it can be given at home by you CPN (Community Psychiatric Nurse). The area will be cleaned with an alcohol swab and injection given. You might feel a slight tingling sensation.

P: What is a CPA?

C: Your care package can be discussed at a CPA where it can be discussed about your medication and if you want to change it

P: What are the side effects?

C: The side effects are not common, but it can cause swelling at the site of the injection. Like the tablets, it can also cause some movement and joint problems (extra pyramidal side effects, but to a lesser degree.

P: What are the alternatives?

C: In addition to the depot, we have the other forms of the treatment, like the talking therapies and social aspects of care

Summarise
Mr Tinker, thank you for talking to me. We have discussed about the possibility of you going on a depot. I have some more information and leaflets for you to read. I would also like you to go and think about what we discussed and we can arrange another appointment for you to come and see me. What do you think?

Do you have any other questions?

GENERAL ADULT PSYCHIATRY

Types of Depot
*1. **Risperidone Risperdal Consta**® start at up to maximum 50mg intramuscularly every 2 weeks*
*2. **Zuclopenthixol Decanoate injection Clopixol** ®*
- *Test dose 100mg dose range 100mg-600mg per week or 2 weeks or 3 weeks or 4 weeks*
- *Side effects*
- *Common: akathisia, movement disorders (EPSE's), Raised prolactin, weight gain*
- *Less common: drowsiness*
- *Uncommon: anti cholinergic effects, sexual dysfunction*
- *Swelling and nodules at injection site*
- *Rare hypotension*
- *Very rare*
- *Urine retention and NMS*

*3. **Palperidone***

© Smartsesh

Nature -Treatment/intervention

Depot

Purpose:
- Schizophrenia
- Injection every 2, 3,4weeks

Effects/benefits
- Don't have to remember to take medication
- Fewer side effects
- Ensure person is well, prevents relapse

Adverse/side effects
- **Swelling at injection site**

Precautions

Alternatives
- Biological
- Medication

Psychological interventions
- Psychoeducation
- Talking therapy like CBT for delusions, improve compliance

Social interventions
- Activities
- Vocational

©Smartsesh

DEPOT MEDICATION	SIDE EFFECTS
Flupenthixol Decoanate Depixol® **(Lundbeck)** *Test dose 20 mg IM* *Upper outer buttock/thigh* *After 7 days- 20mg-40mg every 2-4 weeks* *Max 400mg weekly*	*EPSE's* *Sedating*
Fluphenazine Decoanate **Modecate® (Sanofi-Aventis)** *Deep IM gluteal muscle* *Test dose 12.5 mg* *Then 4-7 days 12.5-100mg* *Every 2-4 weeks*	*EPSE's* *Dystonia, akathisia* *SLE, SIADH, OEDEMA*
Haloperidol Haldol Decoanate ® **(Janssen)** *Deep IM gluteal* *Deep gluteal injection 50mg every 4 weeks* *Up to max 300mg every 4 weeks*	*EPSE'S*
Olanzapine Embonate ZypAdheera *150 mg every 4 week* *Initially 210 mg every 2 weeks* *15 mg Oral -300mg every 2 weeks* *20mg oral – 300mg every 2 weeks*	*Injection site reaction*

Palperidone Invega®(Janssen) **Xeplion ®** Deep IM in deltoid 150 mg day 1 100mg day 8 Recommended 75mg every 4 weeks	*EPSE's*

Pipothiazine Palmitate Sanofi **Aventis ®**	*EPSE's*
Risperidone Risperdal Consta® **(Janssen)** Deep IM deltoid or gluteal 4mg oral- 25mg every 2 weeks 37.5mg -50 mg im every 2 weeks	*Hypertension, Depression,* *paraesthesiae, apathy, weight loss* *Injection site reaction*
Zuclopenthixol Decoanate Clopixol® **(Lundbeck**) Deep im buttock/thigh Test dose 100mg Day 7 200 mg -500mg Every 1-4 weeks	*EPSES'*

GENERAL ADULT PSYCHIATRY

25. NMS- NEUROLEPTIC MALIGNANT SYNDROME

INSTRUCTIONS TO CANDIDATE
You have been asked to see the father, James Brook, of 20 yr. old Oliver Brook. His son has been transferred to the medical ward with NMS – Neuroleptic Malignant Syndrome.

TASK FOR THE CANDIDATE
- Explain his diagnosis and management of NMS.

PAY APRTICULAR ATTENTION TO THE FOLLOWING (MENTAL CHECKLIST)
- Explain NMS- Neuroleptic Malignant Syndrome.
- Explain the symptoms and signs.
- Explain how the diagnosis is made.
- Explain further treatment and management.
- Highlight that immediate treatment is to stop antipsychotic.
- Explain that antipsychotic would need to recommence once settled.
- Explain complaints procedure if necessary.
- Explain that a medical alert will be place for future.

COMMUNICATION SKILLS
- Start the interview by developing rapport and showing empathy.
- Show sensitivity.
- Anticipate a concerned father who was obviously shocked that his son suffered a life threatening reaction to the antipsychotic that was prescribed.

Suggested approach
Introduction
C: Hello, I'm Dr ..... I'm one of the psychiatrists. I know you must be concerned about your son. I have come to talk to you more about what happened, his diagnosis and how we have been treating him.

F: Why did you people allow this to happen?

C: I am sorry. I can see that you are understandably upset about   what happened to your son. If you would allow me, I can explain what happened.

F: They told me it was because of the medication you gave him.

C: You are right. There was a difficult situation whereby he was agitated and putting himself at risk as well as possibly endangering others. As a result we tried other behavioural approaches but it did not help and only then, to calm him down, we prescribed this medication. We carefully weighed the risk and benefits of prescribing this medication and also monitored him physically.

GENERAL ADULT PSYCHIATRY

F: *What is the diagnosis?*

C: The condition that your son has suffered is called NMS. It is an *acronym for Neuroleptic Malignant Syndrome. This is a rapidly progressive side effect of neuroleptic or antipsychotic medication which usually cannot be predicted in advance.*

F: *How common is it?*

C: *It is a rare side effect and can occur in 1 in 100 people. It is known to be more common in males than females.*

F: *What are the causes?*

C: *It is due to a side effect to the antipsychotic medication. There are a few factors which does make a person more vulnerable to get this. These include conditions like dehydration, organic brain disease and hyperactivity of the thyroid gland.*
It occurs more commonly with the following medication: Haloperidol, Trifluperazine, and Clozapine.

F: *What are the symptoms and signs?*

C: *There are three main clinical features which are fluctuations in his blood pressure (BP) and pulse, confusion and muscle stiffness (rigidity.)*
The serious complications are seizures and coma.

F: *What is the prognosis?*

C: *It is a life threatening condition and there is 1 in 500 risk of mortality.*

F: *How did you know that he had this reaction?*

C: *We were closely monitoring his physical condition after prescribing him this medication and we also did some blood investigations. Full Blood Count (FBC), urea and electrolytes and creatinine phosphokinase (CPK).]These levels are usually found to be elevated in this condition.*
We can also do an (EEG) electroencephalogram which shows diffuse slowing.

Differential diagnosis
C: *We did consider and excluded other possible causes for his presentation and excluded for example meningitis, septic shock and malignant hyperthermia*

F: *What are the treatment options available?*

C: *Due to this being a medical emergency, we initially stopped his antipsychotic medication and referred him immediately to the medical team for further management.*

GENERAL ADULT PSYCHIATRY

We had been monitoring his vital signs regularly: for example blood pressure, pulse and temperature. He was also given some intravenous fluids.
We also documented in his notes about this adverse reaction for future reference so that he is not prescribed this particular medication in the future.

The medication options we have available are Bromocriptine, Amantadine, and Dantrolene. We would also consider giving him Benzodiazepines as an additional treatment if he did become agitated.

F: What medication will he be treated with in the future?

C: We will continue to monitor him and review his medication in 2 weeks if he was on oral medication and 6 weeks if he was on intramuscular treatment.
We will recommence him on a low dose
antipsychotic, preferable one which has a lesser chance to cause this reaction.

F: Can I make a complaint?

C: I can only apologise for what has happened and as I have
explained it is a rare side effect, however you are entitled to make a complaint, for which there is a procedure to follow. I can ask the nursing staff to explain this to you.

F: Will he get this again?

C: From the evidence that is available, there is a chance of this happening; however the recurrence rate is much less.

Summarise
I know that you are still concerned about your son. To summarise he has suffered a rare side effect of the neuroleptic medication called NMS for which we are treating him. This has been documented and once he is settled we will need to restart him on another antipsychotic medication.

Information and leaflets
I have some information, leaflets and website addresses that you can read. Please feel free to make another appointment to discuss your son's progress.

GENERAL ADULT PSYCHIATRY

26. GENERALISED ANXIETY DISORDER

INSTRUCTIONS TO CANDIDATE
You have been asked to see this 24 year old lady Natalie Taylor who has been referred by her GP with Anxiety symptoms.

TASK FOR THE CANDIDATE
- Elicit a history with a view of coming to a diagnosis.

PAY PARTICULAR ATTENTION TO THE FOLLOWING (MENTAL CHECKLIST)
- Elicit history of presenting complaint.
- Elicit the psychological symptoms and psychological arousal.
- Elicit the physical symptoms.
- Establish avoidance mechanisms.
- Establish aetiological factors using a biopsychosocial approach.
- Establish any underlying co-morbidity-Agoraphobia, phobias, Depression, Obsessive compulsive disorder (OCD).
- Establish coping mechanisms.

COMMUNICATION SKILLS
- Start the interview by developing rapport and showing empathy.
- Seek to understand the subjective feeling of the individual.

Suggested approach
Introduction
C: Hello, I'm Dr....I'm one of the psychiatrists. Your GP has referred you to see me as you had expressed some concerns. Can you tell me more about that?

P: I sometimes feel terrible and I can't seem to shake that feeling.

C: Sounds like you have been having a difficult time. Can you tell me more about this feeling?

A. History of Presenting Complaint (HOPC) (onset, duration, progression, severity)
- Have there been times when you have been anxious or frightened?
- What was it like?

B. Establish psychological symptoms
- Have you had the feeling that something terrible might happen? (Fearful anticipations)
- Do you ever feel like you on edge? (Irritability)
- Are you sensitive to any noises? (Sensitivity to noise)
- Do you tend to find yourself worrying about simple things? (Repetitive worrying thoughts)
- Can you tell me what these things are that go through

your mind at the time?
- How is your concentration? How is your memory?

C. Establish physical symptoms (autonomic arousal)
Screen for symptoms from each of the following systems
1. Respiratory symptoms
   - Do you have any difficulty breathing? (Breathlessness)
2. Elicit symptoms of hyperventilation syndrome.
   (Weakness, faintness, numbness, tinnitus, tingling of the hands, feet and face, dizziness, headache, carpopedal spasms)
3. Cardiovascular symptoms
   - Have you felt your heart racing? (Palpitations)
4. Gastrointestinal symptoms
   - Have you experienced your mouth being dry? (Dry mouth)
5. Genito-urinary symptoms
   - Increased frequency and urgency of micturition)
6. Neurological symptoms (related to CNS)
   - Blurred vision.
7. Musculo-skeletal symptoms
   - Do you experience yourself having jelly legs and your hands? (Trembling)
8. Sleep disturbance
   - How has your sleep been?
   - Can you remember when did you have this for the first time? (Onset)
   - What was going on in your life at the time? (Trigger)

D. Establish aetiology using a biopsychosocial approach
Biological
- Underlying physical illness - hyperthyroidism

Psychological
- Personality type – Neurotic (worrier)

Social
- Psychosocial precipitators-
- Do you have any worries?
- (Relationship, work, family, finances, health)

E. Establish, if any, underlying co-morbid conditions
- Screen for Depressive symptoms
- Screen for Panic disorder, Obsessive Compulsive
- disorder, any Phobic disorder (Agoraphobia, Social
- phobia, Specific phobia)

F. Coping mechanisms
- Some people tell me when they are under stress they

drink or take street drugs. How about you? (Drug and alcohol)

Summarise
Thank you for talking to me. To summarise, you have told me that you been experiencing some Anxiety symptoms which has been affecting you on a daily basis to the extent that you are no longer able to work.

We have some medication and talking therapies which can help

Support groups and websites
Anxiety UK *works to relieve and support those living with Anxiety disorders by providing information, support and understanding via an extensive range of services, including 1:1 therapy.*

GENERAL ADULT PSYCHIATRY

F41.1 Generalized Anxiety disorder

Anxiety that is generalized and persistent but not restricted to, or even strongly predominating in, any particular environmental circumstances (i.e. it is "free-floating"). The dominant symptoms are variable but include complaints of persistent nervousness, trembling, muscular tensions, sweating, light-headedness, palpitations, dizziness, and epigastric discomfort. Fears that the patient or a relative will shortly become ill or have an accident are often expressed.

Incl.:
Anxiety:
- *neurosis*
- *reaction*
- *state*

Excl.:
Neurasthenia (F48.0)

POSSIBLE VARIATIONS OF THEME
1. 45 yr. old lady referred with Anxiety. Elicit a history with a view of a diagnosis
2. 46 yr. old lady with Hyperthyroidism, presenting with Anxiety symptoms.

GENERAL ADULT PSYCHIATRY

27. PANIC ATTACKS

Suggested approach
Introduction
C: Hello, I'm Dr...I'm one of the psychiatrists. I understand your GP has referred you as you have been experiencing some Anxiety symptoms.

P: I told my GP that it feels like I'm having a heart attack.

C: That must be worrying for you. Can you please describe it to me?

A. History of Presenting Complaint (HOPC) (onset, duration, progression and severity)

Description of Panic attack
- Can you describe what happens?
- How often do you get these attacks? (frequency)
- How long does it last for? (duration)
- Is there anything that will make it better or worse? (triggers)

B. Elicit the psychological symptom?
- What was going through your mind at the time?
- What do you fear might happen?
- Do you feel like you are losing control?

C. Elicit physical symptoms
- Did you notice changes in your body when you were anxious?
- Have you had times when you felt shaky, or your heart pounded, or you felt sweaty and you simply had to do something about it?
- Have you felt like you had butterflies, jelly legs or felt trembling?
- Did you ever notice a change in your breathing?

D. Precipitators
- Are you able to remember what was going on when you had these attacks for the first time?
- When was the first time?
- What do you think brought on the attack?
- How often have you been getting these attacks?
- How are you in between these attacks?

E. Explore for presence of avoidance behaviours
Agoraphobia
- What sorts of things do you tend to avoid that causes you to become anxious?
- Can you please tell me what situations you avoid? How often does this occur in a month? Does it help?
- Do you tend to get anxious in certain situations such as travelling away from home, or being alone?
- Have you been able to get out of the house to the supermarkets or shops?
- Have you been able to travel in a bus or train? (travelling)
- How do you feel if you are meeting people in a crowded area?

F. Impact on daily functioning (anticipatory Anxiety)
- How much does this affect your life? (family, occupation, social)
- Is it preventing you from doing things that you normally enjoying doing?

G. Use a biopsychosocial approach to identify possible aetiological factors
Biological
- Is there any family history of panic attacks or heart attacks?
- Enquire about - current medication, caffeine,
- Enquire about physical illnesses- IBS, thyroid, MVP (mitral valve prolapse)

Psychological
- Personality type - anxious

Social
- Have you had any worries recently?

H. Differential diagnosis
Exclude Depression, OCD, Psychosis

I. Drug and alcohol history
- *How have you been coping?*
- *Some people may drink or take street drugs, how about you?*

Summarise
Thank you for talking to me. To summarise what you have described is typically of what we call panic attacks. They usually occur out of the blue and it feels sometimes like you are losing control. It's reassuring however that you are not having a heart attack. We have a range of treatment options available which are medication, psychological or talking therapies and social aspects of care.

Information and leaflets
I have some information and leaflets which you can take home to read.
Support groups and websites

No Panic
It is an organisation for people with Anxiety problems which provide support to sufferers, their family and carers. Phone helpline and counselling, pop-in centres, CBT self-help books, videos and tapes.

POSSIBLE VARIATIONS OF THEME
A young female referred by A+E doctor as she thought she was having a heart attack. She has a family history of uncle and dad dying of heart attack.

NICE guidelines for panic disorder
- ➢ *CBT psychotherapy-7-14 hours of cognitive behaviour therapy-usually weekly sessions of 1-2 hours, completed in 4 months is recommended.*
- ➢ *Self-help by bibliotherapy and self-help groups and support groups are useful in primary care.*
- ➢ *SSRIs are useful first line drug treatments.*
- ➢ *If no improvement is seen after a 12 week course of SSRIs, imipramine or clomipramine should be considered.*
- ➢ *Benzodiazepines are associated with a worse outcome in the long term and should not be prescribed.*

F41.0 Panic disorder [episodic paroxysmal Anxiety]
The essential feature is recurrent attacks of severe Anxiety (panic), which are not restricted to any particular situation or set of circumstances and are therefore unpredictable. As with other Anxiety disorders, the dominant symptoms include sudden onset of palpitations, chest pain, choking sensations, dizziness, and feelings of unreality (depersonalisation or derealisation). There is often also a secondary fear of dying, losing control, or going mad. Panic disorder should not be given as the main diagnosis if the patient has a depressive disorder at the time the attacks start; in these circumstances the panic attacks are probably secondary to Depression.

Incl.:Panic:
- attack
- state

Excl.:
panic disorder with agoraphobia (F40.0)

F40.0 Agoraphobia
A fairly well-defined cluster of phobias embracing fears of leaving home, entering shops, crowds and public or open spaces, or travelling alone in trains, buses or planes, often with an inability to escape to a safe place. Panic disorder is a frequent feature of both present and past episodes. Depressive and obsessional symptoms and social phobias can also commonly present as subsidiary features. Avoidance of the phobic situation is often prominent, and some agoraphobics experience little Anxiety because they are able to avoid their phobic situations.

Incl.:
Agoraphobia without history of panic disorder
Panic disorder with agoraphobia

GENERAL ADULT PSYCHIATRY

28. PANIC ATTACKS

INSTRUCTIONS TO CANDIDATE
You are about to see the husband Gerald Ross of the lady you had seen previously. The cardiologist has excluded a heart attack. Discuss your diagnosis and management with her partner.

TASK FOR THE CANDIDATE
- Discuss diagnosis and management of panic attacks.

PAY PARTICULAR ATTENTION TO THE FOLLOWING (MENTAL CHECKLIST)
- Reassurance that cardiac investigations are normal.
- Explain diagnosis of panic attack.
- Explain mechanism of panic attack.
- Explain the management using a biopsychosocial approach.

COMMUNICATION SKILLS
- Start the interview by developing rapport and showing empathy.
- Show sensitivity when discussing diagnosis.

Suggested approach
Introduction
C: Hello, I'm Dr....I'm one of the psychiatrists. I have seen your wife and wanted to talk to you more about my assessment and the treatment options available.

P: Hello doctor. We were worried that she was having a heart attack.

C: I can see you are quite concerned. I can reassure you that the cardiologists have seen her and excluded a heart attack. They have completed a tracing of the heart i.e. ECG, some blood tests and these have all come back normal. She is having what we call a panic attack. I will try to explain.

P: What is a panic attack?

C: A panic attack occurs when our body is exposed to a frightening situation and this sets off the fight and flight reaction. This simply means that our body will either stay to fight the situation or would prepare to flee the situation.

As a result we start to breathe faster and this causes the hyperventilation syndrome. As a consequence, there is an increase in oxygen and decrease in carbon dioxide. As a result of the low carbon dioxide this causes a physiological response in our body and causes a tingling sensation in our fingers, faintness, numbness, dizziness and breathlessness. And this perpetuates like a vicious cycle.

We sometimes can mistake this for a heart attack because of the hyperventilation which can increase the tension in our chest muscles and also result in them to becoming sore.

P: How common is it?

C: It occurs in 1 in 100 people and is twice more common in females. It usually has an onset age of between 20-44 years.

P: What are the causes?

C: It is difficult to pinpoint one particular cause in your partner's situation. It can be due to a few associated factors. It is also possible that it happened once that your partner was exposed to a threatening situation that this triggered this reaction. Now even something small in the environment can trigger this and the body is just waiting for the next time, and it's thus like a vicious cycle.

P: What are the treatment options available?

C: There are treatment options available, like medication, psychological or talking therapy and because we know it affects a person's life, we have the social aspect of care.

Biological or medication
The medication options we have are a group of antidepressant medication called SSRI's (selective serotonin reuptake inhibitors)

Would you like to hear more about this? [Elaborate further if necessary]

According to the guidelines we follow (NICE guidelines)
- First line- Fluvoxamine, Paroxetine, Sertraline, Fluoxetine
- Second line- Clomipramine or Imipramine

Like all medication they have do have side effects. Most side effects usually go away.

Common side effects include nausea and sickness, loss of appetite, insomnia, diarrhoea and sexual dysfunction.

More uncommon side effects are dizziness, drowsiness and headache.

Psychological
The psychological or talking therapies that have been shown to be beneficial is CBT or cognitive behavioural therapy.
There are 2 components to this; the behavioural and cognitive parts:-

Explain Cognitive Behavioural Therapy (CBT): The behavioural part:

As we have discussed the hyperventilation can actually trigger a panic attack and make it worse. Therefore by controlling ones breathing, this can help to reduce these unpleasant symptoms. It can help to reduce the number of attacks, shorten the attacks and also cease the attack.

The therapist would teach her some controlled breathing and muscle relaxation exercise. This can be done in an individual or group setting like and Anxiety management training group. We have some useful videos and CD's as well.

Explain CBT: The cognitive part

This is a type of talking therapy which looks at the links between the way how what we think affects the way we feel, causes the behaviours and the physical symptoms

The therapist will help identify these thinking patterns in order to change them to more helpful way.

P: What can I do?

C: Your support and understanding of her condition is vitally important in assisting in her recovery. We also suggest these useful and practical tips.

Something which I do tell people also which is beneficial is simple measures which can be done at anytime and anywhere when she is having a panic attack.
- It is beneficial to breathe into a paper bag.
- Also cupping of the hands over the mouth (and demonstrate) and breathing slowly has shown to be effective.

The **social aspect** would include if necessary more support to you and her.

Information and leaflets

I know I have given you a lot of information; I have some leaflets for you to read. I am happy to see you and your wife again to discuss this further. Do you have any other questions?

Support groups and websites
No Panic

It is an organisation for people with Anxiety problems which provide support to sufferers, their family and carers. Phone helpline and counselling, pop-in centres, CBT self-help books, videos and tapes.

Thank you

GENERAL ADULT PSYCHIATRY

29. CONVERSION DISORDER-BLINDNESS

INSTRUCTIONS TO CANDIDATE
A young girl, Geraldine Fobbs, has presented with sudden loss of vision in left eye.

TASK FOR THE CANDIDATE
Elicit a history of sudden vision loss with a view of a diagnosis.
Perform a Fundoscopy (Alcohol gel and ophthalmoscope are provided).

PAY PARTICULAR ATTENTION TO THE FOLLOWING (MENTAL CHECKLIST)
- Establish history of presenting complaint.
- Establish the nature of the visual disturbance.
- Exclude any other physical symptoms.
- Illustrate La belle indifference.
- Illustrate secondary gain.
- Identify the psycho social stressor.
- Perform a Fundoscopy. –see examination section

COMMUNICATION SKILLS
- Start the interview by developing rapport and showing empathy.
- Seek to understand the subjective experience of the individual.

Suggested approach
Introduction
C: Hello, I'm Dr ....I am one of the psychiatrists. I understand that you have had sudden loss of vision. Can you tell me more about that?

A. History of Presenting Complaint
(HOPC) -onset, duration, progression and severity
- When did this happen? Can you describe this to me?
- In which eye did you become blind?
- Can you tell me what were you doing at the time? What are you able to see or not able to see?
- Establish any other physical associated symptoms e.g. double vision, photophobia, and floaters? Pain?
- Have you experienced anything similar in the past?

B. Precipitators
- What do you think could have caused this?
- Have you been under any stress recently?
- (Enquire about stressors at home, work, and relationships)

C. La belle in difference
- How have you been feeling about your visual loss?

D. Secondary gain
- How have things been at home, school/college/work/friends?

E. Assess for underlying mental illness (Depression)
- *How have you been feeling in yourself? (Mood)*
- *Have you felt like life was not worth living?*

F. Family history
- *Has anyone is your family had similar problems?*

G. Past psychiatric history
- *Have you seen a psychiatrist in the past?*

H. Medical history
- *Have you had physical health problems?*
- *Are you on any medication?*
- *Do you take any street drugs (drug and alcohol history)?*
- *Do you drink alcohol?*

I. Perform Fundoscopy examination-see physical examination section

Summarise
Thank you for talking to me. It appears that you have been under stress recently. This has affected you in that you have suddenly loss your vision in your one eye. I have examined you and thankfully there isn't any abnormality at present. I would like to see you again. I understand that your mother would like to speak to me. Is that all right with you?

30. CONVERSION DISORDER-MANAGEMENT

INSTRUCTIONS TO CANDIDATE
You have been asked to see Cassandra Fobbs, mother of Geraldine Fobbs.
She is concerned about her daughter's sudden loss of vision.

TASK FOR THE CANDIDATE
- *Address her concerns.*
- *Discuss diagnosis and management.*

PAY PARTICULAR ATTENTION TO THE FOLLOWING (MENTAL CHECKLIST)
- *Summarise findings from previous station, including psychiatric assessment and fundoscopy*
- *Emphasise that the physical examinations and investigations are normal.*
- *Explain diagnosis of conversion disorder using body and mind analogy.*
- *Explain possible aetiological factors.*
- *Explain management in terms of biopsychosocial approach.*
- *Emphasise that family need not reinforce her beliefs.*
- *Emphasise prognosis*

COMMUNICATION SKILLS
- *Start the interview by developing rapport and showing empathy.*

Suggested approach
Introduction
C: Hello, I'm Dr....I am a psychiatrist. I understand you are concerned about your daughter, can you tell me more about this?

My findings were: (summary)
It appears that your daughter has had a sudden loss of vision. She has been under stress due to recent circumstances.

I have examined her eyes, and she has been seen by the other doctors that have ruled out any physical problems for example a stroke. The blood investigations and CT scan that were done have all come back normal.
I have also examined her eyes, and have found no abnormality.

M: What is her diagnosis?

C: We call this **Conversion disorder.** Our body and mind is connected, and if one is affected, so is the other. For example if you have a bad day and feel a bit stressed, you may have a headache. So in a sense what it means is that the stress is converted into a physical form. It appears that she has dealt with the current stress by converting it into a physical symptom.

So for her, what she is experiencing in her mind is real, and it's difficult for other people to understand. I can say that this condition is temporary. About 30-60% of people do make full recovery.

M: What are the causes?

C: It's difficult to say what has caused this, but from my experience, it is usually triggered by stress and a number of associated factors working together.

M: How can we treat her?

C: The management is usually a combination of treatments medication, psychological and social.

Biological-investigations and medication
All the Investigations we have done thus far have been normal. We will only carry out further investigations if indicated. At present they are not indicated, but I can speak to my colleagues about this if you wish. Antidepressant medications are indicated if she develops either depressive or PTSD symptoms.

Psychological
There are talking therapies like CBT or cognitive behavioural therapy which has been shown to be beneficial.
In CBT, she will learn how to deal with the traumatic experience and guilt feelings. It will also enable her to cope with her emotions in a mature way. Other forms of treatment are hypnosis and bereavement counselling.

Social
We know that she will require your support and understanding of what she is going through.
There is also the option of carers support if you require this.

M: What else can I do?

C: The important thing is not for you and others not to reinforce the belief of not being able to see.

M: What is the prognosis?

C: From the research that is available, at least 7 out of 10 people do recover.

Information and leaflets
Thank you for talking to me. Do you have any other questions?
I have some more information and leaflets which you can read. I am happy to see you again to discuss your daughter's progress.

CONVERSION DISORDER-MANAGEMENT

Biological Interventions
- *Investigations only if indicated.*
- *Antidepressants are indicated for either depressive or PTSD symptoms.*

Psychological Interventions
- *Psychotherapy/Talking therapy*
- *CBT- cognitive behavioural therapy*
- *Hypnosis*
- *Bereavement counselling*

Social Interventions
- *Support*
- *Carers support*

©Smartsesh

F44 Dissociative [conversion] disorders

The common themes that are shared by dissociative or conversion disorders are a partial or complete loss of the normal integration between memories of the past, awareness of identity and immediate sensations, and control of bodily movements. All types of dissociative disorders tend to remit after a few weeks or months, particularly if their onset is associated with a traumatic life event. More chronic disorders, particularly paralyses and anaesthesias, may develop if the onset is associated with insoluble problems or interpersonal difficulties. These disorders have previously been classified as various types of "conversion hysteria". They are presumed to be psychogenic in origin, being associated closely in time with traumatic events, insoluble and intolerable problems, or disturbed relationships. The symptoms often represent the patient's concept of how a physical illness would be manifest. Medical examination and investigation do not reveal the presence of any known physical or neurological disorder. In addition, there is evidence that the loss of function is an expression of emotional conflicts or needs. The symptoms may develop in close relationship to psychological stress, and often appear suddenly. Only disorders of physical functions normally under voluntary control and loss of sensations are included here. Disorders involving pain and other complex physical sensations mediated by the autonomic nervous system are classified under somatisation disorder (F45.0). The possibility of the later appearance of serious physical or psychiatric disorders should always be kept in mind.

Incl.:
conversion:
- *hysteria*
- *reaction*

hysteria
hysterical Psychosis
Excl.:
malingering [conscious simulation] (Z76.5

GENERAL ADULT PSYCHIATRY

31. SOCIAL PHOBIA

INSTRUCTIONS TO CANDIDATE
You have been asked to see Miss Sarah Ritter, a 25 yr old lady. She has difficulty going out.

TASK FOR THE CANDIDATE
- Take a history with a view of a diagnosis.
- Explore aetiological factors.

PAY PARTICULAR ATTENTION TO THE FOLLOWING (MENTAL CHECKLIST)
- Establish History of presenting complaint (HOPC) onset, duration, severity, progression)
- Identify precipitating factors
- Establish aetiological factors using a biopsychosocial approach
- Elicit diagnostic criteria for social phobia
- Enquire about associated symptoms
- Exclude co-morbid conditions
- Elicit family history
- Elicit coping skills

COMMUNICATION SKILLS
- Develop rapport and show empathy.
- Seek to understand the subjective feeling of the individual.

Suggested Approach
Introduction
C: Hello, I'm Dr ....I'm one of the psychiatrists. Thank you for coming to see me. I understand your GP has referred you as you have been experiencing difficulty in going out? Can you tell me a bit more about this?

P: I know it sounds silly, but I don't like going out.

A. History of Presenting Complaint (HOPC) (onset, duration, progression, severity)
C: Can you tell me more about this? What situations do you have difficulty in going out to?
- What would you be worried about at that time?
- Can you tell me what would be going on in your mind at that particular time?
- Are you able to control these thoughts?
- Are there any other situations you are feeling anxious about?
- [What about public speaking, eating and drinking, being sick, social situations]

B. Enquire about associated symptoms
- Shaking, blushing, wanting to use the toilet.

- *Anxiety in other situations like in writing in public, using public toilets or social situations such as parties.*
- *Can you pinpoint when this all started? (Onset)*
- *How has this impacted on your life, work, family, social, relationships?*

C. Exclude underlying co-morbid conditions
- *Depression, Obsessive compulsive disorder (OCD)*

D. Aetiological factors
Traumatic experience
- *Is there anything in your childhood that sticks out? (Any traumatic incident)*
- *Is there anyone in the family that has anything similar?*
- *Have you ever seen a psychiatrist in the past?*

E. Premorbid personality
- *How would you describe yourself before all of this?*

G. Medical History
- *How is your physical health?*

H. Medication
- *Are you on any regular medication?*

I. Drug and alcohol history
- *How do you usually cope?*
- *Do you drink or take street drugs?*

Summary
Thank you for talking to me. To summarise, what you have told me is that you have an intense fear of going out, especially to social gatherings. There are other situations you have a fear of being in for example giving presentations at work.
We have psychological treatments or talking therapy and medication to help you. What do you think?

Information and leaflets
I have some information and leaflets for you to read. I would like to meet with you again and discuss this further.

Support groups and websites
Shyness & Social Anxiety Treatment Australia: *Information about social Anxiety, the treatment options, group therapy and workshops, support groups, articles, resources and links to other sites.*
Triumph Over Phobia *Runs a national network of self-help groups to help people with phobia or obsessive compulsive disorder (OCD) to overcome their*

problems using graded self-exposure. This means learning how to face up to your fears in a very gradual and structured way so that eventually the Anxiety should decrease.
Thank you

Possible variation of theme
1.36 yr old lady who had a fear of going in public as she might be sick.
2.45 yr. old man who declines social events as he feel he will be ridiculed.

F40 *Phobic Anxiety disorders*

A group of disorders in which Anxiety is evoked only, or predominantly, in certain well-defined situations that are not currently dangerous. As a result these situations are characteristically avoided or endured with dread. The patient's concern may be focused on individual symptoms like palpitations or feeling faint and is often associated with secondary fears of dying, losing control, or going mad. Contemplating entry to the phobic situation usually generates anticipatory Anxiety. Phobic Anxiety and Depression often coexist. Whether two diagnoses, phobic Anxiety and depressive episode, are needed, or only one, is determined by predominance of the symptoms and the temporal relationship between the two conditions

---

F40.1 Social phobias

Fear of scrutiny by other people leading to avoidance of social situations. More pervasive social phobias are usually associated with low self-esteem and fear of criticism. They may present as a complaint of blushing, hand tremor, nausea, or urgency of micturition, the patient sometimes being convinced that one of these secondary manifestations of their Anxiety is the primary problem. Symptoms may progress to panic attacks. Often present in adolescence and are equally common in men and women.
Incl.:
Anthropophobia
Social neurosis

GENERAL ADULT PSYCHIATRY

32. OBSESSIVE COMPULSIVE DISORDERS (OCD)

INSTRUCTIONS TO CANDIDATE
You have been asked to a 25 yr. old man Neville Simpson who has been repeatedly washing his hands. He has been referred to you by his GP.

TASK FOR THE CANDIDATE
- *Elicit history of Obsessive Compulsive Disorder (OCD)*

PAY PARTICULAR ATTENTION TO THE FOLLOWING (MENTAL CHECKLIST)
- *Establish the obsession and rituals.*
- *Establish the severity and impact on his daily functioning.*
- *Establish aetiological factors using a biopsychosocial approach.*
- *Establish the presence of underlying co-morbid conditions.*
- *Establish coping mechanisms*

COMMUNICATION SKILLS
- *Start the interview by developing rapport and showing empathy.*
- *Seek to understand the subjective experience of the individual.*

Suggested approach
Introduction
C: Hello, I am Dr.... I am one of the psychiatrists. I have been asked to see you by your GP. I understand that you have been experiencing some difficulties. Can you please tell me more about this?

P: I wash them to get rid of the germs. I know I am contaminating everything I come in contact with. The only way I can get rid of them, is to wash them.

A History of presenting complaint (HOPC) (onset, duration, progression and severity)
1. Establish the obsessional symptoms
C: Let me ask you more about these thoughts (Please note there can be images, impulses, ideas or ruminations)
- *Can you describe these thoughts you have been having?*
- *Do they keep coming back to you even when you try not to have them? (Intrusive)*
- *Where do they come from? Do these thoughts come from your own mind?*
- *What do you do when you have these thoughts?*
- *Is there anything you do to stop these thoughts?*
- *Do you try to resist these thoughts? (Resistance)*
- *How often do you get these thoughts?*
- *How do they make you feel? (Establish the egodystonic nature)*

2. Establish the compulsive symptoms

- *What happens if you ignore or try to get rid of these thoughts?*
- *Do you try to neutralise these thoughts in any way?*
- *Do you wash your hands repeatedly because you think they are dirty? (Compulsion)*
- *What about spending time on personal cleaning like washing over and over even though you know that they are clean?*
- *Does washing make you feel less anxious? (relief)*
- *How do you decide when to stop washing?*
- *Do you check things to make sure there is no dirt? (checking behaviour)*
- *Do you find you have to keep checking things that you know you have already done? (Like gas tops, doors, switches, etc.)*
- *Are there things you do to prevent coming into contact with dirt and germs?*
- *Do you think these obsessions/compulsions are excessive or unreasonable in any way? (Recognises as unreasonable or senseless)*
- *Do you have any other rituals?*
- *What would happen if you didn't wash?*
- *Can you tell me when this first started? (Onset)*
- *How much time do you spend washing?*

B. These are other OCD symptom dimensions to consider and tailor according to the scenario
Contamination
Aggressive
- *Do you think that you might harm yourself or others in any other way?*
- *What do you do to prevent this happening?*

Sexual/Religious
- *Do you have forbidden or seemingly perverse sexual thoughts/images/impulses?*
- *Are you overly concerned with what is morally right and wrong or blasphemy?*
- *Do you repeatedly check anything because of this?*
- *What about the need to tell or confess?*

Symmetry/ordering/counting/arranging
- *Are there things you have to do in a very precise or exact way?*
- *Do you count or order things to get them in just the right way or symmetrically?*

Hoarding/collecting
- *Do you save/collect things that are of little sentimental or monetary value?*
- *Do you have trouble throwing things away?*

GENERAL ADULT PSYCHIATRY

Somatic
- Are there aspects of your body or health that you are concerned about?
- Do you mirror check or ask for reassurance repeatedly?

Miscellaneous
- Are you a superstitious person?
- Do you have any lucky/unlucky numbers or colours that have special significance?

C. Differential diagnosis to consider
Rule out Depression, Anxiety, Panic attacks, Phobia, Eating disorders, head injury and seizure disorder.

D. Establish impact on functioning
- How has this affected you in your daily life?
- Are there certain things you avoid doing because of this?

E. Establish coping mechanisms
- How have you been coping?
- Do you drink alcohol or take street drugs?

Summarise
To summarise what you have told me is that you have been experiencing these unpleasant thoughts that your hands are contaminated with germs. As a result you repeatedly wash your hands. This has been affecting you and you have not been able to work or go out socially.

We have some medication and psychological treatments that are helpful. What help would you like?

I have some information and leaflets for you.
Support and websites
OCD Action
A leading national charity for people with OCD, body dysmorphic disorder, compulsive skin picking and trichotillomania.

OCD UK
OCD-UK is a leading national charity, independently working with and for people with Obsessive-Compulsive Disorder (OCD).

OCD spectrum disorders to consider

- *Are you concerned about your physical health? (Hypochondriasis)*
- *Do you have any repetitive, seemingly driven behaviour such as nail biting (Tourette's syndrome)*
- *Stereotypic movements (skin picking, nail biting, scratching, body rocking)*
- *Have you had sudden movements or made sounds that you were unable to control?*
- *What about things like eye blinking, grunting, sniffing or snorting.*
- *How often do these movements or sounds occur?*
- *Have you ever pulled your hair, leaving bald patches or leaving you with thin hair?*

(Trichotillomania)

©Smartsesh

F42 Obsessive-compulsive disorder

The essential feature is recurrent obsessional thoughts or compulsive acts. Obsessional thoughts are ideas, images, or impulses that enter the patient's mind again and again in a stereotyped form. They are almost invariably distressing and the patient often tries, unsuccessfully, to resist them. They are, however, recognized as his or her own thoughts, even though they are involuntary and often repugnant. Compulsive acts or rituals are stereotyped behaviours that are repeated again and again. They are not inherently enjoyable, nor do they result in the completion of inherently useful tasks. Their function is to prevent some objectively unlikely event, often involving harm to or caused by the patient, which he or she fears might otherwise occur. Usually, this behaviour is recognized by the patient as pointless or ineffectual and repeated attempts are made to resist. Anxiety is almost invariably present. If compulsive acts are resisted the Anxiety gets worse.

Incl.:
Anankastic Neurosis
Obsessive-Compulsive Neurosis

Excl.:
Obsessive-Compulsive Personality (Disorder) (F60.5

NICE guidelines for adults with OCD and BDD

(Adapted from NICE guidance)

- ➢ *In the initial treatment of adults with OCD, low intensity psychological treatments (including exposure and response prevention (ERP)) (up to 10 therapist hours per patient) should be offered if the patient's degree of functional impairment is mild and/or the patient expresses a preference for a low intensity approach. Low intensity treatments include, ERP face to face or over the phone.*
- ➢ *Adults with OCD with mild functional impairment who are unable to engage in low intensity CBT (including ERP), or for whom low intensity treatment has proved to be inadequate, should be offered the choice of either a course of selective serotonin re-uptake inhibitor (SSRI) or more intensive CBT (including ERP) (more than 10 therapist hours per patient), because these treatments appear to be comparably efficacious.*
- ➢ *Adults with OCD and moderate functional impairment should be offered the choice of either a course of a SSRI or more intensive CBT (including ERP) (more than therapist hours per patient), because these treatments appear comparably efficacious).*
- ➢ *Adults with moderate functional impairment should be offered the choice of either a course of an SSRI or more intensive CBT (including ERP) that addresses key features.*

33. OBSESSIVE COMPULSIVE DISORDER (OCD)

INSTRUCTIONS TO CANDIDATE
You have been asked to see this 36 yr. old man Andrew Fowler who suffers from OCD and has not responded to oral SSRI medication. He has been taking it for the past few months and his symptoms are not any better. He has made an appointment with you to discuss the management of his OCD.

TASK FOR THE CANDIDATE
- *Explain the management of Obsessive compulsive disorder (OCD)*

PAY PARTICULAR ATTENTION TO THE FOLLOWING (MENTAL CHECKLIST)
- *Establish his model of Obsessive Compulsive Disorder (OCD)*
- *Explain about the diagnosis of Obsessive Compulsive Disorder (OCD), aetiology and prognosis.*
- *Explain management in terms of biopsychosocial approach.*

COMMUNICATION SKILLS
- *Start the interview by developing rapport and showing empathy.*

Suggested approach
Introduction
C: Hello, I am Dr.... I am one of the psychiatrists. I understand that your GP has referred you because you are experiencing some problems with the medication he has prescribed which has not helped you. To begin with, can you tell me what your understanding is of Obsessive Compulsive Disorder (OCD)?

P: He said that I have Obsessive compulsive disorder (OCD), because I have been getting these unpleasant thoughts of washing my hands excessively.

C: What you have described is OCD. OCD is an acronym for Obsessive Compulsive Disorder. An obsession is when you get thoughts that repeatedly come into your mind, even if you try to keep them out. This causes you to feel anxious, which results in the compulsion, which is when you have to touch, count or repeat the same action like washing over and over again.

P: How common is Obsessive Compulsive Disorder (OCD)?

C: OCD occurs in 2 in every 100 people and is equally common in both men and women. It affects 2-3% of people in their lifetime and usually begins in teenage years or 20's.

P: What causes OCD?

GENERAL ADULT PSYCHIATRY

C: No-one knows for sure what causes Obsessive Compulsive Disorder (OCD). It is known to be hereditary or genetic, and it can run in the families. Usually about 25% of people with OCD also have a close relative with the disorder. From the research available it has been proposed that OCD is due to brain changes, due to the chemical imbalance called serotonin (5HT), which is also found to be low in depressed people.

Other associated causes are due to stress, life changes and personality type. If you are the type of person who is neat, methodical and meticulous, you are more likely to develop OCD.

P: What other treatments are available?

C: OCD can be treated using both medication and psychological or talking treatment.

P: Can you tell me about the medication?

C: The medication that is available is from the group of antidepressants called Selective Serotonin Reuptake Inhibitors (SSRI's). It works on the same chemical imbalance of Serotonin which is also found in Depression. However, having said that, we usually have to use a higher dose in treating OCD and for a longer time.

The names of the antidepressants which are the recommended by the guidelines we follow (NICE- (National institute of clinical excellence), is Citalopram, Sertraline and Clomipramine.

Like all medication they do have side effects. It is not to say that everyone who takes it will get these side effects.

Side effects to mention: stomach upsets like nausea and sickness, headaches and dizziness. It can also affect your sexual function. These side effects are usually related to the dose and are self- limiting.

P: Can you tell me about the psychological treatment?

C: The psychological or talking treatment is called CBT or Cognitive Behavioural Therapy. There are 2 components of this.

The Exposure and Response Prevention (ERP) is the behavioural component of CBT which is beneficial in treating the compulsive behaviours like in your case, washing your hands.

P: What is Exposure and response prevention?

C: The therapist will expose you to the situation you are fearful of being in and at the same time, will prevent you from performing the ritual.

GENERAL ADULT PSYCHIATRY

For example if you wanted to wash your hands, the therapist will expose you to that situation, but will prevent you from washing your hands.

You will make a list with the therapist, from least Anxiety provoking to most Anxiety provoking. The rationale behind this is that if we are exposed to a situation that causes us Anxiety, the Anxiety increases, but if we stay in it long enough it will decrease.

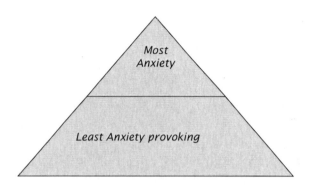

The therapist will also teach you slow breathing exercises and relaxation.

The other component is the Cognitive therapy.
This is effective for the obsessional thoughts. Together with the therapist you will change your reaction to the thoughts instead of trying to get rid of them.

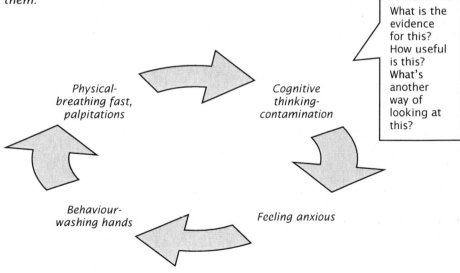

GENERAL ADULT PSYCHIATRY

Summarise

Thank you for talking to me. I have explained to you more about the medication and psychological treatments available for Obsessive compulsive disorder. Here are some leaflets and useful websites addresses.

Support groups and websites

<u>OCD Action</u>

It is a leading national charity for people with OCD, body dysmorphic disorder, compulsive skin picking and trichotillomania.

<u>OCD UK</u>

OCD-UK is a leading national charity, independently working with and for people with Obsessive-Compulsive Disorder (OCD).

GENERAL ADULT PSYCHIATRY

34. BODY DYSMORPHIC DISORDER

INSTRUCTIONS TO CANDIDATE
You have been asked to see a 24 yr. old college student Anthony Costa who was complaining that his eyes were far apart.

TASK FOR THE CANDIDATE
- Elicit a history to come to a diagnosis.

PAY APRTICULAR ATTENTION TO THE FOLLOWING (MENTAL CHECKLIST)
- Establishes the onset, duration, nature and progression of the main complaint.
- Establishes coping mechanisms.
- Establish possible aetiological factors.
- Establish the impact of the pain using a biopsychosocial approach.
- Establishes any underlying co-morbid conditions.

COMMUNICATION SKILLS
- Start the interview by developing rapport and showing empathy.
- Seek to understand the subjective feeling of the individual.

Suggested approach
Introduction
C: Hello, I'm Dr....I am one of the psychiatrists. Your GP has referred you to see me as you had expressed some concerns. Can you tell me more about that?
What are your concerns?

P: My eyes are far apart. Can't you see that, it's so obvious?

C: I understand what you are saying, but I'm more interested to know why you have started to think this.

A. History of presenting complaint (HOPC) (onset, duration, progression, severity)
- Can you tell when did this all start?
- What did you notice first? How do you feel now about it?
- Apart from you, has anyone else commented on this?
- Can you describe what you see when you look into the mirror? How much time do you spend looking in the mirror?
- Do you find yourself comparing differing parts of your body?

B. Coping mechanisms
- Have you tried camouflaging? What do you do? (For example with use of hats, scarf's, and make-up)
- Do you pick your skin?

C. Establish if it is an overvalued idea or delusion
- Who have you seen regarding this? What have they said?
- Have you see an eye specialist?
- What have other people said about this?
- Are you concerned about any other part of your body?
(I.e. Nose, breasts, chest)

D. Impact on daily functioning
- How has it affected your life...your family, social, work, relationships?
- Do you avoid certain situations because of this?

E. Establish possible aetiological factors
Childhood
- Is there anything from your childhood that sticks out?
- Do you have any memorable or unpleasant experiences?

F. Exclude any underlying psychiatric co-morbidity
OCD symptoms, Depression, Anxiety symptoms
- How have you been feeling in yourself?
- How has your mood been?

G. Drug and alcohol history
- How have you been coping?
- Some people might take alcohol and drugs, how about you?

H. Past psychiatric history and family history
- Does anyone in the family have anything similar?

I. Risk assessment
- Do you have any thoughts of wanting to end it all? (Suicidal thoughts)
- Do you have any thoughts of doing something yourself? (For example correcting it themselves)

Summarise
Thank you for talking to me. To summarise you have told me that you believe your eyes are far apart. You have mentioned that this could have possibly been triggered by some unpleasant experience in
your childhood. You have seen an eye specialist who has reassured you that there is nothing wrong.

GENERAL ADULT PSYCHIATRY

We have some treatment options available like medication and psychological treatment which I would like to discuss with you.

BODY DYSMORPHIC DISORDER
A. HOPC (onset, duration, progression, severity)
Coping mechanisms
- *Camouflaging, skin picking*

Establish if an overvalued idea or delusion
Impact on daily functioning
Effect on life...your family, social, work, relationships
Avoidance behaviour
Establish possible aetiological factors
- *Childhood-traumatic experiences*

Exclude any underlying psychiatric co-morbidity
OCD Symptoms, Depression, Anxiety Symptoms
Drug and alcohol history
Past psychiatric history and family history
Risk assessment

POSSIBLE VARIATIONS OF THEME
1. Lady who is concerned that her breasts are too small and is seeking reconstructive surgery.
2. Male who is concerned that his nose is too big, and is seeking reconstructive surgery. He has already attempted to correct this himself.

GENERAL ADULT PSYCHIATRY

35. PTSD - POST TRAUMATIC STRESS DISORDER

INSTRUCTIONS TO CANDIDATE
You have been asked to see this 46 yr. old man Adrian Cook who has recently been in involved in a road traffic accident. He has gone to see his GP as he has been unable to drive and has been distressed by the accident.

TASK FOR THE CANDIDATE
- Elicit history to establish diagnosis.

PAY PARTICULAR ATTENTION TO THE FOLLOWING (MENTAL CHECKLIST)
- Establish life threatening/catastrophic nature of event.
- Elicit core features of PTSD (Post Traumatic Stress Disorder) i.e. intrusive, hyper arousal, avoidance.
- Assess impact on functioning using biopsychosocial model.
- Exclude on-going co-morbid illness e.g. Depression.

COMMUNICATION SKILLS
- Start the interview by developing rapport and showing empathy.
- Assess for maladaptive coping strategies and on-going legal or compensation issues.
- Seek to understand the personal meaning of experience.

Suggested approach
Introduction
I understand you have been going through a difficult time. Would you like to tell me how this all began?

A. History of Presenting Complaint (HOPC) (onset, duration, progression and severity)
Establish the life threatening event

- Can you describe what happened please?
- Can you tell me more about the accident please?
- How long ago did this happen?
- Who was involved?
- Who was driving?
- Where did this happen?
- Have you recently visited the scene of the accident, since the accident?

B. Elicit core symptoms of PTSD (Post Traumatic Stress Disorder)
Re-experience
- Do you get any flashbacks? Are they in the form of unwanted/intrusive images or recurrent thoughts? (Flashbacks)
- Do you have any nightmares?

- *Do you feel like you are reliving the accident?*

Avoidance
- *Do you avoid certain places which remind you of the accident?*
- *Have you been to where the accident occurred?*
- *Tell me how do you travel since the RTA? (Road Traffic Accident)*

Hyper arousal/Startle
- *Do you feel on edge most of the time? (hyper vigilance)*
- *How is your concentration? Have you become more sensitive to noises? (startle response)*
- *How is your sleep? (Sleep)*
- *How is your memory?*
- *Do you get annoyed easily?*

Emotional dysregulation
- *How do you feel in yourself? (Assessing mood)*
- *Are you able to enjoy things you usually do? (Anhedonia)*
- *How do you see the future?*
- *Do you find it difficult to experience normal emotions? (Emotional blunting)*

C. Assess impact using biopsychosocial approach
Biological
- *Have you had any physical health problems?*

Psychological
- *How have you been feeling in yourself?*
- *How do you cope with stress?*
- *Some people use street drugs and alcohol, how about you?*

Social
- *How has this impacted on your work and on family life?*
- *Exclude any co-morbidity.*

D. Premorbid personality
- *How would your friends and family describe you?*

E. Compensation
- *Are you involved in any legal proceedings or any on-going compensation claims, following the incident?*

Summarise
Thank you for talking to me and taking the initiative to approach your GP. From what you have described, it is clear that since the accident you have been distressed by the recurrent nightmares, unpleasant memories, as well as difficulty in sleeping. You have also noticed that you are more on edge, and easily frightened by sudden noises. All these experiences are not

uncommon after an RTA and suggest a disorder like PTSD (Post Traumatic Stress Disorder).

Some useful websites and organisations:
UK trauma group*: has links to a selection of materials which helpful information for the general public and for health professionals about Post Traumatic Stress Reactions*

Charity organisation
http://www.combatstress.org.uk

POSSIBLE VARIATIONS OF THEME
1. 45yr. old man who had recent onset of alcohol problems following an RTA.
2. 37yr old lady who is presenting with overdose following a recent sexual assault.
3 45 yr old war veteran experiencing PTSD symptoms.

GENERAL ADULT PSYCHIATRY

POST TRAUMATIC STRESS DISORDER-PTSD HISTORY
HOPC (onset, duration, progression and severity)
Establish the life threatening event
Elicit core symptoms of PTSD
- Re Experience
- Flashbacks, images, recurrent thoughts, nightmares, any memories?
- reliving
- Avoidance
- Hyper arousal/Startle
- Emotional dysregulation

Establish impact using bio psycho social approach
Biological
Physical
Psychological
- **Mood**

Drug and alcohol history
Social
- Impact on your work and on family life

Premorbid personality
Summarize

©Smartsesh

Nice guidelines for PTSD

➤ Encourages primary care diagnosis and screening-it is probably under diagnosed.
➤ Up to 30% of people exposed to trauma may develop PTSD.
➤ PTSD can also develop in children.
➤ Watchful waiting if symptoms are mild and present for less than 4 weeks after trauma.
➤ Trauma-focused CBT-individual basis as outpatients to be offered to all the severe symptoms present for less than 3 months.
➤ If present for more than 3months (chronic) offer trauma-focussed CBT or EMDR.
➤ If no improvement consider pharmacological treatment.
➤ Paroxetine, mirtazapine for general use; amitriptyline or phenelzine for specialist use.

F43.1 Post-traumatic stress disorder

Arises as a delayed or protracted response to a stressful event or situation (of either brief or long duration) of an exceptionally threatening or catastrophic nature, which is likely to cause pervasive distress in almost anyone. Predisposing factors, such as personality traits (e.g. compulsive, asthenic) or previous history of neurotic illness, may lower the threshold for the development of the syndrome or aggravate its course, but they are neither necessary nor sufficient to explain its occurrence. Typical features include episodes of repeated reliving of the trauma in intrusive memories ("flashbacks"), dreams or nightmares, occurring against the persisting background of a sense of "numbness" and emotional blunting, detachment from other people, unresponsiveness to surroundings, anhedonia, and avoidance of activities and situations reminiscent of the trauma. There is usually a state of autonomic hyperarousal with hypervigilance, an enhanced startle reaction, and insomnia. Anxiety and Depression are commonly associated with the above symptoms and signs, and suicidal ideation is not infrequent. The onset follows the trauma with a latency period that may range from a few weeks to months. The course is fluctuating but recovery can be expected in the majority of cases. In a small proportion of cases the condition may follow a chronic course over many years, with eventual transition to an enduring personality change (F62.0).

Incl.:
Traumatic neurosis

36. SOMATOFORM PAIN DISORDER

INSTRUCTIONS TO CANDIDATE
You have been asked to see this 41 year old man Brian Curtis who has a history of chronic back pain. He had a range of tests and investigations done, but no cause for his pain has been found. He has also been seen in the pain clinic. He is reluctant to see a psychiatrist.

TASK FOR THE CANDIDATE
- *Elicit a history of presenting complaint.*

PAY PARTICULAR ATTENTION TO THE FOLLOWING (MENTAL CHECKLIST)
- *Establishes the onset, duration, nature and progression of the pain.*
- *Establishes associated factors.*
- *Establishes aetiology using a biopsychosocial approach.*
- *Establish the impact of the pain using a biopsychosocial approach.*
- *Establishes any underlying co-morbid conditions.*

COMMUNICATION SKILLS
- *Start the interview by developing rapport and showing empathy.*
- *Seek to understand the subjective feeling of the individual.*
- *Anticipate that he is reluctant to speak to a psychiatrist and use the body and mind analogy to explain your role for seeing him.*

Suggested approach
Introduction
C: *Hello, I'm Dr....I'm one of the psychiatrists. Your GP has referred you as you have been experiencing lower back pain. I wanted to find out more about this.*

P: *I don't know why my GP has asked me to see you. I am not 'mad'.*

C: *As a psychiatrist, we look at how the body and mind is connected and if there is something that affects the mind, it can affect the body and vice versa. I am here to find out more about the pain and how you have been feeling. (Body and mind link)*
Would you like to tell me more about the pain?

A. History of Presenting Complaint (HOPC) (onset, duration, progression and severity)
Establish nature of the pain
- *Can you describe the pain please? For example is it a stabbing, cramping or dull type of pain? (type)*
- *Where is it located? Does it radiate anywhere else? (location)*
- *Is there anything that makes it better? (relieving factors)*
- *Is there anything that makes it worse? (aggravating factors)*
- *When did this all start? (onset)*
- *How long have you been experiencing this for? (duration)*

- *How has this progressed? (progression)*

Establish treatment and investigations thus far
- *Can you take me through the investigations and treatments you have had thus far?*

Summarise
So from what you have told me is that there have been various investigations and treatment, but despite this, there has been no cause found and you are still experiencing this pain.
- *So what do you think is causing this pain?*
- *Is there anything else that could have contributed to this?*
- *Do you have any concerns of any other pain in your body? (somatisation)*
- *Are you worried about any particular illness? (hypochondriasis)*

B. Establish the precipitating factors or triggers
Use a biopsychosocial approach to establish aetiological factors
  1. Biological
- *Do you have any physical health problems?*
- *Have you had any surgery? Have you had any injuries?*
- *Are you currently on any medication?*

  2. Psychological
- *Have you been under any stress recently?*

3. Social
- *Can you tell me about your family?*
- *Are you in any relationship at present?*
- *Do you have any children?*

C. Establish impact on his daily life and seek to understand the subjective feeling of the pain.
- *How have you been feeling in yourself? (Mood)*
- *How has your energy levels been?(energy)*
- *Have you been able to enjoy things you usually would do? What are they?(anhedonia)*
- *How has your sleep been?(biological symptoms)*
- *How has your appetite been? Has there been any change in your weight?*

D. Screen for underlying co-morbid conditions
- *Depression, Anxiety, Somatisation and Hypochondriasis*

E. Past psychiatric history
- *Have you ever seen a psychiatrist in the past?*

F. Coping mechanisms
- *How have you been coping with this?*

GENERAL ADULT PSYCHIATRY

- *Do you drink?*
- *Do you use any street drugs?*

G. Summarise
Thank you for talking to me.
From what you have told me is that you have been experiencing lower back pain for the past six months. You continue to experience this pain despite various investigations and treatments thus far.
I would like to see you again to discuss the treatment options we have available.

POSSIBLE VARIATIONS OF THEME
- *45 yr old man with persistent lower back pain and underlying depressive disorder*
- *35 yr old lady with chronic back pain and depressive symptoms*

SOMATOFORM PAIN DISORDER
A. History of Presenting Complaint (HOPC) onset, duration, progression, severity
Establish nature of the pain
Type, location, relieving factors, aggravating factors
Establish treatment and investigations thus far
Differentiate from Somatisation and Hypochondriasis
B. Establish the precipitating factors or triggers
Use a biopsychosocial approach to establish aetiological factors
1. Biological physical health problems, surgery, injuries, Medication
2. Psychological stressors
3. Social
C. Establish impact on his daily life
D. Screen for underlying co-morbid conditions
- Depression, Anxiety, Somatisation, Hypochondriacal.
E. Past psychiatric history
F. Coping mechanisms-drugs and alcohol use
G. Summarise
©Smartsesh

F45 *Somatoform disorders*

The main feature is repeated presentation of physical symptoms together with persistent requests for medical investigations, in spite of repeated negative findings and reassurances by doctors that the symptoms have no physical basis. If any physical disorders are present, they do not explain the nature and extent of the symptoms or the distress and preoccupation of the patient.

Excl.:
Dissociative Disorders (F44.-)
Hair-Plucking (F98.4)
Lalling (F80.0)
Lisping (F80.8)
Nail-Biting (F98.8)
Psychological Or Behavioural Factors Associated With Disorders Or Diseases Classified Elsewhere (F54)
Sexual Dysfunction, Not Caused By Organic Disorder Or Disease (F52.-)
Thumb-Sucking (F98.8)
Tic Disorders (In Childhood And Adolescence) (F95.-)
Tourette's Syndrome (F95.2)
Trichotillomania (F63.3)

F45.4 Persistent somatoform pain disorder

The predominant complaint is of persistent, severe, and distressing pain, which cannot be explained fully by a physiological process or a physical disorder, and which occurs in association with emotional conflict or psychosocial problems that are sufficient to allow the conclusion that they are the main causative influences. The result is usually a marked increase in support and attention, either personal or medical. Pain presumed to be of psychogenic origin occurring during the course of depressive disorders or schizophrenia should not be included here.

Incl.:
Psychalgia
Psychogenic:
- backache
- headache

Somatoform pain disorder

Excl.:
backache NOS (M54.9)
pain:
- NOS (R52.9)
- acute (R52.0)
- chronic (R52.2)
- intractable (R52.1)

tension headache (G44.2)

GENERAL ADULT PSYCHIATRY

37. HYPOCHONDRIASIS

INSTRUCTIONS TO CANDIDATE
A 45 yr. old fire fighter Christian Young has been referred to the neurologist by his GP with headaches and thought he had a brain tumour. Physical examination and CT scan are unremarkable.

TASK FOR THE CANDIDATE
- *Take a past medical history to arrive at the diagnosis.*

PAY PARTICULAR ATTENTION TO THE FOLLOWING (MENTAL CHECKLIST)
- *Establish the preoccupation of having a brain tumour.*
- *Establish whether it is delusional or overvalued idea.*
- *Assess the impact on activities of daily living and quality of life.*
- *Explore his medical history.*
- *Exclude differential diagnosis.*

COMMUNICATION SKILLS
- *Start the interview by developing rapport and showing empathy.*
- *Seek to understand the subjective feeling of the individual.*
- *Approach this with sensitivity and acknowledge his concerns.*

Suggested approach
Introduction
C: Hello, I'm Dr ...I'm one of the psychiatrists. Your GP has asked me to meet with you to talk about the concerns you have that you may have a brain tumour. Can we perhaps start by talking about the headaches you have been having lately?

History of Presenting Complaint (HOPC) (onset, duration, progression and severity)
- *Can you describe the headaches please?*
- *When did it start?*
- *How has it progressed?*
- *Is there anything that makes it better? (Relieving factor)*
- *Is there anything that makes it worse (aggravating factor)*
- *Any other symptoms i.e. blurred vision, nausea, sickness, neurological-paraplegia, incontinence (associated symptoms)*
- *Why do you think you have a brain tumour?*
- *When did you begin to think this?*
- *Are there any specific symptoms that convince you?*
- *Can you take me through all the tests you have had so far?*

GENERAL ADULT PSYCHIATRY

- *What have you been doing to confirm this belief for example have you been examining yourself?*

Establish whether it is a delusional or an overvalued idea
- *How did you know or work out that this was a brain tumour.*
- *Have you heard or read anything that might explain how you came to believe this?*
- *How convinced are you of this?*
- *Do you think there could be another explanation for this?*
- *What has the neurologist said that it could be?*
- *How do you feel about this? (reassurance)*
- *Have you told your family and friends? What was their reaction?*

Exclude Co-morbidity
- *Exclude Somatisation and Somatoform disorder.*
- *Do you have any other concerns for any other parts of your body?*
- *Do you have any pain anywhere else in your body?*
- *Establish if there are any underlying Depression and Anxiety symptoms.*

Explore if he has specific fears around death and dying
- *What does it mean to you if you do have a brain tumour?*
- *Have you had any concerns about dying?*

Impact on daily life
- *How has this affected you?*
- *Have you been avoiding anything because of your worries?*
- *Have this you stopped you from doing anything?*
- *How are your relationships with friends and family?*
- *How about your social life?*
- *Would you usually describe yourself as a worrier?*
- *I would like to ask you some routine questions about your physical health.*

Elicit a Past medical history
- *Is there anything that sticks out in your childhood?*
- *Did you have any traumatic experience?*
- *Did you have any childhood illnesses?*
- *Did you have any illnesses like Diabetes, Hypertension, and Epilepsy?*
- *Did you have any operations?*
- *Are you on any medication-(benign intracranial hypertension -caused by OCP, tetracycline and Nitrofurantoin)?*
- *Do you have any allergies?*

Family history
- *Is there anyone in your family who had anything similar?*

Risk assessment

GENERAL ADULT PSYCHIATRY

- *Do you sometimes wish you were not alive?(suicidal thoughts)*
- *Have you felt that life was not worth living?*
- *Have you made plans of what you would do?*
- *Have you told anyone?*
- *What is it you think you might do?*
- *What would prevent you from doing this? (Protective factor)*

Summarise
Thank you for talking to me. You have told me that you have been experiencing these headaches and you are now preoccupied that you have a tumour of the brain, despite investigations which have all come back normal.

I would to discuss further how we can help you.

POSSIBLE VARIATIONS OF THEME
1.45 yr. old man who is concerned that he might have contracted AIDS/HIV
2.34 yr. old lady that is worried she has bowel cancer.

GENERAL ADULT PSYCHIATRY

38. HYPOCHONDRIASIS

INSTRUCTIONS TO CANDIDATE
You have been asked to speak to the partner, Sharise Young, of the fire fighter in the previous station, who is worried that he has a brain tumour.

TASK FOR THE CANDIDATE
* Discuss his diagnosis and management with her.

PAY PARTICULAR ATTENTION TO THE FOLLOWING (MENTAL CHECKLIST)
* Summarise findings from the previous station, including a psychiatric assessment.
* Explain the diagnosis of Hypochondriasis.
* Differentiate between overvalued idea and delusional belief.
* Explain possible aetiological factors.
* Explain management in terms of biopsychosocial approach.
* Explain long term prognosis.

COMMUNICATION SKILLS
* Start the interview by developing rapport and showing empathy.
* Show sensitivity.
* Anticipate a concerned partner.

Suggested approach
Introduction
C: Hello I'm Dr ....I'm one of the psychiatrists. I understand you have some concerns about your husband. Can you tell me more about this?

P: He has been worried that he has a brain tumour. Even the other doctors have told him that the brain scan is normal, and they can't find any tumour. I don't know what to do.

C: I can see that this has been difficult for you and you are concerned about him. I will explain.

P: What is his diagnosis?

C: He has what we call Hypochondriasis or also known as a hypochondriac or a health phobia. It is used to describe someone who has a fear or worry of a serious illness. People, who have this condition, continue to believe this, despite being reassured by investigations. Typically they try to self-diagnose; self-examine and become preoccupied with their body. They also doubt the results and investigations which are usually normal.
[Other terms now used if they check the internet it is known as cyberchondria.]

P: How common is Hypochondriasis?

GENERAL ADULT PSYCHIATRY

C: It is something which affects 3 % of the population. Equally common in male and females.

P: What are the causes?

C: There is no one particular cause for Hypochondriasis.
Sometimes it is an illness known to the family and they might have had a relative that has died of this. It can also be triggered by stress.
There is evidence that suggests that it is also due to a chemical imbalance of Serotonin and Noradrenalin (5HT/NA) in the brain.

P: How will you treat him?

C: Our management is usually a combination of treatments available like medication, psychological or talking therapy and the social aspects of care.
Elaborate further on each tailored to her response.
Biological interventions
The medications that are available are a group called antidepressants. They are from the SSRI or Selective serotonin Reuptake inhibitor group. It works by increasing the amount of serotonin or in our body. The names for example are Fluoxetine or Paroxetine. [Elaborate further on this if necessary]

Sometimes if his belief becomes so fixed [delusional] then we would need to consider starting him on an antipsychotic medication. [Elaborate further on this if necessary]

Psychological interventions
C: We do have psychological or talking therapy called CBT or Cognitive behavioural therapy

P: What can I do?

C: Your support and understanding is vitally important to promote his wellbeing and recovery from this illness.

Summary
Thank you for talking to me. Do you have any other questions?

I have more information and leaflets which you can read. I am happy to see you again to discuss your partner's progress and treatment.

Hypochondriasis
Biological
- *SSRI's Fluoxetine*
- *Paroxetine*
- *Antipsychotic*

Psychological
- *CBT*
- *psych education*

Social
- *support*

---

39. DISSOCIATIVE MOTOR DISORDER

INSTRUCTIONS TO CANDIDATE
You are about to see this 45 year old lady Kim Daemon who is in the medical ward, and she has presented with weakness of her left arm.

TASK FOR THE CANDIDATE
- *Assess the HOPC (History of Presenting Complaint) and social history.*

PAY PARTICULAR ATTENTION TO THE FOLLOWING (MENTAL CHECKLIST)
- *Establish history of presenting complaint (onset, duration, progression and severity).*
- *Establish any associated physical symptoms.*
- *Identify psychosocial stressors.*
- *Illustrate secondary gain.*
- *Illustrate La belle indifference.*
- *Exclude any underlying co-morbid mental illness.*

COMMUNICATION SKILLS
- *Develop rapport and show empathy.*
- *Show sensitivity.*

Suggested approach
Introduction
C: Hello, I'm Dr ....Thank you for seeing me. I understand that you came to hospital as you had weakness of your left arm and right leg.
Would you be able to tell me more what happened on that day?

P: I was in bed. Then noticed weakness of my hand

C: Can you tell me more, as to what happened next?

A. History of Presenting Complaint (HOPC) (onset, duration, progression, severity)
- *How long has this been for? (Onset)*
- *Any physical symptoms like pain, headache, slurred speech, pins and needles? (Associated physical symptoms)*
- *Have you had any weakness in any other part of your body? (Focal signs)*
- *Any history of trauma? Any history of epilepsy?*
- *What investigations have you have you had?*
- *What have the doctors told you is wrong?*

B. Identify precipitators/underlying psychosocial stressor
- *Tactfully tease out the possible precipitators*
- *Have you been under any stress recently?*

GENERAL ADULT PSYCHIATRY

- *How are things at home, work, and family?*

C. To illustrate *la belle indifference*
- *How are you feeling about this? (Comment on attitude)*

D. To illustrate Secondary gain
- *How have things been since you came into hospital? (Tactfully prise out the secondary gain)*

E. Past psychiatric history
- *Have you seen a psychiatrist in the past?*

F. Personal and family history
- *Is there anyone in the family that has any similar problems?*

G. Medical History
- *How is your physical health?*

H. Medication
- *Are you on any regular medication?*

Summary
To summarise, from what you have told me, it appears that there has been few stressors at home, work and family. You had sudden paralysis of your left arm. You have had some investigations and they have all come back normal.

Insight
What do you think has caused this? What do you think is wrong?
Sometimes when we are under stress it can cause physical symptoms. For example, when we are stressed it can cause us to have headache. That is when there is something unpleasant to cope with in our unconscious mind, our mind has a way of converting this into a
physical form (body-mind link). I'm wondering if you think there
could be a something similar with you. What do you think? [Insight]

DISSOCIATIVE MOTOR DISORDER -HISTORY
History of presenting complaint HOPC (severity, onset, duration, progression)
Identify precipitator/stressor
Tactfully tease out the possible precipitators
To illustrate la belle indifference
Secondary gain
Past psychiatric history
Personal and family history
Medical History
Medication
Summary
© *Smartsesh*

Possible variation of theme
1. 43 yr old lady who has presented with a 2 day history of not being able to speak.
2. 35 yr old lady who has presented with a 1 day history of blindness in right eye.

GENERAL ADULT PSYCHIATRY

40. DISSOCIATIVE MOTOR DISORDER

INSTRUCTIONS TO CANDIDATE
You have assessed Mrs Kim Daemon you are about to see her husband Mr Simon Daemon who is concerned about her.

TASK FOR THE CANDIDATE
- Discuss the diagnosis and management with her husband.

PAY PARTICULAR ATTENTION TO THE FOLLOWING (MENTAL CHECKLIST)
- Summarise psychiatric assessment from previous station.
- Explain the diagnosis of Conversion disorder using body and mind link.
- Explain the aetiological factors.
- Explain the prognosis.
- Explain the management in terms of biopsychosocial approach.

COMMUNICATION SKILLS
- Start the interview by developing rapport and showing empathy.
- Show sensitivity when discussing wife's condition as he would be feeling partly responsible.

Suggested approach
Introduction
C: Hello, I'm Dr ..... I'm one of the psychiatrists. Thank you for seeing me today. I have seen your wife and I'm sure you are concerned about her. I would like to speak to you more about what I discussed with her and how we will be able to treat her. Before I begin, can you please tell me what your understanding is of how she came to hospital?

H: I just know that she woke up the one day, and she couldn't move her arm and leg.

Summarise from previous station (synopsis from previous station)

C: Since she has been in hospital, they have completed blood and other special investigations to exclude a physical problem. Despite this she doesn't seem reassured. They did also exclude other causes like a stroke which can present in a similar way to how your wife presented.

H: So what is wrong with her? Why is she seeing a psychiatrist?

GENERAL ADULT PSYCHIATRY

C: I am a medical doctor, specialising in the diseases of the mind. As we know, the body and mind are connected, and if one is affected, so is the other and vice versa.
To give you a common example, when you are having a bad day, you might get a headache, and therefore the stress is converted into a physical form. We are all different and we all deal with stress in different ways.

In your wife's case, she has told me that she has been under some stress, i.e. {use the information in previous station}

H: **What is her diagnosis?**

C: It is called Conversion Disorder. This is a disorder where stress is converted into a physical form. In essence, it is not something that she is putting on. I can tell you that she has coped with the stressors in this way and for her what she is experiencing is very real. Sometimes another person in her position would be worried about this

H: **What are the causes?**

C: It is difficult to pinpoint an exact cause in your wife's case, but it is commonly due to an underlying psychological stress.

H: **How common is it?**

C: It is something which is equally common in male and female.

H: **Will she get better?**

C: It is something which has a relatively good outcome. We know that 7 out of 10 people do get better.

H: **What is the treatment available?**

C: There are treatment options available, like medication, psychological or talking therapy and social aspects of care.
I would like to talk about the **psychological or talking therapies.** Something which is effective is CBT or Cognitive behavioural therapy. In her case, the therapist will try to help her find ways of changing and challenging her thoughts. She will see a therapist regularly for up to 16 sessions.

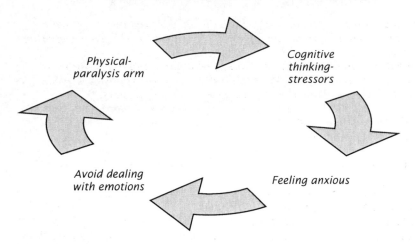

*Physical-
paralysis arm*

*Cognitive
thinking-
stressors*

*Avoid dealing
with emotions*

Feeling anxious

I would also like to see her regularly in outpatients to monitor her progress.

Biological interventions
There is medication *available, but that is only if she develops any other
mental illness like Depression.*
We also know that it affects the home environment, and therefore the **social**
*aspect of care includes your support and understanding of her condition. It is
also helpful, if you try not to reinforce her belief. (I.e. with promoting the use
of the walking stick)*

Summarise
*Thank you for talking to me. From what we have discussed I told you more
about your wife's condition of Conversion Disorder I am happy to see you
again to discuss this further. Do you have any other questions? There are
also these useful organisations and charities. Also these websites
www.rcpsych.ac.uk have useful information.*

Thank you

GENERAL ADULT PSYCHIATRY

41. HEAD INJURY

Suggested approach
Introduction
C: Hello, I'm Dr .....I'm one of the psychiatrists. I understand that you are concerned about your son, Darryl since he had the head injury. I would like to gather some more information about this from you.

A. History of Presenting Complaint (HOPC) (onset, duration, progression, severity)
- Can you describe to me the changes you have noticed? (Changes)
- How has this progressed? Has this been a gradual or sudden change?

Enquire briefly about the head injury
- I understand he had a recent head injury. Can you tell me more about this please?
- Were there any investigations done? (I.e. bloods, brain scans)
- May I know what the results of these investigations were please?

B. Premorbid personality
- How would you describe him before all of this happened?

C. Personality changes
- Has he done anything that was embarrassing? (Prankish behaviour)
- Has he done anything sexually inappropriate? (Disinhibited behaviour)

- *How does he spend his day? (Level of ADL functioning)*
- *Is he able to plan his day? (Planning and organising)*
- *How is his level of self-care? Does he need prompting? (Apathy)*

D. Behaviour
- *Has he been aggressive or agitated? (Aggression)*
- *Has he appeared easily annoyed?*
- *Has he expressed this in any way? (Verbal and physical aggression)*
- *Has he done anything on the spur of the moment? (Impulsive)*
- *Has he had any repetitive movements? (Stereotypes)*

E. Cognitive
- *How has his memory been?*
- *Have you noticed him being forgetful? (Amnesia)*
- *Can you give me some examples?*
- *How is he able to communicate? Has he been repetitive? (Echolalia, later Mutism)*

F. Psychiatric
- *How is his mood? (Depressed)*
- *Has he appeared tearful? (Labile)*
- *Has he had any concerns for his physical health? (Hypochondriasis)*
- *Has he appeared anxious? (Anxiety)*

G. Risk assessment
- *Has he expressed any thoughts of wanting to end it all? (Suicidal thoughts)*
- *Has he expressed thoughts of wanting to harm anyone else?*
- *(Homicidal thoughts)*

H. Past psychiatric history
- *Has he seen a psychiatrist in the past?*

I. Personal and family history
- *Is there anyone in the family that has any similar problems?*

J. Medical History
- *How is his physical health?*

K. Medication
- *Is he on any regular medication?*

Elicit if appropriate Forensic, Psychosexual and Social history

Summary
Thank you for talking to me. To summarise, you have been concerned about Darryl. Since he was injured you have noticed some changes in his personality and his behaviour in that he has become more aggressive. He

spends his day in front of the TV and this is a change from when he previously used to attend college.

I would like to see Darryl and do some further investigations that would pinpoint a cause for these changes. Do you have any questions for me?

Thank you

Possible variation of theme
1. *35 yr. old lady, assaulted in RTA and now presenting with sexually inappropriate behaviour*
2. *29 yr. old male who was recently charged by police for assaulting his neighbour. History is he was assaulted in a pub 2 months ago, and since then there has been a change in his personality.*

FRONT TEMPORAL DEMENTIA

- *History of presenting complaint HOPC(onset, duration, progression, severity)*
- *Premorbid personality*
- *Personality changes*
- *Behaviour changes*
- *Cognitive*
- *Psychiatric*
- *Risk assessment*

©Smartsesh

GENERAL ADULT PSYCHIATRY

42. HEAD INJURY

INSTRUCTIONS TO CANDIDATE
You are about to see this 23 year old gentleman Darryl Raymond, who was assaulted. You have seen his mum and will need to assess him.

TASK FOR THE CANDIDATE
- *Perform a cognitive examination with focus on **Frontal Lobe tests.***

PAY PARTICULAR ATTENTION TO THE FOLLOWING (MENTAL CHECKLIST)
- *Explain purpose of interview and enquire if a chaperone is needed.*
- *Elicit verbal (naming tests) - verbal fluency, proverb testing, similarities and differences and cognitive estimates.*
- *Ask him to perform (Doing tests) -Go no -go-test, Luria motor test.*
- *Elicit Copying tests Alternate sequence.*
- *Examine Primitive reflexes- Glabellar tap, Grasp reflex, Palmomental, pouting.*
- *Summarise and explain need for further investigations.*

COMMUNICATION SKILLS
- *Start the interview by developing rapport and showing empathy.*
- *Anticipate that he could be disinhibited so attempt to gently refocus him on the task you require him to do.*
- *If necessary ask for a chaperone.*

Suggested approach
Introduction
C: Hello, I'm Dr .....I'm one of the psychiatrists. I have seen your mother and today I would like to ask you to do a test of your memory. Is that all right with you?
Please feel free to interrupt me if you are unable to understand me?

S: That's fine.

C: Would you perhaps like a chaperone?

S: No thanks doc.

A. Assessment of Verbal Fluency
- *Can you name as many words starting with the letters 'F','A' and 'S'?*
- *Check for 1 minute*
- *[Normal -15 words per letter in 1 minute]*
- *You can also use categories namely animals, fruits)*
- *Can you name as many animals in one minute?*

GENERAL ADULT PSYCHIATRY

B. Assessment of abstract thinking
Proverb interpretation
- Can you explain what is meant by these proverbs?
- 'Too many cooks spoil the broth'
- 'Don't judge a book by its cover'
- 'A stitch in time saves nine?

C. Similarities and Differences
- Can you explain the similarities and differences between?
- 'Apple and orange'
- 'Table and chair'

D. Assessment of Cognitive estimates
- What is the height of an average English woman?
- How many camels are there in Holland or England?
- How high is a double decker bus?

E. Assessment of Response inhibition and set shifting
- Co-ordinated movements.

F. Luria motor test-Three step test
- Can you copy my actions?
- Show the patient by placing a fist, then edge of the palm and then a flat palm of the opposite hand and repeating the sequence.
- Can you repeat this please?
- Then do this with the other hand. It can be repeated up to five times

G. Alternate sequence
- Can you continue this please?   ----/\-----/\----

H. No don't go
- Can you follow me? If I tap once, you raise one finger. If I tap twice, you tap under the table.

I. Perseveration
- Observe any repetition of particular responses

J. Examination
Primitive reflex- to test frontal lobe release signs
Glabellar tap- taps between the eyebrows, which causes repeated blinking after five or more taps.

Grasping reflex-stroke's patient's palm while distracting the patient and watches for involuntary grasping which can be subtle.
Pouting reflex -taps on a spatula placed on a patient's lips, resulting in pouting.

GENERAL ADULT PSYCHIATRY

Thank you for cooperating with me. I would like to do some further investigations to understand more about what could be the cause for your recent change in your behaviour

---

Frontal Lobe Examination
Naming
- *Verbal fluency*
- *Proverb testing*
- *Similarities and differences*
- *Cognitive estimates*

Doing
- *Go no -go-test*
- *Luria motor test*

Copying
- *Alternate sequence*

Examine
- *Primitive reflexes*
- *Glabellar tap*
- *Grasp reflex*
- *Palmomental*
- *Pouting*

---

43. HAEMATEMESIS

INSTRUCTIONS TO CANDIDATE
You are about to see Mr Aaron White who is a 35 yr old male who has come in with haematemesis. He has been told by the surgeons that they need to do an endoscopy, however he is refusing this. They have asked you to assess his capacity.

TASK FOR THE CANDIDATE
- Assess his capacity.
- Assess his delusional beliefs.

PAY PARTICULAR ATTENTION TO THE FOLLOWING (MENTAL CHECKLIST)
- Establish his understanding and retention of the overall problem and information.
- Establish his understanding of the proposed procedure.
- Establish his understanding of the purpose of the procedure.
- Establish his understanding of the risks.
- Establish whether he is aware of the alternatives to the treatment.
- Establish whether he is able to weigh the pros and cons to come to a decision.
- Establish if he is able to communicate that decision.
- Establish if he has any underlying mental illness.

COMMUNICATION SKILLS
- Develop rapport and show empathy.
- Seek to understand the subjective feeling of the individual.

Suggested approach
Introduction
C: Hello, I'm Dr ....I am one of the psychiatrists working in this hospital. Thank you for agreeing to see me. I understand the surgeons have asked me to see you. They have said that you have come in with vomiting blood. They have also said that you would need to have a procedure done, but you have refused. I would like to ask you more about this, is that all right?

 P: I will tell you what I told them...

C: Thank you. Can you tell me more about the bleeding please?

A. History of Presenting Complaint (HOPC) (onset, duration, progression, severity)
- When did this all start? (Onset)
- How long has it been for? (Duration)
- How has it progressed? (Progression)
- What do you think is wrong?

GENERAL ADULT PSYCHIATRY

B. Exclude any underlying mental illness
- Explore for psychotic or depressive symptoms
- Delusional beliefs- Grandiose, Persecutory, Paranoid
- Auditory/visual/gustatory/tactile hallucinations
- Establish his level of insight

C. Risk assessment

D. Establish his capacity using the 4 main criteria (ref Mental Capacity act 2005)
Establish his overall Understanding of the problem
- What is your understanding of the problem you are having?
- What have the surgeons told you that need to happen?
- Have you been told what the complications would be?
- Have you been told about the benefits of having it done?
- Have you been told what will happen if you don't want to have it done? Would you become ill? Would you be placing your life at risk without it?
- Have the surgeons told you about the alternatives to the proposed treatment?

Establish his Retention of the information
- Are you able to tell me your understanding of what we have discussed thus far?

Establish if he is able to weigh the options or on balance weigh the pros and cons
- Can you tell me why you have refused to the treatment?
- Is there anything worrying you?

Communicate decision
- Can you tell me what your final decision is?

E. Explore relevant history appropriately
Past psychiatric history
- Have you seen a psychiatrist in the past?

F. Personal and family history
- Is there anyone in the family that has any similar problems?

G. Drug and alcohol history
- How do you usually cope? Some people drink or take illicit substances. How about you?

H. Risk Assessment
- Have you had thoughts that life was not worth living? (Suicidal thoughts)
- Have you had thoughts of harming anyone else? (Homicidal thoughts)

GENERAL ADULT PSYCHIATRY

Summary
Thank you for talking to me. To summarise, what you have told me is that you have understood what the surgeons have told you about the endoscopy, and that if you don't have it, you will die. Despite that, you are still refusing. You also believe firmly that the bleeding has special significance, and you do not wish to stop it.

I am concerned about your decision and capacity to make this decision. I will speak to the surgeons and rearrange to come and see you.

HEMATEMESIS
Assess for psychotic symptoms
- Delusional beliefs-Grandiose, Persecutory, Paranoid
- Auditory/visual/gustatory/tactile hallucinations
- Mood symptoms
- Insight

Risk assessment
Assess his capacity
- Understand
- Retain
- Weigh pros and cons
- Communicate decision

Past psychiatric history
Personal and family history
Drug and alcohol history
Risk Assessment
Summarize
©*Smartsesh*

GENERAL ADULT PSYCHIATRY

44. HAEMATEMESIS

INSTRUCTIONS TO CANDIDATE
You have seen this man, Aaron White, to assess his capacity to refuse an endoscopy. You will now be seeing the psychiatry consultant on call.

TASK FOR THE CANDIDATE
- Discuss your management with the consultant.

PAY PARTICULAR ATTENTION TO THE FOLLOWING (MENTAL CHECKLIST)
- Give a psychiatric formulation.
- Highlight the capacity issues.
- Establish possible differential diagnoses.
- Formulate management plan in holistic and biopsychosocial approach.
- Highlight risk issues of Mental illness and underlying physical illness.

COMMUNICATION SKILLS
- Adopt a collegiate approach.

Suggested approach
Introduction
C: Hello, I'm Dr ... I'm one of the psychiatrists. The surgeons referred this gentleman who was admitted with a haematemesis. They have asked me to assess his capacity as he was refusing to have the endoscopy done. I have come to discuss with you more about my assessment, diagnosis and management.

A. Brief synopsis
Summary of demographic data
45 yr old gentleman married, employed, with 2 children. He is presenting with acute psychotic episode and underlying physical illness of haematemesis.

B. Psychiatric assessment
He has the following relevant history
- **Past psychiatric history**
- **Personal and family history**
- **Medical History**
- **Medication**
- **Drug and alcohol**
- **Forensic, Psychosexual, Social**
- **Risk Assessment**

Mental state examination
The following psychotic symptoms were present

C. My differential diagnoses are
- Acute and transient psychotic episode
- Enduring mental illness like Schizophrenia
- Severe Depression with psychotic symptoms

My management plan in holistic or biopsychosocial approach in the immediate, medium and longer term is

Biological interventions
- Investigations
- Collateral history and further information from GP
- Check blood investigations -FBC(Full blood count), U+E(Urea and electrolyte), LFT(Liver function tests), TFT, glucose
- Rating scales-SANS, PANS
- Healthy living advice on general wellbeing
- Address the underlying risk factors
- Diet
- Exercise
- Smoking cessation
- Alcohol -treat for alcohol withdrawal symptoms

Medication
According to the guideline that we use antipsychotic treatment bearing in mind the risks of haematemesis. Weigh the risk and benefits when prescribing.

Psychological interventions
We could consider the talking therapy or CBT cognitive behavioural therapy at a later stage. This will help to promote recovery, reduce symptoms and prevent worsening. It can also help to improve motivation, compliance and reduce stress.

Social interventions
Involve the multi-disciplinary team.

Longer term
The aim would be to improve the therapeutic alliance and provide regular outpatients with effective community support to promote wellbeing and recovery.

GENERAL ADULT PSYCHIATRY

45. TEMPORAL LOBE EPILEPSY

INSTRUCTIONS TO CANDIDATE
You are about to see this 34 year old gentleman, Aaron Simms, who was referred by his GP with concerns of 'weird turns' he has been having. Additional information: he is on Dosulepin.

TASK FOR THE CANDIDATE
- Please take a history to arrive to a diagnosis.

PAY PARTICULAR ATTENTION TO THE FOLLOWING (MENTAL CHECKLIST)
- Establish history of presenting complaint. (HOPC -onset, duration, progression and severity.)
- Establish aura, preictal, ictal and post ictal phases.
- Identify the aetiological factors using a biopsychosocial approach.
- Conduct a risk assessment.

COMMUNICATION SKILLS
- Develop rapport and show empathy.
- Seek to understand the subjective feelings if the individual.

Suggested approach
Introduction
C: Hello, I'm Dr ....I am one of the psychiatrists. Thank you for coming to see me. I understand that you have mentioned to your GP that you were having some 'weird turns'. Would you be able to describe these for me?

P: I don't remember what happens. My girlfriend is the one that sees this.

C: I can appreciate that you are unable to remember these, but it will help if you tell me what it is that she has said happens?

A. History of Presenting Complaint (HOPC) (onset, duration, progression, severity)
C: Can you describe this please?
- When did this first start?
- How has it progressed since then?
- How often do they occur?

B. Establish different stages of seizure
Aura
- Do you ever have a feeling or sense when this would occur?
- Have you had the feeling that a familiar place is unfamiliar? (Jamais vu)
- Have you had the feeling that an unfamiliar place is familiar? (De ja vu)

- *Do you sometimes misinterpret something for something else? (Illusion)*
- *Some people describe a feeling in their tummy. How about you? (Epigastric sensation)*
- *Do you ever get the feeling that the environment is not real? (Derealisation)*
- *Do you ever feel that you yourself are not real? (Depersonalisation)*
- *Have you ever had any picturesque images? (Panoramic memory)*

Ictal

- *What movements have been observed? (Establish the type of seizure)*
- *How about eye movements?*
- *Do you lose consciousness?*
- *Are you able to remember what happens?*
- *Are you able to hear anything that is going on at the same time?*
- *Is there any biting of your tongue?*
- *Is there any incontinence? Or do you wet yourself?*

Post ictal

- *How do you usually feel after this?*
- *Any: Headache, confusion, injury, incontinence*
- *Also enquire about psychotic symptoms and personality changes*

C. Use a biopsychosocial approach to identify possible triggers or precipitators

- *Are you able to know what usually brings this on?*

Biological

- *Can you tell me more about the medication you are taking?*
- *For example if it is Dosulepin, establish dosage, effects and side effects*
- *Have there been any changes in your dosage? (Increase or decrease)*

Psychological

- *Are you sensitive to light or sounds?*

Social

- *Do you notice that if you are under stress that you can get this?*
- *Do you drink? Any times you had seizures after stopping alcohol?*

D. Personal and family history

- *Is there anyone in the family that has any similar problems?*

E. Medical History

- *How is your physical health?*
- *Has there been a past history of seizures?*
- *Is there any history of febrile convulsions?*
- *Enquire about head injury, stroke, RTA*

F. Risk Assessment
- *Do you drive? Has this ever happened when you were driving?*
- *What work do you do? Do you work with machinery?*

Summarise
Thank you for talking to me. To summarise what we have discussed is that you have been episodes, where you have been experiencing falling down and are unable to respond to your surroundings. It coincided with a recent increase in your medication. I would like to arrange for a special test called an EEG (electroencephalogram).

Temporal Lobe epilepsy
- *Aura*
- *Ictal*
- *Post ictal*
- *Screen for psychotic symptoms*
- *Establish aetiological factors using a biopsychosocial approach*
- *Risk assessment*

GENERAL ADULT PSYCHIATRY

46. BORDERLINE PERSONALITY DISORDER (BPD)

INSTRUCTIONS TO CANDIDATE
You have been asked to see Rachel Cannon a 25 yr old lady who has a history of self harm.

TASK FOR THE CANDIDATE
- Elicit Borderline personality traits.

PAY PARTICULAR ATTENTION TO THE FOLLOWING (MENTAL CHECKLIST)
- Establish presence of Borderline personality traits.
- Identity disturbance: Emotional stability, empty feeling.
- Poor tolerance of frustration.
- Self-harm attempts.
- Mood instability.
- Establish quasi psychotic symptoms.
- Exclude underlying co-morbidity.

COMMUNICATION SKILLS
- Start the interview by developing rapport and showing empathy.
- Show sensitivity.

Suggested approach
Introduction
C: Hello, I'm Dr...I am one of the psychiatrists. I have been asked to come and see you. I understand that you have been experiencing some difficulties lately and I wanted to find out more about that?

A. Establish presence of Borderline personality traits
[Emotional stability, tolerance of frustration, risk behaviours, frustration, fluctuating mood, empty feeling]

Identity disturbance
- How do you feel about yourself? Can you please describe this?
- Optional question, Some people describe to me that they have an empty feeling, is this something you can relate to?

Relationships
- How have your relationships worked out?
- How do you feel when your relationships end? Do you ever feel abandoned?
- What happens when you feel this way?

Self-harm attempts
- How do you usually cope?
- Have you self-harmed? [explore further]

GENERAL ADULT PSYCHIATRY

Impulsive
- *Do you regret certain things you have done?*

Affective instability
- *How has your mood been? Does it fluctuate? (Capricious mood)*
- *How do you cope if someone annoys you?*
- *How do you deal with it if you lose your temper?*

B. Establish quasi psychotic symptoms
Differentiate Pseudo auditory hallucination and true hallucination
- *I would like to ask you some routine questions that I ask everyone who comes to see me. They may appear strange to you.*
- *Do you ever hear voices or see things when there is no one else around?*
- *Can you describe this?*

Dissociation
- *Do you ever feel like you are able to separate yourself from what is happening around you?*

C. Screen for co-morbidity
- *Depression, Anxiety, PTSD.*

D. Aetiological factors
- *Is there anything from your childhood memories that stick out?*
- *This is a sensitive question, but have you ever been sexually abused?*

E. Coping strategies
- *Self-harm as above*
- *Do you drink? Have you experimented with street drugs?*

Summarise
Thank you for talking to me. From what we discussed you have told me that you have had difficulty in some relationships and that you sometimes feel abandoned. You also described 'feeling empty' and in times of stress you have been self-harming. We have a range of treatment options available which I would like to discuss with you.

GENERAL ADULT PSYCHIATRY

References

Gelder, M.G, Cowen, P. and Harrison P.J (2006) Shorter Oxford textbook of psychiatry. 5th edn. Oxford: Oxford University Press.

Sims, A. C. P. (2003) Symptoms in the mind: an introduction to descriptive psychopathology. 3rd edn. Great Britain: Saunders.

Taylor, D., Paton, C., Kapur, S. (2009) The South London and Maudsley NHS Foundation Trust & Oxleas NHS Foundation Trust prescribing guidelines. 10th edn. London: Informa Healthcare.

British Medical Association and Royal Pharmaceutical society (2011), British National Formulary 62, 62nd edn. Great Britain: British Medical Journal Publishing Group and Pharmaceutical Press

WHO. (1992)The ICD 10 classification of mental and behavioural disorders: clinical descriptions and diagnostic guideline. 10th revision: Geneva; WHO

Depression
STARD trial
Bazaire, S-(2003) Psychotropic drug directory 2003/4.Salisbury, Wilts: Fivepin publishing

Bipolar Affective Disorder
NICE Guidelines CG38. The management of bipolar disorder in adults, children and adolescents, in primary and secondary care. Prof N Ferrier. July 2006.

BAP Guidelines. Evidence-based guidelines for the treating bipolar disorder: revised second edition - recommendations for the British Association for Psychopharmacology. Guy Goodwin. Journal of Psychopharmacology 23(4) 2009 346-388

World Federation of Societies of Biological Psychiatry (WFSBP) Guidelines on Bipolar Disorder. All found at www.wfsbp.org. Guidelines for the Treatment of bipolar Depression; Treatment of bipolar mania; Maintenance treatment.

Schizophrenia
Kane J, Honigfield G, Singer J, et al: 1988 Clozapine for the treatment-resistant schizophrenic; a double blind comparison with chlorpromazine (Clozaril collaborative study). Arch. Gen. Psychiatry; 45; 789-796

David A. Gutman, Charles B. Nemeroff, 2005The Clinical Antipsychotic Trials of Intervention Effectiveness (CATIE) Study -- Effectiveness of Antipsychotic

GENERAL ADULT PSYCHIATRY

Drugs in Patients With Chronic Schizophrenia: Efficacy and Safety Outcomes of the CATIE Trial

Schizophrenia and Cannabis
Fattore L, Fratta W. Beyond THC: The New Generation of Cannabinoid Designer Drugs.
Front Behav Neurosci. 2011;5:60. Epub 2011 Sep 21.

Manrique-Garcia E, Zammit S, Dalman C, Hemmingsson T, Andreasson S, Allebeck P. Cannabis, schizophrenia and other non-affective psychoses: 35 years of follow-up of a population-based cohort. Psychol Med. 2011 Oct 17:1-8. [Epub ahead of print]

Fiorentini A, Volonteri LS, Dragogna F, Rovera C, Maffini M, Mauri MC, Altamura CA. Substance-Induced Psychoses: A Critical Review Of The Literature. Curr Drug Abuse Rev. 2011 Dec 1. [Epub ahead of print

OCD-Obsessive Compulsive Disorder
Veale, D (2007) Cognitive behavioural for Obsessive Compulsive Disorder. Advances in psychiatric treatment, 13, 438-86
YBOCS- Yale brown obsessive compulsive scale,

Online resources
Royal college of psychiatrist's health information leaflets for patient's www.rcpsych.ac.uk

Support groups and organisations
MIND
RETHINK
SANELINE

OLD AGE

OLD AGE   -Dr Ehab Hegazi

1. Elderly Psychosis- Assess psychopathology and do cognitive examination – Dr Ehab Hegazi
2. Elderly Psychosis –discuss with brother – Dr Ehab Hegazi
3. Behavioural and psychological symptoms of Dementia
4. BPSD-Collateral history
5. Wandering–risk assessment - Dr Ashaye Kunle
6. Vascular Dementia-Dr Ehab Hegazi
7. Vascular Dementia-Management Dr Ehab Hegazi
8. Vascular Dementia-Capacity Dr Ehab Hegazi
9. Treatment Resistant Depression-collateral history – Dr Manjula Atmakur
10. Treatment Resistant Depression-Lithium Augmentation – Dr Manjula Atmakur
11. Electroconvulsive Depression-ECT-Dr Ehab Hegazi
12. Fronto Temporal Dementia–Dr Mike Walker
13. Frontal Lobe Tests- Dr Mike Walker
14. Dementia-Lewy Body Dementia
15. Alzheimer's Dementia history Dr Arun Jha
16. Alzheimer's treatment Antidementia drugs Dr Arun Jha
17. Psychotic Depression-Dr Ashaye Kunle
18. Elderly man- Indecent exposure –assess Raghavakurup Radhakrisknan
19. Elderly man- Indecent exposure –discuss management
20. Delirium/Acute confusional state-Dr Champa Balalle
21. Delirium/Acute confusional state-Dr Champa Balalle

OLD AGE

1. PARAPHRENIA-ASSESS PSYCHOPATHOLOGY

INSTRUCTIONS TO CANDIDATE
You have been asked to see this 65 yr. old lady, Mrs Hall, who was admitted under section 2 of the Mental Health Act(MHA 1983) (MHA) and is not keen to be in hospital.

TASK FOR THE CANDIDATE
- *Elicit her delusional beliefs.*
- *Perform a mental state examination.*

PAY PARTICULAR ATTENTION TO THE FOLLOWING (MENTAL CHECKLIST)
- *Elicit psychotic symptoms using clustering approach.*
- *Elicit first rank symptoms.*
- *Perform a mental state examination.*
- *Conduct a risk assessment.*
- *Establish risk factors for Paraphrenia.*

COMMUNICATION SKILLS
- *Start the interview by developing a rapport and showing empathy.*
- *Seek to understand the subjecting experience of the person.*
- *Anticipate that she is reluctant to stay in hospital and would also not appreciate being challenged about her belief.*

Suggested approach
Introduction
C: Hello, I'm Dr ....I am a psychiatrist working on this ward. .
I understand that you have been admitted here. I wanted to find out more about what led up to this.

P: 'They should be locked in here not me.'

C: It sounds like you have been going through a difficult time. Can you tell me more about who these people are and why you feel they should be in here?

P: It is my neighbours. They have been trying to kill me. They have been poisoning my food.

C: That must be frightening. How do you know that this is happening to you?

A. History of presenting complaint (HOPC) (onset, duration, progression and severity)
C: What does it taste like?
How would they get access to your food to do this?

227

OLD AGE

P: I only buy packaged food. To me, it tastes like arsenic.

C: So how do you know it is arsenic? Have you been ill?

P: No, I know they are poisoning my food.

C: This sounds very strange. I would like to get to the bottom of this. So what have you been eating?

P: I only eat packaged food.

C: Have you had any weight loss? (Risk to self)

Establish degree of conviction of delusional belief

Recapitulation (an example would be)
C: So what you have told me is that your neighbours have been poisoning your food and it tastes like arsenic. You have not been ill however you buy pre-packaged foods.

So tell me how convinced are you that this is happening? Have you told your family and friends?

P: I am convinced they are doing this to me doctor.

B. Further exploration of first rank symptoms
C: Have you heard them talking about you? (Auditory hallucination)
- *What do they say?*
- *Do they speak directly to you? (2nd person auditory hallucination)*
- *Do they comment on what you are doing? (Running commentary*
- *Do you hear your thoughts spoken aloud? (Gedankenlautwerden-thoughts spoken aloud))*
- *Have you seen anything when there was no-one around? (Visual hallucination)*
- *Have you had any strange sensation on your skin? (Tactile)*

I know this may sound strange, but I want to understand your version of what is happening.
- *Have you felt that your thoughts have been interfered with?*
- *Do they take your thoughts away?*
- *(Thought insertion/broadcast/withdrawal)*
- *Do they control you? Do they control the way you are thinking, feeling, or your movements?(made act/will/volition)*
- *How does this make you feel?*
- *Have you had any strange sensations in your body? (Somatic passivity)*
- *Do they spy on you?*

Screen for depressive symptoms if necessary

C. Risk assessment
- So what have you done about it? What are you planning to do?
- What is preventing you from doing anything?
- Have you had any thoughts of wanting to harm them? (homicidal risk)
- Have you had any thoughts of wanting to harm yourself? (suicidal risk)
- This has been a frightening experience for you, how are you coping now? (Establish if drinking alcohol)

D. Establish the risk factors for Paraphrenia (late onset schizophrenia)

E. Past psychiatric history
- Have you seen a psychiatrist in the past? (Past psychiatric history)
- Does anyone in the family suffer from similar problems as you?? (Family history)

F. Medical history
- Are you on any medication? (Medication)
- Do you have any problems with your hearing or eyesight? (visual/hearing disabilities)
- Do you have any other physical health problems?

G. Social history
- Who do you live with? (social isolation)

Summarise
Thank you for talking to me.
From what you have told me, you are convinced that your neighbours are poisoning your food and they want to get rid of you. You are convinced of this despite no evidence.

You also told me that you hear them talking to you through the walls of your house, when there is no-one else around. You have not been eating. You went to confront the neighbours and they contacted the police, who then brought you here.

Insight
I appreciate what you have said. Sometimes when people are under stress they can have some strange experiences. I am concerned about you and think that you will benefit from a stay in hospital. I would also like you to consider taking some medication.

What do you think about this?

OLD AGE

2. PARAPHRENIA-EXPLAIN MANAGEMENT

> **INSTRUCTION TO CANDIDATE**
> *You have assessed this 65 yr. old lady who was admitted under section 2 of the Mental Health Act (MHA 1983) (MHA). She has been diagnosed with Psychosis and is currently on Olanzapine. Discuss management with brother, Mr Hall.*
>
> ━━━━━━━━━━━━━━━━━━━━━━━━━━━━━━━━━━━━━━
>
> **TASK FOR THE CANDIDATE**
> - *Discuss her management with her brother.*
>
> **PAY PARTICULAR ATTENTION TO THE FOLLOWING (MENTAL CHECKLIST)**
> - *Give a summary of you psychiatric assessment.*
> - *Highlight the risks and legal issues.*
> - *Explain how the diagnosis was made.*
> - *Explain the management using a biopsychosocial approach.*
> - *Explain Community Mental Health team (CMHT) involvement and Care programme approach (CPA).*
>
> **COMMUNICATION SKILLS**
> - *Start the interview by developing rapport and showing empathy.*
> - *Seek to understand the subjective feeling of the relative.*
> - *Anticipate a concerned relative.*

Suggested approach
Introduction
C: Hello, I'm Dr ..... I am a psychiatrist involved in your sister's care.
I understand that you are concerned about her. I have come to speak to you more about the diagnosis and management. Before we begin it will be helpful to find out what your understanding is of her being in hospital.

F: I know that she was worried about her neighbours. She thought that they were going to harm her. She also said she was hearing voices.

C: I can understand what a difficult time this is for you. I am sure you are concerned about your sister. Let me try to explain more about her diagnosis and how we will be treating her.

Start by giving a brief Synopsis of the previous station:
C: Your sister said that her neighbours were trying to poison her. She firmly believes this, despite no evidence. When someone has this extreme conviction, we call this a delusion. She was also hearing voices when no one else was around. This is what we call an auditory hallucination.

F: What is her diagnosis?

OLD AGE

C: These delusions and hallucinations, as I have explained, usually occur in a psychotic illness or Schizophrenia. In old age it is called Paraphrenia. In this illness it usually affects the way a person thinking, feeling and behaviour.

F: How common is it?

C: It is a common illness and occurs 1 in 100. It usually occurs in younger people but can occur in older people.
It is equally common in male and female.

F: What are the causes that have resulted in her getting this?

C: There could be various reasons for this. We have excluded a memory problem and physical problems. We have done memory testing MMSE (Mini Mental State Examination) and blood investigations. It is difficult to pinpoint the exact cause in your sister's case.
In old age the causes are usually problems with hearing, eyesight, and living in isolation.

F: Do they usually have to be treated in hospital?

C: We usually assess the risks and if there is a risk of harm to themselves or others, we consider voluntary admission in hospital. In the cases where a person doesn't want to be admitted and if we feel it is for their safety and the safety of others, we then detain them under the Mental Health Act (MHA 1983).

Your sister refused to come in voluntarily, and we were concerned in your sister's case, as she was not eating and drinking. Due to the risks and concerns for her, we had to use the Mental Health Act (MHA 1983).

F: What are the treatments available?

C: There are treatment options available, like medication, psychological or talking therapy and because we know it affects a person's life, we have the social aspect of care.
Which one would you like to hear more about?

F: I would like to know more about the medication Olanzapine that she is on.

C: We have started her on Olanzapine. It belongs to group of medications called antipsychotics. It works to normalise the chemical imbalance [Dopamine] found in Schizophrenia.

Like all medication, they do have side effects. The more common side effects are drowsiness and weight gain. Less common ones are constipation, dry mouth, peripheral oedema and postural hypotension.

We usually weigh the risks and benefits when treating. We will make sure that we monitor this and do regular blood testing. [It can also cause metabolic syndrome which is characterised by weight gain, diabetes, raised cholesterol]

Psychological intervention
When she is more settled we will look at the psychological or talking therapies; which is called CBT or cognitive behavioural therapy.

In later stages of care we usually involve the older people services for mental health. The team consists of the psychiatrist, psychologist, social worker, occupational therapist and community psychiatric nurse. The community psychiatric nurse will monitor her behaviour and medication.
The occupational therapist will help with assessing her ADL (activities of daily living), her functioning and provide her with advice if appropriate.
The social worker will assist with finances and look at social support or carers. We can also see if we can arrange some day activities to keep her occupied and provide her with some social interaction.

Will she be able to go back home?
C: Our aim is for her to be independent and to live at home. If however this is not possible then we would need to look at the options available. [Elaborate further on residential and nursing placements if necessary]

F: How long will it take for her to get better?

C: It is difficult to say. We hope that the medication will help to calm her. We usually recommend that she continue with treatment for at least 6 months. There is a risk that if she stops medication that she will become unwell again.

F: When will she be discharged?
That depends on a few factors as to how she has responded to medication, the assessments of her daily living skills and the level of support she would require.

We will invite you and her family to the CPA (Care programme approach) meeting. This is usually arranged prior to someone being discharged. It will involve all the people involved in her care and we will discuss her discharge plan arrangements and care package.

It goes without saying that your support and understanding is vital to promote her wellbeing and to promote her recovery. We will keep you informed of her progress at all times.

Summarise
Thank you for speaking to me. I have told you about your sister's diagnosis of Schizophrenia and about the treatment in terms of medication. I am happy to meet with you again to discuss your sister's progress. Do you have any other questions?

OLD AGE

If you require any further information, there are also these useful organisations and charities like MIND, SANELINE and RETHINK.

Thank you

MANAGEMENT - PARAPHRENIA
Immediate
Admission according to risks- informal/detained under MHA 1983
Biological interventions
- *Information gathering-GP, family*
- *Screening-blood investigations –FBC, U+E, LFT, CRP, TFT, urine MC+S, CT scan and MRI of brain if indicated*
- *Rating scales- SANS, PANS, GDS*
- *Cognitive examination-MMSE*
- *Medication- Antipsychotics -as per National institute of clinical excellence (NICE guidelines)*
- *Monitor for side effects- regular blood tests.*

Psychological interventions
- *Psychoeducation*
- *Cognitive behavioural therapy (CBT)*

Social interventions
- *Support Day hospital*

Longer term
- *Support with the older people services for mental health.*
- *To also promote wellbeing and recovery*
- *Attend day activities*

©Smartsesh

OLD AGE

3. BEHAVIOURAL AND PSYCHOLOGICAL SYMPTOMS IN DEMENTIA

INSTRUCTIONS TO THE CANDIDATE
You will be seeing the carer of Mr Barrett, who is a 65 yr. old gentleman living in a residential home. The carers are concerned as he has assaulted a resident and has become increasingly agitated. He has a diagnosis of Alzheimer's Dementia.

TASK FOR THE CANDIDATE
- *Get collateral history from carer*

PAY PARTICULAR ATTENTION TO THE FOLLOWING (MENTAL CHECKLIST)
- *Establish the current concerns of the carer.*
- *Establish details of the incident using an antecedent, behaviour and consequence approach.(ABC)*
- *Establish the aetiological factors using a biopsychosocial approach.*
- *Conduct a risk assessment.*

COMMUNICATION SKILLS
- *Start the interview by developing a rapport and showing empathy.*
- *Acknowledge the distress of the current situation and impact on staff and other residents.*

Suggested approach
Introduction
C: *Hello, I'm Dr ....Thank you for coming to see me. I understand Mr Barrett is currently living in your care home, and there has been a change in his behaviour. I would like to find out more about what happened.*

C: Yes, it's been very difficult. He assaulted one of the residents.

C: *I can see clearly that the situation has become a concern for you, staff and other residents. Can you tell me more about what has happened?*

History of Presenting Complaint (HOPC) (onset, duration, progression, severity)

Behavioural symptoms
- *Have you noticed any other changes in his behaviour?*
- *Have you noticed any changes in his mood?*
- *Has he appeared more irritable?*
- *Any other episodes of aggressive behaviour? (Aggression)*
- *Has he been violent? (Violence)*
- *Has he been shouting?*
- *Have you noticed any changes in his personality? (Personality changes)*

- *Has he appeared to be disinhibited?*

Psychological symptoms
- *How is his memory? (Memory)*
- *How is his mood? (Sad or happy)*
- *Has he appeared to be responding or talking to himself?*

Physical
- *Has he been seen by his family doctor (GP)?*
- *Has he had any falls?*
- *Have you had any tests done- bloods, urine dipstick? (Urinary tract infection)*

Establish aetiological factors:
Biological
- *Has there been any change in his medication?*
- *Has he been experiencing any pain?*
- *Does he have any mobility problems?*

Social
- *Have there been any changes in the home?*
- *Has he been doing activities?*
- *Are there any new residents or carers?*
- *Has he had any family visits?*

Past psychiatric history
- *I understand he has a diagnosis of Alzheimer's. Can you tell me more about this?*

Personal and family history
- *Is there anyone in the family that has any similar problems?*

Risk Assessment- covers the following aspects
- *Self-harm- Has he expressed any thoughts of wanting to die? (Suicidal thoughts)*
- *Self-neglect- Is he eating? Is he taking care of himself?*
- *Aggression.*
- *Wandering- Has he been wandering?*
- *Is he aware of road safety?*

Summarise
Thank you for talking to me. To summarise what you have said is that it appears that there has been a few changes in the environment, and that this could have contributed to a change in Mr Barrett's behaviour. I understand that we will have to do physical investigations to exclude a Urinary Tract Infection (UTI (Urinary tract infection)) I would like to see him and we could discuss the management plans thereafter. Do you have any other questions?

OLD AGE

POSSIBLE VARIATIONS OF THEME
1. 65 yr. old man with Alzheimer's and UTI(Urinary tract infection). He has recently assaulted staff and they are concerned.
2. 65 yr. old man with Dementia, threatening to leave the home.

OLD AGE

4. BPSD- COLLATERAL HISTORY

INSTRUCTIONS TO THE CANDIDATE
You have been asked to see Mr Barrett's son, who is concerned about his father. He has been told that his father was prescribed Olanzapine. He has read some information that this can cause falls in elderly and should not be used. He wants to discuss this with you.

TASK FOR THE CANDIDATE
- *Address the son's concerns.*
- *Discuss his father's management.*

PAY PARTICULAR ATTENTION TO THE FOLLOWING (MENTAL CHECKLIST)
- *Explain the rationale for prescribing antipsychotics in Dementia.*
- *Explain risk/benefit approach to treating his father.*
- *Explain National institute of clinical excellence NICE guidelines recommendations of pharmacological and non-pharmacological management in treatment of Dementia.*

COMMUNICATION SKILLS
- *Start the interview by developing rapport and showing empathy.*
- *Anticipate a concerned and angry relative.*
- *Suggest also reviewing his father if necessary.*

Suggested approach
Introduction
C: Hello, I'm Dr...I'm one of the psychiatrists. I've come to talk to you about your father's condition and treatment. I can understand that this must be a difficult time for you.

S: Why did you prescribe this treatment for my dad? I have read about it and it can be dangerous.

C: I can appreciate you are clearly upset about this. I would like to try and explain more about the condition for which we are treating him and reasons why this was prescribed.

S: What is Dementia?

C: As you know, your father has Dementia. It is a disorder which affects the brain in three main domains namely cognitive, functional and behavioural.

The cognitive aspects are to do with a person's intellect and memory. The functional aspects are to do with managing with day to day tasks for example washing and dressing. The behavioural aspects are the increased aggression and agitation, which are the more difficult ones to treat.

OLD AGE

There was a situation in which there was a risk to both your dad and someone else. Despite staff attempts to manage his behaviour, this continued to be a concern. He was therefore prescribed the Olanzapine as a temporary measure.

Medication is usually reserved for severe cases where there is a risk to the patient or other people.

S: I have read that the medication my father is on can cause strokes.

C: You are quite right; we are aware of this and usually weigh the risks and benefits. There are some treatments used in Dementia that have some benefit. Antipsychotics have a proven risk and a proven benefit.

All drugs have risks, and the antipsychotics in Dementia have clearly established risks.

Other side effects to mention
Like all medication, they do have side effects. The more common side effects are drowsiness and weight gain. Less common ones are constipation, dry mouth, peripheral oedema and postural hypotension.

We usually weigh the risks and benefits when treating. We will make sure that we monitor this and do regular blood testing. [It can also cause metabolic syndrome which is characterised by weight gain, Diabetes, raised cholesterol]

S: How long will he need to be on this medication for?

C: In my opinion the antipsychotic drugs do help although there is this risk. When we start the medication, we would review regularly and stop the medication if it has not been of benefit or the problem has subsided. We would also monitor his heart with a tracing. We usually prescribe this medication as a temporary measure.

S: My father appears to be sedated?

C: Olanzapine can cause that, and I will assess him once we have had our talk, as you are concerned.

Apart from medication, there are other forms of the treatment which are: [non pharmacological methods] I would like to tell you about them. Is that all right?

- Aromatherapy
- reminiscence therapy
- music therapy
- art therapy
- Reality orientation.

- *Others to mention are bright light, dementia care mapping, and validation therapy.*

Leaflets and information
I have some leaflets and more information for you. Please feel free to come and see me again if you need to discuss this further.

Thank you for your time

BPSD-BEHAVIOURAL AND PSYCHOLOGICAL SYMPTOMS IN DEMENTIA (BPSD)
NICE GUIDELINES

Non pharmacological
Sensory stimulation
- Music therapy
- aromatherapy
- Bright light therapy
- Massage/touch
- White noise

Behavioural management
- Differential reinforcement
- Stimulus control

Social contact
- One to one interaction
- Pet therapy-Pat a dog
- Simulated contact eg videos

Exercise
Structured activity programs
Environmental modifications
- Wandering areas

Carer education and support
Combining therapies

©Smartsesh

OLD AGE

5. WANDERING

INSTRUCTIONS TO THE CANDIDATE
You have been informed about Robert Briggs, a 67 yr old man, who
wandered to the local shop and was picked up by the police,. You are
about to see his daughter Sarah.

TASK FOR THE CANDIDATE
- Conduct and assessment of his wandering behaviour and a risk
  Assessment.

**PAY PARTICULAR ATTENTION TO THE FOLLOWING (MENTAL
CHECKLIST)**
- Establish history of presenting complaint (onset, duration,
  progression and severity.)
- Establish underlying cognitive symptoms.
- Conduct a risk assessment.
- Highlight the need for an assessment of needs.
- Assess the possibility of a residential care placement.

COMMUNICATION SKILLS
- Start the interview by developing rapport and showing empathy.
- Show sensitivity.

Suggested approach
Introduction
C: Hello, I'm Dr ......a psychiatrists working in this hospital.
I have been informed that your father was found wandering and brought in
by the police. Can you tell me a bit more about this?

**A. History of Presenting Complaint (HOPC) (onset, duration, progression
and severity)**
- Do you know why he was wandering?
- Has this happened before?
- Has he lost his way home before? How did he get back home?
- Has he ever left the house at unusual times?
- Do you know if he is he aware of his surroundings?
- Do you know if he was looking for something or someone?
- Do you know whether he is in any pain?

B. Enquire about symptoms in each of the following domains
- Cognitive
- Behavioural
- Biological –evidence of physical ill health like urinary tract
  information or head injury
- Psychological
- Activities of daily living(ADL)

OLD AGE

C. Risk Assessment
When conducting a risk assessment it is important to consider the following risks in an elderly person

Self-harm
- Has he ever expressed thoughts of wanting to harm himself?(suicidal thoughts)

Self-neglect
- Is he eating?
- Is he taking care of himself?

Susceptibility to illness
- Has he had any infections recently?(urinary tract infection)

Aggression
- Have there been any changes in his behaviour?

Wandering
- Has he had difficulty finding his way home?

Fire
- Does he leave the cooker on?   Does he smoke?

Falls
- Has he had any recent falls?

Exploitation
- Have people taken advantage of him?

Non compliance
- Is he taking his medication?

Driving
- Does he drive?

Drugs and Alcohol
- Does he drink? If Yes then ask CAGE questions

Recapitulate
It seems from what you have told me, there are some risks. We usually advise the following precautions
- Carry Identity bracelet
- Notify local shops /neighbours
- Notify local police
- Door pendant alarm

OLD AGE

Summarize
Thank you for talking to me
From what you have described, I know that this must be a difficult time for you and you are concerned about your father. There appears to be some risks of your father staying on his own. I think that we would need to do an assessment of needs which is usually done by the social worker. We would also need to consider level of care required which could range from increased home and day care to suitable residential care placement.

RISK ASSESSMENT PNEUMONIC-SAWFEND
- *Self-harm*
- *Self-neglect*
- *Susceptibility to illness*
- *Aggression*
- *Wandering*
- *Fire*
- *Falls*
- *Exploitation*
- *Non compliance*
- *Driving/Road sense*
- *Drugs and Alcohol*

©*Smartsesh*

POSSIBLE VARIATIONS OF THEME
1.67 yr. old lady who is known with Alzheimer's Dementia, in a residential home who is wandering and attempting to leave.
2.68 yr. old man with Alzheimer's Dementia, living at home, and he wandered away from home and went on a train to his birth place.

OLD AGE

6. VASCULAR DEMENTIA

INSTRUCTION TO CANDIDATE
You have been asked to see Rose, wife of Robert Jacobs a 60 yr old man who has recently had a stroke. She has been concerned about his memory.

TASK FOR THE CANDIDATE
- *Elicit collateral history.*

PAY PARTICULAR ATTENTION TO THE FOLLOWING (MENTAL CHECKLIST)
- *Establish HOPC (onset, duration, progression, severity).*
- *Establish details of the CVA Cerebrovascular accident*
- *Establish core criteria for Vascular Dementia*
- *Establish the cardiovascular risk factors.*
- *Conduct a risk assessment.*

COMMUNICATION SKILLS
- *Start the interview by developing rapport and showing empathy.*
- *Show sensitivity.*

Suggested approach
Introduction
C: Hello, I'm Dr...I am one of the psychiatrists. I understand that you have been concerned about your husband's memory of late. Would you like to tell me more about this?

W: Yes, I know he is just not the same since he had the stroke 4 months ago.

A. History of Presenting Complaint (HOPC) (onset, duration, progression and severity)
C: It would be helpful if you could tell me a bit more about your concerns?
- *When did you first notice anything wrong?(gradual/insidious onset)*
- *What did you first notice?*
- *Have there been memory problems?(establish fluctuating course)*
- *Can you give any examples?*
- *What has happened since then?*
- *Have there been any sudden changes?*

B. Establish details of the stroke/TIA Transient Ischemic attack
- *Can I know the details of the stroke/TIA?*
- *Do you know what were the results of his CT scan or MRI scan of the brain? (Evidence on CT/MRI of stroke)*
- *Has he had any mobility problems? (Gait disorders)*
- *Has he had any falls? (Fall)*
- *What treatment has he received thus far?*

- *Has there been any improvement?*
- *Is he incontinent? (Incontinence)*

C. Establish risk *factors for cardiovascular disease:*
- *Hypertension, smoking, diabetes, high cholesterol and heart disease*

In assessing the following
- *establish an acute onset*
- *typically fluctuating course and step wise progression*
- *deficits in executive function rather than short-term memory or language*
- *Patchy preservation of some cortical functions*

D. Amnesia
Short term memory
- *Does he tend to repeat himself?*
- *Does he misplace things?*
- *Does he remember appointments or important dates?*

Long term Memory
- *Can he remember things from a few years ago?*

Lack of visuo-spatial awareness
- *Is he able to find his way home?*

Orientation
- *Are there times when he doesn't know where he is or what time it is?*

E. Agnosia/Visuospatial
- *Does he know who you are?*
- *Is he able to recognise people?*
- *What about people he is less familiar with?*
- *What about close family members?*

F. Aphasia
- *Are there times that he has heard you but hasn't understood you?*
- *Does he have difficulty finding the right words?*

G. Apraxia
If he has had a stroke, establish level of impairment which would have an impact
- *Does he need help with dressing and washing?*
- *Is he able to go shopping and bring back the right things?*
- *Does he manage his own finances?*
- *Can he manage his bank account?*
- *Can he pay his own bills?*

H. Attention and concentration
- *Is he able to concentrate on reading or television?*

OLD AGE

I. Executive functioning
- Can he complete a complicated task?
- For example make a cup of tea?
- Is he able to prepare a meal?

J. Judgement and insight
- Does he drive?
- Do you have any concerns about judgement when driving?

K. Mood
- How has he appeared in himself?
- Have you noticed any changes from extreme happiness to being tearful? (Emotional incontinence)
- Screen for depressive symptoms if necessary

L. Personality changes
- How would you describe your husband before this?
- How would you say he has changed?

M. Differential diagnosis (Lewy body/ Frontotemporal Dementia)
- Has there been at the same time sudden worsening?
- Has he ever seen things that other people can't see, for example children or animals?
- How much does the condition vary from day to day?
- Has there been a change of personality?
- Does he sometimes do inappropriate things that he wouldn't have done before?
- Is he rude or aggressive?

Summarise
Thank you for talking to me. From what you have told me, it appears that since the stroke 4 months ago, your husband has had fluctuations in his memory, and functioning. I would like to see him and do some memory tests. I have some leaflets and information which you might find useful to read

---

POSSIBLE VARIATIONS OF THEME
1. Collateral history from wife of a 76 yr old man who has history suggestive of Mixed Type Dementia-Alzheimer's and Vascular
2. History from a 65 yr old man following a stroke, now presenting as being labile.

NINDS-AIREN (International work group) diagnostic criteria:
1. Dementia.
   Cerebrovascular disease-clinical with CT/MRI evidence.
2. Dementia within 3 months of a stroke or abrupt onset or stepwise course.

OLD AGE

VASCULAR DEMENTIA
Hachinski score *<5 no abnormality detected > 6*
suggestive of vascular dementia

- *Abrupt onset*
- *Fluctuation*
- *History of stroke*
- *Focal signs*
- *Step wise progression*
- *HPT(Hypertension)*
- *Personality changes*
- *Depression*
- *Emotional incontinence*
- *Somatic*
- *ICD 10*
- *Higher cortical function memory*
- *Focal brain damage*
- *History of vascular disease*
  ©Smartsesh

F01 **Vascular dementia**
Vascular dementia is the result of infarction of the brain due to vascular disease, including hypertensive cerebrovascular disease. The infarcts are usually small but cumulative in their effect (i.e. repeated transient ischaemic attacks). Onset is usually in later life and can be abrupt or gradual.

Incl.
arteriosclerotic dementia

F01.0 Vascular dementia of acute onset
Usually develops rapidly after a succession of strokes from cerebrovascular thrombosis, embolism or haemorrhage. In rare cases, a single large infarction may be the cause.

F01.1 Multi-infarct dementia

A gradual onset, usually following a number of ischaemic episodes resulting in an accumulation of infarcts.

Incl.
Predominantly cortical dementia

7. VASCULAR DEMENTIA-MANAGEMENT

INSTRUCTIONS TO THE CANDIDATE
You have been asked to see the wife of Robert Jacobs who has Vascular Dementia. She wanted to find out more about his diagnosis and treatment.

TASK FOR THE CANDIDATE
- Discuss the diagnosis and management of Vascular Dementia.

PAY PARTICULAR ATTENTION TO THE FOLLOWING (MENTAL CHECKLIST)
- Explain the diagnosis of Vascular Dementia.
- Explain the aetiological factors and highlight the risk factors.
- Explain the management using a biopsychosocial approach.
- Explain the prognosis.

COMMUNICATION SKILLS
- Start the interview by developing rapport and showing empathy.
- Show sensitivity.

Suggested approach
Introduction
C: Hello, I'm Dr .... I'm one of the psychiatrists. I have seen your husband, and wanted to discuss more about his diagnosis and treatment options available.

D: What is his diagnosis?

C: Your husband has Vascular Dementia. Dementia is an umbrella term for memory problems. Vascular Dementia is caused by blocked blood vessel which affects the blood supply to the brain. This is commonly due to strokes.

It is the second commonest dementia which affects 10-20% of the elderly population. It is found predominantly in males.

W: What are the causes?

C: The causes for Vascular Dementia are strokes and there are certain risk factors associated with this. They are history of diabetes, smoking, hypertension and high cholesterol.

W: How do you make your diagnosis?

C: In order to make a diagnosis, we need to get a detailed history from the patient, collateral information from the family. We also do examinations and investigations like: physical examination, mental state examination, memory tests, blood investigations and a brain scan (CT scan or MRI scan)

OLD AGE

W: What is the treatment available?

C: Our management is using a biopsychosocial approach or holistic approach.

We usually manage in a multidisciplinary team setting. The team consists of a psychiatrist, a community psychiatric nurse, psychologist, occupational therapist, social worker and physiotherapist.

Biological interventions
Medication
There is no evidence for the use of the Anti-Dementia drugs in Vascular Dementia. We usually treat with Aspirin to prevent any further clots and strokes. We would also look at ways of managing the risk factors such as diabetes, hypertension, smoking and high cholesterol.

If he has a mixed type of Dementia which means someone who has both Vascular and Alzheimer's Dementia then we can consider the use of antidementia medication.

Psychological interventions
We can provide psychoeducation for yourself and the rest of the family to ensure proper understanding of symptoms and the ability to provide needed support.
We can also provide additional advice on how to manage the behaviours like aggression using the non-pharmacological treatments that are available. To mention they are relaxation therapy, aromatherapy reality orientation and reminiscence therapy.

Social interventions
The social aspects of care include the social worker assisting with his finances, activities and any additional support he would require. They will also introduce him to day centre to involve him in social activities. This could also mean looking at the option of for example:
there could be carers that would assist you to take care of him and also organising meals on wheels for him.
The social worker will also look at organising an assessment of needs.
The occupational therapist will do an assessment of his activity of daily living skills.
The CPN will support him in the community with monitoring how he is and also to monitor any side effects with medication.

Other practical measures are:
Zimmer frame to assist with mobility
If there is any risk of him wandering: bracelet and panic alarm.

W: What about his finances?

C: *With regards to finances there would be options of looking at lasting power of attorney (LPA) and advanced directives. A Lasting Power of Attorney is a legal document. It will allow him to appoint someone that he trusts as an 'attorney' to make decisions on his behalf. Attorneys can make decisions for him when he no longer wishes to or when he lacks the mental capacity to do so. A Lasting Power of Attorney cannot be used until it is registered with the Office of the Public Guardian.*
The term advance directive (increasingly being replaced by the term advance decision) means a statement explaining what medical treatment the individual would not want in the future, should that individual 'lack capacity' as defined by the **Mental Capacity Act** *2005.*

Summarise
Thank you for talking to me. I have explained to you that your husband has Vascular type Dementia. I have also explained more about how we will treat him and the support him in the community

In advanced cases, a care home placement might be required to ensure the safety of patient and that his needs are properly met.

I have some website addresses like Age UK and leaflets for you to read. Feel free to contact me to arrange another appointment.

Support groups and websites
<u>Help the Aged</u>
<u>Carers UK</u>
Alzheimer's Society

OLD AGE

8. VASCULAR DEMENTIA-CAPACITY

INSTRUCTIONS TO THE CANDIDATE
You have been asked to see Robert Jacobs. He has a known diagnosis of
Vascular Dementia and has been admitted into hospital. He has been
refusing to allow the carers into his home.

TASK FOR THE CANDIDATE
- Assess his capacity to consent to carers and treatment.

**PAY PARTICULAR ATTENTION TO THE FOLLOWING (MENTAL
CHECKLIST)**
- Establish his understanding and retention of the given
  information.
- Establish his understanding of the proposed procedure.
- Establish his understanding of the purpose of the procedure.
- Establish his understanding of the risks of not having them.
- Establish whether he is aware of the alternatives to the
  treatment.
- Establish whether he is able to weigh the pros and cons to come
  to a decision.
- Establish if he is able to communicate that decision.

COMMUNICATION SKILLS
- Start the interview by developing rapport and showing empathy.

Suggested approach
Introduction
C: Hello, I am Dr.... I am one of the psychiatrists. I have been asked by one
of the nurses on the ward to see you. I understand that there have been
some concerns.

P: I don't know why they say that

C: The information I have been given is that the carers came to your home
today and you did not allow the carers in the house. Why is that?

C: Mr Jacobs, I need to ask you some specific questions related to this if this
is all right with you? Before I begin ...

**A. History of presenting complaint (HOPC) (onset, duration, progression
and severity)**
- Can you tell me how it is that you have come to hospital?

B. Establish his level of self-care
- How have you been taking care of yourself for example cooking,
  feeding, chores, bathing and dressing?

- *How have you been managing with your shopping and paying of bills (Finances)*
- *How do you spend your days?*
- *How have you been taking your medication?*

C. Establish overall understanding of the problem and capacity assessment

C: I understand that your family were concerned and have asked for carers to come assist you?

- *Do you know why this is?*

Capacity assessment to include the following:

- *Establish his understanding of the proposed procedure*
- *Establish his understanding of the purpose of the procedure*
- *Establish his understanding of the risks of not having them*
- *Establish whether he is aware of the alternatives to the treatment*
- *Establish whether he is able to weigh the pros and cons to come to a decision*
- *Establish if he is able to communicate that decision*

Summarise [an example]

Thank you for talking to me. From what you have told me is that you understand that your family is concerned about you. They have asked for carers to come and see you. Despite their concerns, you have not allowed the carers in. I would like you to come and discuss this with you again and also speak to your family.

OLD AGE

9. TREATMENT RESISTANT DEPRESSION (TRD)

INSTRUCTIONS TO THE CANDIDATE
You have been asked to see Mrs Nidhi White about her husband, 67 yr old Oliver White. He has a history of treatment resistant Depression.

TASK FOR THE CANDIDATE
- *Obtain a collateral history.*

PAY PARTICULAR ATTENTION TO THE FOLLOWING (MENTAL CHECKLIST)
- *Establish history of Depression.*
- *Establish Treatment Resistant Depression (TRD).*
- *Establish severity of episodes including all treatments received using a biopsychosocial approach.*
- *Establish whether he had informal or formal admissions.*
- *Do a risk assessment focussing on any history of self-harm attempts.*

COMMUNICATION SKILLS
- *Start the interview by developing rapport and showing empathy.*
- *Show sensitivity.*

Suggested approach
Introduction
C: Hello, my name is Dr... I'm one of the psychiatrists. I have been asked to see you about your husband. I understand he has not been too well. I wanted to find out more about this.

W: Yes, he has been seeing psychiatrists for years.

C: It would be helpful, if you could tell me when he first became ill.

W: It started a while back, when he became redundant.

A. History of presenting complaint (HOPC) (onset, duration, progression, severity)
Establish details of the previous episodes
- *How would you describe how he was at the time?*

B. Medication history (dosage, duration, effects, side effects, combination treatment, compliance)
- *What treatment did he receive?*
- *How long did he take treatment for?*
- *Was he ever admitted to hospital?*
- *Were they informal or formal admissions? (Voluntary or detention under MHA). Can you tell me more about the circumstances around his admissions?*

OLD AGE

- *Did he have any psychological of talking therapy?*
- *Did he ever receive ECT (Electroconvulsive Therapy?)*
- *Did he ever have any self-harm attempts (i.e. overdose or any other forms of self-harm)*

C. Establish aetiological factors using a biopsychosocial approach
Biological
- *Consider hypothyroidism, cardiac, hypertension, diabetes*
- *Co-morbid substance misuse*

Psychological
- *Have you had any worries recently? (Psychosocial stressors)*
- *Does he have any concerns at home, work, financial?*

Social
Any social stressors
On any of these occasions did he attempt to harm himself?

Summarize
Thank you for talking to me. You have told me that your husband has been suffering with Depression for many years and has been on several different antidepressants. Despite this, he still remains depressed. It appears that he has what we call Treatment Resistant Depression. I would like to make an appointment to discuss the treatment options with you both.

POSSIBLE VARIATIONS OF THEME
1.78 yr old male, known with recurrent depressive disorder now suicidal and refusing to eat and drink.
2.67 yr old male, known with Depression, now presenting with nihilistic delusions.

10. TREATMENT RESISTANT DEPRESSION -LITHIUM AUGMENTATION

INSTRUCTIONS TO THE CANDIDATE
You have been asked to see Mr Oliver White who has a history of recurrent Depression.

TASK FOR THE CANDIDATE
- *Explain Lithium Augmentation.*

PAY PARTICULAR ATTENTION TO THE FOLLOWING (MENTAL CHECKLIST)
- *Establish refractory or treatment resistant Depression.*
- *Explain rationale for Lithium according to National institute of clinical excellence NICE guidelines.*
- *Advice on the effects, benefits, side effects, toxicity and precautions of Lithium blood level monitoring.*
- *Inform her of alternative treatment options.*

COMMUNICATION SKILLS
- *Start the interview by developing rapport and showing empathy.*
- *Anticipate that the patient will be concerned due to side effects of medication*

Introduction
Suggested approach
C: Hello, I 'm Dr...I'm one of the psychiatrists. I understand you wanted to find out more about one of medication Lithium which we wanted to start your husband on?

W: Yes. He has been on so many medications and that has not helped.

C: I can see you are concerned about your husband. Your husband has been tried on 2 different antidepressants which he has not responded to and this is what we call Treatment Resistant Depression.

The next medication in line of treatment according to the guidelines we follow is Lithium.
Have you heard about this medication before?

C: Lithium is known as a mood stabiliser and it has been shown to be effective in the treatment of mania to prevent further mood swings for Bipolar Affective Disorder. Lithium can also be used in Treatment Resistant Depressive Disorder to enhance the effects of the antidepressant medication. Treatment Resistant Depression is when a person has been on 2 or more antidepressants, and they continue to have depressive symptoms.

P: How does Lithium work?

C: The exact mechanism is uncertain, but it corrects the chemical imbalance in people who have Depression and Mania.

P: **What are the side effects?**

Shorter term
C: Like all medication, Lithium does have side effects which are variable, dose related, mild and self-limiting. Many people don't get side effects.
Some of the common side effects include slight stomach upset, feeling a sick, metallic taste and it can cause dry mouth. It can also cause you to drink more and pass more urine.

Longer term
The longer term effects include tremor, weight gain, acne or skin rash, it can cause under activity of the thyroid gland and affect the kidney function.

P: **What do we do prior to starting treatment?**

C: Before you start Lithium you will need to have a blood test to check your thyroid function and renal function to ensure that it is safe for you to have Lithium. Lithium can cause the thyroid gland to be underactive in long term use. Lithium is also passed in the urine, so we check your kidney function to ensure there is no problem with your kidney function.

We will check these bloods every 6 months. We usually monitor the level of Lithium in the body to make sure you are on the right dose. Your Lithium level will be done initially weekly and then repeated every 3 months once stabilized. We usually take the bloods 12 hours after the last dose.

P: **What happens if the Lithium level becomes high?**

C: The normal therapeutic range of the Lithium level that we aim for is 0, 6-1mmol/L. But in elderly we try to keep it between 0.4-0.6mmol/L (or at lower limit of the normal range) If the level goes above this, you might have diarrhoea; feel sick, slurred speech, tremor, unsteady gait and confusion. If this occurs, we usually advise that you have to stop your medication immediately and contact your doctor. We also advise that you drink plenty of fluids. We would need to repeat your bloods to check your level.

P: **What skin conditions does Lithium cause?**

C: Lithium can cause acne, psoriasis and eczema.

P: **Is Lithium addictive?**

C: No. There is no evidence to suggest that Lithium causes craving and people to become physically dependent on the medication.

P: **Would he be able to take his other medication with Lithium?**

OLD AGE

C: Some medication like blood pressure and diuretics or water tablets can interact with Lithium. Over the counter pain killers like ibuprofen can also increase its level, so do consult your pharmacist or doctor.

P: How long will he need to take treatment?
This will vary from person to person and also will depend on the indication of use of Lithium.

P: Can I have alcohol with Lithium?

C: There is no known interaction of Lithium with alcohol; however we do advise that you drink moderately if you are taking medication.

P: Can I drive if I am taking Lithium?

C: This will vary from person to person as a result of the Lithium on your level of alertness. You can discuss this with your doctor if you are experiencing any problems. Caution should also be taken if operating machinery.

Practical Tips:
If you are taking Lithium we advise the following because Lithium is affected by fluid in the body and salt.
- Drink plenty of water
- If you go on holiday, to a warm climate ,ensure you drink plenty of water
- Avoid a low salt diet
- Avoid the sauna
- Exercise

Information and leaflets
I know we have spoken a lot. I have some leaflets for you to read and would like to arrange to see you again to discuss your decision.

If he does decide to start the Lithium, then we have the Lithium treatment pack (purple in colour), which consists of an information booklet, Lithium Alert card and a record for the monitoring of the Lithium level.

LITHIUM
Indications: Mood stabiliser.
- Effective in the treatment and prophylaxis of mania in bipolar affective disorder.
- Augmentation for treatment resistant depressive disorder or refractory Depression
- Adjunct to antipsychotics in treatment of Schizoaffective disorder

Route: Oral tablet, dosage
- Camcolit 300mg-400mg, 1-1,5g daily
- Priadel 0, 4 to 1, 2 g

Effects/benefits Treat mania, prevent relapse

Adverse/side effects
- Short term
- Common: slight stomach upset, feeling a sick, metallic taste, dry mouth, polyuria, weight gain
- Longer term effects: include tremor, acne, under activity of the thyroid gland.
- Skin conditions: acne, psoriasis and eczema.

Alternatives
- Consider psychological treatment
- Consider alternative medication

Precautions
- Pre checks blood test to check your thyroid function TFT and renal function to ensure that it is safe for you to have Lithium.
- Repeat TFT and U+E(Urea and electrolyte) bloods every 3 months.
- Lithium level will be repeated every 3 months and is usually done 12 hours after the last dose.
- We start Lithium treatment we start with a low dose and check the level after a week, and make adjustments if necessary.

Lithium Toxicity
- Lithium level 0.8-1, if higher diarrhoea, feel sick, slurred speech, tremor, unsteady gait and confusion.

Practical Tips
- If you are taking Lithium we advise the following because Lithium is affected by fluid in the body and salt.
- Drink plenty of water
- If you go on holiday, to warm climate, ensure you drink plenty of water
- Avoid a low salt diet
- Avoid the sauna
- Exercise
- Lithium treatment pack, which consists of an **information** booklet, Lithium Alert card and a record for the monitoring of the Lithium level.

OLD AGE

11. ELECTROCONVULSIVE THERAPY -ECT

INSTRUCTIONS TO CANDIDATE
You have been asked to see this 64 yr. old gentleman Errol Brown who has been treated for Depression and he has not responded to treatment. You have been asked to explain to him about ECT.

TASK FOR THE CANDIDATE
- Explain ECT.

PAY PARTICULAR ATTENTION TO THE FOLLOWING (MENTAL CHECKLIST)
- Explain rationale for Electroconvulsive Therapy (ECT).
- Explain ECT process, indications, benefits and adverse effects.
- Explain consent issues.
- Obtain informed consent.

COMMUNICATION SKILLS
- Start the interview by developing rapport and showing empathy.
- Anticipate an individual who would be concerned about ECT in general and side effects.

Suggested approach
Introduction
C: Hello, I'm Dr .....I'm one of the psychiatrists. I understand you have been treated with two antidepressants and I think it would be helpful if you were to consider ECT. I would like to talk to you about that. Is that all right with you?

P: I don't want that. That's that shock therapy isn't it?

C: It has been known as shock therapy. I will explain this a bit more.
ECT stands for Electroconvulsive therapy. This means that when a person is asleep under general anaesthetic, a small current is sent to the brain to cause a fit.

P: Why do you use ECT?

C: It is helpful in people who suffer from severe Depression, in whom medication has not proved effective. It is also useful in people where there are serious concerns of physical health because of poor dietary intake if someone has Depression.

P: How does it work?

C: During ECT, a small electric current is passed across your brain. This current causes a fit which has scientific evidence to affect the parts of the brain responsible for our mood, sleep, appetite and your thinking. As a result it is thought to affect the chemical imbalance found in Depression, and normalises them.

OLD AGE

P: How effective is it?

C: At least 7 out of 10 people respond well to ECT. People who have been severely depressed and respond to ECT, find they look forward to the future, and find themselves able to make a good recovery.

P: What are the side effects?

C: The side effects are usually mild and short lasting. Some people experience nausea, headache and muscle pains. Some feel a bit confused for a short while, however this usually wears off.

P: What is the risk of dying?

C: There is a very small risk of dying which is less than if you are having a tooth extraction under general anaesthetic. This risk is 1 in 50 000. Prior to you having the procedure, we will do a detailed physical examination, blood tests and a heart tracing to ensure that it is safe for you to undergo this procedure.

P: Will it affect my memory?

C: The memory problems related to side effects are mostly mild and transient or short lived. You might have difficulty with memory in recognising familiar people. This is usually temporary and most people report this clearing up. There is insufficient evidence to say the longer term effects of memory problems.

P: What happens prior to ECT?

C: You will be seen by an anaesthetist prior to the procedure. You will have to fast overnight. On the morning of the ECT you will be taken to the ECT suite. You will be seen by an anaesthetist, psychiatrist and a nurse.

P: What happens on the day?

C: The anaesthetist will give you an injection to make you sleep and a muscle relaxant. You will be asked to breathe oxygen while some equipment is attached to monitor your blood pressure, heart tracing and brain waves. Once you are asleep 2 electrodes will be placed on your head. A small current will be passed across your head using a machine. This will cause you to have a fit for less than a minute, which, because you are asleep, you will not remember.

Once the anaesthetics wear off, you will regain consciousness and begin to feel a bit fuzzy. You will be taken to the recovery area, and one of the staff will accompany you back to the ward.

OLD AGE

P: What if I don't want to have ECT?

C: We usually hope that you will give informed consent to the procedure by providing you with the information on the procedure, the benefits, side effects and risks.

You can withdraw your consent at any time. We can also suggest alternative treatments such as the psychological or talking treatments and the option of reviewing your medication.
In life threatening conditions we would have to seek the advice from a (SOAD) Second Opinion Doctor and use the Mental Health Act (MHA 1983).

Summarise
Mr Brown, thank you for talking to me. To summarise what we have discussed today is that I have told you more about ECT. I would like you to consider this and will make arrangements to come and see you later about your decision. If you wish you could discuss this with your relative.

Support groups and websites
Royal College of Psychiatrists-www.rcpsych.ac.uk

ECT-ELECTROCONVULSIVE THERAPY NATURE -
Treatment/intervention
Purpose
- *NICE recommendations for severe depressive disorder with life threatening consequences and psychomotor retardation.*
- *ECT given unilateral/bilateral*
- *6-12 treatments twice a week*

Effects/benefits
- *70-75 %treatment response*
- *Improvement in depressive symptoms*

Adverse/side effects
- *Confusion, headaches,*
- *Temporary retrograde and anterograde amnesia, more with bilateral*

Precautions
- *Mortality risk is 1 in 50 000 due to general anaesthetic, same as if getting tooth extraction under general anaesthetic*

Alternatives
- *Psychological treatment with alternative antidepressant*

Smartsesh©

OLD AGE

12. FRONTO-TEMPORAL -DEMENTIA

INSTRUCTIONS TO THE CANDIDATE
You have been asked to see Meera Krishna who is the wife of 60 yr old Raj. Her husband was brought to hospital after he was suicidal and attempted to jump from a bridge.

TASK FOR THE CANDIDATE
- Elicit a history of presenting complaint.

PAY PARTICULAR ATTENTION TO THE FOLLOWING (MENTAL CHECKLIST)
- Establish the history of presenting complaint.
- Establish premorbid personality.
- Establish changes specifically for frontal lobe changes.
- Identify the changes in the following domains: Personality changes, Behaviour, Cognitive, Psychiatric.
- Conduct a risk assessment.

COMMUNICATION SKILLS
- Start the interview by developing rapport and showing empathy.
- Show sensitivity when discussing her husband.
- Anticipate and emotional response.

Suggested approach
Introduction
Hello, I'm Dr ....I'm one of the psychiatrists. Thank you for coming to see me. I understand you have been concerned about the recent change in your husband's behaviour. Can you tell me more about your concerns?

P: He's not the same...

C: I can see you are clearly concerned about your husband. I gather, that you have noticed a change in his personality. Can you tell me when did this all start? (Onset)
- Can you tell me more about what happened?

A. History of Presenting Complaint (HOPC) (onset, duration, progression, severity)
- What are the changes you noticed first? (Changes)
- How is he now? (Progression)
- How has this progressed? Is it gradual or sudden?

B. Premorbid personality
- How would you describe him before all of this?

C. Personality changes

- *Has he done anything that was embarrassing? (Prankish behaviour)*
- *Has he done anything sexually inappropriate? (Disinhibited behaviour)*
- *How does he spend his day? (Level of activity of daily living (ADL functioning)*
- *Is he able to plan his day? (Planning and organising)*
- *How is his level of self-care? Does he need prompting? (Apathy)*

D. Behaviour
- *Has he been aggressive or agitated? (Aggression)*
- *Has he appeared easily annoyed?*
- *Has he expressed this in any way? (Verbal and physical aggression)*
- *Has he done anything on the spur of the moment? (Impulsive)*
- *Has he had any repetitive movements? (Stereotypes)*

E. Cognitive
- *How has his memory been?*
- *Have you noticed him being forgetful? (Amnesia)*
- *Can you give me some examples?*
- *How is he able to communicate? Has he been repetitive? (Echolalia, later Mutism)*

F. Psychiatric
- *How is his mood? (Depressed)*
- *Has he appeared tearful? (Labile)*
- *Has he had any concerns for his physical health? (Hypochondriasis)*
- *Has he appeared anxious? (Anxiety)*

G. Risk assessment
- *Has he expressed any thoughts of wanting to end it all? (Suicidal thoughts)*
- *Has he expressed thoughts of wanting to harm anyone else? (Homicidal thoughts)*

H. Past psychiatric history
- *Has he ever seen a psychiatrist in the past?*

I. Personal and family history
- *Is there anyone in the family that has any similar problems?*

J. Medical History
- *How is his physical health?*

K. Medication
- *Is he on any regular medication?*

L. Elicit if appropriate Forensic, Psychosexual and Social history

OLD AGE

Summary
Thank you for talking to me. To summarise, you have been concerned about husband. You have noticed some changes in his personality and his behaviour in that he has become more aggressive. He spends his day in front of the TV and this is a noticeable change.

I would like to see him and do some further investigations that would pinpoint a cause for these changes. Do you have any questions for me?

OLD AGE

13. FRONTAL LOBE TESTS

INSTRUCTIONS TO THE CANDIDATE
You have been asked to see this Raj Krishna. You have spoken to his wife about the recent changes in his personality.

TASK FOR THE CANDIDATE
- *Please do a frontal lobe test examination.*

PAY PARTICULAR ATTENTION TO THE FOLLOWING (MENTAL CHECKLIST)
- *Assessment of verbal fluency*
  -F, A, S.
- *Assessment of abstract thinking*
  -Proverb testing
  -Similarities and differences
  -Cognitive estimates
- *Assessment of response inhibition and set shifting*
  -Luria motor test
  -Alternate sequencing
  -No don't go test
  -Perseveration
- *Frontal lobe test release signs*
  -Primitive reflexes

COMMUNICATION SKILLS
- *Obtain consent.*
- *Ask if a chaperone is required.*
- *Anticipate that person could be disinhibited and easily distracted.*

Suggested approach
Introduction
C: Hello, I'm Dr .....I'm one of the psychiatrists.
I would like to do some tests with for your memory. Is that all right with you?
Please feel free to interrupt me if you are unable to understand me.
Would you perhaps like a chaperone?

A. Assessment of Verbal Fluency
FAS test
Judges ability to generate categorical lists

Ask the patient to lists words beginning with letter F in one minute. Same with letter A and S. Normal adult should be able to list 15 words/letter in one minute. Total FAS words > 30.
For elderly 10 words/letter/minute is acceptable.

You can also use categories namely animals, fruits)
Can you name as many animals in one minute?

OLD AGE

B. Assessment of abstract thinking
1) Proverb interpretation
Can you explain what is meant by these proverbs?
'Too many cooks spoil the broth'
'Don't judge a book by its cover'
'A stitch in time saves nine?'

2) Similarities and Differences
Can you explain the similarities and differences between?
'Apple and orange'
'Table and chair'

3) Assessment of Cognitive estimates
What is the height of an average English woman?
How many camels are there in Holland or England?
How high is a double decker bus?

C. Assessment of Response inhibition and set shifting
Co-ordinated movements.

1) Luria motor test-Three step test
Motor sequencing:
Luria's three -step test. Tell the patient that you are going to show them a series of hand movements. Demonstrate fist, edge and palm five times on your leg without verbal prompts. Ask the patient to repeat the sequence.

2) Go no go test:
Ask the patient to place a hand on the table. Tap under the table. Tell the patient to raise one finger when you tap once and not to raise the finger when you tap twice. Show the patient how it's done and then do the test.

3) Alternate sequences
Can you continue this please?   ----/\----/\-----

4) Perseveration
Observe any repetition of particular responses

D. Examination
Primitive reflexes
Grasp: Stroke patient's palm from radial to ulnar side. Patient will grasp your other hand.
Pout: Stroke the philtrum or tap a spatula placed over lips.
Palmomental: Stroke patient's thenar eminence and the patient will wince.

OLD AGE

E. Neurological test:
Check for anosmia (olfactory nerve involvement)
Expressive dysphasia (Broca's area involvement

Summarize
Thank you for cooperating with me. From my assessment I would like to do some further tests which could explain the reason for the recent changes in your behaviour.

FRONTAL LOBE TESTING
Naming
- *Verbal fluency*
- *Proverb testing*
- *Similarities and differences*
- *Cognitive estimates*

Doing
- *Go no -go-test*
- *Luria motor test*

Copying
- *Alternate sequence*

Examine
- *Primitive reflexes*
- *Glabellar tap*
- *Grasp reflex*
- *Palmomental*
- *pouting*

Smartsesh®

OLD AGE

14. DEMENTIA- LEWY BODY DEMENTIA- COLLATERAL HISTORY

INSTRUCTIONS TO THE CANDIDATE
You have been asked to see Mr Roger Temple's daughter Fiona. She wants to know more about her father's diagnosis of Lewy Body Dementia.

TASK FOR THE CANDIDATE
- *Explain his diagnosis and management.*

PAY PARTICULAR ATTENTION TO THE FOLLOWING (MENTAL CHECKLIST)
- *Explain the diagnosis of Lewy body Dementia.*
- *Differentiate between Lewy Body Dementia and Dementia of Parkinson's disease.*
- *Explain the DAT scan.*
- *Explain the management using a biopsychosocial approach.*

COMMUNICATION SKILLS
- *Start the interview by developing rapport and showing empathy.*
- *Show sensitivity.*

Suggested approach
Introduction
C: Hello, I'm one of the psychiatrists. I understand that you wanted to find out more about your fathers diagnosis of Lewy Body Dementia and how we are treating him?

D: Hello, yes they have told us he has Lewy body Dementia. I don't know much about this.

C: Let me explain. Please feel free to interrupt me if you do not understand me.

Lewy Body is one of the types of Dementia and it has 3 classic symptoms which are falls, fluctuating cognition and visual hallucinations.

Dementia as you might be aware is a generic term used for people with memory problems.

D: I have heard also about Parkinson's Dementia. Is that the same thing as Lewy body dementia?

C: No. Dementia in Lewy Body (DLB) is a type of dementia that shares characteristics with both Alzheimer's and Parkinson's disease. If the motor symptoms or Parkinson's symptoms occur a year prior to memory symptoms, then it is called Dementia in Parkinson's disease.

D: I understand that my father had to go for a DAT scan. What is that?

C: Yes, the DAT scan is a type of scan used to differentiate between Alzheimer's and Lewy body dementia. However, the DAT scan is unable to differentiate Dementia in Lewy Body and Parkinson's Dementia.

D: So how are you going to treat my father?

C: The treatment is a combination of medication, psychological, behaviour and social treatment.

Biological interventions

We usually advise that we would need to be aware of the risk of falls Also that if necessary we would need to consider ambulatory aids (Zimmer frame, walking stick). We will also monitor fluctuation in consciousness and manage accordingly

Medication:

In terms of medication used in treatment of Lewy Body Dementia, we use a balanced approach or 'watchful waiting'. One of the reasons is the sensitivity to antipsychotic or neuroleptic medication.

- Rivastigmine-it is an antidementia medication which is licensed in the use of Dementia in Lewy Body.
- Quetiapine
- L dopa can cause hallucinations
- Antipsychotics-sensitivity to neuroleptics

Psychological interventions

We advise families of ways to manage distressing hallucinations.

Social interventions

We would get the social worker to assist Support
Psychoeducation
Head gear

Non pharmacological

- Aromatherapy for agitation
- Reminiscence therapy
- Reality orientation

Summarise

Thank you for talking to me. I have spoken to you more about your father's diagnosis of Lewy Body Dementia and how we will be treating him. I have some leaflets and information which you will have to read.

OLD AGE

ANTIDEMENTIA DRUGS- Mechanism : anticholinesterase inhibitors	SIDE EFFECTS
1 Donepezil Hydrochloride Aricept ®(Esai) *Mild to moderate Dementia* *Initially 5mg od at bedtime* *Increased to maximum 10 mg*	**Very Common:** *Nausea, loss of appetite , diarrhoea, dizziness* **Common:** *Muscle cramps, tiredness, increased sweating, insomnia, agitation, , tremor, urinary incontinence and headaches* **Rare:** *Cardiac irregularities, hallucinations, gastric ulcers, rash*
2 Rivastigmine Exelon®(Novartis) *Mild to moderate Alzheimer's or Parkinson's Disease Dementia* *Initially 1.5 mg bd increased by i.5mg at 2 week interval* *Maximum 3-6mg bd*	**Common:** *Nausea, vomiting, diarrhoea, dyspepsia, anorexia, weight loos, increased salivation, abdominal pain, bradycardia, dizziness, drowsiness, headache, Worsening of Parkinson's symptoms(EPSE's)* **Less common:** *Atrial fibrillation, AV block, Depression* **Rare:** *Gastric and duodenal ulceration*
3 Galantamine Reminyl ®(Shire) *Mild to moderate Alzheimer's Dementia* *Initially 4mg bd for 4 weeks* *8mg bd for 4 weeks* *Maintenance 8-12mg*	**Common:** *Nausea, vomiting, abdominal pain, diarrhoea, dyspepsia, anorexia, weight loss, bradycardia, hypertension, syncope* **Less common:** *AV block, hypotension,* **Rare:** *hepatitis, seizures, exacerbation of Parkinson's*
4 Memantine Ebixa®(Lundbeck) **NMDA antagonist** *Moderate to severe Alzheimer's disease* *Initially 5mg od increased in steps of 5mg weekly up to maximum 20mg od*	**Common:** *Constipation, hypertension, headache, dyspnoea, dizziness, drowsiness,* **Less common:** *Vomiting, thrombosis, heart failure, confusion* **Rare:** *seizures, pancreatitis*

OLD AGE

15. ALZHEIMERS DEMENTIA

INSTRUCTIONS TO THE CANDIDATE
You have been asked to obtain collateral history from Mr Barker, who is the son of a 67 yr. old man who has recently had some memory difficulties.

TASK FOR THE CANDIDATE
- *Elicit Collateral History to with a view of a diagnosis.*

PAY PARTICULAR ATTENTION TO THE FOLLOWING (MENTAL CHECKLIST)
- *Establish HOPC (onset, duration, progression and severity).*
- *Establish core criteria for Dementia.*
- *Establish the presence of the 4 A'S (Amnesia, Agnosia, Aphasia, Apraxia).*
- *Establish aetiological factors using a biopsychosocial approach.*
- *Conduct a risk assessment.*

COMMUNICATION SKILLS
- *Start the interview by developing rapport and showing empathy.*

Suggested approach
Introduction
C: Hello, I'm Dr .....I'm one of the psychiatrists. I gather that you must be concerned about your father. His GP has informed me that the family has recently noticed that he is having some memory difficulties. Sometimes, as part of our assessment we need to get more information from family in order to understand what could be wrong with him. It would therefore be helpful if you could tell me a bit more about these memory difficulties?

S: My dad is just forgetful. At first we didn't think much of it, but it seems to be getting worse of late.

C: Can you tell me more about what you have noticed?

A. History of Presenting Complaint (HOPC) (onset, duration, progression and severity)
- *When did you first notice anything wrong? (Onset and duration)*
- *Can you give me some examples of his memory difficulties?*
- *What has happened since then? (Progression)*
- *Have there been any other sudden changes?*

B. Amnesia
Short term memory (STM)
- *Does he tend to repeat himself?*
- *Does he misplace things?*
- *Does he remember appointments or important dates?*

C. Long term Memory
- *Can he remember things from a few years ago?*

D. Orientation
- *Are there times when he doesn't know where he is or what time it is?*
- *Are there times when you have noticed that he is confused? (Episodes of confusion)*

E. Agnosia/Visuospatial
- *Does he know who you are?*
- *Is he able to recognise people? (Prosopagnosia)*
- *What about people he is less familiar with?*
- *What about close family members?*

F. Visuo spatial awareness
- *Is he able to find his way home?*
- *Is he aware of his surroundings?*

G. Aphasia
- *Are there times that he has heard you but hasn't understood you?*
- *Does he have difficulty finding the right words? (Nominal dysphasia)*

H. Apraxia
- *Does he need help with dressing and washing? (Dressing dyspraxia)*
- *Is he able to go shopping and bring back the right things? (Activity of daily living skills)*
- *Does he manage his own finances? (Finances)*
- *Can he manage his bank account?*
- *Can he pay his own bills?*

I. Attention and concentration
- *Is he able to concentrate on reading or television?*

J. Executive functioning
- *Can he complete a complicated task?*
- *For example make a cup of tea?*
- *Is he able to prepare a meal?*

K. Judgement and insight
- *Does he drive?*
- *Do you have any concerns about judgement when driving?*

L. Differential diagnosis (exclude vascular/Lewybody/ Frontotemporal Dementia)
- *Have there been any strokes /mini strokes?*
- *Has there been any falls?*
- *Has there been at the same time sudden worsening?*
- *Has he ever seen things that other people can't see, for example children or animals?*

OLD AGE

- *How much does the condition vary from day to day?*
- *Has there been a change of personality?*
- *Does he sometimes do inappropriate things that he wouldn't have done before?*
- *Is he rude or aggressive?*

Summarise
Thank you for talking to me. It appears that your father has been experiencing some memory problems, difficulties in managing with day to day chores and in taking care of himself. He also appears to be more irritable of late and has found difficulty in getting home on one occasion. I would like to assess him and do some memory testing [MMSE and CT scan or MRI of the brain]

I have some leaflets and websites addresses which you might find useful.

ALZHEIMERS DEMENTIA –COLLATERAL HISTORY
HOPC (onset, duration, progression and severity)
Amnesia
Short term memory
- *Repetitive*
- *Misplacing*
- *Appointments and dates*

Long term Memory
- *Birthdays*
- *Lack of visuo spatial awareness*

Orientation
- *Confusion*

Agnosia-recognition of people
- *Visuospatial awareness-awareness of his surroundings*

Aphasia-*difficulty in finding the right words*
Apraxia
- *Dressing, ADL activity of daily living skills, finances, domestic*

Attention and concentration
Executive functioning
Planning, organising, *able to make a cup of tea*
Judgement and insight
Differential diagnosis:
- *Lewy Body Dementia-falls, fluctuating consciousness, visual hallucinations*
- *Vascular Dementia-history of strokes*
- *Fronto temporal Dementia –changes in personality, aggressive behaviour*

©**Smartsesh**

OLD AGE

POSSIBLE VARIATIONS OF THEME
1. You have been asked to see a 72 yr old man who has recently wandered from his house and was picked up the police.
2. You have been asked to see a 65 yr old lady who has recently been forgetful and misplacing her belongings.

ICD F00* Dementia in Alzheimer's disease (_G30.-+_)
Alzheimer's disease is a primary degenerative cerebral disease of unknown aetiology with characteristic neuropathological and neurochemical features. The disease usually has an insidious in onset and develops slowly but steadily over a period of several years.

F00.0* Dementia in Alzheimer's disease with early onset (_G30.0+_)
Dementia in Alzheimer's disease with onset before the age of 65, with a relatively rapid deteriorating course often with marked multiple disorders of the higher cortical functions.

Incl.:
Alzheimer's disease, type 2
Presenile dementia, Alzheimer's type
Primary degenerative dementia of the Alzheimer's type, presenile onset

F00.1* Dementia in Alzheimer's disease with late onset (_G30.1+_)
Dementia in Alzheimer's disease with onset after the age of 65, usually in the late 70s or thereafter. Characterised by a slow progression, with memory impairment as the principal feature.

Incl.:
Alzheimer's disease, type 1
Primary degenerative dementia of the Alzheimer's type, senile onset
Senile dementia, Alzheimer's type

F00.2* Dementia in Alzheimer's disease, atypical or mixed type (_G30.8+_)
Incl.:
Atypical dementia, Alzheimer's type

F00.9* Dementia in Alzheimer's disease, unspecified (_G30.9+_)

NICE guidelines for Alzheimer's Dementia

(Adapted from NICE guidance)
> ➤ *Alzheimer's Dementia must be diagnosed in a specialist clinic by a specialist (psychiatrists, neurologists, physicians with a special interest in care of the elderly)*
> ➤ *Carers' views at baseline must be sort.*
> ➤ *For anti-dementia medication the patient must have moderate Alzheimer's Dementia only (MMSE between 10 and 20).*
> ➤ *Cognition (MMSE), global and behavioural functioning including ADLs should be assessed at baseline and every 6 months after commencing treatment. Carers' views should be sought.*
> ➤ *The drug should be continued only while the patient's MMSE score is above 10 and their level of functioning and behavioural condition remains at a level where the drug is considered as having a worthwhile effect.*

Non pharmacological
- *Aromatherapy*
- *Reminiscence therapy*
- *Pat a dog*
- *Music therapy*
- *Art therapy*
- *Reality orientation*
- *Bright light*
- *Dementia care mapping*
- *Validation therapy*

OLD AGE

16. ALZHEIMERS DISEASE

INSTRUCTIONS TO CANDIDATE
You are asked to see Farah Dawson, the daughter of Mr Barker who has been diagnosed with Alzheimer's Dementia.

TASK FOR THE CANDIDATE
- Explain his diagnosis and management of Alzheimer's Dementia.

PAY PARTICULAR ATTENTION TO THE FOLLOWING (MENTAL CHECKLIST)
- Explain diagnosis of Alzheimer's Dementia.
- Explain the aetiological factors.
- Explain the symptoms and signs.
- Explain the management using a biopsychosocial approach.
- Explain the prognosis.

COMMUNICATION SKILLS
- Start the interview by developing rapport and empathy.
- Impart information in a breaking bad news approach.

Suggested approach
Introduction
C: Hello, I'm Dr ...I'm one the psychiatrists. I understand that you wanted to know more about your father's condition of Alzheimer's dementia. May I ask how much you have been told about his diagnosis?

D: I was told by my mother that my father has Alzheimer's, but I was also told that he has dementia. Has he got both? What is the difference?

C: I understand your concerns, and I will be happy to explain in more detail, if you so wish. Alzheimer's disease is the commonest type of dementia. Dementia is a generic term, and it consists of several types, of which Alzheimer's is one. Your father therefore has Alzheimer's type.

The significance of this diagnosis is that there is some treatment, whereas for some of the other's, there are no specific drugs for other types of Dementia.

The other difference is that usually Alzheimer's disease takes longer and is longer to progress.

D: What is Alzheimer's Dementia?

C: Dementia is a disorder which affects the brain. There are three main domains namely cognitive, functional and behavioural. The cognitive aspects are to do with a person's intellect and memory.

OLD AGE

The functional aspects are to do with managing with day to day tasks for example washing and dressing. The behavioural aspects are the increased aggression and agitation, which are the more difficult ones to treat.

Alzheimer's Dementia *is the commonest type of Dementia. It is a progressive illness with the rapid loss of brain cells.*

D: What is likely to happen when it progresses further?

C: At the moment your father is showing signs of early dementia. He forgets things. He doesn't remember appointments. With the help of your mother, he is still able to function well. If she is not around you will be worried about him generally and his wellbeing and safety.

As the disease progresses he is likely to become more forgetful. He will most probably get muddled with dates. He may not be able to manage his finances and his will for example. Sooner or later, people with this condition develop other distressing symptoms such as being suspicious, agitated and irritable. They also become depressed and sometimes psychotic too. This may result in aggression, night time disturbance. If they are living on their own, all sorts of risks are raised. E.g. cooking, nutrition, incontinence, falls.

D: What are the symptoms and signs of Alzheimer's Dementia?
C: Someone with this condition will initially become forgetful and have difficulty learning new information. You might notice they tend to misplace things or repeat themselves. Later on they have difficulty in communicating, and in completing daily tasks for example getting dressed or preparing meals.

D: What are the causes?

C: The causes for Alzheimer's Dementia are multifactorial. It has a genetic component so it can run in families. People who have Downs's syndrome are at a higher risk, as are people who have had a head injury.

The exact cause of Alzheimer's is not known why he developed this disease. There are several factors usually working together. Older age is the usually the biggest factor, which in association with other factors such as physical ill health, bereavement, alcohol consumption and history of injury to the brain, can further complicate the picture.

D: How likely is it that I can get it?

C: It does have some genetic factor but it is more so if the disease starts earlier in life. If someone develops it before 65, then the risk is 3-4 times increased, that if they developed in old age, which is less. Unfortunately there is no really genetic test available.

OLD AGE

D: How do you diagnose Alzheimer's Dementia?

C: In order to make a diagnosis of Alzheimer's Dementia, we had to take a thorough history of the main difficulties your father was experiencing. We completed a physical examination and blood investigations to exclude any medical problems that can cause memory problems. We also did some memory testing, and he was seen by our psychologist for neuropsychological testing. [MMSE, CAMCOG, CAMDEX]
Finally we did a CT scan of the brain.

D: What are the treatments available?

C: The medications that are available are called antidementia drugs which are available for mild to moderately severe Dementia. They are Donepezil, Rivastigmine, Galantamine and now Memantine.

Our trust has both the memory clinic and medication available.

D: How will this medication help him?

C: Unfortunately the medication is not a cure, however it will help to stabilise the illness. Families usually notice an improvement in memory, mood, motivation, and behaviour. It has been shown to be effective in 6 out of 10 people. It is not curative; it just delays the progression of the condition

D: How does it work?

C: In Alzheimer's dementia, there is a decrease in the chemical in the brain called acetylcholine which is responsible for memory. These medication works to normalise this chemical. (Anticholinesterase inhibitor)

We usually start treatment in the specialist or memory clinic to monitor response to medication. According to the guidelines we follow, we start medication if Mini mental state examination (MMSE) score is 10-20. Before starting treatment we will also do ADL (activity of daily living) assessments and get your view in terms of the treatment.

D: Is there anything else to be concerned about?

C: We will ensure that the medication suits him and he doesn't have a history of COAD, asthma, heart problems or kidney problems. Also find out if he is on any other medication.

D: What are the side effects?

C: Like all medication, they have side effects, however these are usually mild. It can make someone feel sick and nauseous. We therefore recommend taking it with food.

OLD AGE

D: How long will she need to take them?

C: When we start the medication, he will be reviewed in the community by the CPN, who will monitor for side effects. The medication will be reviewed at 3 months and then 6 months. We usually stop the medication if there is no good response to the medication.

D: What other treatment is available?

C: Apart from medication, there are also the psychological and social aspects of care.

There are other things that can be done to support your father and your mother as this can obviously cause her some difficulty (carer distress). In the early stages meals on wheels can be arranged. Carers can come to help them him to take medication on time. They can also ensure he is washing, dressing and having breakfast.

If he requires treatment for other conditions such as Depression, agitation and aggression, he may require treatment.

Later on as the illness progresses, and if he is unable to live independently on his own, we would need to look at alternative accommodation that are available.

I will give you some leaflets and details about age concern and the Alzheimer's disease society. Thank you for coming to see me.

Support groups and websites
Help the Aged
Carers UK

OLD AGE

17. PSYCHOTIC DEPRESSION

INSTRUCTIONS TO CANDIDATE
You are asked t see this lady, Fiona Walkman, who was brought to hospital A+E by her neighbour. She was saying she was found in her back garden trying to build a fire. She also said she was dead.

<hr>

TASK FOR THE CANDIDATE
- *Perform a mental state examination.*
- *Explore her psychotic symptoms and psychopathology.*

PAY PARTICULAR ATTENTION TO THE FOLLOWING (MENTAL CHECKLIST)
- *Establish history of presenting complaint.*
- *Elicit mental state examination.*
- *Establish the presence of Depressive symptoms.*
- *Establish the presence of Psychotic symptoms – nihilistic delusions.*
- *Establish if the delusion is primary or secondary delusional belief.*
- *Conduct a risk assessment.*

COMMUNICATION SKILLS
- *Start the interview by developing rapport and showing empathy.*
- *Seek to understand the subjective feeling of the individual.*
- *Acknowledge that she is saying she is dead.*
- *Ask her how she was before she died as this will create the opportunity to move past her belief.*

Suggested approach
Introduction
C: Hello, I'm Dr ....one of the psychiatrists. I understand that your neighbour brought you in as she was concerned about you. I have been asked to come and see you. Can you tell me what happened?

P:' I am dead...I am dead.'

C: What do you mean you are dead?

P: I am dead, I died?

C: Can you tell me what do you mean by that? How did that happen?

History of Presenting Complaint (HOPC) (onset, duration, progression and severity)
- *How do you know this?*
- *Can you describe this for me? How did you know that you died?*
- *Did you see anything or hear anything?*
- *Are you able to see now?*

OLD AGE

- *Do you have any strange tastes, smells or sensations?*
- *So may I ask how is it that you are able to talk to me?*
- *I would like to understand this. If you died, then may I know who is speaking to me now?*
- *Do you think there could be another explanation for what you are saying?*
- *How convinced are you that this is the case?*

Attempt to establish chronology of events
- *Can you tell me how you were before you died?*

Elicit core depressive symptoms
- *How were you feeling in yourself? (Mood)*
- *How was your sleep? (Biological symptoms)*
- *How were you eating?*
- *Were you able to do things you usually would do?*
- *What were your energy levels like? (Energy)*
- *Do you have any guilt feelings? (Guilty)*
- *How do you see the future?*
- *Have you had thoughts that life was not worth living? (Suicidal ideation)*
- *Did you do anything?*

Elicit psychotic symptoms
- *Were you having any strange experiences?*
- *Did you hear things that no one else could hear or see things that no one else could see?*
- *Have you had any thoughts that someone was going to harm you?*
- *Do you think there is interference with your thinking?*
- *Do you think someone is trying to control you?*
- *Are you concerned about your physical health?*

Past psychiatric history
- *Have you ever seen a psychiatrist in the past?*
- *Have you had anything similar in the past?*

Personal and family history
- *Is there anyone in the family that has any similar problems?*

Medical History
- *How has your physical health been?*

Medication
- *Are you on any regular medication?*

Risk Assessment
- *I understand you were found in your garden building a fire. Can you tell me what your intentions were?*
- *Have you had thoughts of harming anyone else? (Homicidal ideation)*

OLD AGE

- *What are your plans now?*

Summary
Thank you for talking to me. To summarise, what you have told me is that you have been feeling depressed for few weeks. At the time you were experiencing some stress at work and in your current relationship. You have also said that you have died and that you wanted to burn your body.

Insight
I am concerned about you and I think you need to stay in hospital. What do you think? [Enquire if she thinks that neither medication nor inpatient care is appropriate. Does she understand the level of risk from her depressive illness?]
I would like to meet with you again.

Thank you

POSSIBLE VARIATONS OF THEME
1.65 yr. old lady who has not been eating and drinking and says her 'insides are rotting'.
2.74 yr. old man who believes the world is coming to an end and he is responsible for this.

OLD AGE

PSYCHOTIC DEPRESSION: HISTORY
HOPC (onset, duration, progression and severity)
Attempt to establish chronology of events
Elicit core depressive symptoms
- *Mood, lack of energy, lack of interest or anhedonia, self-care*
- *Biological symptoms*
- *Appetite, weight loss, constipation, early morning awakening, worsening of morning mood*

Elicit psychotic symptoms
Nihilistic delusions, guilt, paranoid ideas
Past psychiatric history
Personal and family history
Medical History
Medication
Risk Assessment
- *Suicidal ideation*
- *Homicidal ideation*

Summary
Insight
Cotards syndrome
- *Delires de negations*
- *Psychotic Depression. Described by Jules Cotard.*
- *Depressive symptoms with nihilistic delusions.*

©Smartsesh

OLD AGE

18. INDECENT EXPOSURE

INSTRUCTIONS TO CANDIDATE
You have been asked to see Mr Graham Lewis. He is a 65 yr old man who was brought in by his wife, as there were concerns that he was found urinating in his neighbour's garden and was seen by the neighbour.

TASK TO THE CANDIDATE
- Assess him for reasons for these allegations.

PAY PARTICULAR ATTENTION TO THE FOLLOWING (MENTAL CHECKLIST)
- Establish history of presenting complaint.
- Establish his version of events.
- Establish aetiological factors using a biopsychosocial approach.
- Ask for consent to speak to his wife.
- Assess his level of insight.

COMMUNICATION SKILLS
- Start the interview by developing rapport and showing empathy.
- Anticipate that he would reluctant to acknowledge the incident that occurred.

Suggested approach
Introduction
C: Hello, I'm Dr ....I'm one of the psychiatrists. Thank you for coming to see me. I have been requested to see you by your GP had some concerns. I have been told that the neighbour has said that you exposed yourself to her. I know this is a sensitive matter, but would you be able to tell me what happened today?

P: **She just cannot mind her own business.**

C: You seem obviously annoyed by this and I know this must be difficult for you to talk about. The reason for me seeing you is that this might be out of character for you and we need to get to the bottom of this. From the information given to me, the neighbour has made a complaint that she saw you urinating in the garden. Can you please tell me your version of what occurred on that day?

History of Presenting Complaint (HOPC) (onset, duration, progression and severity)
C: May I ask what made you do that?
- Did you know your neighbour was there?
- Is this something that you usually do?
- How did you feel when you did this?
- Have you been drinking at the time?
-

- *Mr Lewis, I don't mean to be disrespectful, but because of the sensitive nature of the allegation, I need to ask if you got an erection. Did you feel any pleasure? (Arousal)*
- *Has this happened before? (Previous episodes)*
- *Do you think this will happen again?*

Thank you for cooperating with me thus far. Can you tell me what your wife has said about what happened?

Psychosexual history
- *How is the relationship with your wife?*

Establish aetiological factors using a biopsychosocial approach
- *Have you noticed any changes in yourself recently?*
- *Has your wife mentioned any changes in your behaviour?*

Differential diagnosis to consider
- *Learning disability (LD), Hypomania, Bipolar Affective Disorder (BPAD), Dementia, Depression, Head injury.*

Cognitive
- *Have you been forgetful? For example are you able to remember appointments? (Amnesia)*
- *Have you had difficulty expressing yourself?*
- *How have you been caring for yourself? (Activity of daily living functioning)*
- *How about chores around the house?*
- *Who does the finances and pays the bills? (Finances)*

Psychological
- *How have you been feeling in yourself generally? (Mood)*
- *Have you been tearful at all?*
- *How have you been sleeping? (Biological symptoms)*
- *How have you been eating?*
- *This is a routine question I usually ask, have you had any strange experiences like hearing voices or seeing things when there is no one around?*

Behaviour
- *Have you been annoyed easily? (Irritable)*
- *Have you lost your temper at all? (Aggression)*

Physical
- *How is your physical health?*
- *Are you on any regular medication?*
- *Any Diabetes Mellitus (DM), Hypertension, Epilepsy, Head injury, allergies, falls, incontinence, Urinary Tract Infection (UTI).*

OLD AGE

Forensic
- *Have you had any problems with the police?*

Past psychiatric history
- *Have you ever seen a psychiatrist in the past?*

Personal and family history
- *Is there anyone in the family that has any similar problems?*
- *Is there anyone else in your family?*
- *Is there any history of learning difficulties?*

Premorbid personality
- *How would your wife describe you as usually?*

Risk Assessment
- *Have you had thoughts that life was not worth living? (Suicidal ideation)*
- *Have you had thoughts of harming anyone else? (Homicidal ideation)*

Summary
Thank you for talking to me. I know this must not have been easy. To summarise, the neighbour has made this allegation that you have exposed yourself. Because there is a different version of events, I would need to see you again. I want to do some further tests.
would also like to speak to your wife if that is all right with you? [Consent]

OLD AGE

ELDERLY –INDECENT EXPOSURE
History of presenting complaint HOPC (onset, duration, progression and severity)
- *Enquire about the alleged incident*
- *Enquire any previous episodes*
- *Enquire if he had been taking alcohol*
- *Establish if he gained any sexual arousal/pleasure*

Psychosexual history relationship with your wife
Establish aetiological factors using a biopsychosocial approach
Differential diagnosis:
- *LD, Hypomania, SOTP, BPAD, Dementia, Depression, had injury*
- *Cognitive amnesia, aphasia, ADLS, finances*

Psychological
- *Mood, labile, biological symptoms (sleep, appetite, weight)*
- *Screen for psychotic symptoms*
- *Behaviour irritable aggression*
- *Physical health, regular medication*
- *Any DM(Diabetes Mellitus), HPT(Hypertension), Epilepsy, Head injury, allergies, falls, incontinence, UIT*

Forensic
- *Police involvement, charges and convictions*

Past psychiatric history
Personal and family history
Premorbid personality
Risk Assessment

©Smartsesh

POSSIBLE VARIATIONS OF THEME
1.65 yr. old man found being sexually inappropriate with one of the residents in the residential home.
2.66 yr old lady recently presenting with being labile, depressed and presenting with speech abnormalities.

OLD AGE

19. INDECENT EXPOSURE

> **INSTRUCTIONS TO CANDIDATE**
> You have been asked to see Carol, the wife of Mr Graham Lewis. She is concerned about her husband.
>
> **TASK FOR THE CANDIDATE**
> - Get further collateral information.
> - Discuss the management options.
>
> **PAY PARTICULAR ATTENTION TO THE FOLOWING (MENTAL CHECKLIST)**
> - Establish her version of events that occurred and neighbours allegations.
> - Establish if there have been any previous episodes or concerns.
> - Highlight the confidentiality issues if any person is at risk.
> - Establish if there have been any changes in her husband.
> - Use a biopsychosocial approach to elicit possible aetiological factors.
> - Explain the need for further investigations.
> - Explain diagnosis of Frontal lobe Dementia.
>
> **COMMUNICATION SKILLS**
> - Start the interview by developing rapport and showing empathy.
> - Seek to understand the subjective experience of the individual.
> - Anticipate a concerned wife and bear in mind the sensitive nature of presenting complaint.

Suggested approach
Introduction
C: Hello, I'm Dr ..... I'm one of the psychiatrists. I gather you must be concerned about your husband. From the information that I have been given, I understand the neighbour has made allegations about your husband urinating in the garden. Would you be able to tell me more about this?

W: I don't know what's wrong, it's not like him?

C: This is a sensitive issue I know, but I can assure you I have your husband's best interest at heart. Can you tell me what your understanding of what happened is?

History of Presenting Complaint (HOPC) - (onset, duration, progression and severity)
- Where were you when this happened?
- What did you see or hear?
- Can you tell me what your neighbour has said?
- Have you noticed any changes in his behaviour?
- Is there anything else troubling you?

OLD AGE

- *Has he done any other sexual inappropriate things?*
- *If so, can you tell me about this?*

Differential diagnosis to consider in collateral history
- *(LD, Hypomania, SOTP, BPAD, Dementia, Depression, head injury*

Cognitive
- *Have you notice him being forgetful? Can you give some examples? Is he able to remember appointments? (Amnesia)*
- *Does he have difficulty expressing himself?*
- *How has he been caring for himself? (Activities of daily living)*
- *How about chores around the house?*
- *Who does the finances and pays the bills? (Finances)*

Psychological
- *How has he been feeling in himself generally? (Mood)*
- *Have he been tearful at all? (Labiality)*
- *How has he been sleeping? (Biological symptoms)*
- *How has he been eating?*
- *This is a routine question we usually ask, have do you know if he had any strange experiences like hearing voices? Or seeing things when there is no one around?*

Behaviour
- *Has he been easily annoyed? (Irritable)*
- *Has he lost his temper? (Aggression/violence)*

Physical
- *How is his physical health?*
- *Is he on any regular medication?*
- *Any DM (Diabetes Mellitus), HPT (Hypertension), Epilepsy, Head injury, allergies, falls, incontinence, UIT.*

Forensic
- *Has he had any problems with the police?*

Past psychiatric history
- *Has he seen a psychiatrist in the past?*

Personal and family history
- *Is there anyone in the family that has any similar problems?*
- *Is there anyone else in your family?*
- *Is there any history of learning difficulties?*

Premorbid personality
- *How would your husband before all this started?*

OLD AGE

Summary
Thank you for talking to me. I know this must not be easy for you. To summarise you have told me you have noticed some changes in your husband's behaviour and personality. I would like to do some further memory tests and investigations. I think it is too early to say what is wrong, but this change in his behaviour could be due to some abnormality related to the front part of his brain.

What do you think needs to happen?

SOTP –SEX OFFENDER TREATMENT PROGRAMME
Management
Biological or medication is
- *SSRI'S or antidepressants to reduce impulsivity*
- *GNRH (gonadotropin releasing hormone) to reduce testosterone*
- *Like all medication they have side effects*

Psychological or talking therapies are
- *CBT-covert desensitization. Look at the offence cycle and victim empathy.*
- *Psychoeducation*

The social aspect of care includes
- *Support*
- *Day activities*
- *Social services*

MAPPA

©*Smartsesh*

POSSIBLE VARIATON OF THEME
1.65 year old wife of man who was found urinating in the garden .She discloses that he has been inappropriate with their granddaughter.

OLD AGE

20. ACUTE CONFUSIONAL STATE-DELIRIUM

INSTRUCTIONS TO CANDIDATE
You have been asked to see Naomi Ryan who is the daughter of a 76 yr. old man Thomas Blake who has been admitted in the medical ward for confusion.

TASK FOR THE CANDIDATE
- *Obtain a collateral history.*

PAY PARTICULAR ATTENTION TO THE FOLLOWING (MENTAL CHECKLIST)
- *Establish whether the onset is acute or chronic.*
- *Establish aetiological factors using biopsychosocial approach.*
- *Conduct a risk assessment.*
- *Convey diagnosis of Delirium and need for further investigations.*

COMMUNICATION SKILLS
- *Start interview by developing rapport and showing empathy.*
- *Shows sensitivity to carer and acknowledges the distress.*
- *Start with open questions and then closed questions.*

Suggested approach
Introduction
C: Hello, I'm Dr ....I'm one of the psychiatrists. Thank you for coming to see me. I understand that your father was admitted with sudden onset of confusion. Part of our routine assessment it is important to obtain further collateral information from the family. I would like to ask you some more information that might help us understand what has happened to him. I am sure you are concerned about him. Is that all right with you?

D: That's fine

History of Presenting Complaint (HOPC) (onset, duration, progression and severity)
Enquire about circumstances that led to admission to hospital.
- Can you describe what has happened?
- Has this happened before?(previous episodes)
- If so, how was he in between episodes?
- When did this happen?
- Elicit a history to differentiate acute from chronic confused state
- Establish level of consciousness
- Has he been aware of his surroundings (clouded consciousness)
- Are there any fluctuations in his presentation during the day as well as with day and night? (fluctuating consciousness/ sun downing)
- Has he been sensitive to his environment? (hyper arousal)
- Has he been quieter than usual or appeared subdued?
Use clustering approach to elicit symptoms in 3 main domains

OLD AGE

Cognitive impairment
- Have there been any memory problems?

Amnesia
Short term memory
- Does he tend to repeat himself? (Repetitive speech)
- Does he misplace things?
- Does he remember appointments or important dates?

Long term Memory
- Can he remember things from a few years ago?

Lack of visual spatial awareness
- Is he able to find his way home?
- Has he got lost in an unfamiliar surrounding or does he sometimes mix up his friend and family?

Orientation
- Are there times when he doesn't know where he is or what time it is?

Agnosia/Visuospatial
- Does he know who you are?
- Does he sometimes tend to mix up his friends and family?
- Is he able to recognise people?
- What about people he is less familiar with?
- What about close family members?

Aphasia
- Are there times that he has heard you but hasn't understood you?
- Does he have difficulty finding the right words?

Apraxia
- Does he need help with dressing and washing?
- Is he able to go shopping and bring back the right things?
- Does he manage his own finances?
- Can he manage his bank account?
- Can he pay his own bill?

Attention and concentration
- Is he able to concentrate on reading or television?

Executive functioning
- Can he complete a complicated task?
- For example make a cup of tea?
- Is he able to prepare a meal?

Judgement and insight
- Does he drive?
- Do you have any concerns about judgement when driving?

OLD AGE

Behavioural domain
- Has there been a change in his behaviour?
- Has there been any neither aggression nor violence?
- Has he been shouting?
- Has there been any change in his personality?
- Has he done anything inappropriate?

Psychiatric domain
- Has he appeared to be responding to hearing voices when there is no one in the room?
- Has he appeared to be seeing things when there is no one in the room?
- How has he appeared in himself?
- How has he been sleeping? How has he been eating?(biological symptoms)
- Has he been tearful?

Elicit aetiological factors using biopsychosocial approach
Biological
- Has he seen his GP recently? Has he had any recent blood investigations? Has he had any UTI (Urinary tract infection) urinary tract infections?

Psychological
- Has he ever been seen by a psychiatrist in the past?
- Is there a family history of Alzheimer's dementia or Lewy body Dementia?

Social
- Who does he live with?
- Have there been any changes to his surroundings?

Risk factors
- Enquire about the following:
- Fracture, HPT (Hypertension), DM (Diabetes Mellitus), Stroke (CVAs or TIAs, Epilepsy, Medication, Parkinson's, alcohol.

Risk Assessment
- During the interview, establish if any of the following risk factors are present.
- Self-harm/ self-neglect
- Aggression
- Wandering
- Fire
- Falls
- Exploitation
- Non-compliance with medication
- Driving

OLD AGE

Summarise

Thank you for talking to me. The information you have given me is extremely helpful. At this stage we are considering a few possibilities for your fathers' presentation. We will need to complete our assessment with a physical examination and bloods to exclude any infection. It mostly likely is an acute confusional state which we call Delirium. I would like to discuss this further with you. I have some information and leaflets for you.

POSSIBLE VARIATION OF THEME
1. 75 yr old man who has recently sustained a fracture and is now on the orthopaedic ward. He is distressed by visual hallucinations
2. 68 yr old lady known with Alzheimer's Dementia with sudden onset of confusion and hallucinations. Recently has been commenced on steroid treatment for chest problems.

ACUTE CONFUSIONAL STATE/DELIRIUM
HOPC (onset, duration, progression and severity)
Circumstances
- *Previous episodes*

Elicit history to differentiate acute from chronic confusional state
Establish level of consciousness
- *Clouded consciousness, fluctuating consciousness/ sun downing, hyper arousal*

Use clustering approach to elicit symptoms in 3 main domains
Cognitive impairment
- *Amnesia-Short term memory, Long term Memory*
- *Lack of visuo spatial awareness, Orientation, Agnosia/Visuospatial*
- *Aphasia, Apraxia*
- *Attention and concentration*
- *Executive functioning*
- *Judgement and insight*

Behavioural domain
- *Behaviour, violence, shouting, personality, inappropriate*

Psychiatric domain
- *Perceptual abnormalities- visual, auditory hallucinations*
- *Depression- mood, sleep, appetite*

Elicit aetiological factors using biopsychosocial approach
Biological: Risk factors-

- *Fracture, HPT(Hypertension), DM(Diabetes Mellitus), Stroke (CVAs or TIAs, Epilepsy, Medication, Parkinson's, alcohol, infections*

Psychological
- *diagnosis, Family history of Alzheimer's dementia or Lewy body Dementia*

Social
- *Currently living circumstances, changes in environment*
- *Risk Assessment: Self-harm/ self-neglect, Aggression, Wandering, Fire, falls, Exploitation, Non-compliance with medication, Driving*

Summarise-*Need for further bloods and investigation however diagnosis most likely Delirium*
- *Information and leaflets*

OLD AGE

21. ACUTE CONFUSIONAL STATE-DELIRIUM

INSTRUCTIONS TO CANDIDATE
Discuss the management of the 76 yr. old confused man, Thomas Blake, with the consultant.

TASK FOR THE CANDIDATE
- Discuss his management with the consultant.

PAY PARTICULAR ATTENTION TO THE FOLLOWING (MENTAL CHECKLIST)
- Give Psychiatric formulation-demographics, Circumstances of admission, relevant history.
- Consider differential diagnosis of Delirium-organic and non-organic.
- Highlight the risk issues.
- Discuss management using holistic or biopsychosocial approach.
- Show awareness of risk issues and consider possible Legal caveats.

COMMUNICATION SKILLS
- Give a clear and concise history.
- Adopt a collegiate approach.

Suggested approach
Introduction
C: Hello, I'm Dr .....I'm one of the psychiatrists on call. I have been asked to obtain collateral history for a 76 yr. old gentleman who was admitted on the medical ward with a 3 day history of acute confusional state. I wanted to discuss this with you and discuss the management plan

C: Hello, tell me more about him

A Psychiatric formulation
For example
He is a 76 yr. old man who was admitted informally with features of an acute confusional state.
Other relevant details to include are:
- Demographic data: age, occupation, marital status, living circumstances, family details and whether he has any children.
- Psychiatric assessment
He has the following relevant history:
Past psychiatric history, Personal and family history, Medical History, Medication, Drug and alcohol, Forensic, Psychosexual, Social
Risk Assessment
Mental state examination

OLD AGE

He has the following features of an acute confusional state.

Mental state examination
Inattention is very important; hallucinations, disorganised thought, level of consciousness and also comment on whether all above cognitive functions are fluctuating or not.

My differential diagnoses are:
- *Acute confusional state or Delirium.*
- *Acute confusional state superimposed on an underlying Dementia.*
- *Acute psychotic episode.*

Reasons for delirium:
Acute onset, fluctuation in level of consciousness, disorientation, incoherent speech, present of visual hallucinations and disturbance in sleep wake cycle.

Aetiological factors
In terms of biopsychosocial and predisposing, precipitating and maintaining factors are:

Organic causes
- *Drugs (digoxin, warfarin, diuretics, benzodiazepines) and alcohol, Dementia-Alzheimer's, Vascular, Lewy Body Parkinsonism, Dehydration,*
- *Epilepsy, Electrolyte imbalance*
- *Infections*
- *Recent trauma, fracture, head injury, normal pressure hydrocephalus, subdural haematoma*
- *Ischaemic-Stroke, CVA, TIA*
- *Urinary tract infection*
- *Metabolic-DKA diabetic ketoacidosis, uraemia*

Exclude functional causes
Severe Depression, Late onset Psychosis, Delusional disorder.

Management and treatment
My management plan using the holistic or biopsychosocial interventions is in my immediate management, short and longer term management is:

Immediate management
Investigations
- *Information gathering-obtain further collateral history from staff, colleagues, family and GP.*
- *To exclude an underlying medical cause.*
- *Physical examination.*

Biological
- *Urine Microscopy (mc+s).*

OLD AGE

- Bloods FBC (Full blood count), U+E (Urea and electrolyte), glucose, TFTs, LFT (Liver function tests)s, Vitamin B12 and folate, Calcium, bloods for dementia screening, blood cultures.
- Other radiological investigations chest x-ray, ECG, CT scan/ MRI.
- Screening - CAM - Confusion Assessment method (includes acute onset, inattention, disorganised thinking, and altered level of consciousness).
- Medication.

According to NICE guidelines
- General supportive / Practical measures.
- Nurse in a side room.
- Well lit room.
- Familiar staff.
- Orientation aids-clock.

Medication
- Treat the aetiological factor accordingly.
- Delirium Tremens-Chlordiazepoxide reducing regime.
- Infection -Intravenous antibiotics.
- Rehydration /fluids
- If agitation is present- consider using Haloperidol 3-15mg /d oral or im. This is a quiet high dose for elderly; we usually use 1-2 mg and maximum 5 mg at a time. We use the minimum doses and build it up gradually as elderly brain is already in a toxic condition when they have delirium.
- Avoid using Benzodiazepines as this can exacerbate the confusion.
- Dementia –treat according to the type.

Psychological interventions or talking therapies
- In the longer term part of treatment look at psychoeducation for him and the family.

Social interventions
Includes an OT assessment of ADL'S to identify safety issues and also level of independence.
The social worker to do an assessment of needs, assist with finances, carers and other support.
If there were concerns with finances and patient lacked capacity we would need to consider a LPA and have safeguards in place.
A nursing assessment of where this patient would best be placed in a nursing, residential or continuing care placement (continuing care checklist)
- Other legal aspects
- Mental Health Act(MHA 1983)
- Lasting power of attorney/enduring power of attorney
- Court of protection
- IMCA
- In planning for longer term treatment, we would use the MDT
-

OLD AGE

- *Multidisciplinary team approach. The community psychiatric nurse that will support him at home, the psychologist for psychology, occupational therapy for ADL assessments and social worker to assist him with his carers, finances.*

Prognosis
Good prognosis if detected early and treated early;
Usually associated with increased need of rehabilitation, increasing care package, increased institutionalisation

Mortality rate – increased mortality rate sometimes up to 25-30% if not detected early

OLD AGE

Delirium/Acute confusional state
Psychiatric formulation
Demographic data: *age, occupation, marital status, living circumstances, family details and whether they have any children*
Descriptive formulation
- *History of presenting complaint and events leading up to admission*
- **Psychiatric assessment**
- *He has the following relevant history*
- **Past psychiatric history, Personal and family history, Medical History, Medication, Drug and alcohol, Forensic, Psychosexual, Social**
- **Risk Assessment**
- **Mental state examination**
- *He has the following features of an acute confusional state*

My differential diagnoses are-Acute confusional state, Acute confusional state superimposed on an underlying Dementia, Acute psychotic episode
Reasons for delirium:
- *Acute onset, fluctuation in level of consciousness, disorientation, incoherent speech, present of visual hallucinations and disturbance in sleep wake cycle*

Aetiological factors biopsychosocial
Organic causes
- *Drugs (digoxin, warfarin, diuretics, benzodiazepines) and alcohol, Dementia-Alzheimer's, Vascular, Lewy Body Parkinsonism, Dehydration,*
- *Epilepsy, Electrolyte imbalance*
- *L*
- *Infections*
- *Recent trauma, fracture, head injury, normal pressure hydrocephalus, subdural haematoma*
- *Ischaemic-Stroke, CVA (, TIA*
- *Urinary tract infection*
- *Metabolic-DKA diabetic ketoacidosis, uraemia*

Exclude functional causes
Severe Depression, Late onset Psychosis, Delusional disorder
©Smartsesh

OLD AGE

References
Cambridge behavioural inventory for the diagnosis of dementia
Citation: Progress in Neurology and Psychiatry, 2008, vol./is.
12/7(23-25), 1367-7543 (2008)
Hancock P.,Larner A.J.
The Cambridge Behavioural Inventory (CBI) is a short, self-administered informant questionnaire developed to distinguish between the behavioural and psychiatric symptoms of Alzheimer's dementia and fronto-temporal dementia.

Frontotemporal lobar degeneration
Epidemiology, Pathophysiology, Diagnosis and Management
Rabinovici G.D. and Miller B.L.
CNS Drugs (2010) 24(5) 375-398.
Neary D, Snowden JS Gustafson L et al Frontotemporal lobar degeneration: a consensus on clinical diagnostic criteria Neurology 1998 51: 1546-54

Gelder, M.G, Cowen, P. and Harrison P.J (2006) Shorter Oxford textbook of psychiatry. 5th edn. Oxford: Oxford University Press.

Sims, A. C. P. (2003) Symptoms in the mind: an introduction to descriptive psychopathology. 3rd edn. Great Britain: Saunders.

Taylor, D., Paton, C., Kapur, S. (2009) The South London and Maudsley NHS Foundation Trust & Oxleas NHS Foundation Trust prescribing guidelines. 10th edn. London: Informa Healthcare.

British Medical Association and Royal Pharmaceutical society (2011), British National Formulary 62, 62 edition,British Medical Journal Publishing Group and Pharmaceutical Press

WHO. (1992)The ICD 10 classification of mental and behavioural disorders: clinical descriptions and diagnostic guideline. 10th revision: Geneva; WHO

Lishman, WA (1998) Organic psychiatry, 3rd edn.Oxford: Blackwell Science

Folstein, MF., Folstein, S, .E@ Mchugh, P.R (1975) Mini -mental state': a practical method for grading the cognitive state of patients for the clinician, Journal of psychiatric research, 2,189

Prof Sube Banerjee-report
Ballard, C., O'Brien, J., Jame, I and Swann, A (2001) Dementia: NICE guidelines for Dementia

Online resources
Royal college of psychiatrist's health information leaflets for patients

CHILD AND ADOLESCENT

CAMHS- Dr MS Thambirajah

1. Early onset Psychosis-History taking and mental state examination
2. Early onset Psychosis-discuss management with his mother
3. Early onset Psychosis-discuss management with on call consultant
4. Overdose-suicide risk assessment (trigger rape)
5. Overdose-discuss management with ward manager
6. Overdose-suicide risk assessment (precipitator Bullying)
7. Overdose-Bullying-discuss management with consultant
8. ADHD (Attention Deficit Hyperactivity Disorder) – Collateral History from mother
9. ADHD (Attention Deficit Hyperactivity Disorder) – Explain diagnosis and management to father
10. Autism –collateral history from mother
11. Autism –Explain diagnosis and management
12. Enuresis –collateral history

Dr MS Thambirajah, Dr Ken Ma, Dr Meera Roy

CHILD AND ADOLESCENT

1. EARLY ONSET PSYCHOSIS-HISTORY TAKING

INSTRUCTIONS TO CANDIDATE
You are asked to see this 16yr old Paul Banner. His GP referred him as his parents were concerned about him.

TASK FOR THE CANDIDATE
Elicit history for first episode Psychosis.

PAY PARTICULAR ATTENTION TO THE FOLLOWING (MENTAL CHECKLIST)
- *Establish HOPC (onset, duration, frequency and severity).*
- *Establish psychotic symptoms.*
- *Establish presence of Schneiderian first rank symptoms.*
- *Establish presence of negative symptoms.*
- *Conduct a risk assessment.*
- *Elicit aetiological factors using a biopsychosocial approach.*
- *Elicit past psychiatric history, personal history and family history.*

COMMUNICATION SKILLS
- *Start the interview by developing rapport and showing empathy.*
- *Seek to understand the subjective experience of the individual.*

Suggested approach
Introduction
C: Hello, I'm Dr ...I'm one of the psychiatrists. Thank you for coming to see me. I understand that your GP has referred you to see me as your parents were concerned that you were isolating yourself and losing weight. Can you tell me more about this?

P: I think 'they' are after me.

C: I can see you are clearly distressed by them. I can assure you I am here to help you. It would help if you could tell me more about who you are worried about that are after you.

A. History of Presenting Complaint (HOPC) (onset, duration, progression and severity)
C: Can you tell me why you are concerned that they are after you?
- *How do you know this is the case?*
- *Why have you come to that conclusion?*
- *Do you think there could be another explanation for what you are describing?*
- *What have your family said about this?*
- *Is there anything else that is going on or troubling you?*
- *Can you tell me when did this all start? (Onset)*

B. Then systematically explore for specific psychotic symptoms
Elicit Schneiderian FRS

- *Do you think someone is out to harm you, or poison you? (Persecutory delusions)*
- *Are you able to trust people?*
- *Do you think people are dropping hints about you? (Delusions of reference)*
- *Do you see reference to yourself in the TV/radio? (Delusions of reference)*
- *Do you feel you are in control of your thoughts?*
- *Is someone putting thoughts in, taking thoughts out or broadcasting your thoughts? (Thought insertion, withdrawal and broadcast)*
- *Do you think someone is controlling you, controlling the way you feel, controlling your actions? (Made act, made affect and made volition)*
- *Do you have any strange sensations, or feel electricity? (Somatic passivity)*

C. Negative symptoms

- *How have you been feeling in yourself? (Mood)*
- *How motivated are you when you get up in the morning? (Motivation)*
- *Are you able to enjoy things you usually would do? (Anhedonia)*
- *What are they?*
- *Have you been keeping to yourself? (Isolation)*

D. Risk Assessment

- *Have you had thoughts of wanting to end it all? (Suicidal ideation, intent or plans)*
- *Have you had thoughts of wanting to harm anyone else?*
- *(Homicidal ideation, intent or plans)*

E. Identify triggers

- *Have you been under any stress recently? (Stressor)*
- *At work, home, friends, college, relationships? How do you usually cope? Some people drink or take street drugs. How about you? (Drug and alcohol history)*
- *If yes, what have you been taking?*
- *Have you seen your GP for any physical health problems?*
- *Are you on any regular medication? (Medication)*

F. Past psychiatric history

- *Have you ever seen a psychiatrist in the past?*

G. Personal and family history

- *Is there anyone in the family that has any similar problems?*
- *Is there a family history of Schizophrenia, Bipolar Affective Disorder (BPAD) or Depression?*

H. Developmental history
- *Are you aware whether you had any complications at birth? (Perinatal history)*
- *Are you aware of whether there was a delay in any stage of your development compared to other children your age? For example delay in your speech and motor development? (Milestones)*

I. Forensic History
- *Have you been involved with the police?*

Summary
Thank you for talking to me. I know that this has not been easy for you to do. To summarise, what you have told me is that you have been suspicious about people around you and you have been having some strange experiences. You have also been taking some street drugs to cope with this. This has affected you such that you are not able to attend your lectures and you have been isolating yourself.

Insight
We do have medication and talking therapy or psychotherapy that can help. What help do you think you would like?
I would like to meet with you again. I would also like to speak to your parents to get some more information on how you have been. [consent. Is that all right with you?

Thank you

CHILD AND ADOLESCENT

POSSIBLE VARIATIONS OF THEME
1. 16 year old male brought in by parents to A+E as he was suspicious that he was being poisoned
2. 16 year old male, isolating himself and refusing to go out. He has a history of using cannabis.

EARLY ONSET PSYCHOSIS
History of presenting complaint (HOPC)-severity, onset, duration, progression
Impact on his functioning
Then explore for specific psychotic symptoms
- Elicit Shneiderian First Rank Symptoms
- Negative symptoms

Risk assessment –suicidal or homicidal risk
Identify Trigger
Past psychiatric history
Personal and family history-family history of mental illness
Developmental history-delay in motor development
Forensic history
Summarize
Consent
Insight

©Smartsesh

CHILD AND ADOLESCENT

2. EARLY ONSET PSYCHOSIS- MANAGEMENT

INSTRUCTIONS TO CANDIDATE
You have been asked to see the mother, Pamela Banner, of the 16 year old Paul whom you assessed. She is concerned about her son. Her son has given consent for you to speak to her.

TASK FOR THE CANDIDATE
Discuss the management of Schizophrenia.

PAY PARTICULAR ATTENTION TO THE FOLLOWING (MENTAL CHECKLIST)
- *Ascertain that consent has been given.*
- *Acknowledge concerns raised by mother.*
- *Explain diagnosis of Schizophrenia.*
- *Explain the possible aetiological factors.*
- *Reassure that it is not her fault.*
- *Explain management using a biopsychosocial approach.*

COMMUNICATION SKILLS
- *Start the interview by developing rapport and empathy.*
- *Anticipate that giving his mother the diagnosis is in a sense 'breaking bad news.'*

Suggested approach
Introduction
C: Hello, I'm Dr ..... I am one of the psychiatrists. I have seen your son and I know you are concerned about him. I am here to talk to you more about his diagnosis and management. Before I begin, can you tell me what your understanding is of his condition is.

M: I know he is just not the same. He has been staying at home and he has said his mates are after him. One of the nurses said he has Schizophrenia.

C: I will explain to you more about this. Please do feel free to interrupt me if you do not follow me. Schizophrenia is a relatively common illness at it usually affects the way a person thinks, feels and behaves.

Your son has become suspicious about people and has strong beliefs that they are poisoning him despite no evidence for this. This type of thinking is one of the positive symptoms called a delusion. The other positive symptom is hallucinations, when someone hears voices or sees things when there is no one else around.

The other symptoms are the negative symptoms. This means that your son will become less motivated in taking care of himself. He might also isolate himself and not want to talk to anyone.

CHILD AND ADOLESCENT

M: How common is it?

C: It occurs 1 in 100 people. It can develop in the late teens from 15-35 yrs.

M: What are the causes?

C: Like many of the diseases like Hypertension and Diabetes it is difficult to pinpoint one particular cause in your son's case. From the literature that is available it can be due to a few associated factors. It has a genetic component and can run in families. That means if someone in the family has it, then there is a 10 times increased risk of having it.

It is also due to a chemical imbalance of dopamine, Noradrenalin (NA) and serotonin (5HT). It can be caused by birth infections, and the season of birth e.g. winter months.
We know also that using street drugs like cannabis can also trigger an episode. Some people are more sensitive and vulnerable to develop the effects of cannabis and other conditions similar to **Schizophrenia.** We also know that if someone has a diagnosis of Schizophrenia that using cannabis can cause them to deteriorate.

M: Is it my fault?

C: No, it is not your fault. A lot of people in your situation do feel responsible. It's important that you understand his illness and therefore your support plays an important role in his recovery.

M: Will he get better?

C: Our aim is to get your son to lead a normal life as possible. The general rule of thumb is that about a third of people will recover completely. Another third will continue to have episodes with periods of recovery. Another third will continue to have symptoms. It's difficult to say which category he will be in.

We work in a multidisciplinary team (MDT) which consist of the psychiatrists that will look at the medication aspect. The community psychiatric nurse (CPN) that will support him at home; the psychologist for psychological therapy; the occupational therapy to assist him with vocational training and the social worker to assist him with housing and finances.

M: What are the medications available for him?

C: The medications we have are a group called antipsychotic. It works to normalise the chemical imbalance. It helps to make a person think more clearly, weaken the delusions and hallucinations and increase the motivation so that they will be able to take care of themselves.

CHILD AND ADOLESCENT

*Like all medication they have side effects. Would you like to know about that?
[Elaborate further if necessary]
The older generation or typical medication can cause stiffness, shakiness
and restlessness. (Extrapyramidal side effects-EPSEs)*

Risperidone and Olanzapine are the new generation or atypical medication.

*Olanzapine- the more common side effects are drowsiness and weight gain.
Less common ones are constipation, dry mouth, peripheral oedema and
postural hypotension.*

*It can also cause metabolic syndrome where there is raised blood pressure
glucose and cholesterol, diabetes and weight gain.
We will monitor him for these side effects and not everyone will develop these
side effects. We usually start on a low dose and gradually increase this. [also
because [neuroleptic naïve]*

M: How long will he need to continue with this medication?

*C: There is a chance if he doesn't take medication that he will relapse. We
usually advise that he would need to continue it for 1-2 years to prevent
getting unwell. Sometimes it might be the case that he does not respond to
the medication.*

Psychological interventions
*In the longer term other treatment options available are the psychological or
talking therapies called CBT or cognitive behavioural therapy for the
delusions and family therapy. This is usually done at the later stage of
treatment.*

*Another vitally important part is education about his illness, because if
people understand the illness, then this would improve their insight and
engagement with their treatment and this would also promote his recovery. It
is also important that you and the rest of the family learn more about his
illness and we could also provide some support. Relaxation therapy is
important to decrease the stress.*

*The social aspects involve that getting him to a functional level. The
Occupational therapist will maximise his potential to ensure he could possible
return to education and vocational training. We have day centre and
activities, and encourage people to volunteer at MIND.*

M: Does he need to be in hospital?

*C: We usually assess the risks and consider either admission in hospital
either voluntary or on own free will. In cases where a person doesn't want to
be admitted and if we feel it is in their best interest, we will have to use the
Mental Health Act(MHA 1983).*

CHILD AND ADOLESCENT

In later stages of care we usually involve the EIS (Early intervention team) who will be able to provide him support in the community.

Summarise
Thank you for talking to me. To summarise we have discussed more about your son's diagnosis of Schizophrenia and how we are going to be treating him. I have some leaflets for you to read. I am happy to see you again to discuss this further. Do you have any other questions?

Support group and websites
There are also these useful organisations like MIND and charities
Also these websites www have useful information

EARLY ONSET PSYCHOSIS -MANAGEMENT
Schizophrenia-common mental illness
Epidemiology: 1/100, M=F
Aetiology- genetic, environmental, viral infections, street drugs,
Biological interventions
Medication
- Antipsychotic according to National institute of clinical excellence NICE guidelines
- Atypical antipsychotic -Risperidone, Olanzapine, Aripiprazole, Quetiapine side effects metabolic syndrome, weight gain, DM(Diabetes Mellitus)
- Typical Haloperidol side effects stiffness, shakiness, restlessness

Psychological interventions
- Cognitive Behavioural Therapy (CBT) or Family Therapy.
- Psych education
- Relaxation therapy

Social interventions
- Finances
- Day centre , activities
- MIND volunteer
- Vocational services
- Long term
- Early intervention service (EIS)

©Smartsesh

CHILD AND ADOLESCENT

3. EARLY ONSET PSYCHOSIS

INSTRUCTIONS TO CANDIDATE
You have seen this 16 year old male Paul who was referred by his GP. His blood results, urine dipstick and CT scan are all normal.

TASK FOR THE CANDIDATE
- Discuss your assessment and management with the consultant on call.

PAY PARTICULAR ATTENTION TO THE FOLLOWING (MENTAL CHECKLIST)
- Give a psychiatric formulation.
- Highlight aspects of your risk assessment.
- Explain the diagnosis of Schizophrenia and possible range of differential diagnoses considered.
- Explain the management in terms of biopsychosocial approach.

COMMUNICATION SKILLS
- Adopt a collegiate approach.

Suggested approach
Introduction
C: Hello, I'm Dr ....I am the on call psychiatry doctor. I have seen this 16 yr. old male who was referred by his GP as his parents were concerned about him. I would like to present my assessment and management plan with you.

A. Brief synopsis
Psychiatric formulation
Summary
I assessed a 16 yr old college student, who is living with his parents. He is presenting with a 4 month history of paranoia, isolating himself and hearing voices with a gradual decline is his functioning. The other relevant information from his history to highlight is:

B. Elaborate further highlighting the salient features of the psychiatric assessment
He has the following relevant history
- Past psychiatric history
- Personal and family history
- Medical History
- Medication
- Drug and alcohol
- Forensic, Psychosexual, Social
- Risk Assessment

C. Comment on his mental state examination.

CHILD AND ADOLESCENT

The following FRS was present: [elaborate your findings from previous scenario]

D. My differential diagnoses are
- Schizophrenia- duration of symptoms (possible Hebephrenic type)
- Drug induced Psychosis
- Depression with psychotic symptoms

E. My management plan using the holistic or biopsychosocial approach in my immediate management, short and longer term management is:
Immediate management
To consider admission or community treatment
We would need to assess the risk and consider either admission in hospital either voluntary or on his own free will. In cases where a person doesn't want to be admitted and if we feel it is in their best interest, we will have to use the Mental Health Act (MHA 1983).
We could also consider, if the risks are not high, and after obtaining further collateral history from his parents, we could treat and support in the community with the EIS (early intervention services)

Biological interventions
Medical investigations like bloods, CT scan/MRI (done)
Medication
According to National institute of clinical excellence (NICE) guidelines, I will consider starting him on a low dose antipsychotic, bearing in mind for side effects as he would be neuroleptic naive.
The following are the atypical or new generation of antipsychotic medication.

DRUG	SIDE EFFECTS
Risperidone (Risperdal®) 4-6mg max oral/IM	**Common:** headaches, hypotension, restless or agitated and raised prolactin. **Uncommon:** Akathisia, constipation, drowsiness, insomnia, movement disorders, weight gain. **Rare:** blurred vision, NMS, Skin rashes
Olanzapine (Zyprexa®) 20mg	**Common:** drowsiness, weight gain. **Uncommon:** constipation, dry mouth, peripheral oedema, postural hypotension. **Rare:** altered liver function, photosensitivity, and metabolic syndrome.
Aripiprazole (Abilify®) 15-30mg	**Common:** Light-headedness, insomnia, Akathisia, somnolence, tremor, blurred vision, nausea and vomiting, dyspepsia, constipation, headache, asthenia. **Uncommon:** tachycardia, orthostatic hypotension.

CHILD AND ADOLESCENT

The psychological or talking therapies are
- *Cognitive behaviour therapy (CBT) - for the delusions*
- *Family therapy (FT) - to address the high expressed emotions.*
- *Psychoeducation - about the illness, relapse indicators*
- *Relaxation training*

This would also include addressing issues of high expressed emotion, compliance and addressing stigma issues.

Address substance misuse issues if present-cannabis known risk of 6 times increase with moderate use.

The social aspect of care includes
Aim of getting him to a functional level.
- *Occupational therapist will maximise his potential to ensure he could*
- *possible return to education and vocational training.*
- *Encourage day centre and activities.*
- *Encourage people to volunteer at MIND.*
- *Social worker assists with housing, and finances.*

In planning for longer term treatment, we would use the Multidisciplinary approach (MDT) approach and referral to the early intervention services. (EIS)

I would ensure that he has regular follow up in outpatients with a doctor or psychiatrist that will look at the medication. The community psychiatric nurse that will support him at home; the psychologist for psychological therapy; occupational therapy for vocational training and social worker to assist him with housing and finances.

Thank you

Other points
It is important to bear in mind if admission is considered, as of October 2010 serious untoward incident (SUI) if 16 yr old is admitted into a general adult ward.

EARLY ONSET SCHIZOPHRENIA
Biological interventions
Investigations: bloods, CT scan/MRI
Medication
- *According to NICE, start a low dose antipsychotic, bear in mind for side effects as neuroleptic naïve.*
- *Risperidone 4-6mg max oral/IM   side effects less EPSE's, PRL ,weight gain*
- *Olanzapine 20mg   side effects syndrome, DM(Diabetes Mellitus),HPT(Hypertension), Weight gain*
- *Aripiprazole 15-30mg   side effects*
- *Receptors D2 and 5HT2*

Psychological interventions-Talking therapy
- *CBT cognitive behaviour therapy*
- *FT Family therapy*
- *Psych education*
- *Relaxation training*
- *Look at high expressed emotion, compliance , stigma*
- *Address substance misuse issues if present-cannabis known risk of 6 times increased risk.*

The social interventions
- *Aim-get him to a functional level*
- *Occupational therapist- vocational training*
- *Encourage day centre and activities*
- *Encourage to volunteer at MIND*
- *Social worker to assist with finances.*

©Smartsesh

CHILD AND ADOLESCENT

4. OVERDOSE – SUICIDE RISK ASSESSMENT

> **INSTRUCTIONS TO CANDIDATE**
> You are about to see a 16 year old girl Anya Robinson who was brought to A+E by her friend. She had taken an overdose of 70 Paracetamol. Elicit a history of the overdose and perform a suicide risk assessment.
>
> **TASK FOR THE CANDIDATE**
> * Elicit a history and do a suicide risk assessment.
>
> **PAY PARTICULAR ATTENTION TO THE FOLLOWING (MENTAL CHECKLIST)**
> **Establish the overdose**
> * Establish the details of the overdose.
> * Include the following planning, preparation, precaution.
> * Identify what the current precipitator is.
> * Establish past history of Deliberate self har(DSH) and past psychiatric history.
> * Assess her mental state.
> * Conduct a thorough risk assessment.
> * Establish coping skills and support.
>
> **COMMUNICATION SKILLS**
> * Start the interview by developing rapport and showing empathy.
> * Seek to understand the subjective feeling of the individual.
> * Anticipate that she could be reluctant to disclose details of the overdose.

Suggested approach
Introduction
C: Hello, I'm Dr ....I'm one of the psychiatrists. Thank you for agreeing to see me. I understand from the doctor in A+E that you had been brought here as you had taken an overdose. I am sorry to hear that. Are you able to tell me what happened?

P: Hello

A. History of Presenting Complaint (HOPC) (onset, duration, progression and severity)

C: I know this may be difficult for you. Because of what happened I do need to ask you some questions. It will help if you can take me through the event when you took the tablets?

Para suicide
* Where were you at the time?
* What did you do?
* What tablets did you take? How many tablets? [calculate the dosage]

- *Did you take anything else with them? Did you take any alcohol?*

Degree of Preparation
- *How did you get the tablets?*

a) Planning
- *Did you plan to end it all and for how long?*
- *Has it been a spur of the moment?*

b) Suicide note
- *Did you write a note, send text messages, email, Face book, or call anyone?*

c) Last acts
- *What preparation did you do?*
- *Did you bid farewell to anyone?*
- *Have you told anyone?*

2- Circumstances of the overdose
- *When did you take the tablets?*
- *Have you been alone?*
- *What did you do to prevent anyone from finding you?*

Post suicidal attempt
- *How did you feel after taking the tablets?*
- *What did you do next?*
- *Did you make yourself sick?*
- *Did you seek help? How were you discovered?*
- *How did you get to the hospital?*
- *Do you regret that your overdose did not succeed in killing you?*
- *Do you still think about killing yourself?*
- *Is it possible that you might plan to end it all again?*

Suicidal ideation and intent
- *What was your intention?*
- *What were you thinking at the time?*
- *Did you have thoughts of wanting to end it all? Did you believe that that amount would kill you?(lethality)*

B. Current suicide risk
- *How do you see the future?*
- *Do you have thoughts of wanting to end it all?*
- *Did you believe that that amount would kill you?*

C. Precipitating factors
- *Why did you do that?*
- *What sorts of things have been troubling you?*
- *What would you say was the final straw?*

CHILD AND ADOLESCENT

- *How are things at home, school, work, college?*
- *Are you in any relationship?*

D. Recent history of Depression
- *How have you been feeling in yourself?(mood)*
- *How has your energy levels been?(energy)*
- *Have you been able to enjoy things you usually would do? (anhedonia)*
- *How have you been eating?(biological symptoms)*
- *How have you been sleeping?*

E. hopelessness
- *Do you ever feel hopeless?*
- *Do you ever feel that things will not or cannot get better?*
- *Are there times when you cannot see beyond your suffering?*
- *Did you ever wish your life would end?*

Possible scenario of alleged rape
- *I'm sorry to hear this has happened to you. I know this must be difficult to talk about.*
- *Can I ask, have you told anyone else?*
- *Do you the person who has done this?*
- *Do you know if there is anyone else at risk?*

Do not explore in detail to prevent contamination of evidence.
Thank you for sharing this with me. I know how difficult this must be for you. No person should go through anything like this. I will have to speak to my colleagues in social services who will be able to help you and to ensure your safety. Is that all right?

Relevant past psychiatric history
a-Past DSH
- *Can you tell me how you usually cope?*
- *Have you self-harmed in the past? If so, how serious was it?*

b-Past psychiatric history
- *Have you seen a psychiatrist in the past?*
- *Screen for Psychosis*
- *I should ask you routine questions which we ask of everybody? Have you had any strange experiences?*
- *Do you ever seem to hear noises or voices when there is no one around and nothing else to explain it?*

C-Personal and family history
- *Is there anyone in the family that has any similar problems?*

D-Medical History
- *How is your physical health?*

CHILD AND ADOLESCENT

E-Medication
- *Are you on any regular medication?*

F. Social history (establish social support network)
- *With whom do you live?*
- *Is there anyone you can confide in? Is there anyone you feel comfortable to share your problems with?*
- *Who is the one person that you are able to trust?*

Risk Assessment
- *How do you see the future?*
- *Do you thoughts of wanting to end it all?(suicidal thoughts)*
- *What do you think you might do?*

Summarise

Thank you for talking and opening up to me. I know that this must not have been easy. To summarise, you have taken an overdose as a result of the on-going sexual abuse. I know this is a difficult time for you. I can assure your safety and would like you to stay in hospital. I will also be calling my colleagues from social services that will be able to help you. What do you think?

OVERDOSE –SUICIDE RISK ASSESSMENT
- **History of presenting complaint(HOPC)**-severity, onset, duration, progression
- **Para suicide**
- *Preparation*
- *Preparation*
- *Planning*
- *Suicidal ideation and intent*
- *Precautions*
- *Preparatory acts*
- **Post suicidal attempt**

Precipitating factors
- **Regrets**

Past DSH-cutting, ligatures, carbon monoxide poisoning
Past psychiatric history
Personal and family history-family history of suicide
Medical History
Medication
Drug and alcohol history
Forensic, Psychosexual,
Social support-confidant
Risk Assessment-according to severity-mild, moderate, severe

©Smartsesh

CHILD AND ADOLESCENT

POSSIBLE VARIATIONS OF THEME
1. 14 yr. old girl, who took and overdose of 60 Paracetamol. Recent history of mother being admitted to psychiatric unit and she was raped by her stepfather.
2. 13 yr. old girl, who took an overdose of 70 Paracetamol due to a breakup with his girlfriend.

SOCIAL SERVICES INVOLVEMENT
- ➢ It is imperative that social services are involved
- ➢ They will be able to conduct a comprehensive assessment and gather information about the social circumstances
- ➢ They will liaise with the police.
- ➢ A joint strategy meeting will be held to discuss possible placement
- ➢ There is also the use of the child protection enquiry-Section 47 of the Child act 1989.

CHILD AND ADOLESCENT

5. OVERDOSE -SUCIDE RISK ASSESSMENT

INSTRUCTIONS TO CANDIDATE
You have assessed this 16 year old girl, Anya Robinson, who has taken an overdose. Discuss your management with the ward manager.

TASK FOR THE CANDIDATE
Discuss management with the ward manager.

PAY PARTICULAR ATTENTION TO THE FOLLOWING (MENTAL CHECKLIST)
- Give a summary of your psychiatric assessment.
- Highlight the risk issues present.
- Explain your management using a holistic or biopsychosocial approach.
- Discuss multi agency involvement.
- Establish any child protection issues.

COMMUNICATION SKILLS
- Start the interview by developing rapport and showing empathy.
- Use a collaborative approach towards keeping the patients best interests at heart.

Suggested Approach
Introduction
C: Hello, I'm Dr ...I'm one of the psychiatrists. I have seen the young 16 yr old girl, who has taken a serious overdose. I would like to discuss this with you.

W: Thank you for coming. Do you think you can discharge her please?

Brief synopsis- Psychiatric formulation
C: It appears she has taken this overdose due to an acute stress reaction .She has disclosed to me in confidence that she has been allegedly sexual abused. **I did not explore this further to prevent contamination of evidence.**

I understand your pressures on the ward. I think you will agree with me that we have a duty of care to this young girl and that at present ensuring her safety is paramount. We can formulate a management plan jointly and continue to keep her as an inpatient on this ward as this is now the place of safety.

My management plan in terms of holistic or biological, psychological and social approach is:

We will need to inform child and family services as well as social services, who will contact the police to investigate this further.

CHILD AND ADOLESCENT

Biological interventions
- *There is no current indication for medication as she has no evidence of an underlying mental illness, and we will allow for the therapeutic milieu settling the crisis*
- *We will need to continue to monitor her mental state and assess for evidence of underlying mental illness.*
- *We need to continue with on-going risk assessment*
- *We need to keep her on 1:1 nursing observations for 24 hours and assess regularly with risk assessment and downgrade accordingly.*
- *The police will investigate further and do the physical, a vaginal swab and genital examination.*
- *Visits should be monitored and prevent contact with the alleged perpetrator. Security to be contacted if this person insists on visiting her*

Psychological
- *We will need to continue to provide her with support.*
- *We can consider counselling at a later stage.*

Social
- *Social services to be contacted who will contact the police.*
- *We need to liaise with her family about her progress.*
- *Depending on who the alleged perpetrator is, if it is a family member or stranger, we would have to manage accordingly.*

In longer term, she would need psychotherapy or talking therapy. There is the possibility of her developing Depression, Post Traumatic Stress Disorder (PTSD), Anxiety symptoms after this, so she will need to be supported in the community by the CAMHS. There are also the voluntary organisations that can assist.

Thank you

CHILD AND ADOLESCENT

MANAGEMENT- OVERDOSE CSA
Admission informally
Biological interventions
- *Therapeutic milieu to settle*
- *Medication for underlying mental illness*
- *Nursing observations*
- *Visits*
- *Risk assessments*

Psychological investigations
- *Support*
- *Counselling*
- *Psychotherapy*

Social interventions
- *Social services*
- *Police -criminal charge*
- *Family*
- *Separation care order*
- *Joint strategy meeting*

©smartsesh

CHILD AND ADOLESCENT

6. OVERDOSE -SUICIDE RISK ASSESSMENT

INSTRUCTIONS TO CANDIDATE
You are about to see a 16 year, Tara Cooper, old who was brought to A+E by her friend. She had taken an overdose of 70 Paracetamol. Elicit a history of the overdose and do a risk assessment.

TASK FOR THE CANDIDATE
- Elicit a history and do a suicide risk assessment.

PAY PARTICULAR ATTENTION TO THE FOLLOWING (MENTAL CHECKLIST)
- Give a summary of your psychiatric assessment.
- Highlight the risk issues present.
- Explain your management using a holistic or biopsychosocial approach.
- Discuss multi agency involvement.
- Establish any child protection issues.

COMMUNICATION SKILLS
- Start the interview by developing rapport and show empathy.
- Seek to understand the subjective feeling of the individual.
- Anticipate that she could be reluctant to disclose details of the overdose.

Suggested approach
Introduction
C: Hello, I'm Dr ....I'm one of the psychiatrists. Thank you for agreeing to see me. I understand from the doctor in A+E that you had been brought here as you had taken an overdose. I am sorry to hear that. Are you able to tell me what happened?

P: Hello

A. History of Presenting Complaint (HOPC) (onset, duration, progression and severity)
C: I know this may be difficult for you. Because of what happened I do need to ask you some questions. It will help if you can take me through the events when you took the tablets?

Para suicide
- Where were you at the time?
- What did you do?
- What tablets did you take? How many tablets?
- Did you take anything else with them? Did you take any alcohol?

Degree of Preparation
- Where did you get the tablets?

CHILD AND ADOLESCENT

Planning
- Did you plan to end it all and for how long?
- Has it been a spur of the moment?

Suicide note
- Did you write a note, send text messages, email, Face book, or call anyone?

Last acts
- What preparation did you do?
- Did you bid farewell to anyone?
- Have you told anyone?

2) Circumstances of the overdose
- When did you take the tablets?
- Have you been alone?
- What did you do to prevent anyone from finding you?

Post suicidal attempt
- How did you feel after taking the tablets?
- What did you do next?
- Did you make yourself sick?
- Did you seek help?
- How were you discovered?
- How did you get to the hospital?
- Do you regret that your overdose did not succeed in killing you?
- Do you still think about killing yourself?
- Is it possible that you might plan to end it all again?

Suicidal ideation and intent
- What was your intention?
- What were you thinking at the time?
- Did you have thoughts of wanting to end it all?(suicidal thoughts)
- Did you believe that that amount would kill you?(lethality)

Current suicide risk
- How do you see the future?
- Do you have thoughts of wanting to end it all?
- Did you believe that that amount would kill you?

Precipitating factors
- Why did you do that?
- What sorts of things have been troubling you?
- What do you think was the final straw?
- How are things at home, school, work, college?
- Are you in any relationship?

CHILD AND ADOLESCENT

Recent history of Depression
- How have you been feeling in yourself? (Mood)
- How has your energy levels been? (Energy)
- Have you been able to enjoy things you usually would do? (Anhedonia)
- How have you been eating? (Biological symptoms)
- How have you been sleeping?

Hopelessness
- Do you ever feel hopeless?
- Do you ever feel that things will not or cannot get better?
- Are there times when you cannot see beyond your suffering?
- Did you ever wish your life with end?

Possible scenario of bullying
- I'm sorry to hear this is happening to you. I know this must be difficult to talk about.
- Can you tell me what they are doing to you?
- Who is doing this?
- Have you confided in anyone else?
- When did this all start?
- Enquire about the types of bullying.

Physical
- Have they been assaulting you? Have they been taking things off you?

Verbal
- Have they been calling you names?

Emotional
- Have they been doing anything else? Have they been spreading rumours?

Past DSH
- Can you tell me how you usually cope?
- Have you self-harmed in the past? If so, how serious was it?

Past psychiatric history
- Have you ever seen a psychiatrist in the past?

Screen for Psychosis
- I should ask you routine questions which we ask of everybody? Have you had any strange experiences?
- Do you ever seem to hear noises or voices when there is no one around and nothing else to explain it?

Personal and family history
- Is there anyone in the family that has any similar problems?

CHILD AND ADOLESCENT

Medical History
- *How is your physical health?*

Medication
- *Are you on any regular medication?*

Social history (establish social support network)
- *With whom do you live?*
- *Is there anyone you can confide in? Is there anyone you feel comfortable to share your problems with?*
- *Who is the one person that you are able to trust?*

Mental state examination
Assess for Depressive, Psychotic and PTSD Symptoms
- *How have you been feeling in yourself? (Mood)*
- *How has your energy levels been? (Energy)*
- *Have you been able to enjoy things you usually would do? (Anhedonia)*
- *How have you been eating?(biological symptoms)*
- *How have you been sleeping?*
- *Have you lost weight?*

Post-traumatic stress disorder PTSD symptoms
- *Have you been having any nightmares? Any flashbacks? (flashbacks)*
- *Do you avoid going to school? (Avoidance)*
- *Do you feel you are on edge? (hyper vigilance)*
- *How has your concentration been?*

Risk Assessment
- *How do you see the future?*
- *Do you have thoughts of wanting to end it all?*
- *What do you think you might do?*

Summarise
Thank you for opening up to me. I know that this must not have been easy. To summarise, you have taken an overdose as a result of the on-going bullying. I know this is a difficult time for you.

Insight
I think that maybe it would be better if you considered staying hospital .What do you think?

OVERDOSE –SUICIDE RISK ASSESSMENT

History of presenting complaint(HOPC)-*severity, onset, duration, progression*

- **Para suicide**
- *Preparation*
- *Preparation*
- *Planning*
- *Suicidal ideation and intent*
- *Precautions*
- *Preparatory acts*
- **Post suicidal attempt**

Precipitating factors

- **Regrets**

Past DSH-*cutting, ligatures, carbon monoxide poisoning*
Past psychiatric history
Personal and family history-*family history of suicide*
Medical History
Medication
Drug and alcohol history
Forensic, Psychosexual,
Social support-confidant
Risk Assessment-*according to severity-mild, moderate, severe*

©Smartsesh

POSSIBLE VARIATIONS OF THEME
1. 16 yr old boy who took an overdose of paracetamol in the context of being bullied that he is a homosexual. He has an underlying Depression.
2. 16 yr old girl who took an overdose of paracetamol for being bullied about being fat.

CHILD AND ADOLESCENT

7. OVERDOSE-BULLYING

INSTRUCTIONS TO CANDIDATE
You have seen this 16 year old girl, Tara Cooper, who is in the paediatric ward for taking an overdose. She admits that this was precipitated by bullying at her school. You have spoken to her parents and they want her to be admitted to hospital. Discuss your management with the consultant psychiatrist.

TASK FOR THE CANDIDATE
- *Discuss management of overdose and bullying with consultant.*

PAY PARTICULAR ATTENTION TO THE FOLLOWING (MENTAL CHECKLIST)
- *Give a psychiatric formulation of your assessment.*
- *Establish your differential diagnosis.*
- *Highlight the precipitating factors.*
- *Explain your management using a biopsychosocial approach.*
- *Highlight any child protection issues.*

COMMUNICATION SKILLS
- *Adopt a collegiate approach.*

Suggested approach
Introduction
C: Hello, I'm one Dr ...I'm one of the psychiatrists. I have seen the young 16 yr old girl, who has taken a serious overdose. I would like to discuss this with you.

Summary
16 year old who is presenting with having taken a serious overdose. (Include all details about the overdose)
The overdose was precipitated by on-going bullying. Comment on type of bullying-(physical, emotional, mental).

A. Brief synopsis
Psychiatric formulation
She has the following relevant history
- *Past psychiatric history*
- *Personal and family history*
- *Medical History*
- *Medication*
- *Drug and alcohol history*
- *Forensic, Psychosexual, Social history*
- *Risk Assessment (low, intermediate, high)*
- *Protective factors*

CHILD AND ADOLESCENT

B. Mental state examination
- *Comment on whether evidence of Depression, Psychosis or Post Traumatic Stress Disorder (PTSD) Symptoms Present.*
- *Evidence of suicidal thoughts, ideation or plans*

C. My differential diagnoses are:
- *Moderate to severe Depression with PTSD secondary to bullying*
- *Adjustment disorder*
- *Acute stress reaction*

D. My management plan using the holistic or biopsychosocial approach in my immediate management, short and longer term management is:

Immediate management
To consider admission or community treatment
We would need to assess the risk and consider either admission in hospital either voluntary or on own free will. In cases where a person doesn't want to be admitted and if we feel it is in their best interest, we will have to use the Mental Health Act (MHA 1983).

A possible scenario could be:
I have discussed this with her parents and they feel they will not be able to manage the situation due to the current risks and they feel that she it would be in her best interests for her to be managed on the ward. The period of admission will also allow for the therapeutic milieu settling the crisis.

Biological interventions
- *According to NICE(National institute of Clinical Excellence) guidelines for her to remain in hospital for 24 hours*
- *Get further collateral information from GP, family, teachers*
- *Routine bloods investigations*
- *Medication*
- *She can be treated if there is any underlying co-morbid condition e.g. Depression or PTSD.*
- *She will need to be placed on nursing observations*
- *We would need to do regular risk assessments*
- *We will also continue to monitor her mental state*
- *Part of the management would include emotional support*

The psychological or talking therapies are
- *CBT cognitive behaviour therapy*
- *Psychoeducation*
- *Relaxation training*

The social aspect of care includes
- *Liaising with her school*
- *Most schools should have an anti-bullying policy and therefore this protocol should be initiated following a meeting with her parents, teachers and school psychologist.*

CHILD AND ADOLESCENT

- *Depending on the nature of bullying, the involvement of the social services.*

*In planning for **longer term treatment**, we would use the MDT approach.*

SOCIAL SERVICES INVOLVEMENT
- ➤ *Depending on the nature and severity of the bullying, this should be raised as a child protection issue*
- ➤ *Liaise with school about the anti-bullying policy*

BULLYING
- *Bullying is when a child is picked on by other children or a group of children. It can affect a child*

Effects of bullying
- *Physical complications*
- *Psychological complications*
- *Depression*
- *Anxiety*
- *Decreased concentration*
- *Avoid school or cause of school refusal*
- *PTSD Post traumatic stress disorder*

Types of bullying
- *Physical*
- *Emotional*
- *Verbal*

Incidence
- *It occurs 1 in 100*

Management of bullying
School
- *Anti-bullying policy-obtainable from the department of education and skills*

Home
- *Parents-Need to listen*
- *Avoid blaming child*
- *Reassurance*

Other professionals
- *Social services*
- *Children, school and family services*
- *Educational psychologist*

©Smartsesh

CHILD AND ADOLESCENT

Overdose –Bullying management
- Brief synopsis /Psychiatric assessment
- HOPC
- Para suicide
- Precipitators
- She has the following relevant history
- Past psychiatric history
- Personal and family history
- Medical History
- Medication
- Drug and alcohol
- Forensic, Psychosexual, Social
- Risk Assessment(low, intermediate, high)
- Protective factors

Mental state examination
- Comment on whether evidence of Depression, Psychosis or PTSD symptoms present.
- Evidence of suicidal thoughts, ideation or plans

My differential diagnoses are
Immediate management
To consider admission or community treatment
Biological interventions
- According to NICE guidelines for her to remain in hospital for 24 hours
- Get further collateral information from GP, family, teachers
- Routine bloods investigations
- Rating scales-MADRS/BDI/BECKS/strengths and difficulty questionnaire
- Medication
- She can be treated if there is any underlying co-morbid condition e.g. Depression or PTSD.
- nursing observation
  - Regular risk assessments
- We will also continue to monitor her mental state
- Part of the management would include emotional support

©Smartsesh

The *psychological or talking therapies are*
- CBT cognitive behaviour therapy
- Psychoeducation
- Relaxation training
- The **social** aspect of care includes
- Liaising with her school
- Most schools should have an anti-bullying policy and therefore this protocol should be initiated following a meeting with her parents, teachers and school psychologist.
- Depending on the nature of bullying the involvement of the children, schools and family services.
- In planning for longer term treatment, we would use the MDT approach- CAMHS
- Services

©Smartsesh

CHILD AND ADOLESCENT

8. ADHD (Attention Deficit Hyperactivity Disorder)-COLLATERAL HISTORY

INSTRUCTIONS TO CANDIDATE
You have been asked to see the mother Nisha Singh of an 8yr old boy Kamal as she has concerns that he is 'hyper'.

TASK FOR THE CANDIDATE
Elicit a collateral history with a view of a diagnosis

PAY PARTICULAR ATTENTION TO THE FOLLOWING (MENTAL CHECKLIST)
- *Elicit the history of presenting complaint (onset, duration, severity and duration)*
- *Establish the core features of ADHD(Attention Deficit Hyperactivity Disorder)*
- *-Hyperactivity*
- *-Inactivity*
- *-Inattention*
- *Screen for co-morbid conditions*
- *Conduct a risk assessment*

COMMUNICATION SKILLS
- *Start the interview by developing rapport and showing empathy.*
- *Show sensitivity and seek to understand the impact her son's behaviour is having on the family dynamics.*

Suggested approach
Introduction
C: Hello, I'm Dr ...I am one of the psychiatrists. Thank you for coming to see me. I understand from your GP that you have had concerns about your son?

M: He is 'hyper'.

C: I gather that you have been finding it difficult to manage him at home. Can you tell me more about what concerns you have?

A. History of Presenting Complaint (HOPC) (severity, onset, duration, progression)
Elicit the history to demonstrate the 3 core features of ADHD

(Attention Deficit Hyperactivity Disorder)
1. Hyperactivity
- *Do you find he is always on the go? (Hyperactive)*
- *How he is around the dinner table for example, is he able to sit still? (Restless) What does he do?*
- *Can you give examples of him being restless? Is he fidgety?*
- *Does he interrupt you for example if you are on the phone?*

CHILD AND ADOLESCENT

2. Impulsivity

- Is he able to wait his turn?
- Does he do things without thinking? (Impulsive)
- Does he do things on the spur of the moment?
- Has he done anything concerning?
- For example running across the road and causing accidents at home?
- How would you say his road sense is?

3. Inattention

- How long is he able to concentrate on a task? Can you give me some examples? (Commonly parents will mention Games like WII and XBOX; however these are not good indicators. Ask specifically for school work, activities)
- Would he be able to follow a 3 stage command: for example if you asked him to take his shoes off, hang his coat and then sit at the table?
- How is he with his homework? Does he make any mistakes? Is he easily distractible?

B. Establish Pervasiveness: Behaviour should be present at school, home and social settings
School
- What have teachers said about him?

Hyperactivity
- Is he able to sit still in the classroom?

Impulsivity
- Have they mentioned whether he interrupts in the classroom?

Inattention
- What have the teachers said about his performance?

Social
- How is he if you take him shopping, or for parties?
- When did this all start? (Onset)
- How do you compare him to other children?[Establish if there are other siblings]
- How have you been managing these behaviours?

C. Aetiological factors
Elicit possible aetiological factors using the bio-psychosocial approach
Biological
- Complications at birth, low birth weight, epilepsy
- Genetic- family history
- Smoking in pregnancy

Psychological
- Underlying co-morbidity for example learning disability.

Social
- Poorer socio-economic conditions.

D. Developmental history
Perinatal history
- How was your pregnancy?
- Were there any complications at birth?
- How were his developmental milestones?
- Can you describe his temperament?
- Did he have any childhood illnesses?
- Did he require hospitalisation?
- Has he been statemented? (To exclude learning difficulties)

E. Differential diagnosis
Conduct disorder
Has he been truanting?
Has he got in trouble at school or with the police?

Autistic spectrum disorders
Does he have friends?
Does he have any particular interests or repetitive behaviours?

Learning disability
Is he achieving his school work at his level?

Depression
Does she appear happy or sad?
Has he been doing things he usually enjoys doing?
Has he been isolating himself?

F. Past psychiatric history
Has he ever seen a psychiatrist in the past?

G. Drug and alcohol history
This is a rather sensitive question, but is there any chance he has come into contact with street drugs?

Summarise
Thank you for talking to me. To summarise, it appears that your son has been overactive, restless, and impulsive. He has decreased attention at school and at home and is easily distractible. This could be explained by ADHD (Attention Deficit Hyperactivity Disorder) - Attention Deficit Hyperactivity Disorder. I would like to see him to do further assessments, and with your permission contact his school to complete a Connors questionnaire.

I have some information and leaflets for you and I am available if you wish to meet with me to discuss this. Do you have any questions?

Thank you

CHILD AND ADOLESCENT

POSSIBLE VARIATIONS OF THEME
1.10 yr. old boy referred for poor development at school. He has been expelled from school. Family history of ADHD (Attention Deficit Hyperactivity Disorder)
2. 14 yr. old boy who has mild learning disability and possible ADHD (Attention Deficit Hyperactivity Disorder).

CHILD AND ADOLESCENT

ADHD (Attention Deficit Hyperactivity Disorder) –COLLATERAL HISTORY

History of presenting complaint (HOPC)-severity, onset, duration, progression

Elicit core features of ADHD (Attention Deficit Hyperactivity Disorder)

- **Hyperactivity**-restless, fidgety
- **Impulsivity**- jumps queues, blurts answers
- **Inattention**- distractible, careless, forgetful

Developmental history

- Perinatal History
- Pregnancy
- Complications
- Developmental milestones
- Temperament
- Childhood illnesses, hospitalisation
- School attendance

Aetiological factors

- **Elicit using the biopsychosocial approach**
- **Biological**
- Complications at birth, low birth weight, epilepsy
- Genetic family history
- Smoking in pregnancy
- **Psychological**
- Underlying co-morbidity
- **Social**
- Poorer socio economic

Differential diagnosis

- Conduct disorder(CD)
- Autistic spectrum disorders
- Learning difficulties
- Depression

Past psychiatric history

Drug and alcohol history

Current medication

©Smartsesh

CHILD AND ADOLESCENT

9. ADHD (Attention Deficit Hyperactivity Disorder) -MANAGEMENT

INSTRUCTIONS TO CANDIDATE
You have been asked to see the father Viresh Singh of the 8yr old boy,
who has been concerned about her son being 'hyper'.

TASK FOR THE CANDIDATE
- Explain the diagnosis and management.

PAY PARTICULAR ATTENTION TO THE FOLLOWING (MENTAL CHECKLIST)
- Explain the diagnosis of ADHD (Attention Deficit Hyperactivity Disorder).
- Explain the aetiological factors, prognosis.
- Explain the management using a holistic or biopsychosocial approach.

COMMUNICATION SKILLS
- Start the interview by developing rapport and showing empathy.
- Show sensitivity.

Suggested approach
Introduction
C: Hello, I'm Dr ...I am one of the psychiatrists. Thank you for coming to see me. I have spoken to your wife about your son.   I wanted to come and tell you more about your son's diagnosis and the treatment options available. Before we begin, it would be helpful for you to describe to me how he is at home?

F: He is on the go all the time and a bit 'hyper' if you ask me. What is his diagnosis?

C: From the assessments that we have carried out, he has what we call **ADHD (Attention Deficit Hyperactivity Disorder).** Have you heard about this?
If so can you tell me what is your understanding of this?

F: Well he is on the go all the time and that's what we have been telling the GP that he is hyperactive.

C: I will explain:
ADHD (Attention Deficit Hyperactivity Disorder) is an acronym for Attention deficit hyperactive disorder. This is a term used in the US and in the UK we use the term Hyperkinetic disorder.
It is used to describe children with 3 main groups of symptoms. They can present as restless, fidgety, have difficulty concentrating and are impulsive for example they might act without thinking.

F: How did you make the diagnosis?

CHILD AND ADOLESCENT

C: There is no simple test to diagnose ADHD (Attention Deficit Hyperactivity Disorder). The diagnosis is usually made in a specialist setting by child psychiatrist, or by a paediatrician. We use the information we get from parents and also get some reports called Connors scale completed by the teachers.

F: How common is it?

C: It occurs in 1 in 100 and 3 times more common in boys.

F: What are the causes?

C: It is difficult to pinpoint one particular cause. From the literature we have we know it can be hereditary or genetic. That means it can run in families. It can be caused by complications at birth like brain injury and low birth weight. It is common to see this also with people who have epilepsy. It is a developmental disorder which affects part of the brain which is involved in focussing attention, organising and behaviour.

F: What treatment is available?

C: We use a combination of treatment which includes behavioural, social and medication.

Which one would you like to hear more about?

F: I have heard about this Ritalin®

C: The name of the medication we use is called Ritalin® or Methylphenidate. It is from a group of medication called stimulants due to the way in which it works.

It works to normalise the chemicals in the brain. The beneficial effects are that it makes children calmer, more focussed, increased attention and reduces the hyperactivity.

From my experience parents notice a difference in their children's behaviour. The medication provides a window of opportunity for them to learn better at school, find homework enjoyable and make more friends.

Like all medication they have side effects. Would you like to hear more about that now?

F: Yes

C: There are side effects, like with all medicines, however it is not to say that he will develop these side effects. These can vary from person to person and depends on their response to the medication.

Methylphenidate or Ritalin® can cause tummy aches, headaches, and sleep disturbance. In the longer term it can also cause growth suppression.

We have safeguards against these side effects and do the following:
-allow for drug free weekends
-monitor weight and height regularly in the clinic to identify it is stunting a child's growth.

We also have the Psychological therapy or talking therapy:
The psychological forms of treatment include
- *Behavioural management. We encourage parents to use the behavioural reward system to reward positive behaviour i.e. reward charts*
- *Psychoeducation*
- *Your understanding of this condition is vital in managing your child's condition*
- *Parent training programmes*

Because we know how difficult it can be to manage these behaviours we have these programmes to educate parents.

Social interventions
The social aspects of treatment include:
- *School based interventions*
- *This is where we would liaise with the school to provide specialised support at school e.g. if your child has difficulty in learning the teacher can adjust the teaching style more tailored to your child and also provide more one to one support.*
- *Social skills training has been found to be beneficial with improving a child's self-esteem, temper tantrums and aggression.*

Other forms of treatment which are currently being researched are:
-Feingold diet
-Avoid additives
There is no evidence to suggest that doing this will help for hyperactivity. We do advise parent that if they notice that there is anything in their child's diet that they have noticed affects their behaviour, and then they should avoid this.

F: What is the prognosis or chances my child will get better?

C: The general rule of thumb is that we do know that usually that ¾ of children do improve by the teenage years and only about a ¼ will go on to continue to have symptoms in adulthood.

Summarise
Thank you for talking to me. To summarise we have discussed more about ADHD (Attention Deficit Hyperactivity Disorder) and the treatment options available for your son. I am happy to make another appointment if you wish

to discuss this with your partner to discuss what you have decided about the treatment options available. Is that all right?

Information and leaflets
I have some information and leaflets that you can take home and read. I have some details of groups and websites that are helpful

Thank you

ADHD (Attention Deficit Hyperactivity Disorder) –EXPLAIN MANAGEMENT
Summarise findings
Diagnosis ADHD (Attention Deficit Hyperactivity Disorder)
- 3 core features
- Hyperactivity
- Impulsivity
- Inattention
- Pervasive –home, school and social
- Causes- genetic, injury to the brain, learning disabilities

Diagnosis made
- Specialist CAMHS or paediatrics
- Physical, bloods, tests

Management
Biological interventions
- Stimulant according to NICE
- Methylphenidate
- Others Dexamphetamine
- Atomoxetine
- Clonidine
- Side effects

Psychological interventions
- Behavioural
- Reward positive behaviour
- Psych education
- Parent training programmes

Social interventions
- School based interventions
- Social skills training
- Conference
- Child special education needs
- Other Feingold diet
- Avoid additives

Prognosis
- Usually settles mid-teens
- ¼ continue as adults

©Smartsesh

CHILD AND ADOLESCENT

ADHD (Attention Deficit Hyperactivity Disorder)

MEDICATION	SIDE EFFECTS
METHYLPHENIDATE Ritalin ®(Novartis) Equasym XL ®((Shire) 18 mg od then increased to maximum 54mg Concerta XL®(Janssen) 10 mg od up to maximum 100mg Medikinet XL (Flynn) 10 mg od up to maximum 100mg	**Common:** Abdominal pain, nausea, vomiting, diarrhoea, dyspepsia, dry mouth, anorexia, reduced weight, tachycardia **Less common:** Constipation, dyspnoea, confusion, reduced height **Rare:** Angina, sweating, visual disturbance
ATOMOXETINE Strattera® 6-18 yrs 40mg daily for 7 days increased 80 mg daily Maximum 120 mg daily	**Common:** Nausea, diarrhoea, dry mouth, abdominal cramps, anorexia, **Less common:** Anxiety, hostility, tremor **Rare:** hepatic disorders
DEXAMFETAMINE	**Common:** Nausea, diarrhoea, dry mouth, abdominal cramps, anorexia, weight loss **Less common:** Anxiety, confusion, restlessness, hypertension **Rare:** angle closure glaucoma

CHILD AND ADOLESCENT

10. AUTISM

INSTRUCTIONS TO CANDIDATE
Mrs Rachel Stephens has been concerned about her 6 year old son's Thomas's speech development.

TASK FOR THE CANDIDATE
- Take a history with a view of a diagnosis.

PAY PARTICULAR ATTENTION TO THE FOLLOWING (MENTAL CHECKLIST)
- Establish history of presenting complaint (onset, duration, progression and severity).
- Elicit a developmental history.
- Elicit the core features in the 3 main domains for autism.
- Establish the qualitative impairments in communication
- Establish the qualitative impairment in social interaction:
- Establish Restricted repetitive and stereotyped patterns of behavior, interests and activities:

COMMUNICATION SKILLS
- Start the interview by developing rapport and showing empathy.
- Show sensitivity and seek to understand the subjective feeling of the mother.

Suggested approach
Introduction
C: Hello, I'm Dr ...I'm one of the psychiatrists. I understand you have some concerns about your son. Can you tell me more about this?

M: Hello Doctor. Yes I have started to worry about him. I thought he might have hearing problems, but his hearing has been tested and is normal. His speech is still not very clear.

A. History of Presenting Complaint (HOPC) (onset, duration, progression and severity)
- Tell me more about his speech, how does he communicate?
- When were his first words: then ask specifically when he started babbling, when he spoke 1 word; 2 words; sentences.
- Did he ever repeat words (echolalia)? Does he get words mixed up e.g. calling himself you instead of me, is he monotonous?
- Is he able to tell you what he wants? Is he able to tell you about things that have happened for e.g. at school? Can others understand what he says or only people close to him?

B. Elicit some developmental history
Perinatal history
- Can you tell me about your pregnancy?
- Was it planned or unplanned? Were there any complications?

- *Do you have any other children?*
- *How was your delivery?*
- *How was he when you took him home?*
- *How was he sleeping? (Sleep)*
- *How was he if there was a change in his routine? (Routine)*
- *How was he feeding? (Feeding)*
- *Would he make eye contact during feeding? (Avoidance gaze)*
- *How was he with weaning?*
- *Any sensitivity with smells, textures? (Sensitivity to textures)*
- *Enquire about developmental milestones*
- *When did he first smile, crawl, sit, and walk? (Developmental milestones)*
- *Did he enjoy being picked up and cuddled?*
- *Did you notice any clumsiness?*
- *How did he respond if you played for example peek-a-boo?*
- *Would he point to objects as part of sharing his interest? (Shred or joint interest)*
- *Is he able to communicate his needs?*
- *Is he able to understand you?*
- *Are you able to have a 2 way conversation?*
- *Does he interrupt conversations? How is he at turn taking?*

C. Elicit the three domains for Autism
Impairment in Communication (as elicited above)
Impairment in Social interaction
- *Does he stare at people or get into their personal space?*
- *How does he play? Does he share his toys? Does he play with his siblings, if any?*
- *Does he have friends? How is he at making friends? Is he a loner?(solitary play)*
- *How would he react if someone got hurt? (Empathy)*
- *How about imaginative play? (Decreased imaginative play)*
- *Did he have imaginary friends?*

Stereotype interests and repetitive behaviours
- *Does he have any particular interests? (Stereotyped interests)*
- *How about rocking, spinning or hand-flapping?*
- *Does he have any preference for a particular toy/object?*
- *How would he play with his toys? Would he line things up? For example would he line trains or cars?*
- *Is he set in his way? How does he cope with change? (Routine)*

Summary
Thank you for talking to me. From what you told me about your son, it appears that he has some difficulty in his communication, his social interactions and some repetitive behaviour. I would like to see him and refer him to my colleagues in the team like the SALT (speech and language therapist) and educational psychologist for further assessment.

CHILD AND ADOLESCENT

Do you have any other questions? I have some leaflets and information which you can take home to read.

Thank You

F84 Autism
A total of six (or more) items from (a), (b), and (c), with at least two from (a), and one each from (b) and (c)
1. Qualitative impairment in social interaction:
- *impairments in nonverbal behaviors such as eye-to-eye gaze*
- *failure to develop peer relationships*
- *lack of spontaneous seeking to share enjoyment, interests*
- *achievements*
- *lack of social or emotional reciprocity*

2. Qualitative impairments in communication:
- *delay in the development of spoken language*
- *marked impairment in sustain a conversation*
- *idiosyncratic language*
- *lack of social imitative play*

3. Restricted repetitive and stereotyped patterns of behavior, interests and activities:
- *stereotyped and restricted patterns of interest*
- *inflexible nonfunctional routines or rituals*
- *stereotyped and repetitive motor mannerisms*
- *preoccupation with parts of objects*

Delays with onset prior to age 3 years

The disturbance is not better accounted for by Rhett's Disorder or Childhood Disintearative Disorder

---

Other diagnostic assessments FOR Autistic spectrum conditions
- *ADI-R Autism Diagnostic Interview, Revised*
- *ADOS Autism Diagnostic Observation Schedule*
- *DISCO The Diagnostic Interview for Social and Communication Disorders designed by Wing and Gould*

Screening Tools for Aspergers syndrome
- *Autism Spectrum Quotient (ASQ)*
- *Empathy Quotient(EQ)*
- *Childhood Autism Spectrum Test(CAST)*
- *AAA   Adult Asperger Assessment tool (Baron-Cohen et al 2005)*

*These are screening tools available from the **Autism Research Centre** website.*

CHILD AND ADOLESCENT

11. AUTISM

INSTRUCTIONS TO CANDIDATE
You have been asked to see the mother, Rose Watson, of a 6 yr. old boy Thomas Watson who has been diagnosed with Autism. She wants to find out more about this from you.

TASK FOR THE CANDIDATE
- *Explain his diagnosis and management.*

PAY PARTICULAR ATTENTION TO THE FOLLOWING (MENTAL CHECKLIST)
- *Explain diagnosis of autism.*
- *Explain the clinical features of Autism in the 3 main domains.*
- *Explain the aetiology and prognosis of Autism.*
- *Explain the management using a biopsychosocial approach.*

COMMUNICATION SKILLS
- *Start the interview by developing rapport and showing empathy.*
- *Show sensitivity when discussing the diagnosis which in a sense is like breaking bad news to a parent.*

Suggested approach
Introduction
C: Hello, I'm Dr....I'm one of the psychiatrists. Thank you for coming to see me today. I understand you wanted to know about your son's diagnosis of Autism? Can you tell me what your understanding of Autism is?

M: I have heard from a friend whose son has this. I know it can affect the way he speaks and behaves.

C: Yes, that's partly correct. I will explain this to you. Please do interrupt me if you do not understand me. Autism is a neurodevelopmental disorder used to describe children who have difficulties in 3 main areas or domains .They are difficulty in communicating, socialising and they have repetitive behaviours.

They are part of a group of disorders called the Autistic Spectrum disorders. The term neurodevelopmental means they are caused by abnormalities in the way the brain develops and works. They affect approximately 1 in 100 children and young people.

C: I have heard of Asperger's syndrome, is that the same?

Asperger's is similar to Autism; however the speech development is normal. The typical speech is described as being 'pedantic'. They might have some other difficulties like clumsiness. You might have heard also that these are *usually people with an above average IQ (intelligence quotient) and are usually therefore high functioning.*

M: How is it diagnosed?

C: It is usually diagnosed in a specialist setting using a multi-disciplinary approach. This will include assessments made by various members of the team. The team consists of the psychologist, speech and language therapist, child psychiatrist, paediatrician and occupational therapist.
We usually have to take a developmental history which means simply looking at the first 3 years of a child's development i.e. from pregnancy to 3 years. We also, do a physical examination and bloods.

M: How common is it?

C: It has been shown to be more common in males with a male to female ratio of 4:3.

M: What are the causes?

C: It is difficult to pinpoint an exact cause in your son's case and it could be due to various reasons. It has a genetic component, in that it can run in families. If there is someone in the family that has Autism, then there is a risk of getting it. It can also be due to certain genetic syndromes.
Getting the diagnosis is an important step to and also trying to understand the behaviours which will help in the management.

What is the treatment for Autism?
Unfortunately there is no known cure for Autism. Our management consists of behavioural, psychological and social aspects. In some cases we can use medication. This is only indicated for severe cases, and if there is any other underlying condition for example if a child has ADHD (Attention Deficit Hyperactivity Disorder), or Depression, then we would treat accordingly. Sometimes children can also present with challenging behaviour and then we would need to treat that.

We work within a multidisciplinary team approach. There will be several people involved in the care of your child with ASD (Autistic spectrum Disorder), such as a speech and language therapist, psychologist, occupational therapist and a medical doctor (paediatrician or child psychiatrist).

Psychological
Psychoeducation:
We find that it is important for families to learn more about the condition, managing behavioural difficulties, and assist in their child's developing social communication and emotional skills

CHILD AND ADOLESCENT

There are various approaches available to help with communication and learning and for children with ASD (Autistic spectrum Disorder). It is often better to use this as early as possible. There might also be specialist courses on parenting, parent support groups,

Social aspects could include the following
- *Education assessment*
- *Individual help*
- *Structured routine and activities*
- *Support to parents- love, understanding and consistent approach*
- *Respite*
- *Disability allowance*

Education *Children and young people with ASD (Autistic spectrum Disorder) often need some special educational support. This may be in a special school, or in a mainstream school.*
Also advice on how to help the wider family and more general advice about benefits, for example, from local child health services and independent organisations such as the National Autistic Society

Summarize
Thank you for talking to me. I have told you more about your son's condition of Autism and how we will be treating him with the behavioural approaches, improving his communication and social skills. We can also look at support from the social services in terms of his schooling.

I have some leaflets and website addresses which you may find some information. I would like to arrange to see you again.

Support groups and organisations
National Autistic Society
MENCAP

CHILD AND ADOLESCENT

12. ENURESIS

INSTRUCTIONS TO CANDIDATE
You are about to see the father who is concerned about his 8yr old daughter Chloe Simmons has been wetting the bed.

TASK FOR THE CANDIDATE
- *Take a history to come to a diagnosis.*

PAY PARTICULAR ATTENTION TO THE FOLLOWING (MENTAL CHECKLIST)
- *Establish history of presenting complaint (HOPC) onset, duration, severity and progression.*
- *Establish primary or secondary enuresis.*
- *Establish possible aetiological factors using biopsychosocial approach.*
- *Establish any other underlying issues.*

COMMUNICATION SKILLS
- *Start the interview by developing rapport and showing empathy.*
- *Acknowledge the distress to parent and impact on family.*

Suggested approach
Introduction
C: Hello, I'm Dr ....I'm one of the psychiatrists. Thank you for coming to see me. I understand that there have been concerns with your child wetting the bed. I would like to ask you more about that is that all right?

P: Hello. Yes, we have been concerned as she has recently started wetting the bed.

C: I can see that you are quite concerned about her. It would help, if you could tell me more about what has been happening?

History of Presenting Complaint (HOPC) (onset, duration, progression and severity)
- *Can you describe the bedwetting incidents? (Bedwetting)*
- *How frequent has it been? (Frequency)*
- *Doe it occur at day or night? Or both? (Nocturnal or diurnal enuresis)*
- *What restrictions have you made prior to bedtime? (Bedtime restrictions)*

Precipitators
- *Do you know what was going on around the same time when this started?*
- *Have you noticed any change in behaviour at school/home/social? (Behavioural changes)*
- *Has there been any change in the family?*

- *Does he/she have any brothers or sister?*

Exclude an organic cause
- *Is there any history of her having urinary tract infections?(UTI(Urinary tract infection)'s)*
- *Does she have any structural abnormalities/congenital abnormalities?(anatomical abnormalities)*

Toilet training
- *At what age was he/she potty trained?(potty training)*
- *When was she dry at night?*
- *Were there any significant accidents reported?*
- *How was this dealt with?(to establish consistent/inconsistent discipline)*

Past psychiatric history
- *Has she seen a psychiatrist in the past?*

Personal and family history
- *Is there anyone in the family that has any similar problems?*

Summary
Thank you for talking to me. To summarise, what you have told me is that your child has been bedwetting. This seems to have coincided with a few changes at home which could have contributed to her bedwetting. There are behavioural approaches which have been shown to be beneficial. I would like to see you again to discuss this further?

Thank you

POSSIBLE VARIATIONS OF THEME
1.10 yr. old boy who has recently started bedwetting and having nightmares.
2.9 yr. old girl with recent changes in her behaviour and bedwetting. Suspicion of sexual abuse (CSA).

ENURESIS

History of presenting complaint (HOPC)
- Establish whether it is nocturnal or diurnal enuresis
- Frequency
- Fluid restrictions at bed time

Precipitators
- Behavioural changes noticed
- Any stressors
- Identify if organic cause for aetiology
- History of UTI(Urinary tract infection)'S
- Structural abnormalities of the genitourinary system(congenital or anatomical abnormalities)
- Toilet training
- Age continence achieved
- Dry at night
- Any accidents

Past psychiatric history
Personal and family history

MANAGEMENT –ENURESIS
Biological interventions
Practical aspects:
- **Dietary restrictions:** Ensure child does not drink close to bedtime.
- Parent to take child to the toilet.
- **Praise for nights when they have been dry**
- **Biological**

Medication Imipramine (SSRI)
Psychological interventions
- Behavioural approach - bell and pad or enuresis alarm from the specialist clinic
- Reward chart –star chart

Social interventions
- **Support and psychoeducation**
- **Attending Enuresis clinic**

©Smartsesh

CHILD AND ADOLESCENT

CAMHS

References
Gelder, M.G, Cowen, P. and Harrison P.J (2006) Shorter Oxford textbook of psychiatry. 5th edn. Oxford: Oxford University Press.

Sims, A. C. P. (2003) Symptoms in the mind: an introduction to descriptive psychopathology. 3rd edn. Great Britain: Saunders.

Taylor, D., Paton, C., Kapur, S. (2009) The South London and Maudsley NHS Foundation Trust & Oxleas NHS Foundation Trust prescribing guidelines. 10th edn. London: Informa Healthcare.

British Medical Association and Royal Pharmaceutical society (2011), British National Formulary 62, 62nd edn. Great Britain: British Medical Journal Publishing Group and Pharmaceutical Press

WHO. (1992)The ICD 10 classification of mental and behavioural disorders: clinical descriptions and diagnostic guideline. 10th revision: Geneva; WHO

Attention deficit hyperactivity disorder. Diagnosis and management of ADHD (Attention Deficit Hyperactivity Disorder) in children, young people and adults. Guideline number 72. 2009. http://guidance.nice.org.uk/CG72/Guidance/pdf/Englis

Simon Baron-Cohen, Autism and Asperger Syndrome, the facts

M. S. Thambirajah Developmental Assessment of the School-Aged Child with Developmental Disabilities: A Clinician's Guide

Foundation provides information and support to parents and carers of individual with severe learning disabilities

LEARNING DISABILITY

LEARNING DISABILITY- Dr Nilofar Ahmed
Dr Nauman Khalil

1. *Challenging behaviour-Collateral history from carer –Dr Ashok Roy/Dr Jay Thamizhirai*
2. *Downs syndrome- Collateral history to differentiate Dementia and Depression –Dr Meera Roy /Dr Kamalika Mukherji*
3. *Downs syndrome - Bruising –get collateral history from carer- Dr Rajnish Attavar*
4. *Indecent exposure –history taking –Dr Asif Zia*
5. *Indecent exposure –discuss with mother –Dr Asif Zia*
6. *Asperger's syndrome-history taking-Dr Paul Bradley*
7. *Epilepsy-history taking- Dr Nauman Khalil*
8. *Arson –Dr Regi Alexander*

LEARNING DISABILITY

1. CHALLENGING BEHAVIOUR IN LEARNING DISABILITY

INSTRUCTIONS TO CANDIDATE
You are the psychiatry doctor on call. The staff at the local residential home has called you due to their concerns of a 34 yr old man Simon Barbell with moderate learning disability. They are concerned about recent changes in his behaviour. Please take a history of their current concerns.

TASK FOR THE CANDIDATE
- Elicit collateral history from carer on challenging behaviour.

PAY PARTICULAR ATTENTION TO THE FOLLOWING (MENTAL CHECKLIST)
- Elicit a history of challenging behaviour using an antecedent, behavioural and consequence approach.
- Identify the aetiological factors using a biopsychosocial approach.
- Conduct a risk assessment.
- Get carers view as to possible cause for challenging behaviour.

COMMUNICATION SKILLS
- Start the interview by building rapport and show empathy.
- Acknowledge the carers concern and distress.

Suggested approach
Introduction
C: Hello, I'm Dr ....I'm one of the psychiatrists. I understand that you have some concerns regarding Mr Thompson. I gather you and the staffs have been experiencing some difficulty in managing his behaviour. Can you tell me more about this?

M: Hello Doctor. That's right; we are really concerned about him. He is usually very pleasant and this recent change in behaviour is out of character. The staff is finding his behaviour difficult to manage.

C: From what you are telling me, it seems like there has been a change is his behaviour. Can you tell me more about the changes that you and the other staff have noticed?

A. History of Presenting Complaint (HOPC) (onset, duration, progression and severity)
- What happened? (Behaviour)
- When did this all start?
- Have there been any episodes of aggression?

Use behavioural analysis (A, B, C) approach
Antecedent

- What was he doing before this happened? (Trigger)

Behaviour
- What happened?
- What was the behaviour like?(examples include- aggressive gestures, pushing, rocking, stereotyped, ritualistic behaviour, banging, self-injurious, sexually inappropriate, personal behaviours, spitting, smearing)
- Who was involved?
- Was he able to communicate what happened?(form of communication-Makaton sign language)
- How serious was it?
- How did staff manage the incident?

Consequence
- How was he after this happened? (Consequences)
- Did he require any as required medication (enquire about prn or as required)
- Did he show any regret/remorse for his behaviour?(regret/remorse)
- Was this reported?
- What was the damage?
- How have other service users reacted to this?(retaliation)

B. Past history of challenging behaviour
- Has this happened in the past?
- Can you describe what happened?
- What worked in the past?

I would like to ask you some more specific questions to try to identify what the cause for this change in his behaviour could be.

C. Use the biopsychosocial approach to identify the aetiological factors in a learning disability patient
Biological
Screen for any developmental disorders and underlying co-morbid conditions
- What is his diagnosis? Any genetic conditions e.g. Downs, Lesch Nyan?
- What is his level of learning disability? (Mild, moderate, severe, profound)
- Does he have a diagnosis of ASD (Autistic spectrum Disorder) or ADHD (Attention Deficit Hyperactivity Disorder)?

Medical conditions
- Has he had any physical health problems? Has he seen his GP recently?
- Does he have any bowel problems? (Constipation)
- Does he have any history of falls or injury?

- *Does he have Epilepsy, DM (Diabetes Mellitus), HPT (Hypertension), UTI (Urinary tract infection) and Thyroid?*
- *Is he on any regular medication? (Medication)*
- *Have there been any changes in his medication?*

Further exploration of Epilepsy:
- *Is his Epilepsy under control?*
- *What type of Epilepsy does he have? (For example: absences, tonic-clonic, myoclonic, TLE (Temporal Lobe Epilepsy), status epilepticus)*
- *What is the frequency of his seizures?*
- *When was did he have his last seizure?*

Psychological
- *How has he appeared in his mood? (Irritable or tearful or anxious)*
- *Has he experienced any setbacks recently? Are there any bereavement issues? (Stressors)*
- *Has he been isolating himself? (Social isolation)*
- *How has he been sleeping? (Sleep)*
- *How has he been eating? (Appetite)*
- *Has he appeared to be responding to voices? (Auditory hallucinations)*
- *Has he appeared to be seeing things? (Visual hallucinations)*
- *How has his concentration been? (Concentration)*
- *Have you noticed any change in his memory? (Memory)*

Social
- *What is his weekly routine? (Routine)*
- *How has he been caring for himself i.e. personal hygiene? (Personal care)*
- *What activities does he engage in? (Activities)*
- *Is he attending day services? (Day services)*
- *Has there been any significant change in the residential home or day services?*
- *Has he been targeted by other service users?*
- *Possible changes: change of carer; new resident; change in his room; anything related to family and friends*

D. Risk assessment
- *Has he ever expressed thoughts of wanting to end it all? (Suicidal thoughts)*
- *Has he expressed thoughts of wanting to harm anyone else? (Homicidal thoughts)*
- *Have you been concerned that he would try to abscond? (Absconsion risk)*
- *Has he had a past history of violence? (Violence)*

LEARNING DISABILITY

E. Carer's view
Thank you, the information you have given me is extremely helpful. What would you say in your view could have resulted in this recent change in his behaviour?

Summarise
To summarise, Mr Barbell is a known resident with moderate learning disability. There has been a noticeable change in his behaviour, which staffs are now finding it difficult to manage despite behavioural approaches. It is possible that there are a few factors (biopsychosocial) that could have contributed to this.

So form what we have discussed, can you tell me what would be the best way forward?
I would like to see him to do some further investigations and review his medication.
Do you have any questions for me?

Thank you

LEARNING DISABILITY

CHALLENGING BEHAVIOUR IN LEARNING DISABILITY
History of presenting complaint (HOPC) (onset, duration, progression and severity)
Use behavioural analysis (A,B,C)
- *Antecedent-Establish behaviour*
- *Behaviour- establish seriousness*
- *Consequence-outcome*
- *How it was managed.*

Screen for any developmental disorders and underlying co-morbid conditions-i.e. *Attention Deficit Hyperactivity disorder ADHD (Attention Deficit Hyperactivity Disorder), Autistic Spectrum Disorder ASD (Autistic spectrum Disorder), genetic conditions*
Possible aetiological factors
- *Use biopsychosocial approach to identify the aetiological factors in a learning disability patient*
- *Biological-medical conditions-Diabetes, Hypertension HPT(Hypertension), Urinary tract infection UTI(Urinary tract infection) ,Thyroid*
- *Further exploration of Epilepsy*
- *Psychological*
- *Assess for mood and psychotic symptoms*
- *Social*
- *Routine/activities*
- *Changes in environment*

Risk assessment
Carer's view
Summarise

© Smartsesh

POSSIBLE VARIATIONS OF THEME
1. *34yr. old man with moderate LD, self-harming and suicidal.*
2. *27yr. old lady with moderate LD, with challenging behaviour. Additional information- recent bereavement.*

LEARNING DISABILITY

2. DOWNS'S SYNDROME-DEPRESSION VS DEMENTIA

INSTRUCTION TO CANDIDATE
You are about to see Mrs Geraldine Barlow. The GP has referred her 34 yr old son Christopher who has Down syndrome, as there has been a sudden change in his presentation following a fall.

TASK FOR THE CANDIDATE
Elicit a collateral history to differentiate Depression from Dementia.

PAY PARTICULAR ATTENTION TO THE FOLLOWING (MENTAL CHECKLIST)
- *Elicit history to differentiate Depression from Dementia.*
- *Establish premorbid functioning.*
- *Establish aetiological factors using a biopsychosocial approach.*

COMMUNICATION SKILLS
- *Start the interview by developing rapport and show empathy.*
- *Acknowledge the carers distress.*

Suggested approach
Introduction
C: *Hello, I'm Dr ....I'm one of the psychiatrists. Thank you for coming to see me. I gather your GP has referred your son to me, as you expressed some concerns about him. Can you tell me more about this?*

M: **I'm very worried Doctor. He's just not the same.**

A. History of presenting complaint (HOPC)-onset, duration, progression and severity
C: *You appear to be worried about him. I gather things have been difficult for you. Could you tell me when did this all start? (Onset)*
What are the changes you have noticed?

Establish premorbid functioning
- *Have you noticed a change in his personality? (Personality changes)*
- *How has he been before this change in his behaviour? (Premorbid personality)*
- *What is his daily functioning like now? (ADL functions)*
- *How does he spend his day?*
- *Does he attend day services or work? (Activities)*
- *If so, has the staff raised concerns?*

LEARNING DISABILITY

B. Identify possible aetiological factors
Use biopsychosocial approach to identify the aetiological factors in a learning disability patient.
Biological

- *I understand he was seen by the GP. Has he had any physical health problems?*
- *Has he had any trauma or head injury? (Falls)*
- *Is he on any regular medication? (Medication)*
- *Have there been any investigations done by the GP?*
- *Further exploration of constipation, infections, heart problems and thyroid.*
- *Does he have fits?*
- *Check sensory functions for example onset of cataract, hearing problems or if visual not working*

Epilepsy

- *Further exploration of epilepsy.*
- *Is his Epilepsy under control?*
- *What type of Epilepsy does he have? (For example: absences, tonic-clonic, myoclonic, TLE(Temporal Lobe Epilepsy), status epilepticus)*
- *What is the frequency of his seizures?*
- *When was the last seizure?*

Psychological
Need to differentiate Depression from Dementia.

C. Cognitive (4 A's)
I.   Amnesia

- *Have you noticed any memory difficulties?(memory)*
- *Can you give me some examples of his forgetfulness?*
- *How has it progressed?(progression)*
- *Has it come on suddenly or gradually?*

II.   Apraxia

How is he able to take care of himself?

III. Aphasia

- *Has he had difficulty in expressing himself?*
(Understanding and production of language and word finding problems)

IV.   Visual Agnosia

- *Is he able to recognise his family members? (prosopagnosia)*
- *Does he mistake things for example gets confused between tea bag and other objects when making tea)*

V.   Other Executive function

- *Is he able to make a cup of tea?*
- *How is his budgeting?*
- *How is his planning and organising?*

LEARNING DISABILITY

Assess for mood symptoms
- *How does he appear in his mood (tearful, anxious, and irritable)?*
- *How has he been sleeping? (Biological symptoms)*
- *How has he been eating?*
- *Has he been isolating himself? (Social isolation)*
- *Have you noticed if he is having any strange experiences?*
- *For example hearing voices when there is no one else around? Or seeing things when there is no one else around?*
- *Or maybe talking to himself? (Self-talk)*
- *How is his concentration? (Concentration)*

Risk assessment
- *Is he able to go out independently?*
- *Has he ever lost his way home? Has he been wandering? (Wandering)*
- *Have you been concerned about his safety at all? (Safety)*
- *This is a rather sensitive question that we usually ask, but has he expressed thoughts of wanting to end it all? (Suicidal thoughts)*

Past psychiatric history
- *Has he ever been seen by a psychiatrist in the past?*

D. Personal and family history
- *Is there anyone in the family that has similar problems?*

Summarise
Thank you for talking to me. To summarise, what you have told me is that there has been a change in your son's behaviour. You have also noticed that he is more forgetful. He has also had a recent history of collapsing.
I would like to arrange to see your son and order some investigations. I would like to meet with you again if you wish. Do you have any questions for me?

Thank you

LEARNING DISABILITY

DOWNS'S SYNDROME-DEPRESSION VS. DEMENTIA
History of presenting complaint- *(HOPC) onset, duration, progression and severity*
Differentiate Depression from dementia
Premorbid functioning
Identify possible aetiological factors
    Use biopsychosocial approach to identify the aetiological factors in a learning disability patient.
- **Biological**
- **Psychological**

Cognitive
Assess for mood symptoms
Risk assessment
Past psychiatric history
Personal and family history
Summarise
Background
Lennox gestaut syndrome
                        ©Smartsesh

DOWNS SYNDROME
Genotype: Trisomy 21
Phenotype:
- *Facial-flat occiput, oblique palpebral fissures, epicanthic flds, small mouth and teeth, high arched palate, short borad hands, hypotonia*
- *Cardiac-Congenital heart disease(septal defects)*
- *GIT duodenal obstruction*
- *ENDOCCRINE –hypothyroidism*
- *HAEMATOLIGIC- leukaemia*
- *ENT*
- *CNS Alzheimer's changes*
- *Epilepsy*
- *Infancy West syndrome*
- *Early adulthood 20's Partial epilepsy*
- *Later 40's Lennox Gestaut syndrome*

                ©Smartsesh

LEARNING DISABILITY

3. DOWNS SYNDROME -BRUISING

Suggested approach
Introduction
C: Hello, I'm Dr ....I am a psychiatrist. Thank you for coming to see me. I understand that you and the staff have concerns about Mr Brown. Would you be able to tell me more about the nature of your concerns?

C: We have noticed that he had some bruising.

A. History of Presenting Complaint (HOPC) (onset, duration, progression and severity)
- Can you tell me more about what happened?
- When did you first notice the bruising? (onset)
- Can you describe this please?
- How severe is it? (progression)
- Has he had this before? (past history)

B. Identify possible aetiological factors
Use biopsychosocial approach to identify the aetiological factors in a learning disability patient

Biological
- Has he had any injuries? Has he had a bump to his head?
- Does he have any physical illnesses? Any history of bleeding disorders? E.g. Von Willebronds disease?
- Does he have any repetitive behaviour?
- What medication is he on?

Exploration of Epilepsy
- *If present, does he have a history of epilepsy?*
- *Is his Epilepsy under control?*
- *What type of Epilepsy does he have? (for example: absences, tonic-clonic, myoclonic, Temporal Lobe Epilepsy(TLE(Temporal Lobe Epilepsy)), status epilepticus)*
- *What is the frequency of his seizures?*
- *When was the last seizure?*
- *Is he on any regular medication? Have there been any changes in his medication?*
- *Does he take medication regularly?*

Psychological
- *Have you noticed whether he appears happy or sad? (mood)*
- *Has he been isolating himself? (social isolation)*
- *Has he been tearful at all? (crying)*
- *Has he had any aggressive outbursts? (aggression/violence)*
- *Has he expressed that he wanted to harm himself? (suicidal ideation)*

Social
- *Are you aware of anything that is happening at home?*
- *Do we suspect that he could be abused? Is he vulnerable?*
[Enquire more specifically about details of this-possible unexplained injuries, or suspicious injuries)
- *Has social services been in contact?*
- *If he is attending day centre, have they mentioned anything at day centres? (day activities)*

C. Previous episodes
- *Has this happened before?*

D. Past psychiatric history
- *Has he ever been seen by a psychiatrist in the past?*

E. Personal and family history
- *Is there anyone in his family that has any similar problems?*

F. Risk assessment
- *Have there been any concerns for his safety?*

Summarise
Thank you for talking to me. It has been most helpful. To summarise, what you have told me is that Mr Brown has recently been presenting with bruises. He has a history of seizures, and there have been some recent changes in his medication. I would like to assess this further.

I would like to meet with you again.

Thank you.

> **DOWNS –BRUISING**
>
> **History of presenting complaint (HOPC)-**onset, duration, progression and severity
> - **Details about the bruising**
>
> **Identify possible aetiological factors**
>
> **Use biopsychosocial approach to identify the**
>
> **aetiological factors in a learning disability patient**
> - **Biological-physical illnesses, Epilepsy**
> - **Psychological**
> - **Depressive and psychotic symptoms**
> - **Social**
> - **Changes in the environment**
>
> **Past psychiatric history**
> **Personal and family history**
> **Summarise**
>
> ©*Smartsesh*

POSSIBLE VARIATIONS OF THEME
1.36 yr. old man who has a history of bruising and recent changes to his epilepsy medication
2.36 yr. old lady with bruising and possible issues of safeguarding due to physical abuse in the home

LEARNING DISABILITY

4. INDECENT EXPOSURE IN LEARNING DISABILITY

INSTRUCTIONS TO THE CANDIDATE
You have been asked to assess a man with mild learning disability. He and his girlfriend have now found out that she is pregnant. He has had a conviction of indecent exposure a year ago. He has asked to come and see you as he was told by the social workers that the baby will be taken into care immediately after birth. Take a relevant history.

TASK
- Elicit a history.
- Address his concerns.

PAY PARTICULAR ATTENTION TO THE FOLLOWING (MENTAL CHECKLIST)
- Establish details of pregnancy and feelings around his parenting capacity.
- Acknowledge his concerns and explain to him about post birth assessment.
- Establish history of exhibitionism.
- Conduct a risk assessment including recidivism.

COMMUNICATION SKILLS
- Start the interview by developing rapport and showing empathy.
- Anticipate a distressed man with learning disability.
- Pitch the level of the interview at his level of understanding.
- Acknowledge his concerns and seek to understand the subjective experience.

Suggested approach
Introduction
C: Hello, I'm Dr... I'm one of the psychiatrists. I understand you have asked to see me as you had some concerns about your girlfriend's pregnancy. It must be worrying for you. Can you tell me about your girlfriend and your relationship?

P: My girlfriends name is X and we have been together for x time.

C: How many months pregnant is she and how is coping with everything?
- How are you both feeling about the pregnancy? Are you looking forward to the baby?
- Do you have any other children?
- What do you think about having any more children?
- Are you getting any support from your family? (Support)
- How are you usually able to take care of yourself? For example shopping, cleaning and are you on any benefits? (ADL Activity of daily living)
- Do you think you need more help and support than you are getting?

- *Can you tell me more about these worries about your baby being taken away?*

P: My girlfriend's social workers told me this.

C: From my experience, they usually don't take babies away unless there is a reason. The social workers will usually have a meeting with you, your girlfriend and few other people before and after the baby is born. They will see how you are able to take care of your baby and what help you and your girlfriend would need.

At the meeting we can also discuss for the future about family planning. If you wish we can arrange a meeting with your girlfriend, and your social workers, and we could talk more about this? **(This will incorporate the parenting assessment and parenting capacity)**

Throughout the interview continue to reassure him that the baby is not automatically taken away.

History of Presenting Complaint (HOPC) (onset, duration, progression and severity)
- *I understand you have been charged with exposing yourself in the past. If it not too difficult would you are able to tell me more about this?*
- *What has happened? How many times has this happened?*
- *Are you worried it might happen again?*
- *If you are finding it difficult to talk about this now, we can arrange to talk more about this some other time. It would help if you could tell me more about this?*

Further exploration of indecent exposure
- *Can you tell me more how you go about exposing yourself?*
- *Where do usually go?*
- *What do you do? (Exhibitionism)*
- *Who is usually around? What age groups? Any preference for male, female or children? (Target groups)*
- *How do feel? What do you think about the person?*
- *Do you get aroused? Do you get an erection? What do you do?*
- *Do you masturbate? (Masturbation)*
- *Ado you have any fantasies/porn? (Fantasies/porn)*
- *Do you ever feel like taking it further? Has this ever happened?*
- *Have you ever followed anyone? (Stalking behaviour)*

Identify triggers
- *What usually causes you to do this? (Trigger)*
- *How do you usually cope? (Coping)*
- *Some people usually cope with drinking and street drugs. How about you? (Drug and alcohol)*
- *What can we do now to help you?*

LEARNING DISABILITY

Forensic History
- *Have you ever been caught? What charges?*
- *Have you had any other involvement with the police?*
- *How about past sexual offences?*
- *Have you had a history of violence?*
- *Do you have any other convictions or pending charges?*
- *Are you on probation? (Enquire about probation)*

Psychiatric
- *How long have you been receiving support from the Community Learning Disability Team (CLDT)?*

Risk assessment
Self
- *Have you ever had thoughts of wanting to end your life?(suicidal thoughts)*

Others
Recidivism
- *What do you intend to do now?*

Insight
- *What can we do to help you now?*

Summarise

Thank you for talking to me. To summarise what we discussed, you have been concerned about your girlfriend's pregnancy and that you thought the baby will be taken away. From my experience this does not automatically occur. The social services will come to your house to see you and will assess if you are able to take care of your baby.

I appreciate you talking to me about exposing yourself in public. I would like to offer you another appointment to address this issue. What help would you like with this?

Thank you

LEARNING DISABILITY –INDECENT EXPOSURE

Enquire about some background information
- Pregnancy
- Assess his view of current pregnancy and being a father
- Assess his functioning i.e. Activities of daily living ADL's
- Reassurance –baby not taken away

Explain about Parenting assessment and parenting capacity

HOPC (Severity, onset, duration, progression)
- Further exploration of indecent exposure
- Identify possible triggers

Forensic history

Risk assessment

Past Psychiatric history

Plan for further management and willingness to accept help

©Smartsesh

POSSIBLE VARIATIONS OF THEME
- 27 yr. old with moderate learning disability, recently found out his girlfriend is pregnant. He has been caught exposing himself

LEARNING DISABILITY

5. INDECENT EXPOSURE

INSTRUCTIONS TO CANDIDATE
You have been asked to see the mother of the learning disability patient whom you assessed in the previous station. She is upset and wants to know why her son's partner was not sterilised.

TASK FOR THE CANDIDATE
- Address the mother's concerns.
- Explain further management.

PAY PARTICULAR ATTENTION TO THE FOLLOWING (MENTAL CHECKLIST)
- Explain about your assessment with son.
- Explain sterilisation is not routinely performed on learning disabled.
- Explain further management with CLDT.
- Advise on contraception.
- Son to engage in Sex offender Treatment Programme SOTP.
- Offer her a Carers' assessment.

COMMUNICATION SKILLS
- Start the interview by developing rapport and showing empathy.
- Show sensitivity when discussing these issues.
- Anticipate a distressed mother, who has her own issues of raising a learning disabled child.

Suggested approach
Introduction
C: Hello, I'm Dr .. I'm one of the psychiatrists. I have seen your son and he has given me permission to speak to you. I understand that you wanted to talk to me about this. I will try my best to see how we can help you and your son in this situation.

M: I don't know why they have allowed this to happen. They should sterilise his girlfriend. Why don't they do that?

Brief synopsis from previous station tailored according to the mother's response
C: I can see you are clearly upset about this situation with your son. I will try my best to explain. I have seen your son and he has spoken about his feelings about his girlfriend's pregnancy.
From my experience, even though they both have learning disability, this still gives them the **rights** to make this decision. It doesn't mean that if someone has learning disability, that this decision is taken away from them. A person with learning disability decisions should be respected.

LEARNING DISABILITY

Sterilisation is something only done with consent. The process is by application to the court in terms of a legal framework and there usually has to be a strong reason for this. This can also be done by instructing a solicitor. (Sterilisation)

M: They both have learning disability. I still don't know how they are allowed to make this decision to have children?

C: In order for any person to make a decision, we usually assess their parenting capacity. That is a test which has four main parts to it. In this process of assessing capacity, we assess whether the person is able to understand what it is to be a parent, whether they are able to retain the information, whether they are able to weigh the risks and benefits, and lastly whether they are able to communicate this decision. We usually do our best to assess whether they have capacity to make this decision. We will need to assess his views of being a parent. (Parenting capacity)

C: We can offer your son and his girlfriend support from the social services. The social services can do their parenting assessments per and post birth assessments. They will also try to identify what level of support your son and his girlfriend would require.

M: What support will they receive?

C: I can assure you that I and the multidisciplinary team, including social services will do our best to act on behalf of your son's best interest. I can arrange if you wish and with permission from your son to have a meeting with the social workers to discuss the level of support required and what assistance can be offered. Part of our work with learning disability people is to provide advice on contraception and family planning.
Do you have any other questions?

M: How will my grandchild be if they both have parents have learning disability?

C: I know this must be a concern for you. From the evidence that is available if both parents have learning disability, the child will not have an IQ less than either of their parents. So that is reassuring in a sense.

C: Your son has also mentioned about his exposing himself and he is willing to get help for this. Would you like to know more about the treatment options available? (Elaborate on SOTP -Sex Offenders Treatment Programme)

Summarise
Thank you for talking to me. To summarise, you have had concerns about your son and his girlfriend's pregnancy. I will arrange for a meeting with the social services where we can discuss this further and provide advice on family planning.

LEARNING DISABILITY

I know this must be a lot for you to take on board. We can offer you some support and carers assessment. There are also some charity organisations and voluntary organisations.

INDECENT EXPOSURE DISCUSSION WITH THE MOTHER
Sterilisation- on done in extreme cases
- Need consent or application to court

Parenting capacity
- Understand, retain, weigh risks and benefits and communicate decision

Pre and post birth assessment
Assess level of functioning
Social services
Contraception
- Advice on family planning

Carers assessment and voluntary organisations
- **Indecent exposure –SOTP**
- **Summarise**

©Smartsesh

POSSIBLE VARIATIONS OF THEME
1. You are seeing the mother of the man in the previous station, who wants his girlfriend sterilised.
2. You are seeing the mother of the girlfriend, who is demanding her daughter is sterilised.

LEARNING DISABILITY

6. ASPERGERS-HISTORY

INSTRUCTIONS TO CANDIDATE
You have been asked to see this 27 yr old man David Brown who a software developer. He has been referred by his GP as he has been experiencing difficulty at his new job with his co-workers.

TASK FOR THE CANDIDATE
- Elicit history to come to a diagnosis.

PAY PARTICULAR ATTENTION TO THE FOLLOWING (MENTAL CHECKLIST)
- Establish the history of main complaint (onset, duration, severity and progression)
- Establish the core features of Aspergers syndrome
- Establish the qualitative impairment in social interaction
- Exclude language development delay
- Qualitative impairments in verbal or non-verbal communication
- Establish the restricted stereotyped interests and repetitive behaviours and activities
- Supplement this with a developmental history (see Autism station-p.409)
- Screen for co-morbid mental illness i.e. Depression, Anxiety, OCD.

COMMUNICATION SKILLS
- Start the interview by developing rapport and showing empathy.
- Seek to understand the subjective experience of the individual.

Suggested approach
Introduction
C: Hello, I am Dr.... I am one of the psychiatrists. I understand that your GP has referred you as you have been experiencing some difficulty at your new work place.

P: Yes doc, I can't seem to get on with any of the people there?

C: Can you tell me what do you mean by that?

P: I can't seem to get on with anyone there, even though I do make the effort.

C: I can see this is distressing to you. It would be helpful if maybe I could ask you more specific questions about your relationships with people in general.

A. Elicit core features of Asperger's syndrome in the 3 main domains:
1. Establish the qualitative impairment in social interaction
- Can you tell me about your relationships in general? How have they turned out?

- *Do you have any close friends?*
- *Do you usually find it difficult to make or keep friends?*
- *How do you feel about socialising in groups?*
- *Some people tell me that they prefer their own company. How about you? Do you tend to isolate yourself?*
- *Do you have any difficulty maintaining eye contact when you are conversing with someone? Do you perhaps tend to avoid eye contact?*
- *If you were in company, would you be able to understand other people's feelings? For example, if someone was upset of got hurt, would you know when to comfort them? How would you know? What would you do?*

First 3yrs of life [usually obtained as part of developmental history]
- *Were you able to show joint interest if someone pointed at something?*
- *How would you have communicated your needs? Were you able to gesture if you needed something?*

2. Qualitative impairments in verbal or non-verbal communication
Exclude language development delay [to distinguish this from Autism]
Typically 'pedantic or stilted speech'
- *How are you able to communicate with others?*
- *Do people ever have difficulty understanding you? Or do you perhaps have difficulty understanding others?*
- *Have you ever found yourself saying the wrong thing in a social setting?(faux pas)*
- *Do you have any difficulty interpreting what others say? For example would you be able to understand if someone made a joke? Or would you perhaps take the 'literal' meaning of a joke?*
- *Are you aware when you are in conversation that the other person might get bored or that they might want to talk?*

First 3 yrs. of life [usually obtained as part of developmental history]
- *Are you aware of whether you had any delay in your speech development? [First words, sentences, echolalia, pronominal reversal of you and I]*

3. Establish stereotyped Interests and repetitive behaviour
- *Are there certain things that you are interested in?*
- *If yes, what are they?*
- *How much time would you spend on this interest? What is it that you do?*
- *Have you ever done things repeatedly? For example positioning objects in the house?*
- *If there was any change to your daily routine, how would you cope with this?*
- *[Establish history of any repetitive movements ie hand or finger flapping, spinning, rocking body]*

LEARNING DISABILITY

First 3 yrs. of life
- How would you cope with any changes to your routine?

B. Screen for co-morbidity like Depression, Obsessive Compulsive disorder (OCD) and personality disorder)

Summarise
Thank you for talking to me. From what we have discussed it appears that you have been experiencing difficulty in social interactions. You also have some unusual interests and have become an expert in astronomy. I would like to see you again and do some further assessments as I think you could possibly have Asperger's syndrome. In order to complete this assessment I would need to get some more information about the first 3 years of your life, possibly from one of your parents.

POSSIBLE VARIATIONS OF THEME
1. 45 yr. old mathematician with Asperger's and Depression.
2. 26 yr. old man with Asperger's syndrome and suicidal.

LEARNING DISABILITY

SCREENING TOOLS FOR ASPERGERS SYNDROME
- *Autism Spectrum Quotient (ASQ)*
- *Empathy Quotient(EQ)*
- *Childhood Autism Spectrum Test(CAST)*
- *AAA   Adult Asperger Assessment tool (Baron-Cohen et al 2005)*

*These are screening tools available from the **Autism Research Centre** website.*

Other diagnostic assessments FOR Autistic spectrum conditions
- *ADI-R   Autism Diagnostic Interview, Revised*
- *ADOS   Autism Diagnostic Observation Schedule*
- *DISCO   The Diagnostic Interview for Social and Communication Disorders designed by Wing and Gould*

F84.5 Asperger's syndrome

A disorder of uncertain nosological validity, characterized by the same type of qualitative abnormalities of reciprocal social interaction that typify autism, together with a restricted, stereotyped, repetitive repertoire of interests and activities. It differs from autism primarily in the fact that there is no general delay or retardation in language or in cognitive development. This disorder is often associated with marked clumsiness. There is a strong tendency for the abnormalities to persist into adolescence and adult life. Psychotic episodes occasionally occur in early adult life.

Incl.:
Autistic psychopathy
Schizoid disorder of childhood

LEARNING DISABILITY

7. EPILEPSY-HISTORY

INSTRUCTIONS TO THE CANDIDATE
You have been asked to see Barry Rowland, a 27 yr old man who is known
with epilepsy.

TASK FOR THE CANDIDATE
- Elicit history of seizures.

**PAY PARTICULAR ATTENTION TO THE FOLLOWING (MENTAL
CHECKLIST)**
- Establish the history of presenting complaint (onset, duration,
  frequency and severity)
- Establish the phases of seizures (aura, pre ictal, ictal and post
  ictal)
- Establish the risk factors associated with seizures
- Conduct a risk assessment

COMMUNICATION SKILLS
- Start the interview by developing rapport and showing empathy.
- Seek to understand the subjective experience of the individual

---

Suggested approach
Introduction
C: Hello I am Dr.... I am one of the psychiatrists. I have been asked by your
GP to see you as you have recently been experiencing some fits.

**A. History of presenting complaint (onset, duration, severity and
progression)**
- Can you describe to me what happens?
- How does it usually start?

B. Aura:
- Are you able to know when you are about to have a seizure?
- How do you know when you are about to have a seizure?
- Do you get a sensation or feeling in your tummy? (Epigastric
  sensation)
- Do you smell anything or see anything?

C. Pre ictal phase

D. Seizures
- How often do these seizures occur?
- Does the fit start in one part of the body and then spreads to the rest
  of the body?
- Are they associated with loss of consciousness/falling to the
  ground?(loss of consciousness)
- Is there any limb jerking or tongue biting? (Tongue biting)

- *Do you lose control over body functions? Do you wet yourself?(incontinence)*
- *How long does an attack last? (Duration)*
- *Are you able to recall what happens during the seizures? (Amnesia)*

E. Post ictal state
- *How do you feel after the seizure? Do you feel confused? (Confusion)*
- *Do you experience distortion in shape and distance of objects?*
- *Do things appear shrunken or larger than normal? (Micropsia/macropsia)*
- *Do you experience déjà vu (feelings of familiarity) or jamais vu (feelings of unfamiliarity)?*
- *Ask about depersonalisation or derealisation.*
- *History of absence seizures*
- *Ask about brief staring spells and automatism.*

F. Establish aetiological factors using a biopsychosocial approach
1. Biological
- *Have you ever had a history of febrile seizures as a child? (Febrile seizures)*
- *Have you ever had a head injury?*
- *Are you sensitive to loud noises? (Loud noises)*
- *How about when you are exposed to lights or when watching television? (Watching TV flickering lights)*

Drug and alcohol history
- *Do you drink? Have you ever had seizures related to you stopping drinking? (Delirium Tremens or alcohol withdrawal seizures)*
- *Do you use any street drugs?*
- *Are you on any medication?*
- *Have you been taking it regularly? (Compliance)*

2. Psychological
- *Have you been under any stress recently?*

3. Social
- *What work do you do? Do you operate any machinery?*

G. Screen for psychotic symptoms
- *Do a mental state examination for post ictal psychotic symptoms*

I. Establish impact on daily functioning
- *Has these seizures affected you daily functioning? If yes, then how?*
- *What does it restrict you from doing?*

J. Risk Assessment
- *Do you drive?*
- *Have you ever seizures while driving?*

Summarize

Thank you for talking to me. From what we have discussed it is most likely you are experiencing seizures. I would like to arrange for an EEG electroencephalogram to investigate this

Do you have any questions?

LEARNING DISABILITY

TYPES OF SEIZURES

a. **Myoclonic jerks**: brief twitching or jerky movements of a muscle or group of muscles.

b. **Absence seizures**: also called petit mal. Patients blank out, stare and may blink repeatedly. At times eyes also role up. These seizures last for seconds and are not preceded by any warning signs. Patients are alert immediately after the attack. Common between the age groups of 4-14. 70% resolve by the age of 18.

c. **Atonic seizures**: also known as drop attacks. During the attack there is loss of muscle tone, resulting in fall to the ground or dropping things. Lasts for seconds.

d. **Tonic**: muscle tones are increased which manifests as stiffening of the muscles. Consciousness is generally preserved. Commonly occur during sleep.

e. **Clonic:** alternate contraction and relaxation of muscles resulting in rhythmic jerking movements. Clonic seizures are rare and usually occur with tonic seizures as tonic clonic.

f. **Tonic clonic**: also known as grand mal seizures. Usually last between 1-3 minutes. Muscle groups first stiffen. This may be associated with a cry or shrieking sound. There is loss of consciousness and patient falls to the ground. Tongue biting, cyanosis and jerking movements are commonly witnessed. As the body relaxes urinary incontinence may occur. Patient is drowsy or confused after the attack.

g. **Simple partial**: can be motor or sensory. In motor seizures, jerking of a muscle group may manifest of a part of the body. In sensory seizures, patient may be able to smell or taste things. Numbness and pins and needles are common.

h. **Complex partial**: associated with aura, automatism (purposeless movements- patients pick at the air or their clothes), loss of consciousness, déjà vu, patients repeat phrases, stare blankly or behave oddly. Complex [atrial may become secondary generalised.

i. **Secondary generalised:** starts as partial and then becomes generalised. Associated with loss of consciousness.

LEARNING DISABILITY

8. ARSON-HISTORY

INSTRUCTIONS TO CANDIDATE
You have been asked to see an 18 year old man Andrew Gates
Who has set fire to the residential home that he was living in?

TASK FOR THE CANDIDATE
- Elicit history to establish a provisional diagnosis.
- Elicit a risk assessment.

PAY PARTICULAR ATTENTION TO THE FOLLOWING (MENTAL CHECKLIST)
- Establish the fire setting event and the circumstances
- Establish possible precipitators using a biopsychosocial approach
- Elicit psychiatric history with view of a provisional diagnosis BPD(Borderline Personality disorder), Depression, Conduct disorder)
- Consider non psychiatric causes for example relationship difficulties,
- Elicit a history with view of a diagnosis.
- Conduct a risk assessment.

COMMUNICATION SKILLS
- Start the interview by developing rapport and showing empathy.
- Acknowledge the nature of the incident and need to enquire about details.
- Anticipate reluctance to disclose information.

Suggested approach
Introduction
C: Hello, I'm Dr ...one of the psychiatrists here and thank you for seeing me. You may know this but I have been asked to see you because of this incident with the fire at your residential home. I need to clarify what happened with you. Perhaps you could take me through what happened.

A. History of presenting complaint (HOPC) -onset, duration, progression, severity

1. Antecedent
- What happened before you started the fire?

2. Behaviour
- So what did you do exactly? (Arson)
- Did you take any precautions?
- Was it planned or impulsive?
- How did you feel after lighting the fire? Did you feel any pleasure?
- Sometimes some people get sexually aroused, has this ever been true for you? (Sexual arousal)
- How did you feel after this? (Regrets/remorse)

- *Include non-psychiatric causes?*

3. Consequence
- *What did you do?*
- *Did you speak to the police?*
- *Has this ever happened in the past? (Past fire setting history/fascination with fire)*

B. Aetiological factors
Use a biopsychosocial approach to elicit aetiological factors
Biological
- *Any family history of criminality.*
- *Any Learning disabilities/ASD (Autistic spectrum Disorder).*

Psychological
- *Check for Hellman's triad-(bedwetting, fire-setting, cruelty to animals), CSA (child sex abuse).*
- *In general do you feel safe?*
- *I need to ask something very sensitive, have you ever been sexually abused?*

Social
- *How have things been at home?*

C. Assess mental state at the time of the offending behaviour
Screen for underlying mental illness
- *Establish presence of Borderline personality traits Depression, Bipolar affective disorder, Psychosis, Learning difficulties*

D. Risk assessment

Include the following
1. Past risks
- *Past history of arson.*
- *Drug and alcohol history.*
- *Forensic history.*

2. Current risks
- *Identify any current risks*

3. Future risks
- *Recidivism*
- *What do you intend to do?*

Address in each
- *Risk to self.*
- *Risk to others.*
- *Risk to property.*

Summarise

Thank you for talking to me. To summarise, you have told me that you set fire your home. You have been setting fire since a young age and this is usually is triggered at times when you become stressed.
What help would you like?

Thank you

LEARNING DISABILITY

ARSON
Elicit history and Risk assessment
A. HOPC (onset, duration, progression, severity)
    1. Antecedent-*trigger*
    2. Behaviour- *pyromania*
    3. Consequence-*damage, remorse*
B. Aetiological factors
Use a biopsychosocial approach to elicit aetiological factors
    1. Biological *criminality, learning difficulties*
    2. Psychological *Hellman's triangle- bedwetting, cruelty to animals,*
CSA
    3. Social *stressors*
C. Assess mental state at the time of the offending behaviour
Screen for underlying mental illness
        • *Establish presence of Depression, bipolar affective disorder,*
          Psychosis and borderline personality traits
D. Risk assessment
    1. Past risks
      • *Past history of arson*
      • *Drug and alcohol history*
      • *Forensic history*
    2. Current risks
      • *Risk to self*
      • *Risk to others*
      • *Risk to property*
    3. Future risks
    • *Recidivism*
               ©Smartsesh

POSSIBLE VARIATIONS OF THEME
*1 Variation of theme-18 yr old boy with moderate learning disability
and antisocial personality disorder who set fire to the library.
2 18 yr old lady with mild learning disability who set fire in her
room, and she has a history of emotionally unstable personality
disorder.*

References
Forensic learning disability
Plant, A., McDermott, E., Chester, V. & Alexander, R.T. (2011). Substance misuse among offenders in a forensic intellectual disability service. Journal of Learning Disabilities and Offending Behaviour, 2 (3) 127-136.

Alexander, R.T., Hiremath, A., Chester, V., Green, F.N., Gunaratna, I.J. & Hoare, S. (2011). Evaluation of treatment outcomes from a medium secure unit for people with intellectual disability. Advances in Mental Health and Intellectual Disabilities, 5 (1) 22-32.

Alexander, R.T., Green, F.N., O'Mahony, B., Gunaratna, I. J., Gangadharan, S. K. & S. Hoare. (2010). Personality disorders in offenders with intellectual disability: a comparison of clinical, forensic and outcome variables and implications for service provision. Journal of Intellectual Disability Research, 54 (7) 650–658.

Alexander, R. & Cooray, S. (2003). Diagnosis of personality disorders in learning disability. British Journal of Psychiatry, 182, 28-31.

Down's Syndrome and Dementia
Lott, I. T., Dierssen, M. (2010) Cognitive deficits and associated neurological complications in individuals with Down's syndrome. The Lancet Neurology 9 (6):

Epilepsy
Ring, H., Zia, A., Bateman, N., Williams, E., Lindeman, S. & Himlok, K. (2009).How is epilepsy treated in people with a learning disability? A retrospective observational study of 183 individuals. Seizure, 18 (4) 264-268.http://www.seizure-journal.com/article/S1059-1311(08)00235-5/ab

NICE (2004). The diagnosis and management of the epilepsies in adults and children in primary and secondary care
.http://www.nice.org.uk/nicemedia/pdf/CG020fullguideline.pdf
Fitzgerald, B. & Ring, H. (2009). Epilepsy, mental health, adults with learning disability- reviewing the evidence. Psychiatry, 8 (11) 422-424.
http://www.psychiatryjournal.co.uk/article/S1476-1793 (09)00166-9/abstract

Royal College of Psychiatrists. DC-LD: Diagnostic Criteria for Psychiatric Disorders for Use with Adults with Learning Disabilities/mental Retardation (Occasional paper)
http://www.rcpsych.ac.uk/publications/collegereports/op/op48.aspx

Diagnostic Manual-Intellectual Disabilities (DM(Diabetes Mellitus)-ID): A Textbook of Diagnosis of Mental Disorders in People with Intellectual Disabilityhttp://www.dmid.org/

LEARNING DISABILITY

Other reading
Valuing People Now: A new three year strategy for people with learning disabilities., Department of Health 2009.
Death by indifference
Martian in the playground by Clare Sainsbury (understanding the school child with Aspergers syndrome)
The curious incident of the dog in the night by Mark Haddon(Aspergers)
The girl with the dragon tattoo by Stieg Larson

Online resources
Royal college of psychiatrist's health information leaflets for patient's
www.rcpsych.ac.uik
http://www.rcpsych.ac.uk/publications/booksbeyondwords.aspx

FORENSIC PSYCHIATRY

FORENSIC- Dr MS Thambirajah, Dr Piyal Sen

1. Indecent exposure-risk assessment
2. Morbid Jealousy – History taking
3. Morbid Jealousy – Discuss with wife
4. Morbid Jealousy –Discuss with consultant
5. Morbid Jealousy – Displacement
6. Arson-History- History Taking
7. Erotomania – History taking
8. Erotomania – Discuss management with nurse
9. Erotomania – Discuss management with consultant
10. Violence Risk Assessment- history taking
11. Paedophile- Risk assessment
12. Assault on the ward- history taking
13. Assault on the ward- Discuss management

FORENSIC PSYCHIATRY

1. INDECENT EXPOSURE

Instructions to the candidate
You are asked to see a 45 yr old gentleman Robert Cook who has been
exposing himself. He has gone to see his GP as he is concerned that he will
be caught by the police.

TASK FOR THE CANDIDATE
- Elicit a psychosexual history.
- Elicit a risk assessment.

MAIN POINTS TO CONSIDER
- Confidentiality and need to disclose if persons at risk.
- Establish the nature and severity of exhibitionism.
- Conduct a risk assessment and assess dangerousness.
- Establish if any underlying co-morbid mental illness.
- Elicit risk factors of recidivism.

Communication skills
- Develop rapport and show empathy.
- Anticipate some difficulty in disclosing information and
  engagement.
- Acknowledge the sensitivity of the nature of the exposing
  behaviour.
- Preface personal questions.

Suggested approach
Introduction
C: Hello, I 'm Dr ....I'm one on the psychiatrists. I have been asked to see you
by your GP. Before we proceed, whatever we discuss is confidential. ....
[However if at any stage there appears to be a risk to someone, I will have to
disclose this information.]
Would you like to tell me more about your concerns?

P: I went to see my GP as I was worried about doing it again.

C: I appreciate you coming to see me. I can understand this might not be
easy for you. I will have to ask you some personal questions. Can you tell
me more about what you are worried about doing?

A. **History of presenting complaint (HOPC)-onset, duration, progression,
and severity**
Psychosexual history
1. Includes the offending behaviour- Exhibitionism
- Can you tell me more about how you go about exposing yourself?
- Where have you been doing it usually??(target groups)
- What do you do?
- Are these planned or impulsive?

FORENSIC PSYCHIATRY

- *Who is usually around? What age groups? Do you have any preference for male, female or children?*
- *How do they feel? How do you react? What was their reaction?(arousal pattern)*
- *Do you get aroused? Do you get an erection? What do you do exactly?*
- *Do you ever masturbate?(masturbatory habits)*
- *Do you have any fantasies? Do you use pornography?(pornography and fantasies)*
- *Have you ever felt like taking it a step further? For example wanting to have intercourse with the person? Has this ever happened?(risk taking behaviours)*
- *Have you ever followed anyone?(stalking)*

C: I understand that you went to see your GP, what made you do that?

2. Brief psycho sexual history
- *I would like to ask some questions about your earlier years. Can you tell me about when you reached puberty?(puberty)*
- *Can you tell me about your first sexual experience?*
- *What is your sexual orientation?(heterosexual/homosexual)*
- *Can you tell me about your sexual relationships?*
- *Can you tell me about your current sexual relationship?*
- *This is a rather personal question, but have you had any sexual difficulties?*
- *Have you noticed a change in your desire?*
- *Do you have problems with premature ejaculation or with erection?*
- *History of child sexual abuse(CSA)*

3. Establish presence of other Paraphilia
a) Transvestism
- *Do you cross-dress?*
- *Do you ever wish to be a member of the opposite sex?*

b) Fetishism
- *Do you get excited by inanimate objects like shoes?*

B. Forensic History
- *Have you had any involvement with the police?*
- *Have you had past sexual offences?*
- *Do you have a history of violence?*
- *Do you have any convictions or pending charges?*

C. Past Psychiatric History
- *Have you ever seen a psychiatrist in the past?*

D. Premorbid Personality
- *How would you describe yourself?*

E. Social history

FORENSIC PSYCHIATRY

- *Can you tell me who is in your family?*
- *Do you work?*

F. Mental state examination
a) Establish the cognitive distortions
- *Denial, minimisation*
- *Guilt, fantasies*
- *Lack of remorse*
- *Lack of victim empathy*

b) Establish the presence of underlying mental illness
Exclude Depression, Anxiety, Psychosis

c) Screen for suicidal ideation, intent or plans

G. Risk assessment
a) Risk to self
Have you been feeling depressed when you thought of
- *Have you ever had thoughts that life was not worth living?(suicidal thoughts)*
- *What are you planning to do? What are your intentions?*

b) Risk to others
- *How likely is that you would do this again?(Recidivism)*
- *Access to children -i.e. what work do you do?*
- *Have you ever used violence against others*
- *Weapons/violence*

c) Other
- *Drug and alcohol history*
- *Past forensic history*

Summarise
Thank you for talking to me and opening up about your exposing behaviour. From what we have discussed, you have told me that you have been exposing yourself for the past five years. You have not yet been caught by the police; however you are now worried about being caught, because of your increased urges. I would like to discuss the treatment options we have available. What help do you think you would like?

FORENSIC PSYCHIATRY

INDECENT EXPOSURE
HISTORY TAKING AND RISK ASSESSMENT
A. HOPC (onset, duration, progression, severity)

2. Psychosexual history
Arousal pattern, target groups, risk –obscene calls, sexual assault, rape, violence, stalking
3. Other paraphilia-a) Transvestism, b) Fetishism, c) Voyeurism
Puberty, first sexual experience, early morning erections, sexual relationship, Marriage or current sexual relationship, sexual difficulties
CSA
B. Forensic History
Offences, convictions, pending charges
Violence
C. Past Psychiatric history
D. Premorbid Personality
©Smartsesh

POSSIBLE VARIATIONS OF THEME
1. 45 yr. old man exposing himself and is now suicidal and depressed.
2. 45 yr. old man who is exposing himself. He has been caught by the police and brought to the hospital.

FORENSIC PSYCHIATRY

2. MORBID JEALOUSY

INSTRUCTIONS TO THE CANDIDATE
You have been asked to see this 46 yr old gentleman Alex Norman who was referred by his GP. He has expressed some symptoms of Anxiety as he has recently started to believe that his wife is having an affair.

TASK FOR THE CANDIDATE
Elicit a history and conduct a risk assessment.

**PAY PARTICULAR ATTENTION TO THE FOLLOWING (MENTAL CHECKLIST)*
- *Establish his concerns of infidelity.*
- *Establish whether it is delusional or an overvalued idea.*
- *Establish underlying mental illness.*
- *Establish the risk he poses to his partner and risk to 3rd party.*
- *Establish past forensic history.*
- *Assess his insight and need to come into hospital.*

COMMUNICATION SKILLS
- *Establish rapport and show empathy.*
- *Anticipate that he would be guarded about his beliefs.*
- *Tactfully prise out his beliefs without antagonising him.*
- *Patient is bound to be angry.*

Suggested approach
Introduction
C: *Hello, I'm Dr ....I am a psychiatrist. I have been asked to see you by your GP. I understand you have been experiencing some Anxiety symptoms. I would like to talk to you more about this and perhaps how we can help you. Is that all right with you?*

P: **Hello Doctor. It's my wife. I think she's having an affair.**

C: *I can see this is something that is upsetting you. I appreciate you talking to me. Can you tell me more about this please?*

A. HOPC (onset, duration, progression, severity)
- *Can you tell me more about your suspicions?(infidelity)*
- *Why do you suspect she is having an affair?*
- *What evidence do you have for her unfaithfulness?(evidence)*
- *What sorts of things have you been doing to produce some evidence?(producing evidence)*
- *For example-have you been checking her mobile, email, handbag, underwear...*
- *Have you been following her?(stalking behaviour)*
- *How much time have you spent looking for evidence?*

FORENSIC PSYCHIATRY

B. Mental state examination
1. Differentiate whether it is an overvalued idea or a delusional belief
- *How do you know this is the explanation?*
- *How convinced are you this is happening?*
- *Could there perhaps be another explanation for this?*
- *Do you think perhaps that your mind could be playing tricks on you?*
- *How does this make you feel?*

2. Establish presence of underlying mental illness
- *How has your mood been recently?(mood)*
- *How have you been sleeping?(biological symptoms)*
- *How have you been eating*
- *Have you lost weight?*
- *Have you been having any unusual experiences?*
- *For example, some people if they are stressed can hear voices when no one is around?(auditory hallucinations)*
- *Or they might see things when no one is around?(visual hallucinations)*
- *Have you had any such experiences?*
- *Have you ever felt that life was not worth living? (suicidal ideation))*

C. Aetiological factors
Use a biopsychosocial approach to identify the possible aetiological factors
1. Biological
- *Are you on any medication? Do you have any physical health problems?*

2. Psychological
- *Have you ever seen a psychiatrist in the past?*

3. Social
- *How have you been coping?*
- *Some people take drugs and alcohol, how about you?(drug and alcohol history)*

4. Precipitating factors or triggers?
- *Have you been under any stress recently? (stressors)*

D. Psychosexual history
- *Tell me about your other relationships?*
- *Have you had anything similar in the past?*
- *How is your current relationship going?*
- *This is a rather personal question, but do you have any sexual difficulties?*

E. Past forensic history
- *Have you been involved with the police in the past?*

FORENSIC PSYCHIATRY

F. Risk assessment
1. Past risk
- Tell me about your previous relationships?
- Have there been any problems?
- [Identify historical risks]

2. Current risk
- How have your feelings towards your wife been recently?
- Have you discussed this with her?(confrontation)
- What has she said?
- Has there been any violence in your relationship?
- Do you know the other person? (3rd party risk)
- Do you have any children?
- Have you ever felt that life was not worth living?(suicidal ideation)

3. Future risk
- What have you been planning to do about this?
- Have you had thoughts of harming anyone else?(homicidal ideation)

Summarise
Thank you for talking to me. I understand that you have been going through a rather difficult time. It looks like you are convinced about that your partner is having an affair. I am concerned that you may be under stress and would like to see how we can help you. We do have some treatment options available like medication and talking therapies to help.

Insight
I think it might be better for you to be in hospital, what do you think?

POSSIBLE VARIATIONS OF THEME
1. You could be referred someone with a delusional or non-delusional jealousy associated with sexual problems, alcohol dependency, domestic violence, Depression, associated with Dissocial personality disorder or substance misuse
2. Morbid jealousy- 32yr. old banker experiencing Anxiety symptoms at work.
3. Morbid jealousy- 46yr. old male who has a history of assaulting previous partners. He was brought in by police as he suspects his wife of having an affair. He assaulted her earlier that day.

MORBID JEALOUSY

A. HOPC (onset, duration, progression, severity)
- Enquire about suspicions of infidelity
- Evidence for this
- Producing some evidence
- Checking behaviours –mobile, email, letters, underwear, following her

B. Mental state examination
- Differentiate whether it is an overvalued idea or a delusional belief
- Elicit mood, Anxiety and psychotic symptoms
- Suicidal and homicidal ideation

C. Aetiological factors
  1. Biological
  - Medication, physical health problems
  2. Psychological
  - Past history of mental illness-Schizophrenia, BPAD
  3. Social
  - Drugs and alcohol dependence
  4. Precipitating factors or triggers

D. Past psychiatric history

E. Psychosexual history
- Past relationships
- Current relationship
- Children
- Sexual difficulties

F. Past forensic history

G. Risk assessment
  1. Past-violence, convictions
  2. Current – violence,
  3. Future - intentions

Admission to hospital

©Smartsesh

FORENSIC PSYCHIATRY

3. MORBID JEALOUSY- [ASSOCIATED WITH STRESS AT WORK- DISPLACEMENT]

INSTRUCTION TO CANDIDATE
Another possible variation of morbid jealousy. This 45 yr old gentleman Alex Norman has been referred for Anxiety at work.

TASK FOR THE CANDIDATE
- Elicit history to come to a diagnosis.

PAY PARTICULAR ATTENTION TO THE FOLLOWING (MENTAL CHECKLIST)
- Establish the link of displacement.
- Establish the presence of infidelity.
- Establish whether it is delusional or overvalued idea.
- Establish underlying mental illness.
- Establish the risk he poses on his partner and risk to 3rd party.
- Elicit past forensic history.
- Assess need to come into hospital.

COMMUNICATION SKILLS
- Establish rapport and show empathy.
- Anticipate that he would be guarded about his beliefs.
- Tactfully appraise his beliefs without antagonising him.
- The candidate would need to identify that his current problems at home are being displaced at work.
- The candidate would need to explore the Anxiety symptoms and then ask tactfully about things at home.

Suggested approach
Introduction
C: Hello, I'm Dr ....I am a psychiatrist. I have been asked to see you by your GP. I understand you have been experiencing some Anxiety symptoms. I would like to talk to more about this and perhaps how we can help you.

P: I told my GP I have been anxious...

C: Can you tell me more about this?

P: It's when I am at work. I don't know why this is.

C: I can see that this is worrying you. In my experience if people are worried about something, then it can be that this could transfer to when they are at work for example. (Displacement)
- Is there anything else troubling you?
- How are things at work?
- How are things at home?
- How is your relationship?

- *Do you get anxious at work?*
- *Can you describe this please?*

P: Things have been difficult with my wife. I think she is having an affair?

A. HOPC (onset, duration, progression and severity)
- *Can you tell me more about your suspicions? (infidelity)*
- *What evidence do you have of her unfaithfulness?*
- *What sorts of things have you been doing to produce some evidence?(producing evidence)*
- *For example-have you been checking her mobile, email, handbag, underwear...*
- *Have you been following her?(stalking behaviour)*
- *How much time have you spent looking for evidence?*

B. Mental state examination
1. Differentiate whether it is an overvalued idea or a delusional belief
- *How do you know this is the explanation?*
- *How convinced are you that this is happening?*
- *Could there perhaps be another explanation for this?*
- *Do you think that maybe your mind could be playing tricks on you?*

2. Establish presence of underlying mental illness
- *How has your mood been recently?(mood)*
- *Have you ever felt that life was not worth living?(suicidal ideation)*
- *How have you been sleeping?(biological symptoms)*
- *How have you been eating?*
- *Have you lost weight?*
- *Have you been having any unusual experiences?*
- *For example, some people if they are stressed can hear voices when no one is around?(auditory hallucinations))*
- *Or they might see things when no one is around?(visual hallucinations)*
- *Have you had any such experiences?*

C. Aetiological factors
Use a biopsychosocial approach to identify the possible aetiological factors
1. Biological
- *Are you on any medication? Do you have any physical health problems?*

2. Psychological
- *Have you ever seen a psychiatrist in the past?*

3. Social
- *How have you been coping?*

- *Some people take drugs and alcohol, how about you?(drug and alcohol history)*

4. Precipitating factors or triggers?
- *Have you been under any stress recently?(stressors)*

D. Psychosexual history
- *How have your other relationships been?*
- *Have you had anything similar in the past?*
- *Tell me about your current relationship?*
- *This is a rather personal question, but do you have any sexual difficulties?*

E. Past forensic history
- *Have you been involved with the police in the past?*

F Risk assessment
1. Past risk

2. Current risk
- *How have your feelings towards your wife been recently?*
- *Have you discussed this with her?*
- *What has she said?*
- *Has there been any violence in your relationship?*
- *Do you know the other person? (3ʳᵈ party risk)*
- *Do you have any children?*

3. Future risk
- *What have you been planning to do?*

Insight

Summarise
Thank you for talking to me. From what we have discussed today, I understand that you have been going through a rather difficult time. One explanation for what you are experiencing is that the problems at home appear to be displaced or transferred in a sense to when you are at work. You are convinced that your partner is having an affair. I am concerned that you may be under stress and would like to see how we can help you. The treatment options we have available are medication and talking therapies to help you.
I think it might be better for you to be in hospital, what do you think?(insight)

Thank you

FORENSIC PSYCHIATRY

FORENSIC PSYCHIATRY

4. MORBID JEALOUSY

INSTRUCTIONS TO THE CANDIDATE
You are about to see the partner of the man Alex Norman you assessed in the previous station. She is concerned about him.

TASK FOR THE CANDIDATE
- Discuss his diagnosis and management.

PAY PARTICULAR ATTENTION TO THE FOLLOWING (MENTAL CHECKLIST)
- Obtain collateral history.
- Provide information on the diagnosis of Morbid Jealousy.
- Highlight the risks he poses to herself and possible 3rd party.
- Discuss management using holistic or the biopsychosocial approach.
- Explain the need for admission either informally or detained under MHA(Mental Health Act)

COMMNUICATION SKILLS
- Establish rapport and develop empathy.
- Acknowledge the distress of this on her and partner.
- Establish a common ground for acting in best interests of her partner using a collaborative approach.
- Tactfully impart information about the diagnosis and risks.

Suggested approach
Introduction
C: Hello, I'm Dr ..... I am one of the psychiatrists. I have seen your husband and wanted to talk to you about my assessment and management. Before I begin, can I ask what your understanding is of what the current difficulties are with your husband?

W: I don't know. He is just not his usual self?

C: I gather that this must be a difficult time for you.
- Can you tell me more about what is happening at home?(stressors)
- Have you noticed any changes in his behaviour?(behavioural changes)
- How has his mood appeared in general?(mood)
- How does he usually cope? Does he drink?(coping skills)
- What type of person is he usually?(premorbid personality)
- How is the relationship between the two of you?(relationship)
- Has he lost his temper at all?(aggression)
- Has he ever been violent?(violence)

Summarise from previous station

C: Thank you for sharing this information with me. From my assessment with him, he has strong feelings for you. He has expressed to me that he believes that you are having an affair. *[Elaborate further depending with the information from previous station]*

W: Why would he say that?

C: I know this must be difficult to hear. I will explain about this more in detail, so that you can understand that it is actually the illness that is making him like this.

W: What is the diagnosis?

C: He has what we call '**Morbid Jealousy.**' This is when someone believes that their spouse is being unfaithful and is having an extramarital affair
He has misinterpreted some events and is quite convinced you are having an affair and being unfaithful, despite there being no evidence for his beliefs. This fixed belief is what we call a delusion of infidelity.

W: How common is it?

C: It is more common in females than males

W: What are the causes?

C: We cannot pinpoint one particular cause and it can be due to a few associated factors working together. From the evidence we have, it can occur in different mental illnesses like Schizophrenia, Psychosis, BPAD and Alcohol Dependence. Also people with certain suspicious or paranoid personalities are more vulnerable to develop this.
In your husband's case, I understand he has a history of drinking alcohol and has been previously treated for a mental illness.

I need to tell you also that I am concerned about the risk to you and the other person whom he is suspecting you of having an affair with. There is a risk that he can harm either you or the other person.

W: How are you going to treat him?

C: We usually assess the risk and consider admission to hospital either voluntary or alternatively we use the Mental Health Act(MHA 1983) (MHA). We usually attempt to use the least restrictive method. In cases where a person doesn't agree to be admitted, if we feel it is in their best interest, and if there is a risk of harm to him or others, we will have to use the Mental Health Act(MHA 1983) (MHA.).*[Explain further the legal caveats if necessary]*

FORENSIC PSYCHIATRY

In this case as I have highlighted our concern is your safety which is paramount as well as treating your husband. Because of the high risk he will need to be admitted to hospital for further assessment and treatment.

W: What are the treatment options available?

C: The treatment options available are medication, psychological or talking therapy and social interventions.

1. Biological interventions or medications are antipsychotics
We will start him on some antipsychotic medication and monitor him for side effects. We follow the NICE (National institute of clinical excellence) guidelines and use the atypical group of antipsychotics.

The antipsychotic medication we can commence him on is either of the following i.e. Risperidone, Olanzapine, Quetiapine or Aripiprazole. Like all medication they do have side effects. However not all people get these side effects. We will monitor him for these side effects.

We would also need to address any underlying problems. For example if there is any history of alcohol dependence we would need to treat this as well.

2. The psychological interventions or talking therapies are
At a later stage, we can look at the talking therapies available. One example of this is CBT (cognitive behaviour therapy. This therapy looks at how the way he is thinking, is affecting the way he feels and behaves.

We do know that education about a person's illness is important as it will improve compliance with medication and promote recovery. Your understanding and support is vital too.

3. The social interventions include support to you
Due to the risks at present we would suggest gradual reintroduction of visits while he is on the ward.

In longer term, we usually involve the Community Mental Health Team who will use a multidisciplinary team approach to assist with recovery from this illness.

Summarize
Thank you for talking to me. We have discussed about your husband's diagnosis and that due to the current risks to yourself he would need to come into hospital.

I can recommend some useful websites and organisations for you to obtain some more information.

Useful websites and organisations:
There are also these useful organisations and charities like MIND, SANELINE and RETHINK.
Mind: Publishes a wide range of literature on all aspects of mental health.

Saneline: A national mental health helpline offering emotional support and practical information for people with mental illness, families, carers and professionals.

Rethink : National voluntary organisation that helps people with any severe mental illness, their families and care

[To note long term prognosis]
Geographical separation advised

MORBID JEALOUSY- OTHELLO SYNDROME
Diagnosis: Morbid Jealousy-delusions of infidelity
Epidemiology: F>M
Aetiology: Schizophrenia, BPAD, Alcohol Dependence, Persistent delusional disorder
Management –using holistic or biopsychosocial approach
A. Immediate
1. Biological interventions
- **Risk assessment**-self, partner, 3rd party
- **Admission**- informal/MHA
- **Nursing observations**
- **Physical examination**
- **Blood investigations**-FBC(Full blood count), U+E(Urea and electrolyte), LFT(Liver function tests), glucose
- **Medication**
- **Antipsychotic**-NICE Atypical-Risperidone, Olanzapine, Quetiapine, Aripiprazole
- **Antidepressant**
- **Alcohol dependence**-treat if present
2. Psychological interventions
- Psychoeducation
- Counselling
- CBT
- Relapse prevention
3. Social interventions
Promote wellbeing
- Support
- Allow partners visits gradually
- Prognosis –geographical separation
B. Medium and Longer term
MAPPA-Multi-agency public protection panels
Support groups- victim support
Self help
Community Mental Health Team (CMHT) to promote recovery
©Seshni

FORENSIC PSYCHIATRY

5. MORBID JEALOUSY

INSTRUCTIONS TO CANDIDATE
You have assessed the gentleman Alex Norman in the previous station who believes that his wife is having an affair.

TASK FOR THE CANDIDATE
- Discuss management with the consultant

PAY PARTICULAR ATTENTION TO THE FOLLOWING (MENTAL CHECKLIST)
- Give a psychiatric formulation.
- Explain diagnosis of Morbid Jealousy and possible differential diagnoses.
- Highlight the risks he poses to himself, wife and possible 3rd party.
- Discuss management in holistic or biopsychosocial approach.
- Explain need for admission either informally or detained under MHA (Mental Health Act).

COMMUNICATION SKILLS
- Adopt a collegiate approach.

Suggested approach
Introduction
C: Hello, I'm Dr...I'm one of the psychiatrists. I have seen this gentleman who has been referred by his GP as he was suspicious that his wife was having an affair
[Include Demographic data: age, marital status, children, and occupation]

A. Psychiatric formulation- please use information in the previous station using this format:
 Known/no previous contact with mental health services
- **Psychiatric assessment**
- **HOPC**
- **Past psychiatric history**
- **Personal and family history**
- **Medical History**
- **Medication**
- **Drug and alcohol**
- **Forensic, Psychosexual, Social**
- **Risk Assessment(low, intermediate, high)**
- **Protective factors**

Precipitators
For example you could begin as follows and include the format after this
I have seen this 45yr. old man who is employed as a broker. He was referred by his GP with a 3 month history of suspicions that his wife is having an affair. He is not previously known to the psychiatric service.

FORENSIC PSYCHIATRY

B. Mental state examination
- Comment on whether there is any evidence of Depression or Psychosis.
- Delusions of infidelity.
- Presence of threat-control and override symptoms.
- Evidence of suicidal or homicidal thoughts, ideation or plans.

Emphasise presence of threat and risk to his wife

C. My differential diagnoses are
- Persistent Delusional disorder
- Schizophrenia -enduring mental illness
- Bipolar Affective Disorder
- Associated Alcohol Dependence

D. My management plan using the holistic or biopsychosocial interventions in my immediate management, short and longer term management is:

1. Immediate management
- To consider admission according to the severity of risk and nature and degree of mental illness.
- Admission- either informal or formally
- Emphasise the need or admission
- To either inpatient general adult or Psychiatric intensive care unit (PICU) depending on the risks.

a) Biological interventions
- **Risk assessment**-self, partner, 3rd party
- **Nursing observations**
- **Physical examination**
- **Blood investigations**-FBC(Full blood count), U+E(Urea and electrolyte), LFT(Liver function tests), glucose
- **Medication**
- **Antipsychotic-National Institute of Clinical Excellence (**NICE) guidelines Atypical-Risperidone, Olanzapine, Quetiapine, Aripiprazole
- **Antidepressant medication**
- **Alcohol dependence** - treat if present

b) Psychological interventions
- Psychoeducation
- Counselling
- CBT(Cognitive behavioural therapy)
- Relapse prevention

c) Social interventions
- Promote wellbeing
- Support
- Allow partners visits slowly
- Prognosis -geographical separation

2. Medium and longer term management

FORENSIC PSYCHIATRY

- **MAPPA**-Mult- agency Public Protection Panels
- Support groups- victim support
- Self help
- CMHT to promote recovery

Othello Syndrome" comes from the character in Shakespeare's play Othello, who murders his wife as a result of a false belief that she has been unfaithful. Recently some workers have asserted that Othello was deceived rather than deluded about Desdemona's alleged infidelity and thus did not have 'the Othello Syndrome.'

---

6. ARSON

INSTRUCTIONS TO CANDIDATE
You have been asked to see an 18 year old girl Ruth Fable who has set fire to her bedroom in her friend flat.

TASK FOR THE CANDIDATE
- Elicit history to establish a provisional diagnosis.
- Conduct a risk assessment.

PAY PARTICULAR ATTENTION TO THE FOLLOWING (MENTAL CHECKLIST)
- Establish the fire setting event and the circumstances.
- Establish possible precipitators using a biopsychosocial approach.
- Elicit psychiatric history to establish a provisional diagnosis (Borderline personality disorder (BPD),Depression, Conduct disorder (CD).
- Consider non psychiatric causes for example relationship difficulties.
- Elicit a history with view of a diagnosis.
- Conduct a risk assessment.

COMMUNICATION SKILLS
- Start the interview by developing rapport and showing empathy.
- Acknowledge the nature of the incident and need to enquire about details.
- Anticipate reluctance to disclose information.

Suggested approach
Introduction
C: Hello, I'm Dr ...one of the psychiatrists here and thank you for seeing me. You may know this, but I have been asked to see you because of this incident with the fire in your bedroom. I need to clarify what happened with you. Perhaps you can take me through what happened?
A. History of Presenting Complaint (HOPC) (onset, duration, progression, severity)

1. Antecedent
- What happened before you started the fire?

2. Behaviour
- So what did you do exactly?(arson)
- Did you take any precautions?
- Was it planned or impulsive?
- How did you feel after lighting the fire? Did you feel any pleasure?
- Sometimes some people get sexually aroused by fires, has that ever been true for you?(sexual arousal)

FORENSIC PSYCHIATRY

- *How did you feel after this?(regrets/remorse)*
Include non-psychiatric causes?

3. Consequence
- *What exactly did you do?*
- *Did you speak to the police?*
- *Has this ever happened in the past?(past fire setting history/fascination with fire)*

B. Aetiological factors
Use a biopsychosocial approach to elicit aetiological factors
1. Biological
- *Family history of criminality*
- *Learning disabilities/Autistic spectrum Disorders(ASD)*

2. Psychological
- *Check for Hellman's triad-(bedwetting, fire-setting ,cruelty to animals), CSA(child sex abuse)*
- *In general do you feel safe?*
- *I need to ask something very sensitive, have you ever been sexually abused?*
3. Social
- *How have things been at home?*

C. Assess mental state at the time of the offending behaviour
Screen for underlying mental illness
Establish presence of borderline personality traits Depression, Bipolar affective disorder, Psychosis

D. Risk assessment
Include the following
1. Past risks
Past history of arson.
Drug and alcohol history.
Forensic history.

2. Current risks
- *Identify any current risks*

3. Future risks
- *Recidivism*
- *What do you intend to do?*
Address in each
- *Risk to self.*
- *Risk to others.*
- *Risk to property.*

FORENSIC PSYCHIATRY

Summarise

Thank you for talking to me. To summarise, you have told me that you set fire to paper in your bedroom and you now regret doing this. This was triggered by an unpleasant memory. You have a history of setting fire in the past. I would like to see you again to discuss more about how we could help you.

Thank You

FORENSIC PSYCHIATRY

ARSON
Elicit history and Risk assessment
A. HOPC (onset, duration, progression, severity)
   1. Antecedent-*trigger*
   2. Behaviour- *pyromania*
   3. Consequence-*damage, remorse*
B. Aetiological factors
Use a biopsychosocial approach to elicit aetiological factors
   1. Biological *criminality, learning difficulties*
   2. Psychological *Hellman's triangle- bedwetting, cruelty to animals,*
CSA
   3. Social *stressors*
C. Assess mental state at the time of the offending behaviour
Screen for underlying mental illness
- *Establish presence of Depression, bipolar affective disorder, Psychosis and borderline personality traits.*

D. Risk assessment
   1. Past risks
- *Past history of arson*
- *Drug and alcohol history*
- *Forensic history*

   2. Current risks
- *Risk to self*
- *Risk to others*
- *Risk to property*

   3. Future risks
- *Recidivism*

©*Smartsesh*

POSSIBLE VARIATIONS OF THEME
   1. Variation of theme-18 yr old boy with antisocial personality disorder who set fire to the library.
   2. 18 yr old lady who set fire in her room, and she has a history of emotionally unstable personality disorder.

FORENSIC PSYCHIATRY

7. EROTOMANIA

Suggested approach
Introduction
C: Hello, I'm Dr... I'm one of the psychiatrists. I've been told you have come to see one of the nurses. I also understand that you had a weapon on you. Do you still have it? If so, can you please place it on the floor or hand it over to the security.

P: I want to see Nicola. Can you call her for me?

C: I will do my best to help you, but can you please tell me if you still have the knife with you?

A. History of Presenting Complaint (HOPC) -onset, duration, progression and severity
Establish the relationship to the object of affection
- You mentioned you came to see the support worker. Can you tell me how you came to know her?

410

FORENSIC PSYCHIATRY

- *Where did you meet her?*
- *What is your relationship with her?*
- *Why do you think she is in love with you? (Erotomania)*
- *Have you tried to contact her?*
- *For example calling her, emailing, sending cards, letters or following her?*
- *Has she returned any of these?*
- *Do you have her details?*
- *Do you know where she lives?*
- *Do you have her mobile number?*
- *What else do you know about her?*
- *What are your plans?*
- *Do you have any fantasies about her? Do you masturbate? (fantasies)*

Degree of conviction
- *How convinced are you that she reciprocates your feelings?*
- *What makes you say that?*
- *I'm just wondering , do you think there could be another explanation, for example maybe she was doing her job and you might have misinterpreted this?*

B. Past psychiatric history
- *Have you seen a psychiatrist in the past?*

C. Medical history
- *How is your physical health?*

D. Current medication
- *Are you on any medication?*

E. Psychosexual history
- *Have you had anything similar to this in the past?*
- *How have your relationships worked out for you in the past?*

F. Premorbid personality
- *How would you describe yourself?*

G. MENTAL STATE EXAMINATION
1. Establish the presence of psychotic, depressive or neurotic symptoms
- *How have you been feeling in yourself?(mood)*
- *Sometimes when people are stressed they have strange experiences. Do you have any?(to establish threat-control and override symptoms)*
- *Do you hear voices when there is no one around?(auditory hallucinations)*
- *Do you see things when there is no one there?(visual hallucinations)*

2. Establish the erotomanic delusion

H. Risk assessment
1. Past risk
Forensic history
- Have you been involved with the police in the past?
- Do you have any convictions or pending charges?
- Do you have any history of violence or assault?

2. Current risk
Risk to the victim and third party
- I wanted to clarify if you have followed her? Do you know if she has any family? Does she have a boyfriend?(3rd party)
- What is it you intend to do then?
- Hypothetically, if she doesn't reciprocate, what do you intend to do?
- Have you had thoughts of wanting to harm others?(homicidal ideation)

Drug and alcohol history
- How do you cope? Some people drink or using street drugs?
- How about you?

Risk to self
- Have you had thoughts that life was not worth living?(suicidal ideation)

3. Future risk
- What are you planning to do?

Summarise
Thank you for talking to me. To summarise, you have told me you came to see this support worker and you're convinced she is in love with you. She has however not reciprocated these feelings. I am concerned about this. I think that you have been under a lot of stress and that you might benefit from staying in hospital.

Insight
What do you think?

Thank You

EROTOMANIA
History taking and assess dangerousness
A. History of Presenting Complaint (HOPC) (onset, duration, progression, severity)
- Establish the nature of relationship
- Reciprocity
- Attempts to contact-email, letters, calls, stalking
- Intentions

B. Past psychiatric history
- Previous contact with psychiatrist

C. Medical history
- physical health

D. Current medication

E. Psychosexual history
- Previous relationships
- Sexual difficulties

F. Premorbid personality

G. Mental State examination
- Assess for mood, psychotic and depressive symptoms
- Presence of threat and override symptoms

H. Risk assessment and dangerousness
1. Past risks- Forensic history
2. Current risks-Drug and alcohol history, access to weapons.
   DSH
3. Future risks- recidivism-victim and Third party
©Smartsesh

POSSIBLE VARIATIONS OF THEME
1. Man demanding to see nurse he met in A&E and he wants to take her home. He has a bag with him with handcuffs.
2. Man demanding to see nurse and he have made threats to harm anyone who attempts to stop him from seeing her. He has a bag with him with a knife in it.
3. non psychiatric cause-You have to see a man who is demanding to see the nurse and his has antisocial personality disorder(ASPD)

FORENSIC PSYCHIATRY

8. EROTOMANIA

INSTRUCTIONS TO CANDIDATE
You are about to see the support worker Nicola Thorpe who the man Eric Simpson you previously assessed demanded to see. You have also been informed that he has absconded and the police are looking for him.

TASK FOR THE CANDIDATE
- Discuss this with the support worker.

PAY PARTICULAR ATTENTION TO THE FOLLOWING (MENTAL CHECKLIST)
- Assess Confidentiality issues.
- Highlight the risks and that her safety is paramount.
- Explore avenues of supporting her and keeping her safe.

COMMUNICATION SKILLS
- Emphasise risk to her.
- Start the interview by developing rapport and showing empathy.
- Anticipate a frightened victim who requires reassurance.
- Be sensitive when explaining the risk issues.

Suggested approach
Introduction
C: Hello, I'm Dr ...I'm one of the psychiatrists. I have seen this man who came looking for you. I can understand this must be stressful for you. Can I first establish what it is that you know about the situation?

N: I know that this man is looking for me and he came here with a knife. I have now been told that he has absconded.

Highlight the risk issues
C: I can see this must be distressing to you. I can assure you that your safety is important. . I am concerned too. We have followed the protocols and have informed the hospital security and police of his absconsion.
Are you able to tell me more about the problems he has been causing you?

N: I don't know him. I have only seen him once in A&E when he came for Anxiety symptoms. What is his diagnosis?

C: Because of the high level I need to break confidentiality to warn of the level of risk disclose the information that he has come to the Accident and Emergency to look for you. From what he tells me, it appears he's convinced that he is in love with you. He mentioned meeting you a few weeks ago.

N: I didn't give him any impression that I am in love with him. I treated him the same way I do all my patients.

FORENSIC PSYCHIATRY

C: I'm sure this is difficult for you to take on board and I can assure you, you have done nothing wrong. He has somehow misinterpreted your professional duties and actions and this has led him to believe he is in love with you.

He has been under stress and seems his belief is quite strong and delusional at present. He has what we call Erotomania.

N: What is Erotomania?

C: This is when someone becomes convinced that someone is in love with them.

N: I heard that he has absconded. What do I do now?

C: Can you tell me about where you live and work? We need to take action to prevent him having any contact with you either in hospital or outside hospital. You need to take it up with the police and also let your family about this. We need to let the managers know and they can advise us on what needs to happen

N: What are you planning to do with him?

C: We will have to assess him and do a Mental Health Act(MHA 1983) assessment.
We are concerned for your safety at present. It would be advisable for you to speak to the police, as they would be the best to advise you on the precautions you would need to take.
Do you have someone with you?

N: When would I be able to come back to work?

C: It might be useful for you to speak to your manager and consider taking some time off. I will come and speak to them if you wish
You should also think of seeing your family GP if you find you find are not coping well with this.

Other Advice to ensure safety:
- There are some useful organisations -victim support
- Also you would need to take precautions to ensure that you are not being followed.

Summarise
Thank you for talking to me. I know this must not be easy for you. I have informed you of our concerns as this gentleman believes that he is in love with you. At present your safety is paramount and therefore we will assist you in the necessary steps towards ensuring this.

Do you have any other concerns?

EROTOMANIA

DISCUSS MANAGEMENT

A. **Diagnosis- delusion of love**
B. **Epidemiology M:F**
C. **Aetiology**
D. **Management-Holistic or Biopsychosocial approach**
   1. Biological intervention
   Setting- admission informal/Mental Health Act(MHA 1983) 1983 (MHA)
   Nursing observations
   Medication –atypical antipsychotic
   2. Psychological intervention
   CBT
   Counselling
   Psycho-educational groups
   3. Social interventions
   Support
   Longer term
E. **Multi-Agency Public Protection Panel (MAPPA)**
   Victim support
   ©Smartsesh

EROTOMANIA (DE CLEREMBAULT'S SYNDROME)
➢ Person believes that someone is in love with them.
➢ The person may be superior, a public figure or celebrity, less frequently someone of equivalent status.
➢ When the lover denies any feelings for the patient and rejects all approaches , further delusional elaborations occur
➢ Perceives the lover cannot openly acknowledge this love and must communicate with secret messages and signs.
➢ More common in woman than men.
➢ In the long term, even legal ways will have no effect on the patient's belief and do little to modify their behaviour.
➢ Patient may pose a significant risk to the lover.
   ©Smartsesh

FORENSIC PSYCHIATRY

9. EROTOMANIA

INSTRUCTIONS TO CANDIDATE
You have seen this man who came to see the nurse whom he believes is in love with him. You have been asked to discuss this case with the Psychiatry consultant on call.

TASK FOR THE CANDIDATE
- Discuss management with the consultant

PAY PARTICULAR ATTENTION TO THE FOLLOWING (MENTAL CHECKLIST)
- Highlight confidentiality issues.
- Highlight the risks to the nurse.
- Consider differential diagnosis.
- Highlight admission required and detention under MHA.

COMMUNICATION SKILLS
- Adopt a collegiate approach

Suggested approach
Introduction
C: Hello, I'm Dr...I'm one of the psychiatrists. I have seen this 45 year old man who was requesting to see one of our psychiatric support workers. I would like to discuss my assessment and management plan with you. (Include demographic data: age, marital status, occupation)

A Brief Synopsis
Psychiatric formulation
Include the following details
- Psychiatric assessment
- History of presenting complaint(HOPC)
- Identifiable precipitants
- Past psychiatric history
- Personal and family history Medical History
- Medication
- Drug and alcohol history
- Forensic, Psychosexual, Social, Premorbid personality
- Risk Assessment(low, intermediate, high)
- Protective factors

For example: begin with the following summary and then continue with the format
I've been asked to assess a 45yr. old man who has a 3 month history of erotomanic delusions of the support worker who treated him in the assessment unit, despite no evidence to substantiate this, he remains fixed in his beliefs.

B Mental state examination
- Comment on the presence of depressive, Anxiety or psychotic symptoms.
- Comment on Erotomanic delusion.

C My differential diagnoses are:
- Enduring mental illness like Schizophrenia.
- Bipolar Affective Disorder.
- Alcohol Dependence.

D. My management plan using the holistic or biopsychosocial approach in my immediate, medium and longer term management is:

Immediate management
Setting
- I will take into consideration the current risks and his current mental state and I will consider admission either informally if he was willing to be admitted.
- In the event that he was not agreeing to come in as an informal patient I would arrange for a Mental Health Act(MHA 1983) (MHA) assessment.

Biological interventions
- Regular nursing observations to monitor his mental state and risks
- Physical examination
- Blood investigations like Full Blood count(FBC)), U+E(Urea and electrolyte), Liver function tests(LFT), glucose, urine drug screening
- Other special investigations -CT/MRI , CXR and ECG if indicated
- Medication -I will consider commencing him on an antipsychotic preferably an atypical antipsychotic according to the National institute of clinical excellence (NICE) guidelines.
- They would be less likely to cause Extra-pyramidal side effects (EPSE). I would need to bear in mind other potential side effects like Metabolic Syndrome.
- I would consider using either of these Atypical antipsychotics- Risperidone, Olanzapine, Aripiprazole or Quetiapine
- My choice would be guided by his previous history of medication, also looking at his patient profile and to ensure that there are no contraindications to prescribing this medication.
- I would also prescribe the medication for Rapid Tranquilisation should he require this.

In the medium and longer term management
I would consider psychological and social interventions:
Psychological interventions
- Cognitive behavioural therapy (CBT) for the delusions and to improve compliance with medication.
- Counselling

FORENSIC PSYCHIATRY

- *Psycho-educational groups-Engage him in understanding his illness, identifying relapse indicators, address compliance issues to promote effective recovery.*

Social interventions
For the victim
- *I would recommend support for the victim and manage appropriately.*

For him
- *Multi-agency public protection panel (MAPPA). I would ensure that he is on the MAPPA.*
- *I would also consider using a Multi-Disciplinary Approach with him being on the care plan approach (CPA) and also receiving support from the Community Mental Health Team(CMHT)*

FORENSIC PSYCHIATRY

10. VIOLENCE RISK ASSESSMENT

INSTRUCTIONS TO CANDIDATE
You are about to see a 34 yr old man Nigel Hunt who was admitted into hospital following an assault on his wife.

TASK FOR THE CANDIDATE
- Conduct a risk assessment.

PAY PARTICULAR ATTENTION TO THE FOLLOWING (MENTAL CHECKLIST)
- Enquire more about the index offence(IO)
- Establish the mental state at the time of offence.
- Establish current feelings and intentions.
- Conduct a comprehensive risk assessment.
- Identify possible aetiological factors.

COMMUNICATION SKILLS
- Start the interview by developing rapport and showing empathy.
- Anticipate that he will be reluctant to engage and could be guarded.
- Avoid antagonising him.

Suggested approach
Introduction
C: Hello, I'm Dr I'm one of the psychiatrists. I understand that you were admitted yesterday following an incident at your home. I would like to ask you more about this if that is all right with you?

Can you tell me what happened?

A. History of presenting complaint (HOPC) (onset, duration, progression and severity)
Index event
Use a behavioural analysis approach
Antecedent
- What was happening before this occurred?(antecedent)
- What did you do exactly?
- Was this planned or impulsive(planning)

B. Establish what his mental state was at the time
Screen for psychotic symptoms
- Did you have any street drugs or alcohol?(drug and alcohol history)

Behaviour
- What happened exactly?(nature of assault)
- Did you use any weapons?

Consequence
- How serious was this?(consequences)

FORENSIC PSYCHIATRY

- *How do you feel now about this?*
- *Do you have any remorse? Do you have any guilt feelings?(remorse)*

Relationship
- *Can you tell me more about your relationship?*
- *How do you feel now?*
- *Do you bear any grudges?*

C. Use a biopsychosocial approach to identify possible aetiological factors
Biological
- *Family history of criminality.*

Psychological
- *Underlying mental illness.*
- *Non-compliance with medication.*

Social
- *Stressors.*

Past psychiatric history
- *Have you ever seen a psychiatrist in the past*

D. Past forensic history
- *Have you been involved with the police in the past?*
- *Do you have a history of violence and aggression?(violence and aggression)*
- *Do you have convictions or charges? (ABH-Actual bodily harm, GBH-Grievous bodily harm)*
- *Do you have any access to any weapons?*

E. Mental state examination
Establish the presence of threat-control and override symptoms
- *Persecutory or paranoid delusions*
- *Delusions of Control*
- *Thought alienation*
- *Insight -compliance with medication*

Establish low frustration tolerance
- *Do you get angry? How do you usually express this?(loss of temper)*
- *Is it directed at a person, or anything else?*
- *What usually triggers this?*

F. Risk assessment
Include the following
- *Past forensic history*
- *Drug and alcohol history*

Risk to self

FORENSIC PSYCHIATRY

- *Have you felt that life was not worth living? Have you made any plans?(suicidal ideation, intent or plans)*
- *What do you intend to do? How close have you come to it?*

Risk to others
- *Do you have thoughts to harm anyone else?(homicidal ideation, intent or plans)*
- *Children*
- *Weapons*
- *Recidivism*

Insight
What do you think could have caused this incident?

Summarise
Thank you for talking to me. To summarise you have told me that you and your wife were involved in a verbal altercation and this resulted in you assaulting her. You have been on treatment for Schizophrenia and have recently stopped taking your medication. You now regret what has happened. You are now also willing to take your medication.
Do you have any other questions for me?

POSSIBLE VARIATIONS OF THEME
- *Assault on wife – due to morbid jealousy.*
- *Assault on wife – charged for assault.*
- *Assault on wife – non-compliance with medication and relapse of mental illness-Schizophrenia.*

FORENSIC PSYCHIATRY

VIOLENCE RISK ASSESSMENT

History of Presenting Complaint (HOPC) (onset, duration, severity and progression)

Index event

- Use a behavioural analysis approach
- Antecedent
- -Establish what his mental state was at the time
- Behaviour
- Consequence
- Current relationship

Use a biopsychosocial approach to identify possible aetiological factors

- **Biological- Family history of criminality**
- Psychological- Underlying mental illness, Non-compliance with medication
- Social -Stressors

Past psychiatric history

Past forensic history-convictions, pending charges

Mental state examination

- Establish the presence of threat control and override symptoms
- Persecutory or paranoid delusions
- Delusions of Control
- Thought alienation
- Insight –compliance with medication
- Establish Low frustration tolerance, looses tempter, triggers, reaction

Past forensic history

Drug and alcohol history

Risk assessment

- **Risk to others – homicidal ideation, intent or plans**
  - Access to children
  - Weapons
  - Recidivism

©Smartsesh

FORENSIC PSYCHIATRY

11. PAEDOPHILE

Instructions to candidate
You are about to see this 30 yr old gentleman. He was brought in by police as his friend's daughter made allegations that he was inappropriate with her.

TASK FOR THE CANDIDATE
Elicit a history and conduct a risk assessment.

PAY PARTICULAR ATTENTION TO THE FOLLOWING (MENTAL CHECKLIST)
- Explain confidentiality issues.
- Elicit psychosexual history.
- Establish the cognitive distortions that would present in a paedophile.
- Conduct a risk assessment.
- Determine current risks and access to children.

COMMUNICATION SKILLS
- Start the interview by developing rapport and showing empathy.
- Anticipate that he may be reluctant to disclose actual events.
- Preface sensitive questions.

Suggested approach
Introduction
C: Thank you for seeing me. I understand from the information given to me, that the police have brought you here as there were concerns expressed by your friend's daughter. She said that you were inappropriate with her. Would you be able to tell me more about this?

P: I don't know what she has told them.

C: I would also like to share a piece of information that we do with everybody. Whatever we discuss is confidential, however if there is a risk of harm to anyone else then I would need to disclose this.

Because of the nature of the allegations, I do need to ask you some personal questions.

A. History of Presenting Complaint (HOPC) (onset, duration, progression and severity)
- Can you tell me what happened today?
- How did you end up having your friend's daughter?
- Can you tell me more about this? How often do you do this?
- Do you come in contact with any other children?
- Where were you today? How long were you with her?
- How did you spend the time?
- At any point did you come in physical contact with her?

FORENSIC PSYCHIATRY

Explore the allegations of sexual assault
- *Did you ask her to touch your genitals?*
- *Did you get aroused?(arousal pattern)*
- *Did you get an erection?(erection)*
- *If so, what did you do then?*
- *Did you masturbate?(masturbation, fantasies)*

B. Cognitive distortions *(minimisation, denial, lack of victim empathy)*
- *What did you think she wanted?*
- *Do you think that she liked that?*
- *Have you had any fantasies about her?*

C. Past history of sexual offending
- *Has this happened before?*
- *Can you tell me more about that?*
- *Were there any charges? Do you have any pending charges?*
- *I need to ask you, some people might say that having this interaction with a child is not appropriate. What would you say?*

D. Psychosexual history
Because of the nature of these allegations, I would like to also ask you some personal questions.
- *Can you tell me about your puberty?(puberty)*
- *Can you tell me about your first sexual experience?*
- *How did it progress from there?*
- *Do you have any particular preference for male or female? Do you prefer children?(Heterosexual or homosexual, or prefer children, age groups)*
- *Can you tell me about your relationships?(relationships)*
- *Are you presently in any relationship?*
- *Do you have sexual fantasies?(sexual fantasies)*
- *Do you use pornography?(pornography)*
- *Do you use the internet? Have you had contact with a paedophile ring?*
- *Do you masturbate?*
- *Do you have any sexual difficulties?(sexual difficulties)*
- *Do you get any early morning erections?(erections)*

E. Past psychiatric history
- *Have you seen a psychiatrist in the past?*

F. RISK ASSESSMENT
Risk of harm to self
- *This must be a difficult time for you, have you had thoughts that life was not worth living? Have you made any plans? How close have you come to it?(suicidal ideation))*

Risk to others
- *Forensic history*

FORENSIC PSYCHIATRY

- *Have you had a history of violence or aggression?*
- *Access to children*
- *Weapons*
- *What work do you do?*
- **Future risk**
- *Recidivism*
- *Have you had thoughts of harming others?(homicidal ideation)*

G. Drug and alcohol history
- *How do you cope? Some people drink or take street drugs?*

Summary
Thank you for talking to me. I would like to summarise what you have told me.

You told me that you were babysitting for your friend and this is something you occasionally do. Her versions of events are that you know that she has made allegations that you have touched her inappropriately. However you have denied doing this. There has been one episode in the past similar to this.

I would like to see you again as there have been versions of the alleged incident which we would need to explore further.

Do you have any questions for me?

POSSIBLE VARIATIONS OF THEME
1. *37 yr. old IT Manager brought in by police. Neighbour's son made allegations that he touched him inappropriately.*
2. *45 yr. old man who was found at work viewing child pornography. He is now depressed and suicidal.*

FORENSIC PSYCHIATRY

PAEDOPHILE HISTORY
HOPC (onset, duration, progression, severity)
- Sexual allegation
- Contact with the victim
- Contact with any other children
- Arousal pattern- erection, masturbation, fantasises
- Cognitive distortions (minimisation, denial, lack of victim empathy)

Past history of sexual offending
Psychosexual history
- Puberty first sexual experiences, sexual orientation-Heterosexual or homosexual, or prefer children, age groups), relationship, sexual fantasies, pornography, internet , paedophile ring
- Masturbation , sexual difficulties
- Early morning erections

Past psychiatric history
Risk assessment
- Risk of harm to self-suicidal ideation ,intent or plans
- Risk to others
- Forensic history -violence or aggression
- Access to children
- Weapons
- Occupation
- Recidivism

Drug and alcohol history
Summarise

©Smartsesh

FORENSIC PSYCHIATRY

12. ASSAULT ON THE WARD

INSTRUCTIONS TO CANDIDATE
You have been asked to see this man Justin Perero known with Schizophrenia who is under section 2 of the Mental Health Act(MHA 1983) (MHA). He has assaulted one of the nursing staff.

TASK FOR THE CANDIDATE
Elicit history and conduct a risk assessment.

PAY PARTICULAR ATTENTION TO THE FOLLOWING (MENTAL CHECKLIST)
- Ensure safety of all is paramount.
- Establish the severity of assault and mental state at the time.
- Assess fitness to be interviewed.
- Conduct a comprehensive risk assessment.
- Identify aetiological factors using biopsychosocial approach.
- Follow the protocols if deemed necessary i.e. informing police.
- Advice debriefing for all involved.

COMMUNICATION SKILLS
- Start interview by developing rapport and showing empathy.
- Anticipate that he could be reluctant or guarded to disclose details.

Suggested approach
Introduction
C: Hello, I'm Dr ....I'm one of the psychiatrists. Thank you for seeing me. I understand that there was an incident on the ward where one of the staff members was assaulted. I would like to find out your version of what happened? Is that all right with you?

N: I already spoke to the other nurse.

C: I understand that this might be difficult to talk about, but it would help if we can try and see what happened. This will help us to see how we move forward from this.

A. History of Presenting Complaint (HOPC) (onset, duration, progression and severity)

Behavioural analysis using A, B, C approach
C: Can you tell me what happened exactly?

Antecedents
- What happened just before the assaulted?(antecedent)

Behaviour

FORENSIC PSYCHIATRY

- *What did you do?(behaviour)*
- *Is it something that was planned or impulsive?(planning)*
- *Were there any weapons used?*

Consequence
- *Did you have any injuries?*
- *Do you know what injuries the nurse sustained?*
- *How do you feel now about what happened?*
- *Do you feel any remorse?(remorse)*
- *Do you have any guilt feelings?(guilt)*

B. Assess for possible triggers
- *Can you tell me why do you think this happened?*
- *Why did you think you hit the nurse?*

Biological
- *Exclude underlying physical illness*
- *How has your physical health been?*
- *How have you been coping? Have you been drinking or had any street drugs?*

Psychological
Mental state examination

C. Identify threat-control-override symptoms? (Auditory hallucinations and persecutory delusions)
- *Can you tell me how have you been feeling in yourself?*
- *This is a routine question I ask everybody. Have you been having any strange experiences?*
- *Have you been hearing voices when there is no one else around?(auditory hallucinations)*
- *Have you been seeing things that no one else can see? (visual hallucinations)*
- *Have you been feeling like people are annoying you? Do you feel that there is someone out to harm you?(persecutory)*
- *Are you concerned for your safety?*
- *Do you feel that there is interference with your thinking?(thought alienation)*
- *Do you feel that you are in control of your thoughts?(delusions of control)*
- *Do you feel someone is trying to control you?(delusions of control)*

D. Compliance and insight
- *How are you feeling about taking medication?*

E. Social history
- *Have there been any changes in the environment?*

FORENSIC PSYCHIATRY

F. Forensic
- Have you been involved with the police in the past?
- Do you have a history of violence and aggression?
- Do you have convictions or charges? (ABH-Actual bodily harm, GBH-grievous bodily harm)
- Do you have any access to any weapons?

G. Risk assessment
- Have you had thoughts of wanting to end it all?(suicidal ideation, intent, plans)
- Have you had thoughts of wanting to harm anyone?(homicidal ideation, intent or plans)
- Past forensic history.
- Risk of harm to self, others and property.
- Recidivism.
- Drug and alcohol.

H. Assess fitness to be interviewed-use the following criteria
- Do you understand the charges?
- Would he be able to follow the relevant procedure for being interviewed?
- How does he feel about this now?
- Does he understand the consequences of being found guilty?

Summarise
Thank you for talking to me. To summarise what we have discussed, it appears that you acknowledge that you assaulted the nurse, and this could have been due to several factors you mentioned. You do feel remorseful about what happened. You know that it is possible the nurse will want to press charges and the police will need to interview you to get your version of events.

I will speak to the ward manager and see how we are going to manage this further. Do you have any questions for me?

FORENSIC PSYCHIATRY

ASSAULT -RISK ASSESSMENT AND FITNESS TO BE INTERVIEWED
History of presenting Complaint (HOPC) (, onset, duration, progression, severity)
- Behavioural analysis using A, B, C approach
- Antecedents
- Behaviour
- Consequence
- Assess for possible triggers

Biological –underlying physical illness
Psychological
- Mental state examination
- Identify threat-control and override symptoms
- Compliance and insight- medication?

Social –changes in the environment
Forensic
Risk Assessment
- Past forensic history
- Risk of harm to self, others and property- suicidal, homicidal

Fitness to be interviewed
- Doe he understand the charges?
- Does he understand the consequence of pleading guilty or not guilty?
- Is he able to follow the interview process?
- How does he feel about this now?

© Smartsesh

Possible variations of theme
1. Assault on staff and patient needs to be transferred to PICU due to escalating risks.
2. Assault on staff and patient still agitated, aggressive and threatening.

FORENSIC PSYCHIATRY

13. ASSAULT ON THE WARD

INSTRUCTIONS TO CANDIDATE
You have assessed the patient who assaulted one of the staff on the ward.
You are about to see the ward manager Darren Curtis who has asked to see you.

TASK FOR THE CANDIDATE
Discuss management with the ward manager.

PAY PARTICULAR ATTENTION TO THE FOLLOWING (MENTAL CHECKLIST)
- Identify the possible triggers from ward manager using an A, B, C approach.
- Propose to have a debriefing.
- Discuss details of your psychiatric assessment and formulation.
- Discuss collaboratively management in terms of biopsychosocial approach.
- Discuss risk management issues.
- Discuss fitness to be interviewed.

COMMUNICATION SKILLS
- Acknowledge concerns and distress to staff and patient.
- Establish common ground in working towards deescalating the situation.
- Ensure ward manager that safety of all is paramount.

Suggested approach
Introduction
C: Hello, I'm Dr .....I'm one of the psychiatrists. Thank you for talking to me. I gather that there was a serious incident where one of your patients assaulted one of your nurses. I have seen him and have come to discuss with you more about my assessment and management.

WM: Thank you Doc. This is a serious situation, can we get him out of here.

C: I understand that this must be a difficult for you and your staff. It would be helpful if you can you tell me what is your understanding of what happened?
How is the nurse who was assaulted?

WM: The nurse told me that he hit her for no apparent reason and there were witnesses to this. I have sent the nurse home as she didn't require any further medical attention.

C: I gather from you have told me, it was a serious incident and I understand you have followed the necessary protocols and informed the police.

FORENSIC PSYCHIATRY

WM: Yes, we have.

C: I will explain my findings with you and we can discuss the risks at presents. We can also discuss how best we will be able to contain this situation, whilst maintaining safety of all.

Summary
C: From my assessment with him, I used a behavioural analysis to identify what the possible triggers could be. He explained to me what he was doing at the time when the incident occurred.
(use information in previous station to summarize the assault)

For example start with the following and add the relevant information obtained in the previous station.
The possible triggers identified in my opinion are a combination of factors. I understand that he has a known past psychiatric and forensic history. I did also assess his mental state and looked specifically for psychotic symptoms which could have contributed to his behaviour. (You can elaborate on your findings)

WM: So what do we do with him now?

C: I would like us to formulate this management plan collaboratively

Management plan in terms of biopsychosocial approach is:
Biological interventions
Investigations
- *First and foremost we would need to exclude any physical causes by doing some blood investigations.*
- *Also exclude use of illicit substances by doing a urine Drug screening.*
- *Ensure incident form completed and DATIX.*
- *Body mapping indicating if there are any injuries.*
- *Seclusion policy-follow protocol if necessary.*

Medication
C: We can consider using antipsychotics as per Rapid Tranquilisation (RT) protocol after all de-escalation techniques have been tried. We could use oral or intramuscular medication-use Haloperidol, Lorazepam or Aripiprazole and monitor for side effects. We can also follow the RT protocol and monitor his vitals accordingly.

Other practical aspects once he is settled are to consider the following:
- *Allow for time out.*
- *We also need to arrange a debriefing for all the staff that was involved in this.*
- *We need to monitor his behaviour using behavioural analysis approach-A,B,C*
- *Engage him in occupational therapy*

- *Engage him in activities/diversion techniques. For example going out of the ward to play pool, games, play station*
- *Have close nursing observations 1:1 to minimise frustration*

If the risks escalate, we can refer him to a forensic or PICU (Psychiatric intensive care unit)

WM: I'm not sure if the nurse is going to press charges. The police might ask us if he is fit to be interviewed.

C: I did assess his fitness to be interviewed using the following criteria:
- *Doe he understand the charges?*
- *Would he be able to follow the relevant procedure for being interviewed?*
- *How does he feel about this now?*
- *Does he understand the consequences of being found guilty?*

Summarise
Thank you for talking to me. To summarise what we have discussed the possible triggers for the assault and identified the current risks. The nursing staff will continue to monitor him and you will follow the rapid tranquilisation policy. If the risks escalate, we will need to consider transfer to a PICU.

Do you have any other questions for me?

FORENSIC PSYCHIATRY

ASSAULT-MANAGEMENT
Summary of previous station- *assault, aetiological factors, mental state examination, risk assessment*
Management plan in terms of biopsychosocial approach is:
Biological interventions
- *Investigations*
- *Exclude physical causes by doing some blood investigations.*
- *Also exclude use of illicit substances by doing a urine dipstick*
- *Ensure incident form completed and DATIX*
- *Body mapping indicating if there are any injuries*
- *Seclusion policy-follow protocol if it deemed necessary that he continues to require this.*
- *Medication*
- *We can consider using antipsychotics as per rapid tranquilisation(RT) protocol after all de-escalation techniques have been tried. We could use oral or intramuscular medication-use Haloperidol, Lorazepam or Aripiprazole and monitor for side effects. Do vital checks.*
- *Other practical aspects*
- *Allow for time out.*
- *debriefing for all the staff that were involved in this.*
- *monitor his behaviour using behavioural analysis approach-A,B,C*
- *Engage in occupational therapy*
- *Engage in activities/diversion techniques eg going out of the ward to play pool, games, play station*
- *Have close nursing observations 1:1 to minimise frustration*
- *If his behaviour continues and the risks escalate, we can refer him to forensics and PICU.*

Assess fitness to be interviewed criteria:
- *Does he understand the nature of assault?*
- *Does he understand the consequence of being guilty or not?*
- *How he feel as about this?*
- *Would he be able to follow the procedure of being interviewed?*

Summarise

©Smartsesh

FORENSIC PSYCHIATRY

References
Gelder, M.G, Cowen, P. and Harrison P.J(2006) Shorter Oxford textbook of psychiatry. 5th edn. Oxford: Oxford University Press.

Sims, A. C. P. (2003) Symptoms in the mind: an introduction to descriptive psychopathology . 3rd edn. Great Britain : Saunders.

Taylor, D., Paton, C., Kapur, S. (2009) The South London and Maudsley NHS Foundation Trust & Oxleas NHS Foundation Trust prescribing guidelines. 10th edn. London: Informa Healthcare.

British Medical Association and Royal Pharmaceutical society(2011), British National Formulary 62, 62nd edn. Great Britain :British Medical Journal Publishing Group and Pharmaceutical Press

WHO.(1992)The ICD 10 classification of mental and behavioural disorders: clinical descriptions and diagnostic guideline. 10th revision : Geneva; WHO

Webster CW, Douglas KS, Eaves D and Hart SD(1997) HCR-20:Assessing risk for violence. Mental Health, Law and Policy Institute, Simon Fraser University, British Columbia, Canada.

Taylor PJ(1985) Motives for offending among violent and psychotic men. British Journal of Psychiatry, 147, 491-498.

Swanson JW, Borum R, Swartz MS and Monahan J(1996) Psychotic symptoms and disorders and the risk of violent behaviour in the community. Criminal Behaviour and Mental Health, 6, 317-338.

Link BG and Stueve A(1994). Psychotic symptoms and the violent/illegal behaviour of mental patients compared to community controls. In J. Monahan and HJ Steadman(Eds) Violence and mental disorder: Developments in risk assessment(pp. 137-159). Chicago: University of Chicago Press.

Seminars in Forensic psychiatry, Gaskell
Seena Fazel and John Danesh. Serious mental disorders in 23 000 prisoners: a systematic review of 62 surveys. Lancet 2002; 359:545-50. http://eprints.ouls.ox.ac.uk/archive/00001002/

Fazel S, Grann M, Carlstrom E, Lichtenstein P, Langstrom N. Risk factors for violent crime in schizophrenia: A national cohort study of 13,806 patients. J Clin Psychiatry 70:362-369

Support groups and websites

MIND: provides information on the Mental Health Act (MHA 1983)

Suggested reading

FORENSIC PSYCHIATRY

Cleckley, M.D., Hervey (1982). The Mask of Sanity (Revised ed.). Mosbey Medical Library.

^ Meloy, J. Reid (1988). The Psychopathic Mind: Origins, Dynamics, and Treatment. Northvale, NJ: Jason Aronson Inc. p. 9.

The Jones Mental Health Act(MHA 1983) manual

Mental Health Act (MHA 1983) Code of Practice: The Code of Practice provides guidance on how the Mental Health Act (MHA 1983) 1983 should be applied Care Quality Commission: Mental Health Act (MHA 1983) leaflets available where patients are detained.

Mental Health Tribunals for England

Mental Health Review Tribunals for Wales

ADDICTIONS

ADDICTIONS- Dr Zahoor Syed

1. Opiate dependence-history–Dr Zahoor Syed

2. Delirium Tremens–Assess psychopathology-Dr Christos Koumistidis

3. Delirium Tremens– Discuss management with orthopaedic nurse-Dr Christos Koumistidis

4. Alcohol Dependence-Dr Zahoor Syed

5. Methadone in pregnancy-Professor Fabrizio Schifano

6. Methadone in pregnancy-Professor Fabrizio Schifano

7. Alcohol and Depression-Professor Fabrizio Schifano

8. Cannabis and Schizophrenia-Professor Fabrizio Schifano

ADDICTIONS

1. OPIATE DEPENDENCE

INSTRUCTIONS TO CANDIDATE
You are about to see this 35 yr old man Herbert Drake who has been referred by the Accident and emergency (A+E) Registrar. He has been demanding methadone. Elicit a history.

TASK FOR THE CANDIDATE
- *Elicit a substance misuse history*

PAY PATICULAR ATTENTION TO THE FOLLOWING (MENTAL CHECKLIST)
- *Establish details of current Methadone prescription.*
- *Establish longitudinal history of illicit substance misuse.*
- *Elicit dependence criteria.*
- *Establish impact using biopsychosocial approach.*
- *Conduct a risk assessment including psychological, forensic and medical risks.*
- *Determine insight and motivation.*

COMMUNICATION SKILLS
- *Start the interview by developing rapport and showing empathy.*
- *Anticipate that you could be dealing with someone who could be withdrawing from illicit substance misuse.*
- *Anticipate that he would be demanding Methadone.*

Suggested approach
Introduction
C: Hello, I'm one of the psychiatrists. Thank you for coming to see me today. I understand from the doctor that has just seen you that you have asked for Methadone. I'm here to see how I can help you.

P: Doc, I need it now!!

C: I appreciate that you seem to be distressed. I will do my best to see how I can help. As you are aware I will have to do a urine drug screening to confirm you are on Methadone. Will you be willing to give me a urine sample?

P: Sure, anything Doc.

C: In order for me to help you I would need to establish more about your history of using street drugs. I need some more details as to know more about why you need the methadone.

A. HOPC (onset, duration, progression, severity)
Establish the reason for requiring Methadone
- *Can you tell me where you are getting Methadone from? Can you tell me what dosage you are taking?(dosage)*

- *Which services usually prescribe this?*
- *Which pharmacy do you usually collect this from? Are you being supervised or unsupervised?*
- *When did the pharmacy dispense the last dose?*
- *How long have you been on Methadone?*
- *Are you on any other prescribed medication?*
- *When was the last time you had any Methadone? Have you had anything else?*
- *I'm just wondering how your supply has run out today?*

Thank you, you have been very helpful. Would you be able to tell me more about when you first started using street drugs?

B. Longitudinal history
- *Can you tell me what type of drugs you use? What else do you use? Ask categorically about each of the following: cannabis, cocaine, cocodamol, heroin, amphetamine, morphine, methadone, pain killers, speed, ecstasy, benzodiazepines, and dihydrocodeine dhc, ketamine, mephedrone and legal highs*
- *Do you drink any alcohol? (if yes, explore further)*

For each type of substance
- *Can you tell me which drug you started with first?*
- *When did you start using it?*
- *Which drug did you try next?*

Tailor your enquiry to the scenario
For example in this scenario
- *How often do you use heroin?(frequency)*
- *How do you use it? (Smoking, snorting, chasing, injecting)*
- *How much heroin do you use on a typical day? (ounces)*
- *How much would you use in a typical week?*
- *On average how much do you spend on heroin in a week?*

If injecting
- *When did you start injecting? How often do you inject?*
- *Do you share needles? With whom do you share needles?*
- *May I please have a look at your arms? (examine paraphernalia sites for any evidence of recent use e.g. feet and groin)*

Typical day
- *Can you take me through a typical day i.e. from the time you get up in the morning until the evening?*

C. Establish dependence criteria
Tolerance
- *What is the maximum you have had on a day?*
- *Has the dose you need for a kick gone up lately?*

ADDICTIONS

Withdrawal symptoms and withdrawal relief
- *What would happen if you miss a dose? How do you manage it?*
- *Do you experience withdrawal symptoms upon waking up?*
- *Do you get body aches, stomach cramps, muscle aches, feeling nauseous and sick, yawning?*

Compulsion
- *Are you finding it difficult to control the amount you use once you have started?*

Craving
- *Are you any having cravings?*

Risk assessment
- *Have you had a history of deliberate or accidental overdoses?*

D. Impact using biopsychosocial approach
Biological
- *Have you had any physical complications from injecting?(e.g. abscesses, infections)(infective endocarditis)*
- *Have you ever been admitted to hospital?*
- *Have you had any tests for hepatitis or HIV infection?*
- *I need to ask you some intimate questions. Are you sexually active? Do you practice safe sex?*

Psychiatric
Establish past history of overdoses
Overdoses
- *Have you had any accidental overdoses?*

Abstinence
- *Have you attended any groups? (Narcotic anonymous)*

Treatment
- *Have you had any treatment in the past?*
- *Establish whether it was substitution treatment or detoxification?*
- *Have you had any mental health problems?*

Forensic
- *Do you have any pending court actions or charges?*
- *Do you have any previous convictions?*

Social
- *Who else is in your family? Do you have any children?*
- *Is there any involvement with social services?*
- *Is there anyone else living with you that is using street drugs?*

Work
- *Are you working?*

ADDICTIONS

Finances
- *Do you have any financial difficulties?*
- *Are you receiving any benefits?*

E. Insight and motivation
- *Do you think you have a problem?*
- *What would you like to do about your problem?*
- *What help would you like from us?*
- *How motivated are you to do this?*
- *On a scale of 1-10 how motivated are you to do something about this?*

F. Summarise
Advice and management plan
Thank you. To summarise, you have told me that you have been using heroin and are now on Methadone. As you are aware we do need to do a urine test to confirm your heroin use. I will not be able to give you methadone today; however I will refer you to your local Community Drug and alcohol team (CDAT), and ensure a key worker is allocated for you.

POSSIBLE VARIATIONS OF THEME
1. *Assess a 34yr. old male who has a history of polysubstance misuse and Depression.*
2. *Assess the social history and the impact of illicit substance misuse.*

ADDICTIONS

2. DELIRIUM TREMENS

> **INSTRUCTIONS TO CANDIDATE**
> You are asked to see this 60 year old man Jeremy Baker who has been admitted on the medical ward. He appears distressed and agitated. He has also been threatening to leave the ward. You have been asked by the nurse in charge to do a psychiatric review.
>
> **TASK FOR THE CANDIDATE**
> * Perform a mental state examination.
>
> **PAY PARTICULAR ATTENTION TO THE FOLLOWING (MENTAL CHECKLIST)**
> * Establish orientation and level of consciousness.
> * Elicit mental state examination.
> * Identify possible aetiological factors.
>
> **COMMUNICATION SKILLS**
> * Start the interview by developing rapport and showing empathy.
> * Anticipate a distressed and frightened person.
> * Periodic reassurance to calm patient.
> * Acknowledgement of possible distress.

Suggested approach
Introduction
C: Hello, I'm Dr ....I'm one of the psychiatrists. I have been asked by the medical staff on this ward to come and see you.

P: Could be distracted and responding.

C: I can see you appear distressed. I can assure you I am one of the psychiatrists and I am here to help you.

P: See that, the spiders, they are all over. Can't you see it?

C: I'm sorry I can see you are clearly distressed. Unfortunately I cannot see what you are seeing. Can you describe to me what you are seeing? (Visual hallucinations)

A. Use clustering approach to elicit psychotic symptoms
Elicit hallucinations in all modalities
* Where do you see it? How clear is it?
* How many spiders do you see?
* Do you see anything else?
* Do you see animals, insects, small people (Lilliputian), or elephants?
* Do you see any spots? (micropsia/macropsia)
* If you close your eyes do you still see it?
* How often do you see it?

ADDICTIONS

- *Apart from you, does anyone else see them?*
- *Do you feel the spiders on you? (tactile hallucination)*
- *Do you hear them? Do you hear any strange noises? Do you hear whispering? Do you hear voices? (auditory hallucinations)*
- *Do you smell any strange smells? (olfactory hallucinations)*

Delusions of control
- *Do you feel that anyone is trying to control you in any way? (delusions of control)*
- *Do they interfere with your thinking?*

Delusions
- *Do you feel that someone is out to harm you?(persecutory and paranoid)*
- *How convinced are you?*

B. Assess for mood symptoms
- *How have you been feeling in yourself?(mood)*

C. Establish level of Cognition
Orientation
- *Do you know where you are?*
- *Do you know what the day is?*
- *Do you know what the date is?*
- *Do you remember what you had for breakfast? Short term memory(STM)*
- *Can you repeat for me apple, table and penny?(Registration)*

D. Risk assessment
- *You appeared distressed. Has there been any time you felt like life was not worth living?(suicidal thoughts)*
- *What do you think you will do?*
- *What plans have you made?*
- *Have you thought about harming anyone else?(homicidal thoughts)*

E. Aetiological factors
Use biopsychosocial approach to identify possible aetiological factors
Biological
- *How has your physical health been?*
- *Are you on any medication?*
- *Have you had any seizures? (different seizures from alcohol induced seizures)*
- *Can you tell me about whether you drink?*
- *If yes, have you experienced anything similar to this in the past?*
- *When was your last drink?*
- *Are you having withdrawal symptoms? (for example sweating, shakes, tremors, nauseous, feeling sick)*
- *Are you having any cravings?*

ADDICTIONS

Psychological
- *Have you ever seen a psychiatrist in the past?*

Social
- *Can you tell me about your family? Whom do you live with?*

Summarise
Thank you for talking to me. You are clearly distressed by what you are experiencing. I will come and speak to you again, once I have spoken to the staff on the ward and had a look at your blood tests.

DELIRIUM TREMENS- MENTAL STATE EXAMINATION
Use clustering approach to elicit psychotic symptoms
Mental state examination
- *Elicit hallucinations in all modalities*
- *visual hallucinations*
- *tactile hallucination*
- *auditory hallucinations*
- *olfactory hallucinations*
- *Delusions of control*
- *Delusions of control*
- *Delusions -persecutory and paranoid*
- *Assess for mood symptoms*
- *Cognition*
- *Orientation*
- *Repetition*

Risk assessment
Aetiological factors
- *Use biopsychosocial approach to identify possible aetiological factors*
- *Biological*
- *Physical health*
- *medication*
- *seizure*
- *Alcohol history*
- *Psychological*
- *Social*

Summarise

©Smartsesh

POSSIBLE VARIATIONS OF THEME
1.46 yr old man admitted to medical ward. He has a history of alcohol dependence and features suggestive of Delirium Tremens.
2.46 yr old man admitted to the orthopaedic ward with a fractured femur. History of alcohol dependence.

ADDICTIONS

3. DELIRIUM TREMENS

INSTRUCTIONS TO CANDIDATE
You have seen this 54yr old gentleman Jeremy Baker on the medical ward and the nurse on the ward wants to know how he will be managed. She is concerned as he has been distressed and threatening to leave the ward.

TASK FOR THE CANDIDATE
- Discuss the management with the nurse.

CHECKLIST
- Summarise findings.
- Exclude organic and functional differential diagnoses.
- Management in holistic or biopsychosocial interventions.
- Consider the legal caveats.
- Offer psychiatric support.

COMMUNICATION SKILLS
- Start the interview by developing rapport and showing empathy.
- Acknowledge the distress and concerns of this case.
- Adopt a collegiate approach

Suggested approach
Introduction
C: Hello, I'm one of the psychiatrists. I have seen Jeremy who was referred to my team. I would like to discuss my findings and discuss the management plan. Before I do this though, would you be able to tell me your understanding of how he has been presenting?

N: Well we think he is psychotic and have been finding it difficult to manage on the ward.

C: I understand from what you are saying that it has been difficult to manage him. Let me explain my psychiatric assessment. My understanding is that he has been admitted following a recent fall. Since then he has been presenting with confusion, agitation, poor memory and is distressed by visual hallucinations.
From my assessment it appears he is displaying features of Delirium Tremens.

He has clouded consciousness, tremors, visual and auditory hallucinations and raised temperature. Delirium Tremens is a life threatening emergency condition and requires emergency medical treatment. He seems best treated on this ward.

I did consider other differential diagnoses.

ADDICTIONS

Blood investigations have excluded an infection. The symptoms are also not typical of a mental illness like Schizophrenia or acute psychotic episode. However we will bear in mind of these diagnoses.

N: What is the prognosis?

C: As I have mentioned it is a life threatening condition. Mortality rate if not treated is 38%.

N: How do we treat him?

C: Our management is in terms of biological, psychological and social approach.

Biological interventions
- Management on the medical ward as it is a medical emergency.
- Monitoring of vitals.(Blood pressure, pulse, temperature respiratory rate)
- Practical aspects that need to be addressed.
- -Nurse in a side room.
- -Ensure adequate lighting.
- -Familiar staff.
- -Orientation aids- i.e. clock to minimise distress.
- **Legal Caveats**: If he tries to leave, we need to assess the risk at the time and can if necessary use a section 5(2) or assess capacity. We however will endeavour to always use the least restrictive method.

Medication
- Start a Chlordiazepoxide reducing regime according to CIWA-Ar) score
- (collateral history to start –as required medication)
- Check his Liver function tests (LFT)
- Lorazepam and Oxazepam can also be considered.
- Antipsychotic medication
- Haloperidol
- Pabrinex® -2 amps three times daily intravenously to prevent Wernikes Encephalopathy.
- Oral Thiamine 100mg three times daily
- Monitor for seizures
- Treat with Carbamazepine for alcohol induced seizures and per rectal(PR) Diazepam if necessary
- Monitor for other withdrawal symptoms
- Analgesia if required

Longer term management
Psychological interventions
- Education to family to explain
- Risk of abrupt withdrawal or discontinuation
- Importance of aftercare and link with community services

- *Counselling*
- *AA-Alcoholic anonymous-12 step programme*

Social interventions
- *Support*
- *Assess ADL(Activity of daily living)*

Long term
- *Discuss with alcohol liaison service, liaise with community services.*

CIWA Ar scores

Cumulative Score

0-8	*No medication is necessary*
9-14	*Medication is optional for patients with a score of 8-14*
15-20	*A score of 15 or over requires treatment with medication*
>20	*A score of over 20 poses a strong risk of Delirium*

DELIRIUM TREMENS -MANAGEMENT

Acute onset of fluctuating consciousness, tremors and visual and auditory hallucinations and raised temperature. It is a life threatening emergency condition and requires medical treatment.
Differential diagnoses to consider
- *Blood investigations have excluded an infection. symptoms not typical of a mental illness like Schizophrenia or acute psychotic episode*

Prognosis-Mortality rate if not treated is 38%
- *Monitoring of vitals*
- *Practical aspects that need to be addressed:*
- *Nurse in a side room*
- *Good lighting*
- *Familiar staff*
- *Orientation aids- clock to minimise distress*
- *If he tries to leave, we need to assess the risk at the time and can use a section 5(2) or assess capacity. We always use the least restrictive method.*

©Smartsesh

ADDICTIONS

Management is in terms of biological, psychological and social approach.
Biological interventions
Medication

- Start a Chlordiazepoxide reducing regime(CIWA-Ar score)
- as required medication
- Check his Liver function tests (LFT(Liver function tests))
- Alternatives : Lorazepam, and Oxazepam
- Antipsychotic medication-Haloperidol
- Pabrinex –2 amps tds intravenously to prevent Wernicke's encephalopathy.
- Oral Thiamine 100m,g tds po
- Monitor seizures-Treat with Carbamazepine
- Other symptoms vomiting
- Offer analgesia.

Medium term management
Psychological interventions

- Education to family to explain
- Risk of abrupt withdrawal or discontinuation
- Importance of aftercare and link with community services
- Counselling
- AA-Alcoholic anonymous-12 step programme

Social interventions

- Support
- Assess ADL(Activity of daily living)

Longer term management

- Discuss with alcohol liaison service, liaise with community services.

©Smartsesh

ADDICTIONS

4. ALCOHOL DEPENDENCE

INSTRUCTIONS TO CANDIDATE
You have been asked to see Mr Angus Green who is a 45 yr old man who has been referred by his GP with history of alcohol dependence. His recent blood tests showed elevated liver function tests (LFT (Liver function tests)'s). His wife has threatened to leave him.

TASK FOR THE CANDIDATE
- *Elicit a history of alcohol dependence.*
- *Assess his insight and motivation.*

PAY PARTICULAR ATTENTION TO THE FOLLOWING (MENTAL CHECKLIST)
- *Establish details of alcohol dependence.*
- *Establish longitudinal history of alcohol use.*
- *Elicit alcohol dependence criteria and Edwards and gross (1976) criteria tolerance, withdrawal, relief drinking, stereotyped pattern, compulsion, primacy, rapid reinstatement).*
- *Establish impact using biopsychosocial approach.*
- *Conduct a risk assessment including psychological, forensic and medical risks.*
- *Determine insight and motivation.*

COMMUNICATION SKILLS
- *Start the interview developing rapport and showing empathy.*
- *Anticipate that he would be in denial about his alcohol dependence and that he would not be forthcoming about this.*

Suggested approach
Introduction
C: Hello, I'm Dr... I am a psychiatrist. I understand that your GP has referred you to see me as your recent blood test results were raised. I would like to discuss this with you. Is that all right?

P: He said my liver functions tests were abnormal and I should stop drinking.

C: From my experience, sometimes if these test results are abnormal, it can be related to a person's drinking habits. Can you tell me about your drinking habits?

A. History of Presenting Complaint (HOPC) (onset, duration, progression, severity)

Longitudinal history
- Can you tell me when you first started to drink?
- What types of drink did you have?

ADDICTIONS

* How has it progressed since then?

Typical day
* Can you take me through a typical day?
* What time would you have your first drink?
* How does that progress through the day?
* How much would you consume on a typical day?
* How much alcohol would you consume on average in a week?
* **(Assist him in calculating units consumed daily and then weekly according to percentage of alcohol, frequency and amount consumed)**
* **[Enquire if he is aware of what the recommended levels for safe drinking are]**
* And what about weekends? Does the amount vary?

B. CAGE questions [2 or more positives indicate alcohol misuse]
* Have you ever felt that you ought to **cut down** your drinking?
* Have people **annoyed** you by criticizing your drinking?
* Have you ever felt **guilty** about your drinking?
* Have you ever had a drink first thing in the morning (an **eye opener**) to steady your nerves or get rid of a hangover?

C. Dependence syndrome
Establish core features of alcohol dependence syndrome including Edwards and Gross criteria
Tolerance
* Do you feel you need to drink more to feel the effects of alcohol?

Withdrawal
* What happens if you miss a drink?
* Do you get any shakes, tremors, sweats, (withdrawal symptoms)
* How do you cope then?
* Have you ever had any seizures?
* Have you ever heard voices or seen things when there was no one else around? (Delirium Tremens or Alcoholic Hallucinosis)

Relief of withdrawal
* Do you need a drink first thing in the morning?

Compulsion
* Do you have difficulty controlling the amount you drink?

Inability to control
Primacy
* Would you say that this has taken priority over other things in your life?

ADDICTIONS

Reinstatement
- *Have there been periods where you have tried to stop? What happened?*

Stereotype
- *Where do you usually drink? Is it socially? (Pub, parties, family gatherings) or do you prefer to drink alone?*

Narrowing of repertoire (drinking only one brand of alcoholic beverage)

Use despite knowing harmful effects
- *Do you know the effects of alcohol?*

D. Impact using a biopsychosocial approach
Biological
- *How has your physical health been?*
- *Have you had any recent blood tests?*

Psychological
- *Screen for depressive symptoms, symptoms of Alcoholic Hallucinosis*

Social
- *How has this affected your work?*
- *How has this impacted your family life?*

E. Forensic history
- *Have you had any problems with the police?*
- *Any drink and driving charges?*

F Family history
- *Is there anyone in the family that has any similar problems?*

G Risk Assessment
- *This is a rather sensitive question that we routinely ask, but have you had thoughts that life was not worth living? (Suicidal thoughts)*
- *Have you had thoughts of harming anyone else?*

H Insight and motivation
- *Would you agree that you have an Alcohol problem?*
- *What do you want to do about it?*
- *What do you think would happen if you don't act?*
- *Why would you act at this point?*
- *What support will you need?*

Summary
Thank you for talking to me. I know this must not have been easy. I have some information and leaflets for you to read. There are also these useful websites and support groups like Alcoholics Anonymous. If you wish to see

ADDICTIONS

me again, feel free to make an appointment to discuss this further. Thank you

Support groups and websites
AA- Alcoholics anonymous
FRANK

Stages of Change Model-Diclemente and Prochaska
- ➢ **Pre-contemplation**- *abuser doesn't believe there is a problem, however recognized by other*
- ➢ **Contemplation**- *individual is able to weigh the pros and cons and considers that change might be necessary*
- ➢ **Decision:** *point reached where decision is made to act (or not to act) on issue of substance misuse*
- ➢ **Action:** *user chooses a strategy for change and pursues it*
- ➢ **Maintenance:** *gains are maintained and consolidated. Failure may lead to relapse*
- ➢ **Relapse**
- ➢ *Return to previous pattern of behaviour*
                    ©Smartsesh

ALCOHOL HISTORY
Longitudinal history
Typical day
Dependence syndrome-Edwards and Gross criteria
- • *Tolerance*
- • *Withdrawal*
- • *Compulsion*
- • *Craving*
- • *reinstatement*
- • *primacy*
- • *stereotype*

Impact on daily functioning
- • *Biological -Physical complications*
- • *Psychological-Depression, Alcoholic Hallucinosis*
- • *Affected-Family, social, work*

Forensic history-*drink and driving charges*
Family history -*alcoholism*
Other –*illicit substance misuse*
Risk assessment
Insight and motivation
                    ©Smartsesh

ADDICTIONS

POSSIBLE VARIATIONS OF THEME
1.46 yr. old man who was referred by GP with elevated liver functions. Establish alcohol dependence and discuss results with him.
2.45 yr old man referred by GP with alcohol dependence. Do a risk assessment.

ICD 10 CRITERIA Alcohol dependence
A Diagnosis of dependence should be made if three (3) or more of the following have been experienced or exhibited at some time during the last year.
(1) A **strong desire or compulsion** to take the substance
(2) Difficulties in **controlling substance** taking behaviour in terms of its onset, termination or levels of use.
(3) Physiological **withdrawal state** when substance has ceased or been reduced, as evidenced by either of the following: characteristic withdrawal syndrome
(4) Evidence of **tolerance,** such that increased doses of the psychoactive substance are required in order to achieve effects originally produced by lower doses
(5) Progressive **neglect of alternative pleasures** or interests because of psychoactive substance use and increased amount of time necessary to obtain or take the substance or to recover from its effects
(6) Persisting with substance use despite clear evidence of overtly **harmful consequences (physical or mental)**

ACAMPROSATE **Campral EC®(Merck Serono)** **666MG TDS**	Common Nausea, vomiting, abdominal pain, fluctuation in libido Rare bulbous skin reactions
DISULFIRAM **Antabuse®(Actavis) 200mg daily** **increased to 500mg daily**	Common drowsiness, fatigue, nausea, vomiting, halitosis, reduced libido Rare psychotic reactions
NALTREXONE **Nalorex®(Bristol-Myers Squibb)** **Opizone®(Genus)** **25 mg od on Day 1,then increased** **to 50 mg od**	Common nausea, vomiting, abdominal pain, diarrhoea, constipation, reduced appetite Less common hepatic dysfunction, suicidal ideation Rare hallucinations, tremor,

ADDICTIONS

5. METHADONE IN PREGNANCY

INSTRUCTIONS TO CANDIDATE
You have been asked to assess this 25 yr old lady Sarah Brighton who is known to the Community Drug and Alcohol Team. She has found out that she is pregnant and wants to discuss this with you.

TASK FOR THE CANDIDATE
- *Elicit a drug and alcohol history and social history.*

PAY PARTICULAR ATTENTION TO THE FOLLOWING (MENTAL CHECKLIST)
- *Establish the details of pregnancy.*
- *Establish the drug and alcohol history.*
- *Establish the social history.*
- *Establish her insight and motivation to change.*
- *Conduct a risk assessment*

COMMUNICATION SKILLS
- *Start the interview by developing rapport and showing empathy.*
- *Show sensitivity and understanding of the subjective experience of the individual.*

Suggested approach
Introduction
C: Hello, I'm Dr I'm one of the psychiatrists. Thank you for coming to see me. I understand that you have found out you are expecting. I would like to see how best we can help you.

P: I have found out that I am pregnant.

C: I'm glad you have come to see me today, so we can discuss this further. It will help if I can know more about the details of your pregnancy?

A. History of Presenting Complaint (HOPC) (onset, duration, progression, severity)
Pregnancy
- *When was your last normal period? (LNP)*
- *How do you know you are pregnant? Have you seen you GP, midwife?*
- *How are you feeling about this?*
- *Would you be attending antenatal appointments and scans?*

C: I understand you have come to the drug and alcohol clinic because you wanted to get some advice about this. Can you tell me if you have been using street drugs?

Establish the drug and alcohol history
Longitudinal history

ADDICTIONS

- *What type of drugs do you use?*
- *What else do you use?*
- *Ask categorically about each of the following: cannabis, cocaine, cocodamol, heroin, amphetamine, morphine, methadone, pain killers, speed, ecstasy, benzodiazepines, and dihydrocodeine dhc, ketamine, mephedrone and legal highs?*
- *Any alcohol?*

For each type of substance:
- *How often do you use heroin?*
- *How do you use it? (Smoking, snorting, chasing, injecting)*
- *How much heroin do you use on a typical day? (ounces)*
- *How much would you use in a typical week?*
- *On average how much do you spend on them in a week?*

If injecting
- *When did you start injecting?*
- *How often do you inject?*
- *Have you shared needles? With whom have you shared needles?*
- *May I have a look at your arms? (Examine paraphernalia sites for any evidence for recent use)*

Typical day
- *Can you take me through a typical day i.e. from the time you get up in the morning until the evening?*

Establish dependence criteria
Tolerance
- *What is the maximum you have had on a day?*
- *Has the dose you need for a kick gone up lately?*

Withdrawal symptoms and withdrawal relief
- *What would happen if you miss a dose?*
- *How do you manage it?*
- *Do you experience withdrawal symptoms upon waking up?*
- *Do you get body aches, stomach cramps, muscle aches, feeling nauseous and sick, yawning?*

Compulsion
- *Are you finding it difficult to control the amount you use once you have started?*

Craving
- *Are you having cravings?*

B. Risk assessment
- *Have you had a history of deliberate or accidental overdoses?*

ADDICTIONS

C. Impact using biopsychosocial approach
1. Biological
- Have you had any physical complications from injecting? (E.g. abscesses, infections)
- Have you ever been admitted to hospital?
- Have you had any tests for hepatitis or HIV infection?
- I need to ask you some intimate details, do you practice safe sex?

2. Psychiatric
Overdoses
- Have you had any accidental overdoses?

Treatment
- Have you had any treatment in the past-substitution or detoxification?

Abstinence
- Have you attended any self-help groups - Narcotic Anonymous?
- Have you had any mental health problems?

Forensic
- Do you have any pending court or charges?
- Do you have any previous convictions?

3. Social history
- Can you tell me more about who is in your family?
- Can you tell me about your partner?
- Is there anyone else using street drugs?
- Do you have any other children?
- Any past history of involvement with social services or children, school and family services?

Work
- Are you working?

Finances
- Do you have any financial difficulties?

Insight and motivation
- Do you think you have a problem?
- What is it that you would like to do?
- What help would you like from us?
- How motivated are you for this?

Summarise
Thank you for coming to see me. To summarise, you have now found out you are pregnant and you are motivated to get help with your drug habit. We do have a few options available like substitution with Methadone and also monitoring your pregnancy closely. We would need to consider closely

monitoring you at the time of delivery as well. I have some information and leaflets you can have to read. I am happy to discuss the options further with you and your partner if you wish.

Thank you

POSSIBLE VARIATIONS OF THEME
1.35 yr. old lady on heroin, cocaine and drinking alcohol who is 4 months pregnant and now wants go on substitution treatment
2.26 yr. old lady, now 3 months pregnant and is alcohol dependent. She has had a previous history of seizures.

ADDICTIONS

6. METHADONE IN PREGNANCY

INSTRUCTIONS TO CANDIDATE
You have been asked to see the partner Mr Darren Bright of the lady who had come to see about her pregnancy and illicit substance misuse. He is concerned about her and the baby.

TASK FOR THE CANDIDATE
- Discuss the effects of illicit substance misuse and further management

PAY PARTICULAR ATTENTION TO THE FOLLOWING (MENTAL CHECKLIST)
- Establish his current attitude about the pregnancy and level of support he will be providing
- Explain the in utero effects and teratogenicity effects of illicit substances(namely Heroin, Cocaine and Methadone)
- Explain the possible treatment options
- Emphasise the need for multiagency management during pregnancy and at time of delivery

COMMUNICATION SKILLS
- Start the interview by developing rapport and showing empathy.
- Develop a common ground for collaborative working with his partner and keeping the babies best interest at heart.

Suggested approach
Introduction
C: Hello, I'm Dr... I am a psychiatrist working gin the community drug and alcohol team. Thank you for coming to see me. I've spoken to your partner and she tells me she has found out that she is expecting. I gather you want to discuss this further and look at the treatment options available.

P: Hello Doc, Yes she is pregnant now. I want to discuss this with you.

Pregnancy
C: How do you feel about the pregnancy?
What are your concerns?
P: I am worried the harm the street drugs would do to her and the baby.

C: This is an important issue you have raised. I will try to explain this as best as I can.

From what we know the following are the effects of illicit substances on pregnancy:
Systematically address the perinatal and teratogenic effects of each substance individually:

ADDICTIONS

Heroin *can cause complications in the pregnancy, cause miscarriage and intrauterine death (IUD).*
Heroin and Methadone can cause at the time of birth, neonatal abstinence syndrome or withdrawal syndrome. Symptoms of baby presenting with this is that the baby when born, will be jittery, sneezing, colicky, and have high pitched cry.

Methadone *is not 'teratogenic', meaning it causes no harm to the unborn baby. Therefore we usually consider this as substitution treatment if pregnant women want to abstain from Heroin.*

Cocaine *can however cause some abnormalities in the baby and is therefore 'teratogenic' for example affects the bones of the baby's head and the genitourinary or the kidney and bladder systems. There is also a higher incidence of sudden infant death and miscarriage.*

Alcohol
Depending on the amount of alcohol, this can cause foetal alcohol syndrome (FAS)

C: I know it is a lot of information. Are you able to understand all we have discussed thus far?

It's good that you and your partner have come to talk to me. Your support is vitally important during this period.

P: I am also concerned about social services?

C: This is usually a concern due to the risks on the baby. Social services will only be involved if there are any concerns of neglect or harm to the baby.

P: What do we do now?

C: There are a few treatment options available. This would be dependent on the level of her motivation. This would include biological or medication like Methadone for detoxification.

She would need to engage with both the drug and alcohol services and also the obstetrics team.
With the Community Drug and Alcohol team.
- *She will need to engage with her allocated key worker*

The options are.
- *She can continue with Methadone, as this is safe in pregnancy. Her pregnancy would be considered as high risk and therefore she would require close monitoring.*
- *If she wants to be abstinent then we can consider her being admitted in the ward and monitor her and the baby during the opiate detoxification.*

ADDICTIONS

With the obstetrics team
- *She will need to ensure a healthy diet, and attendance of her appointments with GP, midwife and ultrasound department. The ultrasound is routinely done at 12 weeks and then the anomaly scan is done at 20 weeks to detect any abnormalities in the unborn baby.*

P: I would like to support her.

I'm glad she will be having your support. I know we have talked a lot, and I have some more information leaflets for you. I am happy to make another appointment to see you both to discuss the best way forward.

Thank you

> ➤ **Methadone is not teratogenic, meaning it causes no harm to the unborn baby.**
> ➤ **Heroin and Methadone can cause at the time of birth, neonatal abstinence syndrome or withdrawal syndrome.**
> ➤ **Cocaine can however cause some abnormalities in the baby for example affect the bones of the head and genitourinary systems. There is also a higher incidence of sudden infant death.**
> ➤ **Alcohol**
> ➤ **It causes foetal alcohol syndrome.**

ADDICTIONS

SUBSTITUT)ON THERAPY **Methadone Methadose** **®(Rosemount)** *10mg to 40 g daily increased to* *maximum 60-120mg*	
Buprenorphine **Subutex® (Reckitt Benckiser)** **Suboxone® (Reckitt Benckiser** *0, 8 mg -4 mg od* *2-4 mg daily* *Maximum 12-24 mg daily*	
Lofexidine BritLofex®(Genus) *800 mcg increased to maximum 2.4* *mg*	**Common:** *Dry mucous membranes,* *hypotension, bradycardia, dizziness,* *drowsiness, QT prolongation*
NALTREXONE **Nalorex®(Bristol-Myers Squibb)** **Opizone®(Genus)** *25 mg od on Day 1,then increased to* *50 mg od*	**Common:** *nausea, vomiting,* *abdominal pain, diarrhoea,* *constipation, reduced appetite* **Less common:** *hepatic dysfunction,* *suicidal ideation* **Rare:** *hallucinations, tremor,*

ADDICTIONS

7. ALCOHOL AND DEPRESSION

INSTRUCTIONS TO CANDIDATE
You have been asked to see this 47 yr. old gentleman Mr Frederick Banks who has been treated for Depression. He has also admitted Drinking

TASK FOR THE CANDIDATE
- Establish the link of alcohol and Depression

PAY PARTICULAR ATTENTION TO THE FOLLOWING (MENTAL CHECKLIST)
- Establish briefly current depressive symptoms
- Establish alcohol dependence and longitudinal history
- Establish temporal relationship as to which come first, i.e. Depression or alcohol dependence.
- Conduct a risk assessment.

COMMUNICATION SKILLS
- Start the interview by developing rapport and showing empathy.
- Show sensitivity.
- Anticipate he could be reluctant to discuss his alcohol dependence.

Suggested approach
Introduction
C: Hello, I'm one of the psychiatrists. Thank you for coming to see me today. I understand that you have been seeing your GP and you are currently on antidepressants. I wanted to ask you more about this. Is that all right?

P: Hello Doctor, I have been seeing my GP for this.

C: Can you tell me when did this all start?

A. HOPC (onset, duration, progression, severity)
Establish history of Depression and core features
- How long have you been on the antidepressants?
- How were you feeling in your spirits at the time? (Mood)
- How have you benefited from the medication?
- I understand also that you had some blood tests for your liver and your GP has mentioned that it could possibly be related to your drinking.

Establish alcohol dependence
- I know this is a sensitive issue, but are you able to tell me more about your drinking habits?

Longitudinal history
- When did you first start drinking?

- *What did you have?*
- *How has it progressed since then?*

Typical day
- *Can you take me through a typical day?*
- *Can you tell me what happens from the time you get up till the evening?*
- *Is there anything else that you take, for example street drugs?*

B. CAGE questions [2 or more positives indicate alcohol misuse]
- *Have you ever felt that you ought to **cut down** your drinking?*
- *Have people **annoyed** you by criticizing your drinking?*
- *Have you ever felt **guilty** about your drinking?*
- *Have you ever had a drink first thing in the morning (an **eye opener**) to steady your nerves or get rid of a hangover?*

C. Dependence syndrome
Establish features of dependence syndrome
To note
Edwards and Gross criteria has all criteria
Tolerance
- *Do you feel you need to drink more to feel the effects of alcohol?*

Withdrawal
- *What happens if you miss a drink?*
- *Do you get any shakes, tremors, sweats? (Withdrawal symptoms)*
- *Have you ever had any seizures?*
- *Have you ever heard voices or seen things when there was no one else around? (Auditory hallucinations)*

Relief of withdrawal
- *Do you need a drink first thing?*

Compulsion
- *Do you have difficulty controlling the amount you drink?*

Inability to control
Primacy
- *Would you say that this has taken priority over other things in your life?*

Reinstatement
- *Have there been periods where you have tried to stop? What happened?*

Stereotype
- *Where do you usually drink?*

Narrowing of repertoire

ADDICTIONS

Use despite knowing harmful effects
- *Do you know the effects of alcohol?*

D. Impact using a biopsychosocial approach
Biological
- *How has your physical health been?*
- *Have you had any recent blood tests?*

Psychological
As above

Social
- *How has this affected your work?*
- *How has this impacted your family life?*

E. Forensic
- *Have you had any problems with the police?*
- *Any drink and driving?*

F. Family history
- *Is there anyone in the family that has any similar problems?*

G. Risk Assessment
- *This is a rather sensitive question that we routinely ask, but have you had thoughts that life was not worth living? (Suicidal thoughts)*
- *Have you had thoughts of harming anyone else?*

H. Establish the link of alcohol and Depression and the chronology
Recapitulation
C: From what you have told me it appears that you have been drinking alcohol for x months and this amount has increased. You have also told me that you have also been depressed and as a result been coping with drinking, and you are aware of its depressant effects. I'm wondering, if I can I take you back to when this all started, can you pinpoint which one came first?

I. Insight and motivation
- *Would you agree that you have an Alcohol problem?*
- *What do you want to do about it?*
- *What do you think would happen if you don't act?*
- *Why would you act at this point?*
- *What support will you need?*

Summary
Thank you for talking to me. I know this must not have been easy. I have some information and leaflets for you to read. There are also these useful websites and support groups like Alcoholics Anonymous. If you wish to see me again, feel free to make an appointment to discuss this further. Thank you

ADDICTIONS

ADDICTIONS

8. CANNABIS AND SCHIZOPHRENIA

INSTRUCTIONS TO CANDIDATE
Speak to the mother of 19yr old gentleman who has been admitted and has a diagnosis of Schizophrenia. His mother feels that his illness is due to cannabis.

TASK FOR THE CANDIDATE
- Discuss this with his mother.
- Establish the link with cannabis and Schizophrenia.

PAY PARTICULAR ATTENTION TO THE FOLLOWING (MENTAL CHECKLIST)
- Establish consent given
- Explain the relationship between cannabis and schizophrenia.
- Explain schizophrenia- aetiology, symptoms and signs, prognosis.
- Avoid false reassurance.
- Explain management in terms of biopsychosocial approach.

COMMUNICATION SKILLS
- Develop rapport and show empathy.
- Show sensitivity and anticipate a concerned mother with possible guilt feelings
- Impart information as if you are breaking bad news.

Suggested approach
Introduction
C: Hello, I'm Dr ....I am a psychiatrists working on this ward. Thank you for coming to see me. I understand that your son has been admitted into our hospital last night. He has given me permission to speak to you. I have come to talk to you more about his diagnosis and the treatment options available. I would like to ask you more about that. Is that all right?

M: It's due to the cannabis, but they are saying it is Schizophrenia.

C: I would like to discuss that, but can you tell me how he was when he came in?

M: Ever since he has been smoking cannabis, he has been hearing voices. It's the cannabis right?

C: From the literature available, we know that cannabis can result in someone getting Schizophrenia. The risk is four-six times more if someone has a history of using cannabis. We know also that the effects cannabis is similar to someone who has Schizophrenia.
We usually advise our patients to abstain from using cannabis because if they have Schizophrenia it can make their symptoms worse.

ADDICTIONS

C: I will explain to you more about Schizophrenia. Please feel free to interrupt me if you do not understand me.

Schizophrenia is a relatively common mental illness. It is when someone's thinking, feeling and behaviour is affected and they lose touch of reality. Your son has become suspicious about people and has strong beliefs that they are poisoning him despite no evidence for this. This type of thinking is one of the positive symptoms called a delusion. The other positive symptom is hallucinations, when someone hears or sees things when there is no one else around.

Other symptoms are the negative symptoms where they lose the get up and go of life and people around them might think they are lazy.

M: Who usually gets this?

C: It is serious mental illness that occurs in 1 in 100 people. It can develop in the late teens from 15-35 yrs.

M: What are the causes?

C: It is difficult to pinpoint one particular cause in your son's case. The causes are multifactorial.   From the research that is available it is due to a few associated factors. It has a genetic component and can run in families. That means if someone in the family has it, there is a 10 times increased risk of having it. It is also due to a chemical imbalance of dopamine, Noradrenalin (NA) and Serotonin (5HT) serotonin.

It can be caused by birth infections, season of birth. As we discussed previously, we know also that using street drugs like cannabis can also trigger an episode.

M: Is it my fault?

C: No, it is not your fault. A lot of people in your situation do feel responsible. It's important that you understand his illness and therefore your support and understanding plays an important role in
his recovery.

M: Will he get better?

C: Our aim is to get him to lead a normal life as possible. This however is not always possible. After one relapse the risk is reduced. The general rule of thumb is that 1/3 will recover, 1/3 will remain chronic and 1/3 another episode. It's difficult to say which category he will be in.

We work within a multidisciplinary team approach. We have the psychiatrists that will look at the medication. The community psychiatric nurse that will support him at home, the psychologist for psychology, occupational therapy *for vocational training and social worker to assist him with his finances and housing.*

M: What are the medications available for him?

C: The medications we have are a group called antipsychotic. It works to normalise the chemical imbalance. It helps to make a person think more clearly, weaken the delusions and hallucinations and increase the motivation so that they will be able to take care of themselves.

Like all medication they have side effects. Would you like to know about that?

The older generation medication or typical medication can cause stiffness, shakiness and restlessness.

The newer generation or atypical medication like Olanzapine can cause metabolic syndrome where there is raised blood pressure glucose and cholesterol, diabetes and weight gain.

We will monitor him for these side effects and not everyone will develop these side effects. We usually start on a low dose and gradually increase this.

M: How long will he need to continue with this medication?

C: There is a chance if he doesn't take medication that he will relapse. We usually advise that he would need to continue it for 1-2 years to prevent getting unwell.

M: What are the Psychological treatments that are available?
In the longer term other treatment options available are the psychological or talking therapies called CBT (cognitive behavioural therapy) for the delusions and family therapy. This is usually done at the later stage of treatment.

Another vitally important part is education about his illness, because if people understand the illness, then this would improve their insight and engagement with their treatment. This will also promote his wellbeing and recovery. It is also important that you and the rest of the family learn more about his illness and we could also provide some support. Relaxation therapy is important to decrease the stress.

M: What support will he get?

The social aspects involve that getting him to a functional level. The Occupational therapist will maximise his potential to ensure he could possible return to education and vocational training. We have day centre and activities, and encourage people to volunteer at MIND.

M: Does he need to be in hospital?

ADDICTIONS

C: We assess the risk and consider either admission in hospital either voluntary or on own free will. In cases where a person doesn't consent to this, be admitted and if we feel it is in their best interest and to ensure their safety or the safety of others, we will have to use the Mental Health Act (MHA 1983). (MHA 1983).

In later stages of care we usually involve the EIS (Early intervention services) which would provide the community support.

Summarise
Thank you for seeing me today. I know you are concerned about your son. I have told you more about his illness and the treatment options available like medication, psychological and social aspects of care.

I have some leaflets for you to read. I am happy to see you again to discuss this further. Do you have any other questions?

There are also these useful organisations and charities like Rethink, Mind and Saneline.

There are also some useful websites.
Thank you

MANAGEMENT
Schizophrenia-common mental illness
Epidemiology: 1/100, M=F
Aetiology- genetic, environmental, viral infections, street drugs,
Biological interventions
- Medication
- Antipsychotic NICE
- Atypical-Risperidone, Olanzapine, Aripiprazole, Quetiapine side effects metabolic syndrome, weight gain, DM(Diabetes Mellitus)
- Typical Haloperidol side effects stiffness, shakiness, restlessness

Psychological interventions
- Cognitive Behavioural therapy(CBT) or Family Therapy(FT0
- Psychoeducation
- Relaxation therapy

Social interventions
- Finances
- Day centre , activities
- MIND volunteer
- Vocational services –occupational therapy

Long term
- EIS

©Smartsesh

ADDICTIONS

CANNABIS
- Also know as Marijuana, weed, puff, hash, skunk, dope, gear, spliff, pot, solids
- Comes from the plant Cannabis Sativa
- Skunk is very strong

Composition: tetrahydrocannabinol(THC) and other canabinoids

Form oral – cooked and eaten
- **Smoking –joint**

Description
- Acts on the cannabinoid receptors and increases the level of Dopamine

Effects
- Relaxed, calm, talkative, 'too relaxed or stoned'
- Heightens sensations-colours, taste, and sound
- Hallucinations and sensory distortions
- Cravings or the munchies

Adverse effects
- Memory and concentration
- Psychosis
- Amotivation syndrome
- **Withdrawal symptoms**

Cannabis and Schizophrenia
- Causality
- Risk of developing Schizophrenia is 6 times if moderate use of Cannabis
- Studies-Andreason

© Smartsesh

ADDICTIONS

References
Gelder, M.G, Cowen, P. and Harrison P.J (2006) *Shorter Oxford textbook of psychiatry*. 5th edn. Oxford: Oxford University Press.

Sims, A. C. P. (2003) *Symptoms in the mind: an introduction to descriptive psychopathology*. 3rd edn. Great Britain: Saunders.

Taylor, D., Paton, C., Kapur, S. (2009) *The South London and Maudsley NHS Foundation Trust & Oxleas NHS Foundation Trust prescribing guidelines*. 10th edn. London: Informa Healthcare.

British Medical Association and Royal Pharmaceutical society (2011), *British National Formulary 62*, 62nd edn. Great Britain: British Medical Journal Publishing Group and Pharmaceutical Press

WHO. (1992)*The ICD 10 classification of mental and behavioural disorders: clinical descriptions and diagnostic guideline*. 10th revision: Geneva; WHO

Department of Health (England) and the devolved administrations (2007).

Dependence: *UK Guidelines on Clinical Management*. London: Department of Health (England), the Scottish Government, Welsh Assembly Government and Northern Ireland
Executive

Schifano F. *Drugs: treatment and management*. In: Substance Abuse: Evidence and Experience. Ghodse AH, Herman H, Maj M and Sartorius N (Eds), Wiley-Blackwell, Chichester (UK), 2011 pp. 53-74

Schifano F: *Central nervous system case studies*. In: Dhillon S, Raymond R: Pharmacy case studies. Pharmaceutical Press, London, 2009; pp: 80-102

Winstock A, Schifano F. *Disorders relating to the use of ecstasy, other' party drugs' and khat*. In: Gelder M, Andreason N, Lopez-Ibor JJ, Geddes J (Eds): New Oxford Textbook of Psychiatry, Oxford Press,

Edwards G. & Gross MM, *Alcohol dependence: provisional description of a clinical syndrome*, BMJ 1976; i: 1058-106P

Fattore L, Fratta W. *Beyond THC: The New Generation of Cannabinoid Designer Drugs.*
Front Behav Neurosci. 2011; 5:60. Epub 2011 Sep 21.

Manrique-Garcia E, Zammit S, Dalman C, Hemmingsson T, Andreasson S, Allebeck P. *Cannabis, schizophrenia and other non-affective psychoses: 35 years of follow-up of a population-based cohort*. Psychol Med. 2011 Oct 17:1-8. [Epub ahead of print]

ADDICTIONS

Fiorentini A, Volonteri LS, Dragogna F, Rovera C, Maffini M, Mauri MC, Altamura CA. Substance-Induced Psychoses: A Critical Review Of The Literature. Curr Drug Abuse Rev. 2011 Dec 1. [Epub ahead of print

Kouimtsidis C, Schifano F, Sharp T, Ford L, Robinson J, Magee C. Neurological and psychopathological sequelae associated with a lifetime intake of 40,000 ecstasy tablets. Psychosomatics. 2006 Jan-Feb; 47(1):86-7.

Kouimtsidis C, Reynolds M, Hunt M, Lind J, Beckett J, Drummond C, Ghodse H. Substance use in the general hospital. Addict Behav. 2003 Apr; 28(3):483-99.

Support groups and organisations
Alcoholics Anonymous
Giveupdrinking.co.uk
50 Ways To Leave Your Lager
If you believe you're drinking too much, or you know alcohol is having a detrimental effect on your life, this website can help.
Online resources
www.downyourdrink.org.uk

F10 - F19
Mental and behavioural disorders due to psychoactive substance use
F10. – Mental and behavioural disorders due to use of alcohol
F11. – Mental and behavioural disorders due to use of opioids
F12. – Mental and behavioural disorders due to use of cannabinoids
F13. – Mental and behavioural disorders due to use of sedative hypnotics
F14. – Mental and behavioural disorders due to use of cocaine
F15. – Mental and behavioural disorders due to use of other stimulants, including caffeine
F16. – Mental and behavioural disorders due to use of hallucinogens
F17. – Mental and behavioural disorders due to use of tobacco
F18. – Mental and behavioural disorders due to use of volatile solvents
F19. – Mental and behavioural disorders due to multiple drug use and use of other
Psychoactive substances
©Smartsesh

PSYCHOTHERAPY

PSYCHOTHERAPY –Dr Dinesh Sinha , Dr Furhan Iqbal

1. Footballer- Cognitive distortions-assess-Dr Dinesh Sinha

2. Footballer –Cognitive distortions- Dr Dinesh Sinha

3. Psychodynamic psychotherapy – Dr Dinesh Sinha

4. Psychoanalytic psychotherapy- Dr Dinesh Sinha

5. Cognitive behavioural therapy(CBT) –Dr Furhan Iqbal

6. Interpersonal psychotherapy(IPT) –Dr Furhan Iqbal

7. Systematic desensitization(SD)-Dr Franco Orsucci

8. Exposure and response prevention(ERP)-Dr Furhan Iqbal

9. Psychotherapy-transference –Dr Franco Orsucci

10. Borderline Personality disorder (BPD)
11. Other personality disorders
12. Dialectical Behaviour therapy(DBT)

PSYCHOTHERAPY

1. FOOTBALLER- COGNITIVE DISTORTIONS

Suggested Approach
Introduction
C: Hello, I'm Dr... I'm one of the psychiatrists. I understand that your GP has referred you as you have been experiencing a difficult time getting on the pitch. Can you tell me what happened?

P: I missed the goal

C: It seems you are clearly upset about missing the goal. Let's have a closer look at how you feel and think about missing the goal.
- Can you tell me if there is a footballer who you admire?
- In your knowledge has he never missed a goal?
- Hypothetically, if he has missed a goal in his successful career, is it not realistically possible for you to have the same experience?

(to demonstrate possibly 'all or nothing'/'black or white' or Dichotomous thinking)
Has anyone made any unpleasant comments to you about missing the chance?
- Do you think it has changed their opinion of you as a player? Has anyone mentioned something to this effect or acted differently.
- So David apart from the chance you missed, how did you think you otherwise performed in the match?

475

PSYCHOTHERAPY

Recapitulation (an example would be as follows)
*So David, what you have told me so far is that you were unable to score in the match between Bolton and Leeds and this was the first time. Your team, manager and family have been supportive and have even commended you on your general good performance. But despite this, you are unable to acknowledge any positives from the game, and appear preoccupied on a small aspect of your performance. (**To demonstrate selective abstraction**)*

C: Can you take me through your career thus far?
When did you first start playing football?
How did your career progress?
How many goals you have scored?
How did you get selected to play professional football?
Have you won any prizes or trophies?

Summarize
*To summarize what you have said is that you have had a successful football career thus far, and you have been chosen from a lot of contemporary players to be where you are today. You have scored X number of goals, so it seems you are ignoring all your achievements thus far. [**To demonstrate minimization**]*

C: So tell me now what does it means to you for your career now that you have missed this goal?

P: That is the end of my career doc.

C: David, you are saying that ever since you have missed this goal that you have been extremely distressed to the extent that now you now even have difficulty going on the pitch. And now you think that this is the end of your football career. Now you are even saying that it is the end of you football career.
It seems to me that you might be jumping to the wrong conclusion. What do you think?
*(**To demonstrate arbitrary inference**)*

P: Doc, at this point in time, I just don't know what to think anymore.

C: Thank you David for speaking to me. To summarize what we know is that you have had a successful career thus far, but right now, you seem to minimize all your achievements. You missed a chance to score a goal at a recent game, and you have been excessively preoccupied on it. This has resulted in you focusing on one negative detail and ignoring the positive things that people are saying about you.
We have some talking therapies available which are likely to be helpful with this kind of thinking. What do you think?

F: Anything doc. My football career is everything to me. I am willing to work with you.

PSYCHOTHERAPY

C: I understand that your coach wants to talk to me as he is also concerned. Is it ok for me to discuss this with him? [Consent]

F: Sure doc.

FOOTBALLER –COGNITIVE DISTORTIONS
Establish History of presenting complaint HOPC (onset, duration, progression and severity)
- *Establish the presence of panic attacks.*
- *Elicit selective Abstraction*
- *Elicit minimization and magnification.*
- *Elicit arbitrary Inference.*
- *Elicit dichotomous thinking*

Establish his psychological mindedness
Establish his insight
Summarize

©Smartsesh

POSSIBLE VARIATIONS OF THEME
1. 36 yr old footballer who has missed a goal. He is now depressed and suicidal. Additional information- he is taking steroids.
2. 23 yr. old footballer who is having panic attacks when he goes on the pitch.

PSYCHOTHERAPY

2. FOOTBALLER- COGNITIVE DISTORTIONS

INSTRUCTIONS TO CANDIDATE
You have been asked to see the coach Michael Knight of the footballer you have just seen. He is concerned about his football player and wants to know how you are going to treat him.

TASK FOR THE CANDIDATE
- Explain the cognitive distortions.
- Discuss the management with the coach.

PAY PARTICULAR ATTENTION TO THE FOLLOWING (MENTAL CHECKLIST)
- Ensure that you have taken players consent prior to speaking to the coach
- Explain the cognitive distortions- Selective Abstraction, Maximization, Minimization and Arbitrary Inference.
- Explain management using biopsychosocial approach.
- Emphasis should be placed on the psychological management.
- Acknowledge concerns of using medication.
- Emphasize the need for support from both the coach and the team.

COMMUNICATION SKILLS
- Start the interview by developing rapport
- Establish a common ground for collaborative working with the coach.
- Explain that the process would take time and there is no quick fix solution.

Suggested approach
Introduction
C: Hello I am Dr...I am one of the psychiatrists. I understand that you are concerned about one of your professional players- David whom I have seen today. He has given me permission to speak to you.

Co: Hello Doc. Can we get him back on the pitch?

C: Coach I understand and share your concerns. David wants to get back on the pitch, as soon as possible but he is experiencing what we call cognitive distortions. I will I will explain to you more about what this is

Co: Cognitive what? What is that?

C: He is thinking like how a depressed person thinks. This is different from how I or you would normally think. We call these unhealthy thinking patterns or **'cognitive distortions'**. They are errors of thinking that distort the way

PSYCHOTHERAPY

we experience the world and in doing so the reality can be experienced in a far from helpful way with consequences for how one feels and behaves. (**When you are going to explain it would be good to link it with David's e.g. so when David missed the goal despite having scored many he feels he is a completely and utterly rubbish player.**)

I will try to explain each of them individually (**tailor the information appropriately and use examples from the players personal experience to demonstrate each one. Make sure to include something along the lines of:**

- **Maximization/Magnification**
This is when someone overestimates errors or it is like 'making a mountain out of a mole hill.'

- **Minimization**
This is when someone is underestimating his achievements or performance

- **Selective abstraction**
This is when someone focuses on a specific detail and ignores other more important aspects of the situation.

- **Arbitrary inference**
This is when someone jumps to conclusions i.e. reaches a conclusion which are not based on the available facts or which there is no evidence.

- **Dichotomous thinking**
This is all or nothing, or black and white thinking.
This is also when someone sees events as completely good or completely bad.

If asked, you can elaborate on these cognitive distortions as well
- **Catastrophsisation:** This is when someone views events as disastrous.

- **Overgeneralization:** This is when someone reaches a general conclusion based on a single event.

Co: How are you going to treat him?

C: We do have a range of treatments available which include talking therapy or psychological treatment as well as medication. .

The psychological therapy or talking therapy is called CBT-Cognitive Behavior Therapy. He will need to have a course of 12-20 sessions. During these sessions he will see a therapist who will look at the way he is thinking, which in turn is affecting the way he is feeling, and affecting his behavior. [Elaborate further]

PSYCHOTHERAPY

Elaborate on the behavioral component and taking him onto the pitch tackling avoidance behavior i.e. Systematic Desensitization-(see pg592.) Use the diagram below to explain Cognitive behavioral therapy.

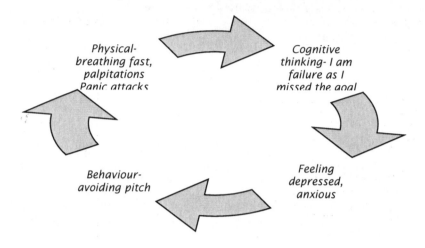

Physical- breathing fast, palpitations Panic attacks

Cognitive thinking- I am failure as I missed the goal

Feeling depressed, anxious

Behaviour- avoiding pitch

Co: What about the medication?

C: We do have the option of starting him on an antidepressant. One of the groups of medication we use is called SSRI's or selective serotonin reuptake inhibitors. [Elaborate further if necessary]

Co: What about the football regulations if he is taking medication?

C: He will need to inform the authorities that he is taking this medication .I can assure you that these are not performance enhancing drugs. However as you know, like all medication they do have side effects. (Elaborate further if necessary)

Co: How can I and the team help?

C: Your understanding and support is essential to promote his recovery. An important part of this process would be that he would need some encouragement from the team. I need to inform you though, that in case he puts too much pressure on himself to get better quickly and returns before he is fully ready then there is a chance that his condition might deteriorate.

Summary
Thank you for talking to me.

PSYCHOTHERAPY

From what we have discussed, you are understandably concerned about David, and the difficulties he has been experiencing. I have explained to you more about the negative thinking driving this problem. We do have medication and talking therapy which can help.

I will give you information and leaflets and there are also websites available.

FOOTBALLER- MANAGEMENT
Explain the cognitive distortions
- Selective Abstraction
- Maximization
- Minimization
- Arbitrary Inference.
- Dichotomous thinking

Discuss management using bio-psychosocial approach
Biological interventions
- Medication-Antidepressants –SSRI's
- FA(football association) regulations

Psychological interventions
- Cognitive behavioral therapy- CBT
- Systematic desensitization

Social interventions
- Support for the coach and team

©*Smartsesh*

PSYCHOTHERAPY

3. PSYCHODYNAMIC FORMULATION

INSTRUCTIONS TO CANDIDATE
You are asked to assess this 35 yr. old gentleman, Donald Peterson, who has been referred to the complex disorder service.

TASK FOR THE CANDIDATE
   Do a psychodynamic formulation.

PAY PARTICULAR ATTENTION TO THE FOLLOWING (MENTAL CHECKLIST)
   - *Establish his understanding of the interview.*
   - *Set the scene.*
   - *Explain more about the initial assessment.*
   - *Elicit relevant history to guide you through for a psychodynamic formulation.*
   - *To include: childhood, family, relationship and social history.*
   - *Establish his coping skills(include drug and alcohol history).*
   - *Explore the commonly used defence mechanisms.*
   - *Establish his psychological mindness and motivation.*
   - *Consider suitability for psychotherapy: ego strength, expectations, open to new ideas, willing to participate.*

COMMUNICATION SKILLS
   - *Seek to understand the subjective feelings of the individual.*
   - *Preface personal questions.*

Suggested approach
Introduction
C: Hello, I'm Dr ...I'm one of the psychiatrists. I understand you have been referred for psychotherapy or talking therapy.
P: Hello, Yes.

Setting the scene
C: For this assessment today, I will need to ask you some personal questions from your early childhood, family and about your current relationships. Is that all right with you?

P: Yes, sure.

A. Guide
   - *Elicit some background history with a view of a psychodynamic formulation.*
   - *This would looking for predisposing, precipitating and perpetuating factors in the biological, psychological and social model*
   - *As you are conducting the interview, think about these to formulate a coherent narrative of psychodynamic formulation*

B. Personal history

PSYCHOTHERAPY

Early history
- What memories do you have of your childhood?
- Is there anything that sticks out as unpleasant?(i.e. sexual abuse)
- Can you tell me about your schooling?
- Did you have friends? Were you bullied or teased as a child?(bullying)

Attachment [construct a genogram]
- Can you tell me more about your family?
- Can you describe your relationships with them?
- Relationship with each, for example mother, father, siblings? (If adopted ask about this.)

Psychosexual history
- Can you tell me about how your relationships have turned out?
- Have you ever been married? Do you have any children?
- So how is your current relationship going?

Psychiatric history
- Have you ever been seen by a psychiatrist in the past?
- Have you had any psychologically therapy? If so, did you find it helpful?
- How do you usually cope with stress?
- Have you ever attempt of self-harm or suicide?

Social history
Enquire about his work; any absences (indicate ego strength)

C. Motivation
- Can you tell me what your expectations are of the talking therapy?
- How motivated are you for this? (motivation)

Summary
To summarize, you have told me about your family, early life, and about your relationships. In addition you have been self-harming as a means of coping with your frustration. You acknowledge that you would like psychotherapy or talking therapy and you are motivated for this.

I will arrange to discuss more about the details of the therapy and the sessions.
Thank you

POSSIBLE VARIATIONS OF THEME
1.49 yr. old lady with BPD (Borderline Personality disorder) and self-harming who has been referred to complex cases. Additional information- was adopted and was sexually abused as a child.

PSYCHOTHERAPY

PSYCHODYNAMIC FORMULATION
Set scene
Establish his understanding of interview
Personal history-perinatal history, attachment, early history- childhood
Early history- schooling, bullying
Family history-mental illness
Psychiatric history – previous contact, suicidal attempts
Psychosexual history- relationships
Coping skills: self-harm behaviors, drug and alcohol use
Insight and motivation
Summarize

©Smartsesh

PSYCHOTHERAPY

4. PSYCHOANALYTICAL PSYCHOTHERAPY

INSTRUCTIONS TO CANDIDATE
You have been asked to see this 34 yr old lady, Karen Higgins, who has been referred for psychoanalytical psychotherapy. She wants to know more about this.

TASK FOR THE CANDIDATE
- Explain Psychoanalytical Psychotherapy.

PAY PARTICULAR ATTENTION TO THE FOLLOWING (MENTAL CHECKLIST)
- Explain the rationale for Psychoanalytical Psychotherapy.
- Explain the structure of psychotherapy.
- Explain the important components i.e. Therapeutic Relationship, Transference, Counter transference, Resistance.

COMMUNICATION SKILLS
- Start the interview by developing rapport and showing empathy.
- Seek to understand the subjective experience of the individual.

Suggested approach
Introduction
C: Hello, I'm Dr ...Thank you for coming to see me. I've come to talk to you more about one of the talking therapies called Psychoanalytical Psychotherapy which we think will be beneficial to you. Before we begin, can you tell me what have been the difficulties recently?

P: I have been treated for Depression and my doctor said that I should consider this talking therapy. Can you tell me more about Psychoanalytical Psychotherapy please?

C: I will explain to you about Psychoanalytical Psychotherapy and about the structure of the sessions

P: What is psychoanalytical psychotherapy?

C: It is a type of the talking therapy in which together with the therapist, you will explore how what's happening in your life today could be connected in some way to your past relationships and conflicts.

P: How will this help me?

C: In essence, you will see a therapist weekly for individual sessions of 50 minutes. It can be done in a group or individual session. The sessions are usually agreed between the two of you and can range up to 2 years. You will see the same therapist at the same time and at the same place.

PSYCHOTHERAPY

During the sessions you can speak freely about whatever comes to mind. This will cause the unconscious or hidden part of our feelings to have some form of expression

The sessions are open for you to bring whatever you like. This may help you to feel free to explore feelings and difficulties that you may not be fully aware of. The work with the therapist could be useful in understanding links between your past experiences and your current problems.

The therapist will then be able to help you make those connections where you would be able to see that whatever is happening in your life today could be driven by the unconscious feelings from your past experiences. If this is happening in the therapy sessions then this could be happening in everyday life.

P: *What is the purpose of this type of talking therapy?*

C: It is a type of talking therapy with the benefits around gaining understanding and there is evidence that this is helpful in patients with Personality disorder, Depression and Anxiety. It is also used when the medication has not helped.

P: *What type of therapist will I will see?*

C: The therapist will be a professional who is trained in this form of therapy. It could be a psychotherapist, psychiatrist, psychologist or a psychiatric nurse.

The other thing to bear in mind is the therapeutic relationship you form with your therapist.

P: *What is the therapeutic relationship?*

C: This is the relationship between you and your therapist. It is like any other relationship; however your therapist is bound by professional ethics. There will be boundaries and the therapist will only disclose certain details about themselves.
There are a few other things that can occur in therapy that you need to bear in mind: Elaborate further on transference, counter transference and resistance.

Transference *It is described as all the feelings that you have towards your therapist which may be linked to past relationships.*

P: *What does this transference mean?*

C: Sometimes in a therapy session you can experience emotions in relation to your therapist; you might for example find yourself getting angry and

PSYCHOTHERAPY

frustrated because the therapist might remind you of a relationship in the past.

Counter transference *is all the feelings the therapist has from his contact with you in the course of therapy.*

Resistance *can sometimes occur. The therapy tries to change the way someone thinks, feels and behaves. If you are not willing to acknowledge this or accept this, then this is called resistance.*

P: What are the contra indications?

C: It is usually not advisable to be carried out on people with Psychosis and Obsessional states.

P: What are the adverse effects?

C: Sometimes people do experience worsening of their symptoms in the beginning of the therapy because of the strong emotions the therapy might bring up. This might also put a strain on their relationships. We usually inform them that this might be a sign that they are actually making progress, and therefore should continue their sessions.

Other possible questions which may need to be addressed
P: What do I do in an emergency?

C: If any emergency situations arise then you would need to seek help from your GP or local community mental health team.

P: What kinds of records or notes are kept?

C: The notes are usually kept separate from the medical notes and your therapist will inform your GP of a summary of your treatment.

P: What are other professionals involved in my care told about me?

C: The information discussed during your session will be confidential. This will only be disclosed if there is a risk to anyone

P: Will I need to stop my medication?

C: If you are on any medication, we usually advise that you can continue with this alongside the therapy.

P: How long will I have to wait?

C: There is a waiting list on the NHS. However there is a list of private therapists if you wish to contact them if you cannot wait.

PSYCHOTHERAPY

P: What if I want to stop these sessions?

C: You can discontinue your sessions with the therapist, but it is a good idea to discuss this first with him/her

Summarise
Thank you for talking to me. To summarize, I have told you about Psychoanalytical Psychotherapy, the rationale for this and how it will benefit you.

Information and leaflets
I have some leaflets and information. There are also some useful websites which you can visit.

PSYCHOANALYTICAL PSYCHOTHERAPY
Purpose
- To look at problems related to childhood experiences

Indications
- Personality disorders, Depression and Anxiety disorders

Sessions
- Form a therapeutic relationship
- Transference
- Counter transference
- Resistance

Structure
- 2-3 times a week for 2 years Trained therapist- Community psychiatric nurse, Psychotherapist , Psychologist

Effects/benefits
- Improves symptoms, relations

Adverse/side effects
- Worsening of symptoms
- Resistance

Summarize
Leaflets and information

©Smartsesh

PSYCHOTHERAPY

5. COGNITIVE BEHAVIOURAL THERAPY-CBT

INSTRUCTIONS TO CANDIDATE
You have been asked to see Mrs Rebecca Hawley who is a 24 yr old lady with a diagnosis of Depression. She has been told about CBT.

TASK FOR THE CANDIDATE
- Explain CBT or Cognitive behavioural therapy to her

PAY PARTICULAR ATTENTION TO THE FOLLOWING (MENTAL CHECKLIST)
- Establish current knowledge of psychotherapy.
- Explain general structure of   CBT
- Explain CBT using hot cross bun diagram adapted form from **Padesky and Mooney, 1990)**
- Explain Becks negative cognitive triad
- Explain Negative automatic thoughts (NAT) or dysfunctional beliefs.
- Explain cognitive distortions or thinking errors.
- Explain general structure of CBT.

COMMUNICATION SKILLS
- Start the interview by developing rapport and showing empathy.

Suggested approach
Introduction
C: Hello, I'm one of the psychiatrists. Thank you for coming to see me today. I understand that you wanted to know more about one of the psychotherapy or talking therapy called Cognitive Behavioural Therapy (CBT). Before we begin can you tell me what your understanding is of this?

P: I heard it is helpful for people that are depressed and it is a type of counselling. What is CBT?

C: You are right in a sense. It is different from counselling. CBT is an acronym for Cognitive Behavioural Therapy. It is a type talking therapy or psychological therapy which involves talking and listening with a therapist.

CBT looks at understanding the links of how our thinking influences the way we feel and behave. For example in Depression people tend to think negatively about themselves. The therapist will help you look at these flaws or errors in your thinking and help you explore why you believe this to be true. Once you are able to identify these flaws or errors, then you will be able to look at ways in which you can change this thinking into a more helpful way, which will eventually improve your mood.

PSYCHOTHERAPY

*Elaborate further using an example. Use the hot cross bun diagram-
Adapted from Padesky and Mooney (1990)*

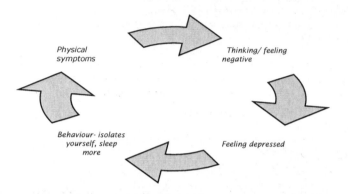

In CBT, in addressing the above as we discussed, the therapist will also assist
you to address the negative views of the self, world and the future. (Becks
negative cognitive triad). [Elaborate further on the reactivation of negative
cognitions when exposed to a critical incident]

How is CBT different from the other talking therapies?
CBT is different in that is focuses on the 'here and now'. It is time limited,
problem focused and goal oriented. It is important in terms of the context of
a person's difficulties and looks at how the current problems are being
maintained.

P: What would I do in the sessions?

C: You will have a fixed number of sessions and in these sessions you will
focus on achieving specific tasks. An integral part of this is for you to
maintain a mood diary to keep a record of your negative thoughts and
thinking errors.

P: What will I need to do in between these sessions?
C: The homework would be negotiated at every session between client and
therapist, so what can be learned in therapy sessions can be reinforced at
home. That is the purpose of the homework.

Later on the therapist will show you how you can actually start changing
these flaws in your thinking and look at alternative ways or explanations.
Eventually you will be able to change them to more helpful type of thinking.
In a sense you will begin to become like your own therapist.

P: How long does CBT take?

PSYCHOTHERAPY

C: You will see a therapist weekly for individual sessions of 50 minutes. It can be done in a group or individual session. The sessions are usually agreed between the two of you and can range up to 12 to 15 sessions. The therapist will be a professional who is trained in this. It could be a psychotherapist, psychiatrist, psychologist or a psychiatric nurse.

P: How effective is CBT?

C: There is good evidence for use of CBT in people with moderate to severe Depression and Anxiety. [National institute of clinical excellence (NICE) recommends CBT] It has also been shown to be effective in combination with medication.

Other possible questions which may need to be addressed

P: What do I do in an emergency?

C: If any emergency situations arise then you would need to seek help from your GP or local community mental health team.

P: What kinds of records or notes are kept?

C: The notes are usually kept separate from the medical notes and your therapist will inform your GP of a summary of your treatment.

P: What are other professionals involved in my care told about me?

C: The information discussed during your session will be confidential. This will only be disclosed if there is a risk to anyone.

P: Will I need to stop my medication?

C: If you are on any medication, we usually advise that you can continue with this alongside the therapy.

P: What if I want to stop these sessions?
C: You can discontinue your sessions with the therapist, but it is a good idea to discuss this first with him/her.

P: How long will I have to wait?

C: There is usually a waiting list on the NHS. However now it is possible to get CBT quicker due to the provision of the government funded programme 'Improved Access to Psychological Therapies' (IAPT).

P: I have heard about computerized CBT, can you tell me more about this?

PSYCHOTHERAPY

C: Computerized Cognitive Behavioral Therapy (CCBT) is a generic term for delivering CBT with the aid of a personal computer. That is used as an alternative to having the therapy face to face with a therapist. [Also recommended by National institute of clinical excellence]

Summarize
Thank you for talking to me. We have discussed about CBT, and how it will help you for your Depression. I would like you to consider this, and we can arrange for another appointment to discuss your decision.

Information and leaflets
There are some useful websites and leaflets if you would like to find out more about this

Websites
British Association of Behavioural and Cognitive Psychotherapies.
Beating the Blues - www.ultrasis.com
Royal College of psychiatrists www.rcpsych.ac.uk

Free online CBT websites
Mood Gym: www.moodgym.anu.edu.au
Living life to the full www.livinglifeto thefull.com
Fearfighter www.fearfighter.com

CBT (COGNITIVE BEHAVIOURAL THERAPY)
Effects: It helps us look at the way we view the world, ourselves and the future. (Negative cognitive triad
Sessions: 12- 16 hourly sessions
Benefits: improved symptoms
Effectiveness: good evidence in combination with antidepressant treatment

---

PSYCHOTHERAPY

6. INTERPERSONAL PSYCHOTHERAPY-IPT

INSTRUCTIONS TO CANDIDATE
You are asked to see this 45 yr. old lady, Rosemary Jacobs, who has been referred for Interpersonal Psychotherapy.

TASK FOR THE CANDIDATE
- Assess suitability for IPT- Interpersonal psychotherapy.
- Explore briefly her depressive symptoms.

PAY PARTICULAR ATTENTION TO THE FOLLOWING (MENTAL CHECKLIST)
- Establish briefly her current depressive symptoms and treatment.
- Assess suitability for Interpersonal psychotherapy
- Highlight the four main components of Interpersonal psychotherapy
    - Role transitions.
    - Interpersonal deficits/sensitivity.
    - Interpersonal disputes.
    - Grief.
    - Explain general structure of IPT.

COMMUNICATON SKILLS
- Start the interview by developing rapport and showing empathy.
- Seek to understand the subjective experience of the individual.

Suggested approach
Introduction
C: Hello, I'm Dr ...I'm one of the psychiatrists. I understand you wanted to find out more about one of the talking therapy, Interpersonal Psychotherapy.

P: Yes. They told me that it might help me.

C: It might be helpful if you can tell me more about how you have been feeling?

A. Assess symptoms of depression
B. Assess her suitability for IPT
- Can you tell me about how your relationships have been?
- Can you tell me if there have been any recent changes?

Summarize (use information that she has provided)
C: From what you have told me, it appears that there have been few changes recently. I will explain to you more about the Interpersonal Psychotherapy and show you how it will be beneficial for you.

P: What is interpersonal psychotherapy?

493

PSYCHOTHERAPY

C: In interpersonal psychotherapy, as the name suggests it helps a person understand how our problems can be related to the way our relationships work. It helps to improve those relationships and to find better ways of coping. It is usually indicated for people who have Depression.

P: How long does it take?

C: It is time limited and treatment focused type of talking therapy. You will be seen by a therapist for 12 to 16 sessions, at the same place and time.

C. Elaborate on the components of Interpersonal psychotherapy
There are four main components which are addressed. I will explain each one in detail. [You can use examples from your discussion to demonstrate each]

1. Role transitions
This is looking at whether there have been subtle changes due to circumstances which have changed. For example if someone has to adjust to maybe their child leaving the home or retirement

2. Interpersonal Deficits or Interpersonal sensitivity
This is the ability for people to develop supportive and lasting relationships, which we find, depressed people have difficulty in.

3. Interpersonal disputes
This involves addressing arguments, disagreements or disappointments in any of your relationships.

4. Grief
This involves looking at bereavement and how maybe a person has not fully recovered from the death of a loved one.

Summarise
Thank you for talking to me. To summarise, I have given you an overview of interpersonal psychotherapy which has four main components. It has been shown to be beneficial for people who have had some difficulties in their relationships. Please have a think about this and I will arrange to see you again if you wish to consider this type of talking therapy.

Information and leaflets
I would like to see you again. I have some more information and leaflets for you to read. There are also some useful website addresses. Do you have any other questions for me?

Thank you

PSYCHOTHERAPY

> **INTERPERSONAL PSYCHOTHERAPY**
> **Key components:**
> - *Grief*
> - *Role transitions*
> - *Interpersonal Deficits*
> - *Interpersonal sensitivity*
> - *Interpersonal disputes*
>
> **Type:** Time limited and treatment focused
> **Sessions:** 12-16 sessions
> **Effects :**
> **Indications :**

PSYCHOTHERAPY

7. SYSTEMATIC DESENSITIZATION

Instruction to candidate
You have been asked to see this 45 year old lady Andrea Hurley who has been suffering from Agoraphobia. She has been informed about systematic desensitization. Please explain this to her.

TASK FOR THE CANDIDATE
- Explain Systematic Desensitization

PAY PARTICULAR ATTENTION TO THE FOLLOWING (MENTAL CHECKLIST)
- Explain systematic desensitization
- Explain rationale for this:
  -Fight and flight reaction
  -Hyperventilation syndrome
- Explain the cognitive therapy component

COMMUNICATION SKILLS
- Start the interview by developing rapport and showing empathy.
- Personalise the therapy with using an example from the individual.

Suggested approach
Introduction
C: Hello, I'm Dr. I'm one of the psychiatrists. I understand that you have been having difficulty in going out. I wanted to talk to you about one of the treatment we use called 'systematic desensitization': In order for me to get a clearer picture of what your difficulties are, can you can you tell me which are the situations you are able to cope in and the situations you find most difficulty in?

P: I have been finding it difficult to go to the local shop around the corner and I am sometimes struggle to go to my appointments, like even this one today.

C: It is clear that this that this has been causing you some distress. Systematic desensitization is one of the behavioral treatment options which have been shown to be effective in treating people like you who have been diagnosed with Agoraphobia with panic attacks.

P: What is this Systematic Desensitization?

C: Systematic desensitization is a type of behavior therapy which has 2 main components to it called 'graded exposure' and relaxation.

PSYCHOTHERAPY

In a nutshell it will involve performing less anxiety provoking behaviors in your mind and then later on, in reality in a more structured way or hierarchical way. This will result in you eventually overcoming the most anxiety provoking problems.

I elaborate further with the use of this diagram. Graded exposure is when we make a hierarchy or list of situations that you are least afraid of; to situations you are most afraid of doing.

For example you mentioned you were least afraid of going to the supermarket, and most afraid of going out to appointments.
If you can look at this diagram,

We will take it one step at a time, at your pace and tackle each situation one by one, so eventually you are able to move on to the next level on this hierarchy.

This is coupled together with relaxation training. The way this works is that we will teach you relaxation training with controlled breathing exercises to help to relax your muscles and decrease the tension.

The rationale by which this works is that we know that 2 incompatible emotions cannot co-exist; that is anxiety and relaxation cannot occur together, so eventually you will be able to face these situations in a more relaxed way.

P: What if I can't go to the therapist?

C: If you have difficulty going to see the therapist the therapist can come to you. The therapist will not put you in a situation that you will not be able to cope with. The therapist will be there to support you.

P: What is the rationale or mechanism behind this treatment?

PSYCHOTHERAPY

C: *When our body is exposed to a threatening situation, this causes the **fight and flight** reaction and either we prepare to stay and fight or we flee the situation. As a result we start to breathe faster and this causes the **hyperventilation syndrome.** It causes the oxygen in our body to increase and the carbon dioxide to decrease. As a result of the low carbon dioxide, this causes a physiological reaction in our body with us feeling some tingling sensation in our fingers, dizziness headaches, numbness, faintness and breathlessness. And this perpetuates like a vicious cycle*

P: How long will this take?
You will see a therapist, weekly for individual sessions about 50 minutes. The sessions are usually agreed between the two of you and usually can range from 8 to 12 sessions.

[For exposure work sometimes sessions have to be longer so a session where you wish to prepare and take someone to the supermarket expose them and help them manage the situation for a sufficient length of time might take longer]

The therapist will be a professional who is trained in this. It could be a psychotherapist, psychiatrist, psychologist or a psychiatric nurse.

Other questions which may need to be addressed:
P: What do I do in an Emergency?

C: *If any emergency situations arise then you would need to seek medical treatment from your GP, emergency service or Community mental health team.*

P: Where are my records or notes kept?

C: *The notes are usually kept separate from the medical notes and your therapist will inform your GP of a summary of your treatment.*

P: What are other professionals involved in my care told?

C: *The information discussed during your session will be confidential. This will only be disclosed if there is a risk to anyone.*

P: Do I still need to take my medication?

C: *If you are on any medication you can continue with this.*

P: How long will I have to wait?

C: *There is a waiting list on the NHS. However now it is possible to get CBT quicker due to the provision of the government funded programme 'Improved Access to Psychological Therapies' (IAPT).*

PSYCHOTHERAPY

What do I do if I want to stop these sessions?

C: You can discontinue your sessions with the therapist, but it is a good idea to discuss this with him or her

Summarize
Thank you for talking to me. To summarize I have told you about 'Systematic Desensitization' and the two components which are the graded exposure and relaxation.

I have some more Information and leaflets which you can take home to read. If you would like to arrange to come and discuss this further with me, I will be happy to make another appointment.

Additional information: Cognitive therapy
The other component of Systematic desensitisation is the cognitive therapy.

Elaborate further using an example. Use the hot cross bun

Diagram-Adapted from Padesky and Mooney (1990)

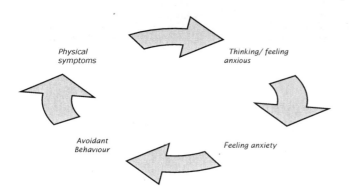

In CBT, or the cognitive therapy component the therapy will assist you to look at the flaws or errors in your thinking which cause you to feel anxious, which in turn results in your avoidant behaviour(ie avoid going out). In essence, as the therapy progresses, you will be able to alter these negative ways of thinking in a helpful way of thinking and eventually when you are faced with similar situations, you will be able change the way you would have reacted or behaved in that situation in a more positive way.

PSYCHOTHERAPY

SYSTEMATIC DESENSITIZATION
Indication Phobias and Anxiety disorders
Sessions 12- 16 sessions
Behavioral and Cognitive component
Rationale
- Fight and Flight
- Hyperventilation syndrome

Behavior therapy
- Hierarchy
- Relaxation training
- Breathing exercises

Cognitive therapy
©Smartsesh

PSYCHOTHERAPY

8. EXPOSURE AND RESPONSE PREVENTION

INSTRUCTIONS TO CANDIDATE
You have been asked to see a 36 yr old male, Nicholas Jeraud, who has been diagnosed with OCD. He wanted to know more about Exposure and Response Prevention (ERP).

TASK FOR THE CANDIDATE
- Explain Exposure and response prevention

PAY PARTICULAR ATTENTION TO THE FOLLOWING (MENTAL CHECKLIST)
- Identify the current model of OCD.
- Explain ERP- behavioural component of CBT.
- Use a diagram to illustrate this (optional)
- Explain the cognitive therapy component.
- Explain general structure of therapy.

COMMUNICATION SKILLS
- Start the interview by developing rapport and showing empathy.

Suggested approach
Introduction
C: Hello, I'm one of the psychiatrists. Thank you for coming to see me today. I understand that you have been diagnosed with OCD. I would like to discuss the psychotherapy available for this condition. It called the Exposure and response prevention therapy.
Before we begin can you tell me what your difficulties are?

P: I can't seem to stop washing my hands because I think they are contaminated.

C: That must be distressing for you. The exposure and response prevention is the behavioural component of CBT (cognitive behavioural therapy) which is beneficial in treating the compulsive
behaviours. In your case the compulsive behaviour includes washing your hands repeatedly.

P: What is Exposure and response prevention?

C: You will make a list with the therapist, from least anxiety provoking to most anxiety provoking situations. The rationale behind this is that if we are exposed to a situation that causes us anxiety, the anxiety increases, but if we stay in it long enough it will decrease.

PSYCHOTHERAPY

The therapist will expose you to the situation you are fearful of being in and at the same time, will prevent you from performing the ritual [use the client's example to illustrate this]
In your case, if you wanted to wash your hands, the therapist will expose you to that situation, but will prevent you from washing your hands.

Cognitive therapy
We have the other component of the CBT or Cognitive behavioural therapy which is effective for the obsessional thoughts. Together with the therapist you will change your reaction to the thoughts instead of trying to get rid of them.

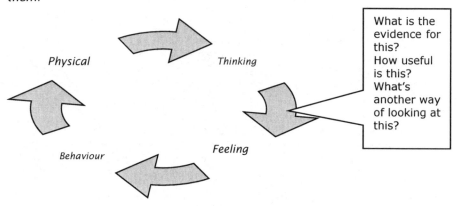

General structure of the psychotherapy
You will see a therapist, weekly for individual sessions for 1 hour .The sessions are usually agreed between the two of you and usually can range from 8 to 12 sessions.

The therapist will be a professional who is trained in this. It could be a psychotherapist,

P: What are the Effects?

C: It has been found to be effective in about 3 out of 4 people with compulsive behaviours and rituals.

P: What can my family do to help?

C: We usually advise that families should be educated more about this. Their understanding and support is good for your recovery. [Elaborate further if you are speaking to a relative, that they should not reinforce the behaviour i.e. sometimes their relative would want them to wash their hands etc.]

Summarise
Thank you for talking to me. To summarise we have discussed CBT for treating your OCD. We looked at exposure and response prevention (ERP) as

one of the treatment options available which would be beneficial for your compulsive behaviours. I would like you to consider this and we can arrange to meet again to discuss this.

Information and leaflets
I know we have discussed a lot. I have some information and leaflets which you can take home to read. There are also some useful websites addresses.

9. TRANSFERENCE

Suggested approach
Introduction
C: Hello, I'm one of the psychiatrists. Thank you for coming to see me today. I understand that you have been attending psychotherapy and I am sorry to hear that you no longer wish to continue with this. It will be helpful if you can start by telling more about when you initially started the sessions.

P: I don't think I am benefitting in any way. In fact I think I am now worse off than when I first started.

Explore details of the psychotherapy
- When did you first start the psychotherapy sessions?
- What were the reasons for starting the therapy?
- How many sessions have you had till now?
- Have you missed any sessions?
- What were you hoping to achieve from the therapy?
- How have you found the therapy so far?
- Do you think it has helped you at all?

Explore her reasons for wanting to discontinue psychotherapy
- So why have you decided that you want to stop your sessions?

Depending on her responses, explain possibilities in psychotherapy
From what we have discussed there could be a number of reasons as to why you feel that you do not want to continue further: Let's explore each one:

In therapy, transference can occur when a client will relate with the therapist as if they were someone from their past relationships. It is not unusual that if

PSYCHOTHERAPY

*this was a difficult relationship, this could cause some unpleasant emotions and therefore you might not want to continue. (**Transference)***

*Sometimes in therapy you unconsciously are not ready to accept change which might manifest itself in behaviour which impedes on the progress of the therapy. This could present as being late for sessions, missing sessions, wanting to stop sessions altogether or change the therapist. (**Resistance)***

*Sometime we advise clients that while undergoing psychotherapy they can actually start feeling worse before they feel better. This could be seen a sign that they are gaining psychological insight into their conscious and unconscious behaviour, and on the way to recovery. (**Adverse effect)***

Summarize
To summarize you have been having therapy for 6 months and now feel that you don't want to continue. We have discussed in detail as to what might be the reasons for the same. We have talked about possible transference, counter transference, or resistance which could be contributing to your decision.

I would like you to reconsider your decision to stop therapy. I would recommend that you discuss these problems with your therapist before making your final decision. However, if after speaking to the therapist you still feel strongly that you don't wish to continue you are entitled to search for an alternative therapist or stop therapy for the time being. If you want we can give you some details about some other available therapists.

PSYCHOTHERAPY

10. BORDERLINE PERSONALITY DISORDER

INSTRUCTIONS TO CANDIDATE
You have been asked to see this 26 yr old lady Caroline Spencer who has been diagnosed with Borderline Personality Disorder (BPD)

TASK FOR THE CANDIDATE
- Explain her diagnosis and treatment.

PAY PARTICULAR ATTENTION TO THE FOLLOWING (MENTAL CHECKLIST)
- Explain Borderline Personality Disorder (emotionally unstable personality disorder).
- Explain possible aetiological factors.
- Explain management using a holistic approach or bio psychosocial approach.
- Explain importance of family support

COMMUNICATION SKILLS
- Start the interview by developing rapport and showing empathy.
- Seek to understand the subjective experience of the individual.

Suggested approach
Introduction

C: Hello, I'm Dr...I'm one of the psychiatrists. I understand you have been referred to our complex case services. I understand you wanted to know more about your diagnosis and what treatment there is available.

P: Yes, doc. They said I have Borderline personality disorder

C: I would like to explain this to you in more detail, but may I ask what your understanding of this is.

P: I seem to self-harm when I am stressed and can't seem to cope with day to day things.

C: Well, in a sense what you have described is characteristic of someone with Borderline or the other term also used emotionally unstable personality disorder. I will explain this to you more in detail.

Our personality is the characteristics or traits that make each of us an individual or unique in a sense. This includes the way we think, feel and behave.

Usually by our late teens or 20's, most of us should have developed our own personality. This will ensure that we have our way of thinking, feeling,

PSYCHOTHERAPY

behaving and interacting with other people in general. Once our personality is developed, this would usually stay the same for the rest of our life.

Borderline personality disorder is a complex condition in which this does not happen. It can present differently in individuals.

P: How common is it?

C: It occurs in 2 in 100 people and is equally common in males and female. . However, in general a larger and more rigorous UK study in 2006 suggested that, at any given time, about 1 in 20 people will have personality disorder.

P: What causes this personality disorder?

C: No one knows for sure what causes personality disorder. There are a few associated factors. It can be due to certain mental health disorders, hereditary, certain brain conditions and upbringing can play a part. {Elaborate on upbringing if necessary- physical or sexual abuse in childhood, violence in the family and parents who drink too much]
P: I know I feel empty inside sometimes, and I just can't express this to anyone.

C: That is characteristic of someone with Borderline personality disorder (BPD). They usually find it difficult to know themselves and do not have a stable sense of their own identity. They experience difficulty in maintaining relationships and the follow a pattern of unstable, brief and intense relationships. They fear abandonment and will attempt by all means to prevent this. Sometimes this can result in them taking overdoses.

P: I do find it difficult to cope and self-harm.

C: This behaviour is a reflection of their impulsivity and difficulty coping with stressful situations. It can sometimes result in suicidal attempts with taking overdoses. They can also experience mood swings, anger outbursts and anxiety symptoms.
We find also that they can sometimes hear voices and begin to feel suspicious about people around them [elaborate further on transient psychotic experiences]

P: I don't mean to be like this doc!

C: Yes, I think it is important to acknowledge this. However what is also important is to understand the impact the distress caused by these actions not only on yourself but also on others. Sometimes people might not understand, and you might feel blamed, victimised and criticised by others. It is important for those close to you to have an understanding of this in order to promote your wellbeing and recovery.

PSYCHOTHERAPY

Another thing we find in relationships is that people with Borderline Personality Disorder cause splitting.

Elaborate further below if essential using a common example i.e. splitting on the ward or in a team
Splitting is a defence mechanism or a means of how we cope with a situation. People with BPD typically tend to cause splitting i.e. they classify people as either all good or all bad [i.e. swing between idealizing and devaluing people in their mind]

P: Why is it that I have this now?

We know that there are certain things in our daily life that can make us more vulnerable or trigger this in a sense. For example:
Misuse of drugs or alcohol
Difficulties' in relationships with your family or partner
Financial difficulties
Anxiety, Depression or other mental health problems
Significant life events
stressful situations

P: What treatment is there available?

C: We have a range of treatment which includes (talking therapies) and or medication.

P: What is the psychological or talking therapy available?
Elaborate further depending on the scenario and tailor information accordingly]

C: The therapies available can vary from shorter term to longer-term therapy can last for years. Some may have to be more than once a week. They all involve different ways of talking with a therapist, but are all different from each other. Some have a clear structure to them, others are more flexible. They include:

Mentalisation – *This combines group and individual therapy. The aim is to help you understand yourself and others better. It is also about being aware and clearer of what's going on in your own mind and in the minds of others.*

Dialectical Behaviour Therapy – *this uses a combination of <u>cognitive and behavioural therapies</u>, with some techniques from Zen Buddhism. It involves individual therapy and group therapy.*

Cognitive Behavioural Therapy – *This involves looking at the links of our thinking, feeling and behaviours. The therapist will assist you in identifying the flaws or errors in your thinking into more helpful patterns of thinking.*

PSYCHOTHERAPY

Schema Focused Therapy - *a type of cognitive therapy that explores and changes collections of deep unhelpful beliefs.*

Transference Focused Therapy - *a more structured type of talking therapy in which the therapist explores and changes unconscious processes. I*

Psychodynamic Psychotherapy - *looks at how past experiences affect present behaviour. It is similar to Transference Focused Therapy, but less structured.*

Cognitive Analytical Therapy – *this is a way to identify and change unhelpful patterns in relationships and behaviour. It is a combination of CBT and psychoanalytical psychotherapy. [Eclectic type]*

Treatment in a therapeutic community – *this is a place where people with long-standing emotional problems can go to for several weeks or months. Most of the work is done in groups. The rationale is that people learn from getting on or not getting on with other people in the treatment group. It differs from 'real life' in that any disagreements or upsets happen in a safe place. People in treatment often have a lot of say over how the community runs.*

P: What medication is there available?

Elaborate further dependent on the scenario]
Antipsychotic drugs (usually at a low dose)
- *Can help with borderline personality disorder if people feel paranoid, or are hearing noises or voices.[transient psychotic experiences]*

Antidepressants
- *Can help with the mood and emotional difficulties that people with borderline personality disorder*
- *Some of the selective serotonin reuptake inhibitor antidepressants (SSRIs) can help people to be less impulsive and aggressive.*

Mood stabilisers
Medication such as lithium, carbamazepine, and sodium valproate can also reduce impulsiveness and aggression.

P: What other support is there?

C: *Our aim is for people with Borderline personality disorder to eventually lead full lives with support. This can be emotional somebody to talk to or practical with help with sorting bills out or arranging things.*

P: Will I get better?
C: *Unfortunately there is no known cure for Borderline personality disorder. There is evidence however that some of the distressing symptoms improve*

slowly with age i.e. impulsiveness, in particular, seem to reduce in your 30s and 40s.

P: What else can I do to help myself?
C: We advise simple, practical things for example like try to unwind when stressed (have a hot bath or go for a walk). You might also want to consider going for yoga, massage or aromatherapy useful.

- Ensure you have plenty of rest and sleep.
- Maintain a balanced diet, with lots of fruit and vegetables.[five a day]
- Avoid drinking too much alcohol or experimenting with street drugs.
- Take some regular exercise, at 3 times a week.
- Occupy yourself and consider a hobby.
- Talk to someone about how you are feeling. This could be a friend or relative or, if preferred, a therapist or counsellor. If you don't have access to a counsellor or therapist, then try your GP.
- In an emergency, try phoning the Samaritans

P: How can my family help?

C: We usually advise that families should be educated more about this. Their understanding and support is good for your recovery.

Summarize
Thank you for talking to me. We have spoken about your diagnosis of Borderline personality disorder and the various treatment options available. I would like to see you again. I will also give you some leaflets and website addresses.

Groups and organisations
Mind
Mind is a leading mental health charity in England and Wales and has extensive information on personality and personality disorder.

Samaritans
Samaritans is available 24 hours a day to provide confidential emotional support for people who are experiencing feelings of distress or despair, including those which may lead to suicide. The website has helpful information about stress and self-harm.

Rethink
Rethink is a leading national mental health membership charity and works to help everyone affected by severe mental illness recover a better quality of life. Has information on personality and personality disorder.

Emergence
Emergence is a service user-led organisation supporting all people affected by a diagnosis of personality disorder, whether you are a service user, carer

PSYCHOTHERAPY

(which is a family member or friend of a service user) or a professional in the field.

Aware
Assists and supports those suffering from Depression (which can occur in those diagnosed with a personality disorder).

BORDERLINE PERSONALITY DISORDER
F60.30 Impulsive type

At least three of the following must be present, one of which must be (2):

1. *marked tendency to act unexpectedly and without consideration of the consequences;*
2. *marked tendency to quarrelsome behaviour and to conflicts with others, especially when impulsive acts are thwarted or criticized;*
3. *liability to outbursts of anger or violence, with inability to control the resulting behavioural explosions;*
4. *difficulty in maintaining any course of action that offers no immediate reward;*
5. *unstable and capricious mood.*

It is a requirement of ICD-10 that a diagnosis of any specific personality disorder also satisfies a set of general personality disorder criteria.

F60.31 Borderline type

At least three of the symptoms mentioned in F60.30 Impulsive type must be present [see above], with at least two of the following in addition:

1. *disturbances in and uncertainty about self-image, aims, and internal preferences (including sexual);*
2. *liability to become involved in intense and unstable relationships, often leading to emotional crisis;*
3. *excessive efforts to avoid abandonment;*
4. *recurrent threats or acts of self-harm;*
5. *chronic feelings of emptiness.*

It is a requirement of ICD-10 that a diagnosis of any specific personality disorder also satisfies a set of general personality disorder criteria.

PSYCHOTHERAPY

11. SUMMARY OF OTHER PERSONALITY DISORDERS

OTHER TYPES OF PERSONALITY DISORDER

Cluster A: 'Odd or Eccentric

Cluster B: 'Dramatic, Emotional, or Erratic'

Cluster C: 'Anxious and Fearful'

CLUSTER A: 'ODD AND ECCENTRIC' GROUP
1 Paranoid Personality disorder
  ➤ suspicious
  ➤ feel that other people are being nasty to you (even when evidence shows this isn't true)
  ➤ feel easily rejected
  ➤ tend to hold grudges
2 Schizoid Personality disorder
  ➤ emotionally 'cold'
  ➤ prefers own company
  ➤ have a rich fantasy world
3 Schizotypal Personality disorder
  ➤ eccentric behaviour
  ➤ odd ideas
  ➤ difficulties with thinking
  ➤ lack of emotion
  ➤ see or hear strange things
  ➤ sometimes related to schizophrenia, the mental illness

©Smartsesh

PSYCHOTHERAPY

CLUSTER B: 'DRAMATIC, EMOTIONAL AND ERRATIC'

1 Antisocial, or Dissocial Personality disorder
- ➢ Callous or unconcern for the feelings of others
- ➢ Low frustration tolerance
- ➢ tend to be aggressive
- ➢ commit crimes
- ➢ find it difficult to make intimate relationships
- ➢ impulsive - do things on the spur of the moment without thinking about them
- ➢ don't feel guilty
- ➢ don't learn from unpleasant experiences

2 Borderline, or Emotionally Unstable Personality disorder
- ➢ impulsive
- ➢ find it hard to control emotions
- ➢ feel bad about yourself
- ➢ often self-harm, e.g. cutting or making suicide attempts
- ➢ feel 'empty'
- ➢ intense relationships but easily lose them and feels abandoned
- ➢ can feel paranoid or depressed
- ➢ when stressed, may hear noises or voices

3 Histrionic Personality disorder
- ➢ over-dramatise events
- ➢ self-centered
- ➢ have strong emotions which change quickly and don't last long
- ➢ can be suggestible
- ➢ worry a lot about appearance
- ➢ crave new things and excitement
- ➢ can be seductive

4 Narcissistic Personality disorder
- ➢ have a strong sense of own self-importance
- ➢ dream of unlimited success, power and intellectual brilliance
- ➢ crave attention from other people, but show few warm feelings in return
- ➢ exploit others ask for favours do not reciprocate

©Smartsesh

CLUSTER C: 'ANXIOUS AND FEARFUL'
1 Obsessive-Compulsive (aka Anankastic) Personality disorder
 ➤ worry or doubt a lot
 ➤ perfectionist - always checking things
 ➤ rigid in what they do
 ➤ cautious, preoccupied with detail
 ➤ worry about doing the wrong thing
 ➤ find it hard to adapt to new situations
 ➤ often have high moral standards
 ➤ judgemental
 ➤ sensitive to criticism
 ➤ can have obsessional thoughts and images (although these are not as bad as those in obsessive-compulsive disorder)
2 Avoidant (aka Anxious/Avoidant) Personality disorder
 ➤ very anxious and tense
 ➤ worry a lot
 ➤ feel insecure and inferior
 ➤ have to be liked and accepted
 ➤ extremely sensitive to criticism
3 Dependent Personality disorder
 ➤ passive
 ➤ rely on others to make their decisions
 ➤ do what other people want them to do
 ➤ find it hard to cope with daily chores
 ➤ feel hopeless and incompetent
 ➤ easily feel abandoned by others

©Smartsesh

PSYCHOTHERAPY

12. DBT-DIALECTICAL BEHAVIOUR THERAPY

Instructions to candidate
You have been asked to see a 35 year old female, Elizabeth Chering, who has a diagnosis of emotionally unstable personality disorder. She has been referred dialectical behaviour therapy .

TASK FOR THE CANDIDATE
- Explain DBT-Dialectical Behaviour Therapy.

PAY PARTICULAR ATTENTION TO THE FOLLOWING (MENTAL CHECKLIST)
- Explain DBT
- Explain the 2 main components
- Explain the rationale for DBT.
- Highlight the different components of DBT.
- Explain general structure of psychotherapy.
- Explain what would occur in an emergency.

COMMUNICATION SKILLS
- Start the interview by developing rapport and showing empathy.

Suggested approach
Introduction
C: Hello, I'm one of the psychiatrists. Thank you for coming to see me today. I understand that you have been referred for dialectical behaviour therapy. Before we begin can you tell me what your understanding is of this?

P: I know they said this is useful for people with BLPD.

C: It is a type of psychotherapy or talking therapy. It uses a combination of cognitive and behavioural therapies with some techniques from Zen Buddhism.

P: What is the purpose?

C: It has proven evidence for treatment of people with emotionally unstable personality disorder

P: What would DBT involve?

C: DBT involves two components: [elaborate further]
An individual component:
An individual component in which the therapist and patient discuss issues that come up during the week, recorded on diary cards, and follow a treatment target hierarchy. Self-injurious and suicidal behaviors take first priority.

515

PSYCHOTHERAPY

Second in priority are behaviors which while not directly harmful to self or others, interfere with the course of treatment. These behaviors are known as therapy-interfering behaviors.

Third in priority are quality of life issues and working towards improving one's life generally. During the individual therapy, the therapist and patient work towards improving skill use. Often, a skills group is discussed and obstacles to acting skillfully are addressed.

B The group therapy component:

The group component in which the group ordinarily meets once weekly for two to two-and-a-half hours and learns to use specific skills that are broken down into four modules: core mindfulness skills, interpersonal effectiveness skills, emotion regulation skills, and distress tolerance skills.

C: There are also four main modules which DBT involve. I will only mention these: [elaborate further if necessary]
The four modules are mindfulness, distress tolerance, emotional regulation and interpersonal affective effectiveness.

Other questions which may need to be addressed:
P: What do I do in an Emergency?

C: If any emergency situations arise then you would need to seek medical treatment from your GP, emergency service or Community mental health team.

P: Where are my records or notes kept?

C: The notes are usually kept separate from the medical notes and your therapist will inform your GP of a summary of your treatment.

P: What are other professionals involved in my care told?

C: The information discussed during your session will be confidential. This will only be disclosed if there is a risk to anyone.

P: Do I still need to take my medication?

C: If you are on any medication you can continue with this.

P: How long will I have to wait?

C: There is a waiting list on the NHS. However now it is possible to get CBT quicker due to the provision of the government funded programme 'Improved Access to Psychological Therapies' (IAPT).

PSYCHOTHERAPY

P: What do I do if I want to stop these sessions

C: You can discontinue your sessions with the therapist, but it is a good idea to discuss this with him or her

Summarize
Thank you for talking to me. We have spoken briefly about the dialectical behaviour therapy and the components. I would like you to think about this as there is good evidence for its benefits in people who have been diagnosed with Borderline personality disorder. We can make another appointment to discuss your decision if you wish. I will also give you some leaflets and website addresses.

	Depression Mild, Moderate and Severe	CBT , IPT behavioural activation
	Depression Mild-Moderate	Counselling , couples therapy
	Panic Disorder	CBT
Step 3 High Intensity Service	Generalised anxiety disorder (GAD) mild- moderate	CBT
	Social Phobia	CBT ,
	Post Traumatic Stress Disorder (PTSD)	CBT , eye movement desensitisation and reprocessing (EMDR)
	Obsessive Compulsive Disorder (OCD	CBT
	Depression Mild-Moderate	cCBT , guided self-help , behavioural activation , exercise
Step 2 : Low Intensity Service	Panic Disorder Mild -Moderate	cCBT , guided self-help , pure self help ,
	Generalised anxiety disorder (GAD) mild- moderate	cCBT , guided self-help , pure self help , psychoeducation groups
	OCD mild - moderate	Guided Self-Help
Step 1 : Primary Care/ IAPT Service	Recognition of Problem	Asessment / Watchful Waiting

IAPT MODEL -Improved Access to Psychological Therapies

PSYCHOTHERAPY

References

Bateman, A.W., Fonagy, P. (2004). Mentalization-based treatment of BPD. Journal of personality disorders, 18, 36-51.

Bateman, A.W., Fonagy, P. (2008). Comorbid antisocial and borderline personality disorders: mentalization-based treatment. Journal of clinical psychology, 64, 181-194 British Medical Association and Royal

Pharmaceutical society (2011), British National Formulary 62, 62nd edn. Great Britain: British Medical Journal Publishing Group and Pharmaceutical Press

Fonagy, P., Bateman, A.W. (2006). Mechanisms of change in metalization-based treatment of BPD. Journal of clinical psychology, 62, 411-430. Freud S,(1959) Collected papaers. New York:basic book

Gelder, M.G, Cowen, P. and Harrison P.J (2006) Shorter Oxford textbook of psychiatry. 5th edn. Oxford: Oxford University Press.

Janowsky, David S. (1999). Psychotherapy indications and outcomes. Washington, DC: American Psychiatric Press. pp. 100.

Marsha M. Linehan. 1993. Skills Training Manual for Treating Borderline Personality Disorder

Marsha M. Linehan. 1993 Cognitive Behavioral Treatment of Borderline Personality Disorder

Linehan, M. M. & Dimeff, L. (2001). Dialectical Behavior Therapy in a nutshell, The California Psychologist, 34, 10-13.

Linehan, M. M.; Armstrong, H. E.; Suarez, A.; Allmon, D.; Heard, H. L. (1991). "Cognitive-behavioral treatment of chronically parasuicidal borderline patients". Archives of General Psychiatry 48: 1060-64.

Freud Mourning and Melancholia (transference and countertransference Melanie Klein
Orsucci,F, (2009).Mind Force On Human Attractions, World scientific publishing co

Veale, D, Willson R (2007) Manage Your Mood. Constable Robinson publishing, London

Sims, A. C. P. (2003) Symptoms in the mind: an introduction to descriptive psychopathology. 3rd edn. Great Britain: Saunders

PSYCHOTHERAPY

Taylor, D., Paton, C., Kapur, S. (2009) The South London and Maudsley NHS Foundation Trust & Oxleas NHS Foundation Trust prescribing guidelines. 10th edn. London: Informa Healthcare.

Veale, D, Willson, R (2005) Overcoming Obsessive Compulsive Disorder. Constable Robinson publishing, London

WHO. (1992)The ICD 10 classification of mentaland behavioural disorders: clinical descriptions and diagnosticguideline. 10th revision: Geneva; WHO

Winnicot, D W (1971) Playing and reality. London: Tavistock publications

Support groups and organisations
Mind
Mind is a leading mental health charity in England and Wales and has extensive information on personality and personality disorder.

Samaritans
Samaritans is available 24 hours a day to provide confidential emotional support for people who are experiencing feelings of distress or despair, including those which may lead to suicide. The website has helpful information about stress and self-harm.

Rethink
Rethink is a leading national mental health membership charity and works to help everyone affected by severe mental illness recover a better quality of life. Has information on personality and personality disorder.

Emergence
Emergence is a service user-led organisation supporting all people affected by a diagnosis of personality disorder, whether you are a service user, carer (which is a family member or friend of a service user) or a professional in the field.

Aware
Assists and supports those suffering from Depression (which can occur in those diagnosed with a personality disorder).

Online resources and websites

Royal College of psychiatrists www.rcpsych.ac.uk
Support groups and organisations

British Association of Behavioural and Cognitive Psychotherapies.
Beating the Blues - www.ultrasis.com
Royal College of psychiatrists www.rcpsych.ac.uk

Free online CBT websites

PSYCHOTHERAPY

Mood Gym: *www.moodgym.anu.edu.au*
Living life to the full www.livinglifeto thefull.com
Fearfighter www.fearfighter.com

EATING DISORDERS

Dr Rajini Rajeswaran
Dr Tony Jaffa

EATING DISORDERS

1. ANOREXIA NERVOSA

Instructions to candidate
You are asked to see a 17 yr. old lady Sarah Cross who was admitted last night informally with hypokalaemia. Her GP was concerned about her recent weight loss.

TASK FOR THE CANDIDATE
- Elicit history of eating disorder.

PAY PARTICULAR ATTENTION TO THE FOLLOWING (MENTAL CHECKLIST)
- Establish current eating pattern.
- Establish the core criteria(weight loss, distorted body image, amenorrhoea, including BMI <17).
- Establish body image perception.
- Elicits compensatory behaviours.
- Establish physical sequelae and effects on hypothalamic pituitary gonadal axis.
- Establish the psychological sequalae of anorexia nervosa.
- Conduct a risk assessment of weight loss and suicidal risk.
- Explores co-morbid symptoms.

COMMUNICATION SKILLS
- Anticipate denial and reluctance to discuss eating difficulties.
- Enquire about eating pattern to latter part of the interview.
- Develop rapport and show empathy.
- Show sensitivity when discussing issues around weight, body image perception and eating habits.

Suggested approach
Introduction
C: Hello, I'm Dr.....I'm one of the psychiatrists. I understand you were admitted to hospital last night and your GP was concerned about your health. Can you please tell me more about what happened that you ended up in hospital?

P: My parents brought me here.

C: Do you know what their concerns were about? (Bound to be denial)

P: I don't know why they were worried.

C: Can you tell me what in particular they were worried about?

P: They were concerned about my weight.

C: How have you been lately?

EATING DISORDERS

- *Have you lost any weight recently?*
- *Can you tell me what your current weight is?*
- *Are you able to tell me your current weight? What is your height? (Calculate BMI WEIGHT/HEIGHT squared)*
- *What was your weight before?*
- *How did you manage to lose this amount of weight?*
- *Have you been concerned about your weight at all? (Preoccupation)*

A. History of Presenting Complaint (HOPC) (onset, duration, progression and severity)
Establishing BMI and eating habit:
1. Typical day
- *Can you take me through a typical day of what you would eat? (typical day)*
- *For example, what do you have in the morning? Do you have any snack before lunch? What do you have for lunch? What would you have for dinner?*

2. Behaviours to counteract fattening effects of food
a) Establish if there are any bingeing episodes
- *Do you sometimes lose control with the amount that you eat?(bingeing)*
- *Can you describe one of those typical instances where you have been overeating? What usually triggers this?*
- *How does it make you feel?*
- *May I ask if you ever make yourself sick? If so, how often? (purging)*

b) Compensatory behaviours
- *Have you been exercising? How often do you exercise? (exercising)*
- *Have you been skipping meals or sometimes starving yourself? Do you avoid certain foods? (starving and abstaining)*
- *Have you been taking water pills or laxatives? (diuretics)*

5. Preoccupation with food
- *Do you find yourself thinking about food?(preoccupation)*
- *Do enjoy cooking?*
- *Do you avoid eating with others?*
- *Do you find yourself count the calories of things that you eat?*

6. Body image distortion
- *What do you feel about your body? (body image perception)*
- *Which part of your body are you most dissatisfied with?*
- *How often do you look in the mirror? What do you see when you look in the mirror?*
- *Do you weigh yourself? How often do you do that?*
- *What would you feel if you gain weight? (morbid fear of gaining weight)*
- *What is your ideal weight? (ideal weight)*

EATING DISORDERS

- *What do other people say about your weight?(establish if overvalued idea)*

7. Endocrine disorder involving the hypothalamic pituitary-gonadal axis
- *I need to ask you a personal question, can you tell me about your periods. Have they been affected at all? (amenorrhoea)*
- *When did you first start with your periods?(menarche)*
- *Are they regular?*

8. Establish any physical complications
- *Have you had any physical health problems?*
- *Have you been admitted to hospital before?*
- *Have you fainted or dizzy? Have you felt tired?(fatigue)*
- *Are you sensitive to cold weather?(sensitivity to cold)*
- *Do you suffer from constipation?(constipation)*
- *Have you recently had any fractures? (fractures)*

B. Aetiological factors
Use biopsychosocial approach to elicit possible aetiological factors
1. Biological
- *Is there anyone in your family who has an eating disorder?*

2. Psychological
Premorbid personality
- *What type of person would your family describe you as?*
- *Would you say you're a perfectionist?*
- *Are appearances important to you?*
- *(associated with Obsessive, Borderline and Anxious personality traits)*
- *How would you describe your family?*
- *How would your family describe you?*
- *With whom are closest to?*
- *Tell me about your relationships with family?*

3. Social
- *Has anyone commented on the way you look or your weight?*
- *Has there been any name calling about your weight?*

C. Exclude Co-morbidity -Depression, Anxiety and OCD
Elicit core features of Depression
- *Sometimes our eating habits can also affect the way we feel. Can you tell me how has your mood been? (mood)*
- *How are your energy levels? (energy)*
- *Have you lost interest in things you usually would enjoy doing? What are they? (anhedonia)*
- *How have you been sleeping? (biological symptoms)*

EATING DISORDERS

Screen for Anxiety and OCD symptoms

D. Risk assessment
 Self-harm/DSH
- I need to ask you some questions about how you see the future? What do you feel about your future?
- Have you ever felt that life was not worth living?(suicidal thoughts)
- Have you had thoughts of wanting to end it all? Have you acted on these?(deliberate self-harm)
- Have you ever cut yourself? Have you ever taken an overdose?
- Starving(include this as part of risk assessment)

Drug and alcohol history
- How do you usually cope? Some people take drink and take street drugs. How about you?

Summarise
Thank you for talking to me. To summarise, you have been concerned about your weight, and have been using various measures to reduce this. This weight loss has now affected your physical health and your mood.

Your mother/family is obviously very worried about you. Are you OK if I speak to them about your condition in general, I won't disclose any of the information that you don't want me to disclose. **(Consent)**

Thank You

NICE guidelines for Eating Disorders
(Adapted from NICE guidance)
Anorexia Nervosa
➤ Drugs should not be used as sole or primary treatment for Anorexia Nervosa.
➤ For Anorexia Nervosa consider cognitive analytic or cognitive behavioural therapies, interpersonal psychotherapy, focal dynamic therapy, or family interventions focused on eating disorders.
➤ Family interventions that directly address the eating disorder are especially useful for children and adolescents with Anorexia Nervosa.
➤ Dietary counselling should not be provided as sole treatment for Anorexia Nervosa.

EATING DISORDERS

Diagnostic Criteria for Anorexia Nervosa F50.1

(Adapted from ICD-10)

(a) Body weight is consistently 15% less (or lower) than that expected for height and age, or body mass index is 17.5 or less. This can be due to either weight loss, or failure to gain weight during growth.

(b) Weight loss is caused by the avoidance of foods perceived to be fattening, along with one or more of the following behaviours: self-induced vomiting, purging, excessive exercise, use of appetite suppressants and/or diuretics.

(c) Distorted body image perception driven by an intense, irrational fear of becoming fat, leads to the desire to remain at a low body weight.

(d) Amenorrhea (abnormal absence of a minimum of three successive menstrual cycles) in women, and loss of libido in men. There may be changes in growth hormone, cortisol, thyroid hormone and insulin.

(e) Puberty in girls and boys may be delayed if the onset of anorexia nervosa is prepubertal, but once recovery from the illness is made, it will often progress normally.

ICD-10 also includes 'atypical' anorexia nervosa, which refers to individuals who show some, but not all, of the characteristics of anorexia nervosa.

EATING DISORDERS

ANOREXIA NERVOSA –HISTORY TAKING

HOPC (onset, duration, progression, severity)
- Establishing BMI and eating habits
- Establish typical day history - all meals
- Calculate BMI (WEIGHT/HEIGHT squared)
- Establish behaviours to counteract fattening effects of food
- Bingeing – triggers, behaviours, calories, emotions
- Compensatory behaviours – Exercising, starving, skipping meals, water pills, laxatives
- Preoccupation with food-calorie counting
- Body image distortion-self-perception of body, morbid fear of fatness
- Endocrine disorder involving the hypothalamic pituitary-gonadal axis physical health - admissions, dizziness, fatigue, constipation, fractures

Aetiological factors-elicit using bio-psychosocial approach
- Biological - family history of eating disorders
- Psychological- dealing with conflicts
- Premorbid personality – Perfectionist, Obsessive, Borderline, Anxious Personality Traits
- Social – friends, relationships

Exclude co-morbidity- Depression, Anxiety and OCD
- Risk assessment -Self harm/DSH, risks of starving

Drug and alcohol history

Summarise
- Consent to speak to parent

©Smartsesh

POSSIBLE VARIATIONS OF THEMES
1. Person with Anorexia nervosa refusing to eat and admitted to the medical ward. Currently has NGT for feeding.
2. Anorexia nervosa with severe depressive disorder and suicidal ideation
3. Anorexia nervosa refusing to have medical investigations
4. Anorexia nervosa with borderline personality disorder

EATING DISORDERS

2. ANOREXIA NERVOSA

INSTRUCTIONS TO THE CANDIDATE
You are asked to see the mother of the young lady, Sarah Cross, whom you assessed in the previous station.

TASK TO THE CANDIDATE
- *Discuss the diagnosis and management with her.*

PAY PARTICULAR ATTENTION TO THE FOLLOWING (MENTAL CHECKLIST)
- *Inform her that her daughter has given consent to speak to her.*
- *Explain diagnosis of Anorexia nervosa-BMI below 17.*
- *Explain management in a holistic or biopsychosocial approach for recovery.*
- *Highlight principles of management of Anorexia Nervosa with recommended weight gain of 0, 5 to 1 kg per week.*
- *Explain the stepped care approach.*
- *Establish premorbid functioning.*

COMMUNICATION SKILLS
- *Start the interview by developing rapport and showing*
- *empathy*
- *Show sensitivity when discussing nature of illness*
- *Understand the possible impact of the family dynamics as contributing the illness.*

Suggested approach
Introduction
C: Hello, I'm Dr .....I'm one of the psychiatrists. Thank you for coming to see me. I have seen your daughter and she has given me permission to speak to you. I know that you must be concerned about her. As you are aware she had been admitted to hospital as there were complications as a result of significant weight loss.

M: I am worried about her. We went to see her GP and the next thing we knew she was being admitted to hospital. Is this the normal presentation? What is her diagnosis?

C: I will explain more about her diagnosis and how we are going to treat her while she is under our care.
She was admitted with a complication of an eating disorder called **Anorexia Nervosa**. The blood tests show that she suffers from, what we call, "hypokalaemia". This is when a salt in our blood called potassium, is low. It can sometimes be life threatening and interfere with the rhythm of the heart. Thankfully by you taking her to her GP we were able to identify this before she had any significant complication.

EATING DISORDERS

M: What is Anorexia Nervosa?

C: Anorexia Nervosa is when someone has an intense fear of gaining weight and becoming fat. They try to lose weight using various methods that can cause harm to the body. It usually starts during the teenage years, affecting 1 fifteen-year-old girl in every 150. Girls and women are 10 times more likely to suffer from anorexia than men.

M: What are the symptoms of Anorexia Nervosa?

C: The classic signs of anorexia are when girls start to worry more and more about their weight and what they eat. They try to lose weight by over exercising, selecting their foods, counting calories and sometimes they may take laxatives or water pills. This makes them tired and weak and has an effect on their menstruation that becomes irregular or stops.

Anorexia nervosa can also result in other physical complications such as brittle bones, hair loss, and in life threatening conditions affecting the heart. Many girls suffering from Anorexia Nervosa also suffer from Depressed Mood, Anxiety or OCD.

M: What are the causes of Anorexia Nervosa?

C: There is no one particular cause for Anorexia Nervosa and it is difficult to pinpoint as to the reasons why your daughter has developed this. It can sometimes be due to a few associated factors. The following are what we commonly see as the causes for anorexia nervosa.
- *social pressure to be thin (from TV, magazines, newspapers)*
- *It has a genetic component and can sometimes run in families*
- *It may be an unhelpful way of coping for some people with emotional difficulties, low self-esteem and/or Depression*
- *It can also be a way of having a sense of control for some people*

M: Is it my fault?

C: No, it's not your fault and you shouldn't blame yourself. No one can pinpoint a single cause as reasons as to why your daughter has developed anorexia nervosa. As we discussed earlier, there are multiple components that contribute to someone developing Anorexia nervosa.

M: What is the treatment?

C: In your daughters cause we had to admit her due to hypokalaemia as a consequence of weight loss. The treatment that is recommended by the guidelines we follow (NICE National institute of clinical excellence) involves a combination of medical, psychological and social aspects of care.

EATING DISORDERS

Our aim is to strike a balance to improve both her nutritional and psychological state. Because at present there are physical health concerns, that would be our main priority of treatment

a) Biological interventions
We usually consider admission to a psychiatric hospital or eating disorder specialist unit if the following are present:
- *Suicidal ideation and risk of suicide or serious self-harm*
- *Rapid and severe weight loss with physical complications*
- *BMI<14*

While she is in hospital, we use a Multidisciplinary Team (MDT) approach with various team members providing care. This team will consist of a psychiatrist, psychologist, dietician, occupational therapist, nurses and an allocated key worker.

The admission is most often voluntary. It is unusual to resort to compulsory treatment. This only happens when the person is severely unwell and is unable to make a decision for themselves or needs to be protected from serious harm.

During the admission her physical health will be closely monitored for any heart, lung or bone problems. She will have regular blood tests, and her weight will be checked, making sure she slowly gains weight progressively. A dietician will be involved, planning her meals according to specific calorie intake.

Nursing staff would provide support with meals, and caring whilst on the ward. During the admission she will be supervised and given care in a structured way.

b) Psychological interventions
It is also important to offer her a space to talk about her feelings and thoughts. This is helpful both during the admission and after discharge. There are many talking therapies that have shown to be beneficial, such as Family therapy, CBT (Cognitive behavioural therapy), IPT (Interpersonal therapy), and Psychodynamic psychotherapy.

c) Social interventions
If you and your daughter consent, staff will be able to liaise with the school and facilitate gradual reintegration into school life.

M: What is the prognosis?

C: The prognosis can depend on many factors such as the age of onset, the duration of the symptoms and a few other factors. Once she is discharged, we will have the community team who will be able to monitor her in the community and provide support to you and your family if necessary. [Relay prognosis tailored to the specific case]

EATING DISORDERS

M: What can I do to help?

C: It is normal for family members to be worried. You can do a lot to help. Learning about the condition, its complications and its treatment is useful. Understanding the illness as well as being available and listening can support your daughter to engage in her treatment plan and promote recovery.

Summarise
Thank you for talking to me. I can only imagine how difficult this must be for you and your family to see Sarah with this severe weight loss and physical complications as a result of this. I will give you some leaflets which will provide you with some more information on Anorexia Nervosa. The website BEAT is useful and has some informative videos. .

I am happy to meet with you again, if you have further questions and/or want to discuss your daughter's progress.

Support groups and websites

ANOREXIA NERVOSA
Epidemiology 1 in 150
- F>M 10 times

Aetiology: social pressure to be thin (from TV, magazines, newspapers), genetic, low self-esteem, Depression

Anorexia Nervosa- intense fear of gaining weight and becoming fat.

Symptoms- worry more about their weight and what they eat.
- Lose weight by over exercising, selecting their foods, counting calories and sometimes they may take laxatives or water pills.
- Menstruation becomes irregular or stops- amenorrhoea

Physical complications brittle bones, hair loss, and in life threatening conditions affecting the heart

Psychological complications Depression sometimes with suicidal ideation, Anxiety and OCD

©Smartsesh

EATING DISORDERS

Management
NICE advice (National Institute of Clinical Excellence) -a step care approach and holistic or biopsychosocial approach to recovery.
Biological interventions
Admission to a psychiatric hospital or eating disorder specialist unit indications are :
Suicidal ideation and risk of suicide or
serious self-harm
Rapid and severe weight loss with physical
complications
BMI<14

- Admission – informal or MHA
- Multidisciplinary Team approach (MDT) - psychiatrist, psychologist, dietician, occupational therapist, nurses and an allocated key worker.
- Monitor physical health, physical examination, regular blood tests
- ovarian scan to assess follicles indicating ovulation
- Weight gain 0.5 kg-1 kg per week
- Dietician

Psychological interventions

- Family therapy
- CBT (Cognitive behavioural therapy)
- IPT (Interpersonal therapy)
- Psychodynamic psychotherapy
- Psychoeducation al groups

Social interventions

- Liaise with the school and facilitate gradual reintegration into school life.
- Prognosis mortality of 10-20 if not treated
- Family and support in understanding the condition

Information/Leaflets

- website BEAT is useful and has some informative videos

©Smartsesh

EATING DISORDERS

3. ANOREXIA NERVOSA

INSTRUCTIONS TO CANDIDATE
You have been asked to speak to the ward manager James Brook about the 17 yr old lady Sarah Cross, who was admitted with hypokalaemia.

TASK TO THE CANDIDATE
Discuss your management plan with the ward manager.

PAY PARTICULAR ATTENTION TO THE FOLLOWING (MENTAL CHECKLIST)
- Establish the current concerns from the ward manager.
- Identify current risks- suicidal ideation, intent or plans.
- Establish the nature of the staff issues i.e. splitting.
- Explain diagnosis of Anorexia nervosa-BMI below 17.
- Explain management in holistic or biopsychosocial approach toward recovery.
- NICE guidelines recommend weight gain of 0, 5 to 1 kg per week.

COMMUNICATION SKILLS
- Adopt a collegiate approach.
- Start the interview by developing rapport and showing empathy for their difficulties the nurses have experienced.

Suggested approach
Introduction
C: Hello, I'm Dr ...I'm one of the psychiatrists. Thank you for referring this young lady on your ward whom I have just assessed. I wanted to discuss my management plan with you. Before I begin, may I ask what your understanding of her diagnosis is?

W: I think we have different views on this ward and it is causing some tension.

C: Most patients with eating disorders are usually difficult to manage. This usually occurs because the person who is suffering with anorexia themselves is in conflict, and thus, creates the defence mechanism of splitting.
I would suggest that in order to address this that maybe we can arrange a meeting to discuss this and this will also allow the staff the opportunity to discuss their views and develop a joint action plan that all members of the staff are agreeing with.

We can adopt a consistent approach and this would help to minimise the splitting.

W: How are we going to treat her?

EATING DISORDERS

C: As you know the: the treatment that is recommended by (NICE National Institute of Clinical Excellence) is a stepped care approach. It involves a combination of medical, psychological and social interventions of care. Our aim is to strike a balance to improve her nutritional and psychological state of the person who has anorexia nervosa.

a) Biological interventions
Admission to a psychiatric hospital/eating disorder specialist unit if the following are present
- *Suicidal- do regular risk assessments and close nursing observations*
- *Weight loss*
- *Physical complications*
- *Admission is either informal or under MHA 1983. Consider section 5(2) if necessary.*

b) Stepped care approach
We use a multidisciplinary approach with various team members providing care. This team would consist of a psychiatrist; there is psychologist, dietician, occupational therapist, nurses and an allocated key worker.

Use of Mental Health Act (MHA 1983) in eating disorders
Considers to be a mental disorder and therefore can use the Mental Health Act (MHA 1983) provided if criteria for admission
Refeeding or tube-feeding can be carried out under the Mental Health Act (MHA 1983).
Nursing staff would provide support with meals; observe for excessive exercising and purging in addition to supporting and caring whilst on the ward.
- *Vitamin supplements and meal plans according to calorie intake.*

c) Physical interventions
- *Supervise eating*
- *Refer to the physician about further management of hypokalaemia*
- *Monitor for exercising, purging and be aware observe for self-induced vomiting*
- *Ensure adequate rest*
- *Ensure gradual weight gain of 0,5-1kg/week*
- *Dietician - advise vitamin, calculate ideal weight and calorie intake.*
- *Bloods and investigations to monitor and get person physically stable Calcium, phosphate, magnesium, Full Blood Count FBC(Full blood count), LFT(Liver function tests)*
- *Bone scan- check for bone density*
- *Ovarian scan to check follicles indicating return of menstrual function*
- *ECG - check for arrhythmias*
- *Monitor for complications that can occur which is 'Refeeding syndrome '*

EATING DISORDERS

d) Pharmacological interventions
- *Rating scales: for Depression and Anxiety-HADS*
- *Medication for co-morbid conditions such as Depression, OCD*

e) Psychological interventions
- *There are talking therapies which have been shown to be beneficial*
- *Cognitive behavioural therapy (CBT)- change the body image perception and fear of fatness*
- *Interpersonal therapy (IPT)*
- *Psycho-education*
- *Psychodynamic psychotherapy*
- *Family therapy(FT)*

f) Social interventions
- *Gradual support in school, to slowly reintegrate back from a period off leave.*
- *Advice on meals*
- *Support with learning*
- *We would need to consider mental health if a person continues to refuse to eat and possible force feeding.*

W: What is the prognosis?

C: Generally the mortality rate is 10-20% if not treated. In her case she has had weight loss and hypokalaemia which increases this risk.

[The long-term prognosis of anorexia nervosa is changeable: the general rule of thumb is a fifth of patients stay severely ill, another fifth of patients recover fully and three fifths of patients have a fluctuating and chronic course (Gelder, Mayou and Geddes 2005).]

Summarise
Thank you for talking to me. To summarise I have explained the management for Sarah in terms of using a holistic approach. The concerns at present would be to monitor her for suicidal and medical risks. When she is more settled we can look at the psychological and social interventions.

As I have mentioned we would need to have a consistent approach and this could be discussed in a professionals meeting. In the interim, if you do require any further advice or assistance, please do not hesitate to contact either me or my team.

EATING DISORDERS

NICE guidelines for Eating Disorders

Anorexia Nervosa

➤ Drugs should not be used as sole or primary treatment for Anorexia Nervosa.

➤ For Anorexia Nervosa consider cognitive analytic or cognitive behavioural therapies, interpersonal psychotherapy, focal dynamic therapy, or family interventions focused on eating disorders.

➤ Family interventions that directly address the eating disorder are especially useful for children and adolescents with Anorexia Nervosa.

➤ Dietary counselling should not be provided as sole treatment for Anorexia Nervosa.

Bulimia Nervosa

➤ Evidence-based self-help programme is first line for Bulimia; as additional option or alternative choice antidepressants can be used in Bulimia.

➤ Antidepressant drugs can reduce frequency of binge eating and purging, but long-term effects are unknown.

➤ Any beneficial effects of antidepressants will be rapidly apparent.

➤ SSRIS (especially fluoxetine) are drugs of first choice for Bulimia Nervosa; effective dose of fluoxetine is higher than for Depression (60 mg daily).

➤ Specifically adapted cognitive behavioural therapy should be offered to adults with Bulimia Nervosa, 16-20 sessions over 4-5 months.

➤ Interpersonal psychotherapy should be considered as alternative to cognitive behavioural therapy, but patients should be informed it takes 8-12 months to achieve similar results.

EATING DISORDERS

4. ANOREXIA NERVOSA

INSTRUCTIONS TO THE CANDIDATE
You have been asked to see this 20yr old lady, Rachel Green, who has a history of anorexia nervosa.

TASK TO THE CANDIDATE
- *Elicit a personal history and family history.*

PAY PARTICULAR ATTENTON TO THE FOLLOWING (MENTAL CHECKLIST)
- *Elicit a history with a view of obtaining aetiological factors for development of anorexia nervosa.*
- *Elicit a personal history with aid of a genogram.*
- *Elicit a family history.*
- *Establish the family dynamics and other relationships.*
- *Establish premorbid functioning.*

COMMUNICATION SKILLS
- *Start the interview by developing rapport and showing empathy.*
- *Anticipate denial and reluctance to discuss family issues and eating difficulties.*
- *Show sensitivity when exploring family dynamics.*

Suggested approach
Introduction
C: Hello, I'm Dr...I'm one of the psychiatrists. I've been asked to see you by your GP. I understand that you have been diagnosed with Anorexia Nervosa and part of this assessment is to discuss the possible reasons of how you could have developed this.

P: Hello Doctor

C: For this assessment I do need to ask you some details from your early childhood and more about your family. Is that all right with you?

A. Family history
Characteristic of family interactions in Anorexia Nervosa include the following: enmeshment, overprotectiveness, rigidity, involvement of sick child in parental conflicts, avoidance of resolution of conflicts. [Minuchin]

Family dynamics
Family structure: draw a genogram to include all members of family
Show awareness if the parents are divorced [nuclear/step/single parent family]
- *Can you tell me about your family? Who are the other people in your family?[in the examination it would be useful to draw a genogram with writing material provide]*

EATING DISORDERS

- *Elicit the structure and composition of the family?[genogram]*

Relationships
- *Can you tell me about your relationships? How do you get along with mum, dad, siblings? (Relationships).*
- *Who are you closest to in your family? Is there anyone you do not get along with?*
- *What is your mother like? How would you describe father? How about your siblings?*
- *Who are you most like in your family?*
- *Do you spend lots of time together(enmeshment)*
- *Do you feel that any of your parents are over involved with you?*
- *Can you tell me about your relationships? Are you in any relationships now?*
- *How do you cope with difficulties in relationships?*

Family history of eating disorder
- *Is there anyone in the family who has any similar problems or eating difficulties? Has anyone been diagnosed with Anorexia Nervosa or Bulimia Nervosa? (family history of eating disorder)*

B. Personal History
Perinatal history
- *Would you be able to tell me about your earlier life? Perhaps start with where you were born. Are you aware of any complications at birth?*
- *Can you tell me more about your childhood?*

Establish any traumatic events
- *What are your childhood memories like? Is there anything that sticks out?*
- *Can I ask you in confidence, have you ever been abused? (Child Sex Abuse-CSA)*
- *Did you have any childhood illnesses? Have you ever been in hospital?*
- *Have you ever been teased about your appearance and weight?*

Psychiatric history
- *Did you have any weight problems when you were growing up?*
- *When did it all start? What treatment did you receive? Did you have any psychological treatment? How about family therapy?*

Establish onset of Puberty
- *I would like to ask some more personal questions, if that's ok. Please tell me if you have any difficulty in answering them?*
- *When did you get your first period? (Menarche)*
- *When was your last period? Are they regular? (Establish amenorrhea)*

Schooling
- *Can you tell me about how you got on at school?*

EATING DISORDERS

Occupational history
- *Can you tell me about your work?*

Premorbid personality
- *How would your family describe you?*
- *Would you say you are a perfectionist or a high achiever?(perfectionist)*
- *How do you feel about yourself?(self-esteem)*
- *Are you overly concerned about your appearance?*
- *Are you in anyway influenced by celebrities and their looks?*
- *Do you know anyone else who has an eating disorder?*
- *Do you have any hobbies?*
- *Are you religious?*
- *How do you generally cope with stress?*

Summarise
Thank you for talking to me. It has been helpful in order to understand reasons as to how you could have developed anorexia Nervosa. To summarise your eating difficulties started at a young age, and it seems to have impacted on your relationships with your family and boyfriend. You have also a family member who had eating difficulties. I would like to see you again to discuss this further.

Thank you

POSSIBLE VARIATIONS OF THEME
1.25 yr. old lady with Anorexia Nervosa who has a family history of Anorexia
Current episode precipitated by recent split from her boyfriend
2.33 yr. old lady, Insulin Dependent Diabetes mellitus IDDM (Diabetes Mellitus) with Bulimia Nervosa.

EATING DISORDERS

EATING DISORDERS

5. ANOREXIA NERVOSA

INSTRUCTIONS TO THE CANDIDATE
*You have seen this 20 yr. old lady Rachel Green with Anorexia Nervosa.
One of the nurses on the ward would like some more information on
aetiological factors of her developing Anorexia Nervosa and also to
discuss the psychological management.*

TASK FOR THE CANDIDATE
* *Discuss aetiological factors and psychological management of
  Anorexia Nervosa.*

**PAY PARTICULAR ATTENTION TO THE FOLLOWING (MENTAL
CHECKLIST)**
* *Convey aetiological factors of Anorexia Nervosa.*
* *Use bio-psycho social approach.*
* *Discuss psychological factors and need for autonomy versus
  pathological family dynamics (enmeshment)*
* *Establish the predisposing, perpetuating and maintaining factors.*
* *Discuss NICE recommendations for psychological therapy.*
* *Discuss biological and social interventions if required*

COMMUNICATION SKILLS
* *Establish rapport with the nurse.*
* *Adopt a collegiate approach.*

Suggested approach
Introduction
C: Hello, I'm Dr...I'm one of the psychiatrists. Thank you for seeing me today.
I've seen one of your patients Rachel, who has a diagnosis of Anorexia
Nervosa. I wanted to come and talk to you more about the reasons for her to
develop Anorexia Nervosa and also about the psychological or talking
therapies that are available.

**N: Hello Doctor. I wanted to find out more about why she could have
developed Anorexia Nervosa?**

C: Yes, I will try to explain. She has what we call Anorexia Nervosa.
It is an eating disorder as you know and it is difficult to pin point one
particular cause.

C: From the history she has given it appears she could have developed this
because of the following aetiological or causative factors:
I will use a biopsychosocial approach mentioning the predisposing,
precipitating and perpetuating factors (Elaborate further using the
information from the previous station)

EATING DISORDERS

Use the following as a guide to approach this:
Biological
- *Family history of eating disorder(Genetic)*
- *Viral illness as a child which required hospitalisation*

Psychological
- *Stressors-exams*
- *Low self esteem*
- *Personality type-perfectionist*
- *Family dynamics-enmeshment-difficulties in individuation and separating from family*
- *Difficulties in communicating needs and using starving as a means for attention*
- *Having a sense of control over their lives including eating*
- *Fear of growing up*

Social
- *Relationships- difficulties with family and heterosexual relationships*

N: Why has she developed this current episode?

C: The triggers from what she has told me appear to be the following stressors. [Use information given by patient in previous station]

N: I wanted to find out more about how we are going to treat her with the psychological therapies?

C: There are a few talking therapies recommended by the NICE guidelines (National institute of clinical excellence). They are CBT, Family therapy, Interpersonal psychotherapy, psychodynamic psychotherapy and cognitive analytical psychotherapy.

I will try to explain each of them in relation to symptom improvement in Anorexia Nervosa.

Cognitive behavioural therapy or CBT [use diagram to explain if necessary]
She will need an assessment for CBT It is a form of therapy which explores the way you think about yourself, the world and others, and how what you do impacts on your thoughts and feelings. In her situation, the therapist will able to further explore her distorted body image, self-esteem and her perfectionism which are contributing to her fear of fatness and weight gain. [Use the hot cross bun diagram to explain if necessary]

IPT or Interpersonal therapy
This form of therapy focuses on the past and present social roles and interpersonal interactions. This is a useful therapy to further identify important relationship difficulties that are linked to her eating disorder.

EATING DISORDERS

Family therapy
If family factors are considered to be important, then she would need an assessment for this. This type of talking therapy is commonly used with children or adolescents suffering from Anorexia Nervosa. It explores the ways in which family dynamics affects ones eating habits.

Psychodynamic psychotherapy
This is a long term therapy where the patient explores, early life experiences, especially those that have been traumatic, previous relationships, conflicts and difficulties in order to initiate change.

Summarise
Thank you for talking to me. Do you any other questions for me?
*I have some information leaflets for you. The website BEAT is useful and has some informative videos. The **Royal College of Psychiatrists** also have useful information leaflets on eating disorders and different types of psychotherapy I have mentioned. Their website address is* **www.rcpsych.ac.uk.**

Anorexia Nervosa-
Aetiological factors using a biological, psychological and social approach with predisposing, precipitating and perpetuating factors
Biological
- *Genetic/family*

Psychological
- *Relationships*
- *Low self esteem*
- *Personality type- Perfectionist*

Social
- *Family*
- *School*

Management
Psychological
- *CBT Cognitive behavioural therapy*
- *FT Family therapy*
- *Focused psychodynamic therapy*
- *IPT Interpersonal psychotherapy*
- *CAT Cognitive analytical therapy*

Summarize

©*Smartsesh*

EATING DISORDERS

6. REFEEDING SYNDROME

INSTRUCTION TO CANDIDATE
*You have been asked to see the community psychiatric nurse Alisha
Downs of a 16yr old girl Sarah who is known with a diagnosis of Anorexia
Nervosa. The nurse has come to see because girl has now become
physically unwell.*

TASK FOR THE CANDIDATE
- *Speak to a nurse about her concerns of young girl.*
- *Discuss with her the diagnosis and management plan.*

**PAY PARTICULAR ATTENTION TO THE FOLLOWING (MENTAL
CHECKLIST)**
- *Consider the possible differential diagnoses.*
- *Including-deterioration in physical complications in Anorexia
  Nervosa (hypokalaemia, renal failure).*
- *Possible infection.*
- *Refeeding syndrome.*
- *Establish the diagnosis of refeeding syndrome
  -By obtaining collateral history illustrating increased calorific
  intake.
  -By establishing the physical complications associated with
  refeeding syndrome.*
- *Convey the diagnosis, mechanism, symptoms and signs of
  refeeding syndrome.*
- *Convey the prognostic factors of increased mortality if left
  untreated.*
- *Explain the immediate medical management of refeeding
  syndrome.*
- *Explain the longer term bio-psychosocial and holistic approach.*

COMMUNICATION SKILLS
- *Start the interview by developing rapport and showing empathy.*
- *Tailor the information to level of fellow medical collegiate.*

Suggested approach
Introduction
C: Hello, I'm Dr...I'm one of the psychiatrists. I understand from the
information I have been given, that you have been recently been caring for
Sarah in the community and that you are now concerned
about her. It would be helpful if you could tell me more about your concerns?

**N: I am concerned about her as we have noticed a few physical
symptoms that have caused us some concerns. She has recently had
swelling of her lips and legs. Her GP did some blood tests last week that
indicated that her phosphate levels were low.**

EATING DISORDERS

Explore the History of Presenting Complaint
HOPC (onset, duration, progression and severity)
Establish any other physical symptoms (chest pain, breathing difficulties)

C: I would like to ask you some more questions about her diagnosis of Anorexia Nervosa and more about the treatment she has been receiving

Establish briefly past psychiatric history of eating disorder
C: Can you tell me for how long she has been diagnosed with Anorexia Nervosa?
- Has she been previously admitted to hospital?
- Do you know the reasons for her admission?
- What is her current BMI?

Establish current community management
- For how long have you been supporting her in the community? What is her current treatment plan? What are her meal plans?
- Have there been any changes in this?
- How much did she weigh last week? And how about this week? [Ask for her weight chart.]
- How much weight has she put on in a week? How many calories has she been having daily?

N: *So doc, what do you think is wrong with her?*

C: From what you have told me thus far and in view of her blood results it appears she has "Refeeding syndrome". Is it something you have come across before?

N: *No. Can you tell me more about it?*

C: Refeeding syndrome as the name suggests occurs if an individual is receiving too much food, too fast.

Refeeding syndrome can be seen in many conditions such as in malnourished patients, patients with cancer on enteral nutrition, gastrointestinal problems, patients suffering from alcoholism and also those suffering from Anorexia Nervosa.

It is a condition that is characterised by a variety of chemical imbalances that occur during the process of refeeding. This is why we need to monitor patients' levels of phosphate, magnesium and potassium closely, especially at the beginning of the treatment. It usually occurs within about 4 days of starting refeeding.

N: **What happens in Refeeding syndrome?**

C: When food is introduced into a body that has been starved, the body has to suddenly shift from fat metabolism to carbohydrate metabolism. This causes

EATING DISORDERS

a shift in the electrolyte and fluid balance. As a result it affects the salts in the body, like potassium, magnesium and phosphates, lowering they blood levels. It causes various serious symptoms.

N: What are the symptoms and signs of refeeding syndrome?

C: There are many signs and symptoms. Patients can suffer from constipation, abdominal pain, vomiting, diarrhoea, twitching, and generalised fatigue. They develop oedema, of their hands, feet, and ankles. They can also suffer from rhabdomyolysis, immunosuppression, hypotension, arrhythmia, and respiratory and cardiac failure. More seriously they can have severe seizures and enter into a coma.

N: What is the management of refeeding syndrome?

C: Refeeding syndrome is considered a serious complication of Anorexia Nervosa.

I will need to arrange to see her and examine her.

*If it proves to be refeeding syndrome then we will need to liaise with the physician. We need for her to come to hospital to be admitted to the **medical ward** for further management and treatment.*

We will have to do a full nutritional assessment (weight, rate of weight loss, dietary intake), and clinical examination:
We will also have to monitor her vitals like Heart rate, BP, RR, level of consciousness, temperature, ECG, cardiac monitoring if necessary

The initial management of refeeding syndrome:
-identification and treatment of any sepsis
-if necessary, carefully restore circulatory volume, monitor her fluid balance, and rehydrate her if she is dehydrated.
-correct electrolyte abnormalities
-correct hypoglycaemia
-manage hypothermia if necessary
-correct and prevent micronutrient deficiencies by administering Thiamine, and Vitamin B strong compound
-her bloods will be done regularly to check electrolyte imbalance
-when stable, feeding can be started with close monitoring

N: What is the prognosis of refeeding syndrome?

C: From the evidence that is available, we know that if it is not recognised early and treated, it can be fatal and can unfortunately lead to death.

Summarise
Thank you for discussing this case with me. To summarise, you have been supporting Sarah in the community. She is known with a diagnosis of

EATING DISORDERS

Anorexia Nervosa. She has been on a meal plan which has recently increased in calories. You have now noticed her to be having some physical symptoms of swelling of her gums and oedema of her legs. Her bloods are also showing some abnormalities.

I think she needs further medical investigations and treatment. We can discuss this further.

POSSIBLE VARIATIONS OF THEME
1. 17 yr. old lady Anorexia Nervosa in the medical ward with complication of refeeding syndrome. Now refusing to eat.
2. 26 yr old lady with Anorexia Nervosa with cardiac complications of Refeeding syndrome.

EATING DISORDERS

INSTRUCTIONS TO THE CANDIDATE
You are about to see a 21 yr. old lady who has a known history of Bulimia Nervosa.

TASK FOR THE CANDIDATE
- Obtain an eating disorder history with a view of eliciting bulimic prognostic factors.

PAY PARTICULAR ATTENTION TO THE FOLLOWING (MENTAL CHECKLIST)
- Consider possibility of bulimia nervosa, and anorexia –bulimia and bulimia nervosa complicated by borderline personality disorder.
- Obtain an eating disorder history in a patient with Bulimia Nervosa.
- Establish the prognostic factors.
- Establish the onset and progression of Bulimia Nervosa.
- Establish the bulimic type.
- Establish any underlying co-morbidity.
- Establish the psychological symptoms associated with prognostic factors.

COMMUNICATION SKILLS
- Develop rapport and show empathy.
- Anticipate denial and reluctance to discuss eating difficulties.
- Show sensitivity.
- Enquire about eating pattern to latter part of the interview.

Suggested approach
Introduction
C: Hello, I'm Dr ....I'm one of the psychiatrists. Thank you for coming to see me. I understand that your GP has referred you as you have been experiencing some eating difficulties.

P: Can I ask you about your weight?

C: Have you had any concerns about your weight?
- What measures have you taken to control your weight?
- What have the results been?
- Have there been fluctuations in weight? (Yo-yo effect)
- Has there been any time when you were underweight? (Enquire for past history of anorexia nervosa)
- Can you tell me what has been your highest and lowest weight? Can you tell me what your height is?
- What do you think your ideal weight should be?

EATING DISORDERS

A. History of Presenting Complaint (HOPC) (onset, duration, progression and severity)
Establishing BMI and eating habit:
1. Typical day
- *Can you take me through a typical day of what you would eat?(typical day)*
- *For example, what do you have in the morning? Do you have any snack before lunch? What do you have for lunch? What would you have for dinner?*

2. Behaviours to counteract fattening effects of food

a) Establish if there are any bingeing episodes
- *Do you sometimes lose control of eating?(binge)*
- *Can you describe a typical instance when you were overeating(bingeing episode)*
- *At what time does this happen?*
- *Can you describe a typical binge? What usually triggers this?*
- *After overeating how does it make you feel?(uncomfortable)*
- *May I ask do you ever make yourself sick? If so, how often?(purging)*
- *How do you make yourself sick?*

b) Compensatory behaviours
- *Have you been on a diet for a while?*
- *Have you been exercising? How often do you exercise?(exercising)*
- *Have you been skipping meals or sometimes starving yourself? Do you avoid certain foods? (starving and abstaining)*
- *Have you been taking water pills or laxatives?(diuretics)*

5. Preoccupation with food
- *Do you feel that you keep thinking about food?*
- *Do you enjoy cooking?*

6. Body image distortion [cross reference to history on anorexia nervosa]
- *What do you feel about your body?(body image perception)*
- *How often do you look in the mirror? What do you see when you look in the mirror?*
- *Do you measure yourself? How often?*
- *How do you feel if you gain weight?*

7. Endocrine disorder involving the hypothalamic pituitary-gonadal axis
- *I need to ask you a personal question, can you tell me about your periods. Have they been affected at all? (amenorrhoea)*

8. Establish any physical complications
- *Have you had any physical health problems?*
- *Have you been admitted to hospital before?*
- *Have you fainted or dizzy? (fatigue)*

EATING DISORDERS

- *Have you felt very tired?(symptomatic of hypokalaemia)*
- *Are you sensitive to cold weather?(sensitivity to cold)*
- *Do you suffer from constipation?(constipation)*
- *Have you recently had any fractures? (fractures)*
- *Ask to look at knuckles (Russell's sign)*
- *Examine the teeth for dental caries and erosions of the enamel?*

B. Aetiological factors
Use biopsychosocial approach to elicit possible aetiological factors
1. Biological
- *Is there anyone in your family who has an eating difficulties*
- *Is there anyone in the family who is overweight?*

2. Psychological
- *What type of person would your family describe you as?*
- *Would you say you're a perfectionist? (associated with Obsessive, Borderline and Anxious personality traits)*

3. Social
- *Have you ever been teased about your weight?*

C. Exclude Co-morbidity -Depression, Anxiety and OCD
Elicit core features of Depression
- *Sometimes our eating habits can also affect the way we feel. Can you tell me how has your mood been? (mood)*
- *How are your energy levels? (energy)*
- *Have you lost interest in things you usually would enjoy doing? What are they? (anhedonia)*

Screen for Anxiety and OCD symptoms

D. Risk assessment
Self-harm/DSH
- *I need to ask you some personal questions about how you see the future? What do you feel about your future?*
- *Have you ever felt that life was not worth living?*
- *Have you tried to harm yourself such as cutting yourself?*
- *Have you had thoughts of wanting to end it all? Have you acted on these?(suicidal thoughts)*
- *Have you ever taken an overdose?*
- *Starving(include as part of risk assessment)*

Drug and alcohol history
- *How do you usually cope? Some people take drink and take street drugs. How about you?*

In obtaining the history as above, focus on eliciting the following Bulimic prognostic factors:
Age of onset

EATING DISORDERS

Bulimic type -purging or non-purging type
Anorexia -Bulimia
Presence of the following psychological factors
- *Self-esteem*
- *Confidence*
- *Co-morbidity - Compulsive behaviour, shoplifting, personality disorder, Depressive symptoms*

Past psychiatric history
Family history of eating disorders
Medical History
Medication

Summarise
Thank you for talking to me. To summarise what you have been fearful of gaining weight from an early age. This has resulted in you having bingeing episodes, and you have cravings for certain foods. As a result you have been using other means of preventing weight gain. You have also been feeling depressed recently.

I have some more information and leaflets which you might find useful. There is also a useful website called BEAT which has some informative videos.

NICE guidelines
Bulimia Nervosa
➢ *Evidence-based self-help programme is first line for Bulimia; as additional option or alternative choice antidepressants can be used in Bulimia.*
➢ *Antidepressant drugs can reduce frequency of binge eating and purging, but long-term effects are unknown.*
➢ *Any beneficial effects of antidepressants will be rapidly apparent.*
➢ *SSRIs (especially fluoxetine) are drugs of first choice for Bulimia Nervosa; effective dose of fluoxetine is higher than for Depression (60 mg daily).*
➢ *Specifically adapted cognitive behavioural therapy should be offered to adults with Bulimia Nervosa, 16-20 sessions over 4-5 months.*
➢ *Interpersonal psychotherapy should be considered as alternative to cognitive behavioural therapy, but patients should be informed it takes 8-12 months to achieve similar results.*

EATING DISORDERS

Diagnostic Criteria for Bulimia Nervosa F 50.2
(Adapted from ICD-10)
(a) The constant obsession with eating and the overwhelming desire for food leads to episodes of eating large amounts of food in short time periods.
(b) There are efforts made to reduce the effect of eating foods perceived as fattening in the form of self-induced vomiting and other purging techniques, alternating episodes of calorie restriction, using appetite suppressants, thyroid preparations or diuretics. People with diabetes may refrain from using their insulin treatment.
(c) There is an intense fear of becoming fat, which leads to the desire to reach a specific body weight much lower than is considered normal or healthy for height and age. In many cases, the bulimia follows an episode of anorexia nervosa, although the period of time between the two disorders may vary considerably.
ICD-10 also includes 'atypical' <u>bulimia nervosa</u>, which refers to individuals who show some, but not all, of the characteristics of bulimia nervosa.

EATING DISORDERS

References

British Medical Association and Royal Pharmaceutical society (2011), British National Formulary 62, 62nd edn. Great Britain: British Medical Journal Publishing Group and Pharmaceutical Press

Gelder, M.G, Cowen, P. and Harrison P.J (2006) Shorter Oxford textbook of psychiatry. 5th edn. Oxford: Oxford University Press.

Nicholls, D and Jaffa, T (2001) Selective eating and other atypical problems. Cambridge university press

Sims, A. C. P. (2003) Symptoms in the mind: an introduction to descriptive psychopathology. 3rd edn. Great Britain: Saunders.

Taylor, D., Paton, C., Kapur, S. (2009) The South London and Maudsley NHS Foundation Trust & Oxleas NHS Foundation Trust prescribing guidelines. 10th edn. London: Informa Healthcare.

WHO. (1992)The ICD 10 classification of mental and behavioural disorders: clinical descriptions and diagnostic guideline. 10th revision : Geneva; WHO

Journal articles
Luck A.J., Morgan J.F., Reid F. et al. (2002) The SCOFF questionnaire and clinical interview for eating disorders in general practice: comparative study. BMJ, 325, 755-756.

Russell, GFM 91979) Bulimia nervosa: an ominous variant of anorexia nervosa

Ratnasuriya et al Anorexia Nervosa Outcome and prognostic factors: 20 years, 1991 Psych

Agras, W. S., Walsh, B.T., Fairburn, C. G., et al (2000) A multicentre comparison of cognitive-behavioural therapy and interpersonal psychotherapy for bulimia nervosa. Archives of General Psychiatry, 57, 459-466.

Online resources
Royal college of psychiatrist's health information leaflets for patient's
www.rcpsych.ac.uk
www.beat.co.uk

Support groups and organisations
Beat

EATING DISORDERS

It is an organisation that campaigns, that challenges the stigma faced by people with eating disorders and that gives people the help and support they need.
www.beat.co.uk

Suggested reading
Anorexia nervosa: hope for recovery Lucy Morley, 2011.05
Breaking Free From Anorexia Nervosa: A Survival Guide for Families. Friends and Sufferers by Janet Treasure (1997) I
Getting Better Bit (e) by Bit (e) by Ulrike Schmidt and Janet Treasure (1993)
Skills-based Learning for Caring for a Loved One with an Eating Disorder: The New Maudsley Method by Janet Treasure, Gráinne Smith & Anna Crane
Anorexia Nervosa: A Survival Guide for Families, Friends and Sufferers by Janet Treasure (1997)
(Last updated: January 2011)

PERINATAL PSYCHIATRY

PERINATAL PSYCHIATRY- Dr Theresa Xeurub.
    Dr M S Thambirajah

1. Puerperal illness-Postnatal Depression

2. Puerperal illness-Postnatal Depression

3. Puerperal illness –Post Partum Psychosis

PERINATAL PSYCHIATRY

1. POSTNATAL DEPRESSION

INSTRUCTIONS TO CANDIDATE
You are about to see Sarah Brown who is, a 25 year old lady who is 6 weeks postpartum. She is crying and appears to be depressed. Her husband has brought her to the accident and emergency department due to concerns of her wanting to harm their baby. Assess her mental state.

TASK FOR THE CANDIDATE
- Elicit history and mental state examination.

PAY PARTICULAR ATTENTION TO THE FOLLOWING (MENTAL CHECKLIST):
- Differentiate between postnatal Depression and puerperal Psychosis.
- Identify risk factors in the prenatal, perinatal and postpartum period.
- Conduct a risk assessment –suicide and infanticide.
- Convey to the patient that it is a serious condition and a high risk situation.
- Establish her insight and the need to come into hospital.

COMMUNICATION SKILLS
- Start the interview by developing rapport and showing empathy.
- Show understanding and sensitivity for her distress.
- Allow time for her to ventilate her feelings.
- Seek to understand the subjective feeling of the individual.

Suggested approach
Introduction
C: Hello, I'm Dr ...I'm one of the psychiatrists. I understand you were brought into hospital by your husband as he had some concerns. I know that this might be difficult for you, but can you tell me what happened that you came to hospital?

P: *'Patient could be tearful and appears distressed.'*

A. History of Presenting Complaint (HOPC) (onset, duration, progression, severity)

C: I can clearly see that this is upsetting you; can you tell me when did this all start?
- Can you tell me about your baby?
- What is your baby's name?

For subsequent questions, personalise the interview by using her baby's name

PERINATAL PSYCHIATRY

A. Explore for risk factors for postnatal Depression/Postpartum Psychosis
This should include factors in the prenatal, perinatal and postnatal period
a) Pregnancy
- Can you tell me more about your pregnancy? Was it a normal delivery? Did you have any complications?

b) Parity
- Is this your first pregnancy or do you have other children?

c) Past psychiatric history
- Have you seen a psychiatrist in the past?
- Are you presently on any medication?

d) Past family history
- Is there any family history of Depression or bipolar disorder?

e) Partners support
- Are you able to talk to the baby's father about your difficulties?
- What level of support are you receiving from the baby's father? Is it sufficient to your needs?

f) Baby bonding
- I would like to ask you more about your baby?
- Please tell me about your baby? Is it a boy or a girl?
- What is his/her name? Can you tell me what your baby is like?
- How do you feel about your baby?
- How is [baby's name] sleeping?
- How do you feel if baby cries?
- How have you been managing to take care of your baby, for example bathing, changing nappies and feeding?

B. Mental state examination
Assess for depressive symptoms
- How have you been feeling in yourself? (mood)
- How have your energy levels been? (energy)
- Is there anything you enjoy doing recently? (anhedonia)
- How have you been sleeping? (biological symptoms)
- What has your appetite been like?
- Are their things that you feel guilty about? Do you have any guilt feelings? (guilt feelings)
- How do you see the future? (suicidal ideation)

Screen for psychotic symptoms [Introduce the subject gently]
Use clustering approach to elicit psychotic symptoms
- I need to ask you some routine questions that we ask everybody?

PERINATAL PSYCHIATRY

Auditory hallucinations
- *Have you had any strange experiences which you could not explain?*
- *Do you ever seem to hear voices or noises when there is no one else around? (auditory or visual hallucinations)*
- *What do they say? How many voices do you hear?*
- *Do you hear your name being called out?*
- *Do they speak directly to you? (second person auditory hallucination)*
- *Do they seem to comment on what you are thinking or doing? (running commentary)*
- *Do they discuss you? Do they argue among themselves? (third person auditory hallucination)*
- *Do they command you or give you orders? (Command hallucination) Do you obey these orders?*
- *I know this must be distressing for you, but can you tell me where do these voices come from?*
- *Where do you hear them?*
- *Are these voices in your mind or can you hear them through your ears*
- *How clear is the voice? Is it as clear as I am talking to you?*
- *Why do you think it says that?*

Assess degree of conviction
- *Do you think there could be another explanation? (degree of conviction)*
- *How convinced are you of this?*
- *Have you told your friends and relatives? What was their reaction?*
- *Do you have any other strange experiences?*

Visual hallucinations
- *Do you see things that other people couldn't see?*
- *Can you describe what you see? How clear is it?*
- *How do you explain that?*

Gustatory/Olfactory
- *Have you noticed any strange tastes or smells recently?*

Tactile
- *Do you have any strange feelings on your skin?*

Delusions
Persecutory/paranoid
- *Do you think there is anyone out to harm you or your baby?*
- *Do you think that someone is spying on you?*

PERINATAL PSYCHIATRY

Establish if she has any concerns for baby, this could form part of her delusional beliefs
- Sometimes some women tell me they have strange thoughts about their baby. They might be concerned about their baby's health? Are there things about [baby's name] that you are concerned about?
- Have you taken him to see the GP?
- What do you think could be wrong?
- Do you think that there is anything wrong with your baby?
- Can you tell me more about it?

Grandiose
- How do you compare yourself to others?

Guilt
- Do you feel guilty?

Nihilistic
- Do you think that there is something terrible that will happen to you or your baby?

Degree of conviction
- How do know this?
- Do you think there could there be another explanation?
- Do you think that maybe your mind maybe playing tricks on you?
- How convinced are you of this?
- Have you told your friends and family? What was their reaction?

Thought Alienation
- Do you feel like there is interference in your thinking?

Thought insertion, withdrawal, broadcast
- Do you think someone in putting thoughts into your head?
- Do you think that someone is taking thoughts out?
- Do you feel your thoughts are being broadcast to others?
- How do you explain that?
- How do you know that?

Passivity phenomena
- Do you feel that someone is controlling the way you think, feel and controlling your action? (Made volition)

C Risk assessment
C: I need to ask you some sensitive questions about how you are feeling about the future?

Risk to self
- What do you think about the future? Have you felt that things have become hopeless?

- *How do you feel as a mother? Do you feel useless or worthless as a mother?*
- *Do you sometimes feel that life is not worth living?*
- *Do you sometimes wish that you could go to sleep and not wake up?*
- *Have you had thoughts of harming yourself? What are your plans?*
- *How close have you come to this?*
- *Have you harmed yourself in the past?*

Risk to baby-infanticide
Sometimes mothers tell me they have worrying thoughts about their baby. Do you have similar thoughts towards your baby?
- *Have you had thoughts about harming your baby?*
- *Tell me more about it. I know it is hard to talk about these matters.*
- *How close have you come to harming him? What have stopped you from doing anything?*

Insight
Can I ask you; having experienced the difficulties that you mentioned, what do you feel your experiences were due to?
What do you think may be the matter with you?
What does your husband and others think?

Summarise
Thank you for talking to me. It appears that you are depressed and you have been experiencing some worrying thoughts. I am concerned that it appears you are ill and are not coping with the birth of your little one. I would like you to stay in hospital where you can take some rest and be treated for the difficulties that you have mentioned.
We do have a mother and baby unit facility unit to ensure that you will not be separated from your baby.

Thank you

POSSIBLE VARIATIONS OF THEME
1.Postnatal Depression with psychotic symptoms- mother is concerned her baby has leukaemia.
2.Postnatal Depression with suicidal risk or infanticide. Mother is 9 months postpartum and 6 weeks pregnant.

PERINATAL PSYCHIATRY

PUERPERAL ILLNESS

History of Presenting Complaint (HOPC) (onset, duration, progression, severity)

Explore for risk factors for postnatal Depression and puerperal Psychosis

- *Pregnancy-complications, delivery*
- *Parity-pervious pregnancies, miscarriages*
- *Past psychiatric history-Depression, Bipolar Affective Disorder(BPAD)*
- *Past family history-increased risk if family history of Depression, BPAD*
- *Partners support and family support*

Establish baby bonding

- *Establish relationship with baby*
- *Coping with newborn*
- *Establish if any concerns for baby*

Mental state examination

- *Assess for depressive symptoms*
- *Use clustering approach to elicit psychotic symptoms*
- *Hallucinations-auditory, visual, gustatory, tactile, olfactory*
- *Delusions-Persecutory/paranoid/Grandiose/guilt/nihilistic*
- *Assess Degree of conviction if delusional*
- *Thought Alienation-Thought insertion, withdrawal, broadcast*
- *Passivity phenomena*

Risk assessment- to self and baby-infanticide

Assess insight and need for admission

Summarise

©*Smartsesh*

PERINATAL PSYCHIATRY

INSTRUCTIONS TO CANDIDATE
You have been asked to speak to the husband David of the lady Sarah Brown whom you assessed in the previous station. Address his concerns and explain further management.

▰▰▰▰▰▰▰▰▰▰▰▰▰▰▰▰▰▰▰▰▰▰▰▰▰▰▰▰▰▰▰▰

TASK FOR THE CANDIDATE
- *Discuss her management with her husband.*

PAY PARTICULAR ATTENTION TO THE FOLLOWING (MENTAL CHECKLIST)
- *Explain her Diagnosis of Postnatal Depression.*
- *Convey to him that it is a serious condition.*
- *Highlight the risks to wife and baby.*
- *Convey that due to risks inpatient treatment is necessary.*
- *Establish safeguarding issues-social services involvement*
- *Establish need for carers' assessment.*
- *Highlight the prognosis and preventative measures for future pregnancies.*

COMMUNICATION SKILLS
- *Start the interview by showing empathy and developing rapport.*
- *Show sensitivity and acknowledge his distress and concern for his partner and baby.*
- *This should be a discussion and not a monologue.*

Suggested approach
C: Hello, I'm Dr ...I'm one of the psychiatrists. I have seen your partner. I know this is a difficult time for you and you are concerned about your wife and baby. I would like to tell you more about her diagnosis and how we are going to treat her. Before we begin, can you tell me what happened?

H: I was worried about her as she has not been the same since our baby was born.

C: I can see this is upsetting for you. I have spoken to her and it appears that she is quite ill. I would like to discuss this further with you.

H: What is her diagnosis?

C: Your wife seems to have what we call **Postnatal Depression (PND)**. It is when mothers feel depressed after the birth of their baby. It occurs most commonly in the first 4 months post-partum and can continue for months and years if left untreated. Mothers usually feel they can't cope with the birth of their little one and can feel guilty.

H: How common is it?

C: It is something which occurs reasonably commonly; about 1 in 8 mothers seem to experience it.

H: What are the causes?

C: It is difficult to pinpoint one particular cause in your wife case. It is usually due to a number of associated factors working together. It can be triggered by stress, lack of sleep, and complications at the time of delivery. Someone who has had a history of Postnatal Depression would also be more vulnerable, and also if there is poor social support.

H: What are the symptoms of postnatal Depression PND?

C: The symptoms are like any other Depression. Women start to feel tearful, anxious, unhappy and useless. They can be irritable, tired and have difficulty sleeping. They can lose their appetite. They will not be able to enjoy things they would usually do, and have decreased interest in sex. They believe they are not good mothers. They can also neglect their child.

H: Will she harm our baby?

C: This is sometimes a concern. When a mother is depressed, it is possible to have such thoughts. In your wife's case, she has told me that she has no intention now of wanting to harm your baby.
We need to bear in mind that if this does occur, that is usually a part of the illness that is causing this. We therefore hope with treatment that she will become better and less likely to have these thoughts. We will also ensure that we take the necessary precautions on this ward to monitor this and ensure hers and your baby's safety.

Management
Setting
C: We would like to admit her to the mother and baby unit facility and the nursing staff would be able to closely monitor her and your baby. I have not asked her yet whether she would stay in hospital voluntarily.

What do you think?

H: I only want what is best for her and my baby.

C: At present we feel the risks are high and that to ensure her safety and that of your baby; she will need to stay in hospital.

H: What is the treatment available for her?

PERINATAL PSYCHIATRY

C: The good news is that Postnatal Depression is eminently treatable. The treatment options available are a combination of medication, psychological or talking therapies and in addition the family will need lots of support

H: What medication will you give her?

C: The group of medication we use are antidepressants. We usually have to weigh the risk and benefits of prescribing this medication if she is breastfeeding. We will consider using an alternative medication which has a lesser chance of passing through the breast milk.

Psychological interventions
Later on, when she is a more settled, we can look at the talking treatments like counselling and cognitive behavioural therapy. This usually looks at how a person's thinking and behaviour could be making someone depressed.

Psychoeducation
We have found that it is helpful if family members learn more about the condition, its complications and treatment. Your understanding of her illness as well as being available and listening can promote her engagement with her treatment plan. This will also be vital to ensure good recovery and to ensure her wellbeing.

Social interventions
I am not sure how much family support you have in terms of grandparents and friends. Because we know how difficult this must be and its impact on you and the family, with the support of our specialist mother and baby team, we can provide more support, and advice on issues relating to taking care of your baby.

Later on, the health visitor can help with advice on breastfeeding, contraception and family planning. [If there are other children in the family... child care for them would be important.]

Other advice we give is to eat a balanced healthy diet, ensure she takes sufficient rest, exercise and to allow for support and love provided by the people close to her.

H: What will happen if it is not treated?

C: Untreated it can last for years especially when the illness is severe. Some women get better without treatment when the illness is mild. Not treating can affect the bonding with your baby, and can put a strain on the relationship. There is also the risk to the child and mother to consider

H: What are the chances of this happening in future pregnancies?

PERINATAL PSYCHIATRY

C: From the evidence we have available it is known that if someone gets Postnatal Depression, then there is a 20-40% chance of having another episode in the next pregnancy.

Summarise
Thank you for talking to me. From what we have discussed I have told you more about your wife's condition, Postnatal Depression and how we will be treating her. Please feel free to contact me to discuss this further.

Support groups and websites
There are also some useful websites and support groups available such as national childbirth trust (NCT) and support group like Meet A Mum Association (MAMA) for mothers suffering from Postnatal Depression.

POSTNATAL DEPRESSION

Depression after birth of baby

Epidemiology occurs in 1/8 women

Aetiology
- Risk factors-parity, pregnancy complications, past psychiatric history, family history, poor social support

Prognosis – 1 previous episode is 20-40%

Management –Biopsychosocial or Holistic approach
- **Immediate and short term**
- **Setting :**
- **consider inpatient or community support**
- **if admission :**
- **Informal admission or use of Mental Health Act(MHA 1983)**
- **Specialist perinatal services –mother and baby unit**

Biological interventions:
- Screening Scales- EPNS(Edinburgh postnatal Depression scale)
- Antidepressants-weigh risk and benefits-Sertraline- not secreted in breast milk
- ECT indicated in severe cases

Psychological interventions:
- Psycho education
- Counselling
- CBT
- Guided imagery

Social interventions :
- Support to family
- Reassurance
- Advice on mothering, bonding
- Longer term management
- Support with perinatal services
- Support with future pregnancies

Information and leaflets

Support groups NCT, Meet a mum association (MAMA)

Websites www.nct

©Smartsesh

POST PARTUM BLUES

After the baby is born, many new mothers have the "postpartum blues" or the "baby blues. Mothers feel more irritable, cries more easily, feels sad and feels confused

The postpartum blues peak three to five days after delivery. They usually end by the tenth day after the baby's birth. Although the postpartum blues are not pleasant, the woman can function normally. The feeling of the "blues" usually lessens and goes away over time

©Smartsesh

PERINATAL PSYCHIATRY

3. POST PARTUM PSYCHOSIS

Suggested approach
Introduction
C: Hello, I'm Dr ...I'm one of the psychiatrists. I understand you were
brought into hospital by your husband as he had some concerns about you.
Can you tell me more about this?

P: She could be distracted and responding to internal stimuli
For example saying 'Sam, go away...'

**A. History of Presenting Complaint (HOPC) (onset, duration, progression,
severity)**
C: I can clearly see that this is upsetting you; can you tell me when this all
started?
- Can you tell me about your baby?
- What is your baby's name?

**For subsequent questions, personalise the interview by using her baby's
name.**

**B. Explore for risk factors for Postnatal Depression/Post-Partum
Psychosis**
**This should include factors in the prenatal, perinatal and postnatal
period**
1. Pregnancy
- Can you tell me more about your pregnancy? Did you have any
complications?

PERINATAL PSYCHIATRY

2. Parity
- Is this your first pregnancy?

3. Past psychiatric history
- Have you seen a psychiatrist in the past?
- Are you on any medication?

4. Past family history
- Is there anyone in the family that had anything similar? Is there any history of Depression or Bipolar Disorder?

5. Partners support
- Are you able to talk about the babies' father?

6. Baby bonding
I would like to ask you more about your baby?
- Can you tell me what your baby is like?
- How do you feel about your baby?
- How have you been coping?
- How does baby sleep?
- How do you feel if baby cries?
- How have you been managing to take care of your baby for example, bathing, changing nappies and feeding your baby?

C. Mental state examination
1. Assess for depressive symptoms
- How have you been feeling in yourself?(mood)
- How have your energy levels been?(energy)
- Is there anything you enjoy doing recently?(anhedonia)
- How have you been sleeping?(biological symptoms)
- How have you been eating?
- Do you have any guilt feelings?(guilt feelings)
- How do you see the future?(suicidal ideation)

2. Screen for psychotic symptoms
Use clustering approach to elicit psychotic symptoms
- I need to ask you some routine questions that we ask everybody?

a) Auditory hallucinations
- Have you had any strange experiences which you could not explain?
- Do you ever seem to hear voices or noises when there is no one else around?
- What do they say? How many voices do you hear?
- Do you hear your name being called out? (second person auditory hallucination)
- Do they speak directly to you?
- Do they seem to comment on what you are thinking or doing? (running commentary)

- *Do they discuss you? (third person auditory hallucination)*
- *Do they argue among themselves?*
- *Do they command you or give you orders? (Command hallucinations). Do you obey these orders?*
- *Where do these voices come from? Where do you hear them?*
- *Are these voices in your mind or can you hear them through your ears?*
- *How clear is the voice? Is it as clear as I am talking to you?*
- *Why do you think it says that?*

Establish degree of conviction
- *Do you think there could be another explanation?*
- *How convinced are you of this?*
- *Have you told your friends and relatives? What was their reaction?*
- *Do you have any other strange experiences?*

b) Visual hallucinations
- *Do you see things that other people couldn't see?*
- *Can you describe what you see?*
- *How clear is it?*
- *How do you explain that?*

c) Gustatory/Olfactory
- *Have you noticed any strange tastes or smells recently?*

d) Tactile
- *Do you have any strange feelings on your skin?*

Delusions
Persecutory/paranoid
- *Do you think there is anyone out to harm you or your baby?*
- *Do you think that someone is spying on you?*

Establish if she has any concerns for baby, this could form part of her delusional beliefs
- *Sometimes some women tell me they have strange thoughts about their baby. They might be concerned about their baby's health? Are you concerned about your baby at all? Have you taken him to see the GP?*
- *What do you think could be wrong?*
- *This is a sensitive question but do you think that something may be wrong with the baby?*
- *Do you think that there is anything abnormal with your baby?*
- *Sometimes some mothers feel that the baby is evil, or be possessed? Is this a possibility?*

Grandiose
- *How do you compare yourself to others?*

Guilt
- Do you sometimes feel guilty about anything?

Nihilistic
- Do you think that there is something terrible that will happen to you or your baby?

Degree of conviction
- How sure are you about this? How do you do knows this?
- Do you think there could there be another explanation?
- Do you think that maybe your mind maybe playing tricks on you?
- How convinced are you of this?
- Have you told your friends and family? What was their reaction?

Thought Alienation
- Do you feel like there is interference in your thinking?

Thought insertion, withdrawal, broadcast
- Do you think someone in putting thoughts into your head?
- Do you think that someone is about taking thoughts out?
- Do you feel your thoughts are being broadcast to others?
- How do you explain that?
- How do you know that?

Passivity phenomena
- Do you feel that someone is controlling the way you think, feel and controlling your action?(Made volition)

D Risk assessment
Risk to self
I need to ask you some sensitive questions about how you are feeling about the future?
- What do you think about the future? Have you felt that things have become hopeless?
- How do you feel as a mother? Do you feel useless or worthless as a mother?
- Do you sometimes feel that life is not worth living?
- Do you sometimes wish that you could go to sleep and not wake up?
- Have you had thoughts of harming yourself? What are your plans?
- How close have you come to this?
- Have you harmed yourself in the past?

Risk to baby - infanticide
Sometimes mothers tell me they have worrying thoughts about their baby. Do you have similar thoughts towards your baby?
- Do you think that baby was better off not being alive?
- Have you had thoughts about harming your baby?
- What plans do you have, and how close have you come to it?
- What would stop you from doing anything?

PERINATAL PSYCHIATRY

Insight
Can I ask you; having experienced the difficulties that you mentioned, what do you feel your experiences were due to?
What do you think may be the matter with you?
What does your husband and others think?

Summarise
Thank you for talking to me. I am concerned that it appears you might not be coping with the birth of your little one and clearly you are very distressed with the various experiences and thoughts you have been having.
I would like you to come into hospital, preferably to a mother and baby unit where you can receive the treatment that you need as well as remaining with your child.
Thank you

POSSIBLE VARIATIONS OF THEME
1. Puerperal Psychosis-risk of infanticide due to delusional belief that baby is possessed and is a demon.
2. Puerperal Psychosis- presentation in a mother with history of BPAD.
3. Puerperal Psychosis- presentation in a mother with schizoaffective disorder.

PERINATAL PSYCHIATRY

PUERPERAL PSYCHOSIS
HOPC (onset , duration, progression, severity)
Explore for risk factors for postnatal Depression/post-partum
Psychosis
- *Pregnancy-complications, delivery*
- *Parity-pervious pregnancies, miscarriages*
- *Past psychiatric history-Depression, bipolar affective disorder*
- *Past family history-increased risk if family history of Depression, BPAD*
- *Partners support and family support*

Baby bonding
- **Establish relationship with baby**
- **Coping with new-borns**
- **Establish if any concerns for baby**

Mental state examination
- *Assess for depressive symptoms*
- *Use clustering approach to elicit psychotic symptoms*
- *Hallucinations-auditory, visual, gustatory, tactile, olfactory*
- *Delusions-Persecutory/paranoid/Grandiose/guilt/nihilistic*
- *Assess Degree of conviction-delusional beliefs*
- *Thought Alienation-Thought insertion, withdrawal, broadcast*
- *Passivity phenomena*

Risk assessment-self and baby –infanticide
Assess insight and need for admission
Summarise
©Smartsesh

PERINATAL PSYCHIATRY

4. POST PARTUM PSYCHOSIS

INSTRUCTIONS TO CANDIDATE
You have seen this lady in the previous station. Her husband Michael Crockett is concerned about her and wants to speak to you.

TASK FOR THE CANDIDATE
- Discuss her management with her husband.

PAY PARTICULAR ATTENTION TO THE FOLLOWING (MENTAL CHECKLIST)
- Explain Diagnosis of Puerperal Psychosis.
- Highlight the risks to his wife and baby.
- Advise admission to mother and baby unit.
- Safeguarding issues-social services involvement
- Assess need for carer's assessment.
- Prognosis and preventative measures for future pregnancies.

COMMUNICATION SKILLS
- Start the interview by showing empathy and developing rapport.
- Show sensitivity and acknowledge his distress and concern for his partner and baby.

Suggested approach
Introduction
C: Hello, I'm Dr ...I'm one of the psychiatrists. I know this must be a difficult time for you. I have seen your wife and I would like to tell you more about her diagnosis and how we are going to treat her? Before we begin, can you tell me what your concerns were?

H: Hello Doctor. I was very worried. She has not been the same since our baby was born. What do you think is wrong with her?

C: I know you must be concerned about your wife and baby. Sometimes when women give birth, they can present with losing touch of reality and start to believe things that are not real. This seems to be the case with your wife. She shows .... [Elaborate on the findings]
We call this **Puerperal Psychosis.** It usually occurs within the first 2 weeks post-delivery.
As part of this illness she has also developed a fixed belief, that your baby is possessed. She is convinced that this is the case and we call this a delusion. I can assure you that it is the illness making her think like this. Unfortunately in her mind this is very real despite no evidence for this.

H: How common is it?

C: This usually occurs in about 1 in 1000 women post-delivery.

H: What are the causes?

PERINATAL PSYCHIATRY

C: It is difficult to pinpoint one particular cause and as to reasons why your wife has developed this. It can be attributed to a number of associated factors working together. It can be triggered by stress, complications at time of delivery. Someone who has a history of Postnatal Depression, Bipolar Affective Disorder or Schizoaffective Disorder would be more vulnerable, and also if there is poor social support. And obviously the birth of the baby is a risk factor as most probably she would not have become unwell otherwise.

H: What are the symptoms of Postpartum/Puerperal Psychosis?

C: The symptoms are like any other Psychosis with those strong beliefs called delusions and sometimes they can hear voices when there is no one else around and we call this a hallucination. They might also behave in a bizarre way, be excitable, unpredictable, and have mood swings.

H: Will she harm our baby?

C: This is a concern if a mother is unwell, however we need to bear in mind that she doesn't mean to have these thoughts. It is the illness causing this. We therefore hope with treatment that she will become better and less likely to have these thoughts. We will also ensure that we take the necessary precautions on the ward to monitor this.

H: How are you going to treat her?

C: Due to the seriousness of the condition and the risks that she is presenting with, and to ensure hers and your baby's safety, I think it is in her best interest for her to be in hospital. She will need to be admitted into a specialist mother and baby unit. There she will be monitored closely and we will take precautions to keep her and your baby safe.
I have not discussed this with her, and hope that we will be able to persuade her to come voluntarily into hospital. We always attempt to use the least restrictive method. If however she does not consent to this, then we will have to detain her under the Mental Health Act (MHA 1983). (Explain caveats of MHA if necessary)

H: What are the treatments available?

C: The treatment options available are a combination of medication, psychological or talking therapies and because it affects the family, the social aspects of care.

1. Medication
We usually treat this mental illness with a group of medication called antipsychotic medication. If she is breastfeeding, we usually have to weigh the risk and benefits of prescribing, and consider an alternative medication which would be safer and which would not pass through the breast milk.

PERINATAL PSYCHIATRY

2. Psychoeducation
We have found that it is helpful if family members learn more about the condition, its complications and treatment. Your understanding of her illness as well as being available and listening can promote her engagement with her treatment plan. This will also be vital to ensure good recovery.

3. Psychological
Later on, when she is a more settled, we can look at the talking treatments like counselling and cognitive behavioural therapy.

4. Social
Because we know how difficult this must be and its impact on you and the family, with the support of our specialist mother and baby team, we can provide more support, and advice on issues like mothering, breastfeeding.

Other advice we give is to eat a balanced healthy diet, ensure she takes sufficient rest, exercise and to allow for support and love provided by the people close to her.

H: What are the chances of this happening in future pregnancies?

C: From the evidence we have available it is known that if someone gets Postpartum Psychosis, then there is a 50-60% chance of having another episode in the next pregnancy. We will however if there are any future pregnancies advise that she will be seen regularly in outpatient appointments, supported with the perinatal services, and reviewed by the obstetrics team.

Summarise
Thank you for talking to me. To summarise, it is important for me to stress the fact that your wife is seriously ill. At present I think it is your wife's best interest to stay in hospital, and we will do our best to ensure hers and your baby's safety.

I have some leaflets for you. There are also some useful websites such as national childbirth trust (NCT) and support groups like sure start and CRY-SIS available. I am happy to meet again with you if have any further questions and to discuss your partners progress.

Social services involvement
An important part of this assessment would include discussion with social services to obtain history and if there were any other child protection or child in need issues.
Urgent referral needs to be made to social services and the police
Need to ascertain if there are any other children at risk
Establish if there is a protective carer/ plan

PERINATAL PSYCHIATRY

PUERPERAL PSYCHOSIS

Puerperal Psychosis-*occurs within the first 2 weeks post-delivery or the puerperium (6 weeks postpartum)*

Epidemiology: *Occurs in about 1 in 1000 women post-delivery*

Aetiology
- *Parity, pregnancy complications, past psychiatric history, family history, poor social support*

Prognosis: *50-60 % risk in future pregnancies*

Management *–Holistic approach*
- *Immediate and short term*
- *Setting :*
- *consider inpatient or community support*
- *if admission :*
- *Informal admission or use of Mental Health Act(MHA 1983)*
- *Specialist perinatal services –mother and baby unit*

Biological Interventions
- *Antipsychotics -weigh risk and benefits*
- *ECT indicated in severe cases*

Psychological Interventions
- *Psychoeducation*
- *Counselling*
- *CBT*
- *Guided imagery*

Social Interventions
- *Support to family*
- *Reassurance*
- *Advice on mothering, bonding*
- *Longer term management*
- *Support with perinatal services*
- *Support with future pregnancies*

Information and leaflets
Support groups NCT, CRY-SIS, and sure start
Websites-www.nct.

ICD 10
Section F53 Mental and behavioural disorders associated with the puerperium, not elsewhere classified, can be used in such circumstances.

PERINATAL PSYCHIATRY

References

British Medical Association and Royal Pharmaceutical society (2011), British National Formulary 62, 62nd edn. Great Britain: British Medical Journal Publishing Group and Pharmaceutical Press

Gelder, M.G, Cowen, P. and Harrison P.J (2006) Shorter Oxford textbook of psychiatry. 5th edn. Oxford: Oxford University Press.

Sims, A. C. P. (2003) Symptoms in the mind: an introduction to descriptive psychopathology. 3rd edn. Great Britain: Saunders.

Taylor, D., Paton, C., Kapur, S. (2009) The South London and Maudsley NHS Foundation Trust & Oxleas NHS Foundation Trust prescribing guidelines. 10th edn. London: Informa Healthcare.

WHO. (1992)The ICD 10 classification of mental and behavioural disorders: clinical descriptions and diagnostic guideline. 10th revision : Geneva; WHO

Journal articles
Daksha Emson: Report into the strategic health authority into the death of Daksha Emson October 2007

Cox J.L., Holden J.M., Sagovsky R. (1987). "Detection of postnatal Depression: development of the 10-item Edinburgh Postnatal Depression Scale". Br J Psychotherapy

Antenatal and postnatal mental health: clinical management and service

NICE Clinical Guideline 45 (2007) National Institute for Clinical Excellence: London.

National confidential enquiry of suicide and homicides

Online resources
Royal college of psychiatrist's health information leaflets for patient's www.rcpsych.ac.uk

EPNDS is used by Midwives and health visitors after delivery. It is used as a screening tool for Postnatal Depression

Support groups and organisations
MAMA -Support group like meets a mum association
CRY-SIS- provide help and support for mothers with crying and sleepless babies.
National Childbirth Trust (NCT)

Suggested reading

PERINATAL PSYCHIATRY

Overcoming Postnatal Depression: A Five Areas Approach (Hodder Arnold [Paperback]
Dr. Christopher Williams (Author), Dr. Roch Cantwell (Author), Ms. Karen Robertson (
Surviving Post-Natal Depression by Cara Aiken- At Home, No One Hears You Scream
The book tells the stories of ten women from very different backgrounds - including the author -who have suffered post-natal Depression. Their stories, told honestly and informally, will be a source of strength and hope for other who sufferers it.

EXAMINATIONS

EXAMINATIONS

1. EXAMINATION OF EXTRA- PYRAMIDAL SIDE EFFECTS OF ANTIPSYCHOTIC MEDICATION

INSTRUCTIONS TO THE CANDIDATE
You have been asked to see a 24 yr old guy Ethan Darwin who is on Haloperidol.

TASK FOR THE CANDIDATE
- Please do an examination for EPSE's or Extra-pyramidal side effects.

PAY PARTICULAR ATTENTION TO THE FOLLOWING (MENTAL CHECKLIST)
- Establish brief history of antipsychotic medication and also Extra-pyramidal side effects(EPSE's)
- Perform a general examination and observation for abnormal movements
- Perform a neurological examination
- Summarise and explain your findings

COMMUNICATION SKILLS
- Obtain consent.
- Ask if a chaperone is required

Suggested approach
Introduction
C: Hello, I 'm Dr ...I'm one of the psychiatrist .I understand that you have been having some problems with your medication. Part of this assessment would be asking you some questions about your medication and then I would like to do an examination.
Is that all right with you?

P: Yes, sure

A. History of presenting complaint (onset, duration, severity and progression)
Establish current history
1. What medications are you currently on?
2. How long have you been on this medication?
3. Has there been any changes in your medication or alteration in dose recently?
4. Have you been drooling?
5. Do you feel as if your thinking has slowed down? (Bradyphrenia)
6. Do you feel restlessness or unable to sit still? (Akathisia)
7. Have you had any difficulty in speaking, eating or breathing? (vocal tics, dysphonia, stridor, dysarthria)
8. Are you able to bear weight?

EXAMINATIONS

9. *Have you noticed any abnormal movements? Has anyone commented if they are present or absent during sleep?*
10. *Have you had any muscle spasms recently? (Dystonia) Does it ever become worse while writing or doing chores?*

Thank you. I would now like to do an examination. Would you like a chaperone?
(Use hand gel provided)
I will be commenting as I go along, please feel free to interrupt me if you do not understand me.

B. General observation
i) Look for abnormal movements
· *Face and neck: Blinking, blepharospasm, oculogyric crisis (eyes rolling upwards), grimacing, puckering or pouting of mouth, lip smacking, tongue protrusion, chewing movements, mouth opening, lateral movements of mouth, lock jaw, torticollis (head and neck tilted to one side).*

· *Upper limb: Tremor, choreoform hand movements (pill rolling or piano rolling), rocking, twisting, and pelvic thrusting.*

· *Lower limb: Foot tapping, crossing and uncrossing of legs, inversion/eversion of feet*

ii) Physical Examination
1. *Make sure there is nothing in patient's mouth. Ask about dentures or chewing gum.*
2. *Ask the patient to open mouth and observe the tongue within the mouth.*
3. *Request the patient to protrude the tongue and observe for any abnormal movements, fasciculation's. Ask the patient to do it twice.*
4. *Ask the patient to sit in a chair with feet on the ground and hands resting on the knees and notice any abnormal movements.*
5. *Ask the patient to extend both arms in front with palms facing downwards. Check for tremors or any abnormal movements.*
6. *Check tone in both hands with wrist supported. Look for cogwheel and lead pipe rigidity.*
7. *Ask patient to touch their thumb with each finger as quickly as possible for 15 seconds. Repeat with other hand.*
8. *Ask the patient to stand up. Look for any abnormalities in posture.*
9. *Ask the patient to hold their arms up by their side and then let them drop to their side freely and quickly. Normally a thud would be heard.*
10. *Ask the patient to walk a few paces. Check if there is an inability to start or stop walking. Check for ataxic gait.*

Summarize
Thank you for cooperating with me. It appears that you have been experiencing side effects with the medication you are on. We call these side effects extra-pyramidal side effects (EPSE). We usually treat this by either

EXAMINATIONS

decreasing the dose of the medication or alternatively give you a medication which counteracts these side effects. The medication is called Procyclidine (anticholinergic)

EXAMINATIONS

Extra-Pyramidal side effects EPSE'S
Dystonia
Prevalence is around 10%.
Dystonia can occur within hours of starting antipsychotics especially in neuroleptic naïve patients and those on high potency medication. Young people are affected more.
It can cause respiratory stridor, breathing difficulties and severe distress.
Treatment: oral or IM Procyclidine 5-10 mg or Benzotropine 1-3 mg.

Pseudo-parkinsonism (tremor, rigidity, salivation)
Prevalence is around 20%.
Onset is within days or weeks of starting or increasing the dose. It occurs more in elderly females and people with neurological problems.
Treatment: Reduce the dose, change to atypical or treat with anticholinergic.

Akathisia
Prevalence is 25%.
It can occur at any time between hours to weeks of commencement of antipsychotics
Treatment: Reduce the dose or stop the drug if intolerable. Change to an atypical.

Treat with Propranolol (5-30 mg), Cyproheptadine or Diazepam/Clonazepam. DO NOT give anticholinergic.

Smartsesh®

EPSE-EXTRAPYRAMIDAL SIDE EFFECTS-TREATMENT
Procyclidine-kemadrine® (GSK), Arpicolin® (Rosemont)
Antimuscarinic drugs
Dosage 2.mg- 5mg 3x daily (maximum 30mg daily)
Side effects
Constipation, dry mouth, nausea, vomiting, tachycardia, dizziness, confusion, euphoria, hallucinations, impaired memory, Anxiety, restlessness, urinary tension, blurred vision and rash.
Contra-indications
Avoid in gastro-intestinal abstraction and myasthenia.
Alternative
Other antimuscarinic drugs-orphenadrine (disipal®) (aspellas), biorphen® (alliance)
Dosage- 150mg daily-maximum 400 mg daily

Smartsesh®

EXAMINATIONS

References

Guy-w-1976-Abnormal Involuntary Movement Scale (AIMS). US Department Health, Education and welfare, Washington DC

Simpson GM, Angus JW, 1970 A rating scale for extra pyramidal side effects Acta Psychiat-Scand

EXAMINATIONS

2 AKATHISIA

INSTRUCTIONS TO THE CANDIDATE
You have been asked to see a young gentleman Mikhail Francessca in A+E who is very restless and very angry. He went to the GP 3 days ago. He was given tablets for Anxiety.

TASK FOR THE CANDIDATE
- *Please do an examination.*

PAY PARTIULAR ATTENTION TO THE FOLLOWING (MENTAL CHECKLIST)
- *History of presenting complaint (HOPC) (onset, duration, severity and progression).*
- *Establish brief history of medication and temporal relationship.*
- *Do a risk assessment.*
- *Conduct an examination as for EPSE's.*

COMMUNICATION SKILLS
- *Obtain consent.*
- *Ask if a chaperone is required.*
- *Anticipate a restless and distressed person who possible might have difficulty in sitting.*

Suggested approach
Introduction
C: Hello I'm Dr...I'm one of the psychiatrists. I understand from the doctor that you have some concerns with your medication. Can you tell me more about this?

A. History of presenting complaint (HOPC) (onset, duration, severity and progression)
- *Can you tell me about the problems you have been having?*
- *Can you tell me what medication you have been taking?*
- *When did you start this and why?*
- *Have you noticed any unusual movements of your body, face and hands and feet?*
- *Have you noticed any rolling of your eyes upwards?*
- *Have you noticed any restlessness of your legs?*
- *How severe has it been?*
- *How has it affected your functioning?*

B. Risk assessment
- *Have you had thoughts of harming yourself? (Suicidal thoughts)*
- *Have you had thoughts of harming anyone else? (Homicidal thoughts)*

C: I would now like to do an examination.
- *Is that all right with you?*
- *Would you like a chaperone?*

EXAMINATIONS

- *(Use hand gel provided)*
- *I will be commenting as I go along, please feel free to interrupt me if you do not understand me.*

C. Physical Examination

1. Make sure there is nothing in patient's mouth. Ask about dentures or chewing gum.
2. Ask the patient to open mouth and observe the tongue within the mouth.
3. Request the patient to protrude the tongue and observe for any abnormal movements, fasciculation's. Ask the patient to do this twice.
4. Ask the patient to sit in a chair with feet on the ground and hands resting on the knees and notice any abnormal movements.
5. Ask the patient to extend both arms in front with palms facing downwards. Check for tremors or any abnormal movements.
6. Check tone in both hands with wrist supported. Look for cogwheel and lead pipe rigidity.
7. Ask patient to tap their thumb with each finger as quickly as possible for 15 seconds. Repeat with other hand.
8. Ask the patient to stand up. Look for any abnormalities in posture.
9. Ask the patient to hold their arms up by their side and then let them drop to their side freely and quickly. Normally a thud would be heard.
10. Ask the patient to walk a few paces. Check if there is an inability to start or stop walking. Check for ataxic gait.

Summarize

*Thank you. From my assessment with you, I think you are experiencing a side effect of the medication you are on. This side effect is called **Akathisia.** It usually occurs in the early stages of treatment.*

We treat this by either decreasing the dose of the medication you are on or alternatively we can change the medication to another medication that would be less likely to cause this side effect.

I can also prescribe Propranolol which can help you for the unpleasant symptoms you are experiencing now.

Akathisia
***Prevalence** is 25%.*
 ***Onset:** It can occur at any time between hours to weeks of commencement of antipsychotics*
***Treatment**: Reduce the dose or stop the drug if intolerable. Change to an atypical.*

Treat with Propranolol (5-30 mg), Cyproheptadine or Diazepam/Clonazepam. DO NOT give anticholinergic.
Propanalol
Inderal® (Astra Zaneca), half-inderal-LA® (Astra Zaneca)

Smartsesh®

EXAMINATIONS

3. THYROID EXAMINATION

INSTRUCTIONS TO THE CANDIDATE
You have been asked to see this 29 yr old lady Clarissa Morrison who has been treated with Lithium.

TASK FOR THE CANDIDATE
- Please do a thyroid examination.

PAY PARTICULAR ATTENTION TO THE FOLLOWING (MENTAL CHECKLIST)
- Elicit a medical history and systematically explores symptoms related to thyroid gland.
- General observation.
- Examination of thyroid gland-inspection, palpation, Auscultation, percussion.
- Examination of the eyes.
- Neurological examination-proximal myopathy and pendulous reflexes.

COMMUNICATION SKILLS
- Obtain consent.
- Ask for a chaperone.

Suggested approach
Introduction
C: Hello, I Dr ....I'm one of the psychiatrists. I have been asked to do an examination of your thyroid gland. Is that all right with you?

A. History of presenting complaint
Enquire about the following in systematic exploration
- Altered bowel habits
- Increased appetite
- Oligomenorrhoea
- Irritability/mood swings
- Dislike of hot weather
- Have there been any changes in your weight recently? Have there been any changes in your appetite?
- How has your energy levels been?
- How have you been able to tolerate cold weather?
- Have you noticed any swelling in your neck?
- May I ask about your periods? Are they regular?

B. Thyroid examination
Ensure that the neck is appropriately exposed. Undo the top 1-2 buttons.

C. General Inspection
- Comment on obesity or weight loss
- Exopthalmos

EXAMINATIONS

- *Dry flaky skin and hair in hypothyroidism*
- *Hair-alopecia*

D. Examination of the hands
- *Check pulse- may be bradycardic or tachycardic*
- *Check for presence of sweating and increase in temperature*
- *Onycholysis (separation of the nail from its bed)*
- *Thyroid acropathy (similar to clubbing)*

Ask the patient to extend his/her arms and hold hands with palms facing down wards. Look for any tremor.

E. Examination of the thyroid gland
1) Inspection
- *Ask the patient to swallow; only goitre or a thyroglossal cyst will rise on swallowing*
- *Note any asymmetry or scars of previous surgery*

2) Palpations
- *Stand behind the patient with thumbs on the back of the neck and patient's head slightly flexed*
- *Gently palpate the neck looking for any abnormality*
- *Have the patient swallow and feel the gland move under your fingers*
- *Palpation of right lobe: ask the patient to turn neck slightly to the right, palpate again with patient swallowing. If thyroid is palpable describe size (feel for the lower border to rule out retrosternal extension), shape (uniformly enlarged or nodular), consistency (soft, rubbery or hard), tenderness (thyroiditis) and mobility (neoplasm: fixed).*
- *Repeat the same for the left lobe.*
- *Palpate for lymph nodes.*

Auscultation
A bruit is a sign of increased blood flow and can be present in thyrotoxicosis.

F. Examination of the eyes
- *Look for lid lag, lid retraction, exophthalmos (examine from the side and above. The eyes should not be visible beyond the supraorbital ridge)*
- *Check eye movements by asking the patient to follow your finger movements without moving their head.*
- *Check reflexes (slow relaxing in hypothyroidism)*
- *Proximal myopathy and*
- *Pretibial myxoedema*

G Cardiovascular examination
- *Signs of cardiac failure*

Summarise

EXAMINATIONS

Thank you for allowing me to examine you. I am concerned that your thyroid gland could be underactive and would like you to have some blood tests done.

Do you have any questions for me?

THYROID FUNCTION TESTS

If you are given thyroid function test results comment on your findings.

- *TSH: 0.5-5.0 mU/l*

- *T3: 1.1-2.8 mol/l*

- *T4: 50-150 mol/l*

Smartsesh®

EXAMINATIONS

4. FRONTAL LOBE TESTS

INSTRUCTIONS TO THE CANDIDATE
You have been asked to see this 25 yr old man Cassidy Mohamed who was assaulted in the pub 3 months ago. He was referred by his GP as his mother had concerns of a change in his personality.

TASK FOR THE CANDIDATE
- Please do a frontal lobe test examination.

PAY PARTICULAR ATTENTION TO THE FOLLOWING (MENTAL CHECKLIST)
- Assessment of verbal fluency
  -F, A, S
- Assessment of abstract thinking
  -Proverb testing
  -Similarities and differences
  -Cognitive estimates
- Assessment of response inhibition and set shifting
  -Luria motor test
  -Alternate sequencing
  -No don't go test
  -Perseveration
- Frontal lobe test release signs
  -Primitive reflexes

COMMUNICATION SKILLS
- Obtain consent.
- Ask if a chaperone is required.
- Anticipate that person could be disinhibited and easily distracted

---

Suggested approach
Introduction
C: Hello, I'm Dr .....I'm one of the psychiatrists.
I would like to do some tests with for your memory. Is that all right with you?
Please feel free to interrupt me if you are unable to understand me?
Would you perhaps like a chaperone?

A. Assessment of Verbal Fluency
- FAS test
- Judges ability to generate categorical lists
- Ask the patient to lists words beginning with letter F in one minute. Same with letter A and S. Normal adult should be able to list 15 words/letter in one minute. Total FAS words > 30.
- For elderly 10 words/letter/minute is acceptable.
- You can also use categories namely animals, fruits)
- Can you name as many animals in one minute?

EXAMINATIONS

B. Assessment of abstract thinking
1) Proverb interpretation
- Can you explain what is meant by these proverbs?
- 'Too many cooks spoil the broth'
- 'Don't judge a book by its cover'
- 'A stitch in time saves nine?'

2) Similarities and Differences
- Can you explain the similarities and differences between?
- 'apple and orange'
- 'table and chair'

3) Assessment of Cognitive estimates
- What is the height of an average English woman?
- How many camels are there in Holland or England?
- How high is a double decker bus?

C. Assessment of Response inhibition and set shifting
- Co-ordinated movements.

1) Luria motor test-Three step test
Motor sequencing:
Luria's three-step test. Tell the patient that you are going to show them a series of hand movements. Demonstrate fist, edge and palm five times on your leg without verbal prompts. Ask the patient to repeat the sequence.

2) Go no go test:
Ask the patient to place a hand on the table. Tap under the table. Tell the patient to raise one finger when you tap once and not to raise the finger when you tap twice. Show the patient how it's done and then do the test.

3) Alternate sequences
Can you continue this please? ----/\------/\-----

4) Perseveration
Observe any repetition of particular responses

D. Examination
Primitive reflexes
Grasp: Stroke patient's palm from radial to ulnar side. Patient will grasp your other hand.
Pout: Stroke the philtrum or tap a spatula placed over lips.
Palmomental: Stroke patient's thenar eminence and the patient will wince.

E. Neurological test:
Check for anosmia (olfactory nerve involvement)

EXAMINATIONS

Expressive dysphasia (Broca's area involvement

Summarize
Thank you for cooperating with me. From my assessment I would like to do some further tests which could explain the reason for the recent changes in your behaviour.

FRONTAL LOBE TESTING
Naming
- *Verbal fluency*
- *Proverb testing*
- *Similarities and differences*
- *Cognitive estimates*

Doing
- *Go no -go-test*
- *Luria motor test*

Copying
- *Alternate sequence*

Examine
- *Primitive reflexes*
- *Glabellar tap*
- *Grasp reflex*
- *Palmomental*
- *pouting*
  Smartsesh®

EXAMINATIONS

5. MINI MENTAL STATE EXAMINATION
FOLSTEIN MF ROBINS EXAMINATION

INSTRUCTIONS TO THE CANDIDATE
You have been asked to see this 67 yr. old Tristan Thomas who has a history of memory problems.

TASK FOR THE CANDIDATE
- Please perform a mini mental state examination.

PAY PARTICULAR ATTENTION TO THE FOLLOWING (MENTAL CHECKLIST)
- Establish orientation to time, place and person
- Check registration (apple, table, penny)
- Do attention and calculation (world or subtract 100-7)
- Establishes recall
- Naming of watch and pen
- Repetition of no ifs ands or buts
- Comprehension- 3 stage command
- Reading-CLOSE YOUR EYES
- Writing a sentence
- Copying 2 intersecting pentagons

COMMUNICATION SKILLS
- Obtain consent.
- Ask if a chaperone is required
- Gives clear instructions

Suggested approach
Introduction
C: Hello, I Dr ....I'm one of the psychiatrists. I have been asked to do a test of your memory.
Is that all right with you?
Would you perhaps like a chaperone?
(Use hand gel provided)
I will be commenting as I go along, please feel free to interrupt me if you do not understand me?
Checks the patient's ability to hear, see, and understand.
- Gives clear instructions.
- Administer and score the MMSE.

A. Orientation
1 Orientation to time/ temporal
- What year is? (Season?), Month? Date? Day?
- Score one point for each.

2 Orientation to place/spatial
- Where are we now? What country? (County?) City/town? Building? Floor of building?

EXAMINATIONS

- *Score one point for each correct answer.*

B. Registration
- *Ask if you can check the individual's memory.*
- *Name three objects (e.g. apple, table, penny) taking 1 second to say each one.*
- *Then ask the individual to repeat the names of all three objects.*
- *Give 1 point for each correct answer.*

C. Attention and calculation
- *Are you better with numbers or words?*
- *Could you spell 'WORLD' please?*
- *Now could you spell the word 'WORLD' backwards please?*
- *One point for each letter in the correct order*

D. Recall
- *What were the three words I asked you to remember?*

E. Naming
- *Show the individual a pen and a watch and ask her to name them.*
- *Score one point for each.*

F. Repetition
- *I want you to repeat exactly what I say.*
- *"No ifs ands or buts."*

G Comprehension-3 stage command
- *Take this piece of paper with your right hand, fold it in half and put it on the floor*

H Reading
- *Write 'CLOSE YOUR EYES' in large letters.*
- *Asks the patient to read it and do what it says.*
- *One point if patient closes his eyes.*

I Writing
- *Ask the individual to write a sentence.*
- *Score one point if the sentence makes sense and has a subject and a verb.*

J Copying
- *Please copy this design.*
- *Draw 2 intersecting pentagons.*
- *One point if the pentagons intersect correctly and the intersections have 4 angles.*

EXAMINATIONS

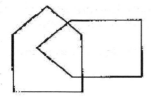

Summarize

Thank you for cooperating with me. How did you think you did?

From my assessment, your score was (score). I would like to do some further testing of your memory.

Mini Mental State examination
- *Orientation to time*
- *Orientation to place*
- *Registration apple, table ,penny*
- *Repetition*
- *Attention WORLD*
- *Naming*
- *No ifs ands or buts*
- *Command 3 stage*
- *Close your eyes*
- *Copy*
- *Sentence*
  Smartsesh®

EXAMINATIONS

6. FUNDOSCOPY

INSTRUCTIONS TO THE CANDIDATE
You have been asked to see this 21 yr. old lady Rochelle Carrere who has come from her father's funeral. She has sudden loss of vision in her left eye.

TASK FOR THE CANDIDATE
- Please do a Fundoscopy examination.

PAY PARTICULAR ATTENTION TO THE FOLLOWING (MENTAL CHECKLIST)
- Explains procedure with Ophthalmoscope.
- Check for visual acuity using Snellen's chart.
- Examine optic disc.
- Identify for any abnormalities.
- Summarises.

COMMUNICATION SKILLS
- Obtain consent.
- Ask if a chaperone is required.
- Express your condolences

Suggested approach
Introduction
C: Hello, I Dr ....I'm one of the psychiatrists. I am sorry to hear about your father. I understand that you have had sudden loss of vision in your left eye.

I have been asked to do an examination of your eyes.
Is that all right with you?
Would you perhaps like a chaperone?
(Use hand gel provided)
I will be commenting as I go along, please feel free to interrupt me if you do not understand me?

A. Neurological examination
1. Optic nerve (2 CN)
- Visual acuity
Test each eye separately
Tell patient that you are going to check their eyesight
Ask them to close one eye and test distant vision using Snellen's chart at a distance of 10 feet
- Visual fields
Sit directly opposite the patient at the same level with your right eye closed approximately one metre away. Ask the patient to cover left eye with left hand, not to move their head and to say yes when they see your finger. The finger should be equidistant from you and the patient. Bring the finger into the field of vision in a curved not a straight line. Repeat with other eye.

EXAMINATIONS

- *Fundoscopy*
Given separately.
- *Accommodation*
Ask the patient to look into the distance and then at the tip of their nose

2. Occulomotor nerve (3 CN), Trochlear (4CN), Abducent nerve (6CN)
Pupillary light reflex
Ask the patient to look into the distance and explain that you are going to shine a light into their eyes. Bring light from below and side. Observe for direct and consensual light reflex.
Repeat with other eye.
Extraocular movements
Tell the patient that you are going to check the movements of their eye muscles. Ask them to follow your finger with their eyes without moving their head and to tell you if they see double. You should again be at a distance of one metre from the patient. Make an H, pausing at the ends of each direction of gaze to observe for nystagmus.

Explain what the procedure involves.
C: I would like to examine the back part of the eye. It will involve dimming the light, and shining a light into the eyes. This will involve me coming quite close to you.

1. Ask the patient to focus gaze on a distant object to prevent constriction of pupils from accommodation. Tell the patient to blink and breathe normally.

2. Turn the ophthalmoscope on to a low-moderate light intensity [preset it to focus on the '0' position and rotate it either clockwise or anticlockwise]

3. Use your right eye to look into the patient's right eye and left eye for the patient's left eye

4. Stand at a distance and look through the ophthalmoscope into the patient's eye from a distance and look for the red reflex

5. Follow the red reflex into the eye angling the light slightly towards the patient's nose.

6. Move close to the patient and locate the optic disc.
- *The normal disc diameter is 1.5 mm.*
- *Note the margin, cup and diameter*
- *Note the vessels and follow the 4 vessels into each quadrant*

7. Examine the fundus as if it were a clock with the disc at the centre. Describe any abnormalities in relation to the disc i.e. 3 o' clock at 2 disc diameters from the disc.

8. Follow the super nasal arcade, the infer nasal arcade, the super temporal arcade and the infer temporal arcade.

EXAMINATIONS

9. Focus on the macula at the end. It is presented temporal to the optic disc.

Summarise
Thank you for cooperating with me.
From my examination of your eyes, I have found no abnormalities at present to explain your sudden loss of vision. [If scenario is for Conversion disorder]

EXAMINATIONS

Optic disc: Normal optic disc is pink with slight pallor on the temporal side. Its margins are well defined. The diameter of the disc should not be more than 50% of the disc

Hard exudates: are well defined and are seen in hypertension, diabetes and retinal vein occlusion

Soft exudates: look like cotton wool

Papiloledema: It is the swelling of the optic disc with blurred margins. Normal cupping of the disc is also lost. Veins become congested. It occurs in increased intracranial pressure, malignant hypertension and optic nerve tumours.

Hypertensive retinopathy: Patches of the ischemia may appear as the blood supply becomes inadequate. Hypertensive retinopathy presents with a 'dry' retina i.e. few haemorrhages, rare oedema and exudates with multiple cotton wool spots whereas diabetic retinopathy presents as 'wet' retina i.e. with numerous haemorrhages, exudates, extensive oedema, and few cotton wool spots.

Group I: narrowing of the retinal arteries

Group II: narrowing of the retinal arteries with areas of focal narrowing and arteriovenous nipping **Group III**: abnormalities as seen in groups I and II along with retinal haemorrhages, hard and soft exudates.

Group IV (i.e., malignant hypertension): All the above along with swelling of the optic nerve.

Diabetic retinopathy: Dot and blot haemorrhages, micro aneurysms, venous dilatation, neovascularisation leading to proliferative retinopathy.

Retinal vein occlusion: Stormy sunset appearance. Engorged veins with large flame haemorrhages and cotton wool spots. In branch vein occlusion changes is confined to a small area.

Retinal artery occlusion: In occlusion of the central retinal artery the retina appears pale and macula becomes prominent and is cherry red in colour.

Senile degeneration: Optic disc normal, unusual pigmentation at the macula. **Drusens** (nodules in the choroid) usually present.

Optic atrophy: Pale optic disc. Occurs in glaucoma, retinal damage and ischemia

EXAMINATIONS

7. ALCOHOL DEPENDENCE

INSTRUCTIONS TO CANDIDATE
The GP has referred this 35 yr old man who has a history of alcohol dependence

TASK FOR THE CANDIDATE
- Please do a physical examination related to alcohol dependence

PAY PARTICULAR ATTENTION TO THE FOLLOWING (MENTAL CHECKLIST)
- General examination
- observe for alcohol withdrawal signs
- Chest examination
- Cardiovascular examination
- Abdominal examination
- Neurological examination

COMMUNICATION SKILLS
- Obtain consent.
- Ask if a chaperone is required.

Suggested approach
Introduction
C: Hello, I Dr ....I'm one of the psychiatrists. I understand your GP has asked me to see I have been asked to do a physical examination.
Is that all right with you?

Would you like a chaperone?

P: No thank you

(Use hand gel provided)

C: I will be commenting as I go along, please feel free to interrupt me if you do not understand me.

A. General Examination
- Withdrawal signs
- Agitation, restlessness
- Tremor (the shakes)
- Autonomic hyperactivity :diaphoresis-raised temperature(hyperthermia) and sweating
- Hypertension, tachycardia
- Tachypnoea
- Bruises, abrasions or scars suggestive of falls or violence
- Spider naevi on trunk , face and arms
- Evidence of self-neglect

- *gynaecomastia*

B. Examination of hands/arms
- *Check pulse and blood pressure*
- *Tremor*
- *Hepatic flap-ask the patient to hold arms straight with hyper extended hands*
- *Palmar erythema*
- *Dupuytren's contracture*
- *Clubbing*
- *Koilonychia*
- *Nicotine stains*

C. Examination of eyes
- *Check extra ocular muscles and rule out nystagmus*
- *Jaundice*
- *Pallor*

D. Mouth
- *Fetor hepaticas*

E. Chest examination
- *Spider naevi*
- *Gynaecomastia*
- *Loss of body hair*
- *Auscultate for heart sounds*

F. Abdominal examination
- *Scratch marks*
- *Caput medusae*
- *Umbilicus everted/inverted*
- *Palpate liver and spleen*
- *Check for ascites*
- *Ask to check the external genitalia for testicular atrophy*

G. Neurological examination
- *Check reflexes*
- *Check for peripheral neuropathy and proximal myopathy*
- *Heel shin/finger nose and dysdiadokinesia*
- *Assess gait*

Summarise
Thank you for allowing me to examine you. Do you have any questions for me? I would like you to go and see your GP and have some blood investigations done more specifically looking at your liver function test.

8. ALCOHOL DEPENDENCE - CEREBELLAR EXAMINATION

INSTRUCTIONS TO THE CANDIDATE
You have been asked to see this 45 yr old man Bremer Davidson who has a history of alcohol dependence.

TASK FOR THE CANDIDATE
- *Please do a cerebellar examination.*

PAY PARTICULAR ATTENTION TO THE FOLLOWING (MENTAL CHECKLIST)
- *Examine for eye signs- nystagmus/opthalmoplegia.*
- *Establish presence of dysarthria or staccato.*
- *Assess for impairment of motor coordination*
  -Past pointing phenomenon-finger nose test
  -Dysdiodokinesia
  -heel shin test
- *Truncal ataxia.*
- *Examine for gait abnormalities*
  -limb ataxia
  -rhombergs test
- *Motor examination of upper and lower limb.*
- *Tone, power, reflexes.*

COMMUNICATION SKILLS
- *Obtain consent.*
- *Ask if a chaperone is required.*

Suggested approach
Introduction
C: Hello, I Dr ....I have been asked to do an examination
Is that all right with you?
Would you perhaps like a chaperone?
(Use hand gel provided)
I will be commenting as I go along, please feel free to interrupt me if you do not understand me?

A. Eye signs
Check for nystagmus or opthalmoplegia

B. Speech
Can you please repeat British constitution? (Dysarthria)

C. Hands
Ask patient to tap the back of their own hand with their other hand repeatedly. (Dysdiadokinesia)

EXAMINATIONS

1) Finger nose test
Ask the patient to touch their own nose with their forefinger and then to touch your finger. Alternate back and forth between their nose and your finger whilst moving your finger. *(Intention tremor and past pointing phenomenon)*

2) Limb ataxia
Ask patient to stretch hands out and observe for hyperpronation of one hand.

3) Heel shin test
Ask the patient to place their heel on the opposite knee and slide it down to their ankle. Ask them to take it back to original position. Repeat on the other leg.

4) Truncal ataxia
Ask the patient to sit up with the arms crossed. *(observe for inability to sit up unsupported)*

D. Examine for gait abnormalities
Ask the patient to stand up and walk heel to toe in a straight line. *(Observe gait)*
Ask patient to stand with their feet together and to close their eyes, while you support with your arm behind them to stop them falling. *(Positive Rhombergs signs)*

E. Motor examination of upper and lower limb
Assess for tone, power and reflexes in upper and lower limbs

---

*Other variation **Neurological examination** in Alcohol dependence*
Neurological Examination
- *Cerebellar Examination*
- *Peripheral neuropathy- Sensory examination*
- *Examine cranial nerves –Examine cranial nerves –for lateral gaze palsy*

  ©Smartsesh

EXAMINATIONS

9. KORSAKOFF SYNDROME

INSTRUCTIONS TO THE CANDIDATE
You have been asked to see this 50 yr old man Heinricht Gustav who has been admitted into the medical ward. He has a history of alcohol dependence

TASK FOR THE CANDIDATE
- Elicit a history with a focus on Korsakoff's syndrome.

PAY PARTICULAR ATTENTION TO THE FOLLOWING (MENTAL CHECKLIST)
- Establish cognitive assessment-orientation.
- Assess short term memory.
- Assess long term memory.
- Demonstrate Confabulation.
- Establish short term memory.
- Establish long term memory.
- Establish autobiographical memory.
- Establish procedural memory.
- Establish working memory.
- Perform cerebellar examination.

COMMUNICATION SKILLS
- Obtain consent.
- Ask if a chaperone is required.

Suggested approach
Introduction
C: Hello, I'm Dr ... I'm one of the psychiatrists. I have been asked to come and see you. It would be helpful if you could tell me more about how you ended up her?

P: I came to see my friend in the Birmingham hospital.

C: can you tell me how you came to the hospital?

A. Establish orientation (elicit some components of the MMSE)
1) Orientation to time
- Year, season, day, date and month

2) Orientation to place
- Country, county, town/village, address or building, floor/ward

B. Enquire about memory
- So how is your memory in general?
- Have you been more forgetful of late?
- Are you able to remember your appointments?

EXAMINATIONS

1. Short term memory (STM)
- Can you tell me what you had for breakfast?

2. Long term memory (LTM)
- Can you tell me when you got married?

3. Autobiographical memory
- Can you tell me when you got married?

4. Procedural memory
- Are you able to ride a bicycle or drive a car?

5. Working memory
- Forward digit span.
- Read a series of numbers to the patient and ask them to repeat the numbers back.
- Read the numbers at one per second and start with three digits in it.
- Normal range 6+-1.
- Backwards digit span
- Repeat string of numbers backwards. (For example, examiner reads 793 and patient reads 397)
- Normal range is 5+-1

Registration and recall of seven item name and address
John Brown, 42 West Street, Luton, Bedfordshire.

Confabulation (patient will fill gaps in his memory. Demonstrate this by saying we would need to collateral history.)
What did you do today?

C. Perform relevant cerebellar physical examination

Summarise
Thank you for talking to me and allowing me to examine you.
From what you have told is that you came to hospital to see a friend. I am concerned about your memory. If it is all right with you I would like to speak one of your relatives to gather some more information.

EXAMINATIONS

10. RESPIRATORY EXAMINATION

INSTRUCTIONS TO THE CANDIDATE
You have been asked to see this 47 yr. old man.

TASK FOR THE CANDIDATE
- Please do a respiratory examination.

PAY PARTICULAR ATTENTION TO THE FOLLOWING (MENTAL CHECKLIST)
- Perform a general examination.
- Systematically examine using the following format.
- Inspection of chest
- Palpation
- Percussion
- Auscultation

COMMUNICATION SKILLS
- Obtain consent.
- Ask if a chaperone is required.

Suggested approach
Introduction
C: Hello, I Dr ....I'm one of the psychiatrists. I understand your GP has asked me to see. I have been asked to do a physical examination.
Is that all right with you?

Would you like a chaperone?

P: No thank you

(Use hand gel provided)

C: I will be commenting as I go along, please feel free to interrupt me if you do not understand me.
Ensure adequate exposure.
Ideally patient will be sitting at the edge of the bed.

A. General examination
Finger clubbing
Cyanosis – Peripheral and Central

B. Chest examination
1. Inspection of chest
Note the respiratory rate
Check for symmetry of chest movements and use of accessory muscles
Note any deformity and shape of chest (barrel shaped in COPD)

EXAMINATIONS

2. Palpation
Ask about tenderness or soreness
Confirm that the trachea is central
Place hands on the posterior aspect of the chest with thumbs touching each other in the midline and ask the patient to inhale deeply. This will confirm symmetry of movement during expansion.
Vocal fremitus is checked by placing the ball of the hand on the back of the chest and the patient is asked to say 999. Move hand from apices to interscapular region to the pulmonary bases. Check on both sides.

3. Percussion
Percussion note is also checked on both left and right sides. Compare one side to the other looking for symmetry. Start from the back again and percuss the apices, interscapular region and the lung bases. Percuss laterally in the mid axillary line. Check percussion note on the anterior aspect again comparing one side to the other.

4. Auscultation
Auscultate apices, interscapular region, bases posterior and the mid axillary region chest comparing one side with the other. Anteriorly auscultate bilaterally superior lobes, right middle lobe and left lingular division of the superior lobe.

Summarise
Thank you for cooperating with me and allowing me to examine you.

EXAMINATIONS

11. CARDIOVASCULAR EXAMINATIONS

INSTRUCTIONS TO THE CANDIDATE
You have been asked to see this 26 yr. old lady.

TASK FOR THE CANDIDATE
- *Please do a cardiovascular examination.*

PAY PARTICULAR ATTENTION TO THE FOLLOWING (MENTAL CHECKLIST)
- *General examination*
- *Chest inspection.*
- *Chest palpation.*
- *Chest auscultation.*
- *Examination of the back.*
- *Examination of the abdomen.*
- *Examination of the legs.*

COMMUNICATION SKILLS
- *Obtain consent.*
- *Ask if a chaperone is required.*

Suggested approach
Introduction
C: Hello, I Dr ....I'm one of the psychiatrists. I understand your GP has asked me to see I have been asked to do a physical examination.
Is that all right with you?

Would you like a chaperone?

P: No thank you

(Use hand gel provided)

C: I will be commenting as I go along, please feel free to interrupt me if you do not understand me.

A. General examination
1. Examination of the hands
- *Check for peripheral cyanosis*
- *Osler's nodes (0.5-1 cm reddish brown painful subcutaneous papules on finger tips, palmar eminences)*
- *Clubbing*
- *Splinter Haemorrhages*
- *Tremor (thyrotoxicosis)*
- *Pulse: rate, rhythm, character, radio radial delay. Character best assessed at the carotid*

EXAMINATIONS

2. Examination of the arms
- IV injection scars
- Take blood pressure

3. Examination of the face
- Malar flush
- Pallor (eyes)
- Xanthelasmas (yellow plaques deposited in the per orbital region)
- Corneal arcus (seen in severe hypercholesterolemia)
- Lips (for central cyanosis)
- High arched palate (seen in Marfan's)

4. Examination of the neck
- Carotid: inspect for carotid pulsations
- Compress one carotid at a time to check for character (fingers behind neck, assess with thumb)
- Check for carotid bruit with bell of stethoscope
- JVP: inspect height with patient at 45 degrees

B. Chest examination
1. Chest inspection
- Scars (mitral valvotomy laterally on left breast)
- Deformities
- Visible pulsations
- Apex beat

2. Chest palpation
- Check for tenderness
- Palpate apex beat for deviation

C. Examination of the back
- Sacral oedema

D. Examination of the abdomen
- Liver palpation
- Splenomegaly (seen in endocarditis)
- Abdominal aortic aneurysm

E. Examination of the legs
- Peripheral oedema

Summarise
Thank you for cooperating with me and allowing me to examine you.
Comment on the positive or negative findings.

EXAMINATIONS

12. EXAMINATION OF CRANIAL NERVES

INSTRUCTIONS TO THE CANDIDATE
You have been asked to see this 29 yr. old man.

TASK FOR THE CANDIDATE
- Please do an examination of the cranial nerves.

PAY PARTICULAR ATTENTION TO THE FOLLOWING (MENTAL CHECKLIST)
- Examine each cranial nerve individually.(cranial nerve 1-12)
- Olfactory nerve (1 CN)
- Optic nerve (2 CN)
- Occulomotor nerve (3 CN), Trochlear (4CN), Abducent nerve (6CN)
- Trigeminal nerve (5 CN)
- Facial nerve (7 CN)
- Vestibulocochlear nerve (8 CN)
- Glossopharangeal nerve (9 CN) and Vagus nerve (10 CN
- Accessory nerve (11 CN)
- Hypoglossal nerve (12 CN)

COMMUNICATION SKILLS
- Obtain consent.
- Ask if a chaperone is required.

Suggested approach
Introduction
C: Hello, I Dr ....I'm one of the psychiatrists. I understand your GP has asked me to see I have been asked to do a physical examination.
Is that all right with you?

Would you like a chaperone?

P: No thank you

(Use hand gel provided)
C: I will be commenting as I go along, please feel free to interrupt me if you do not understand me.

Cranial Nerves
A. Olfactory nerve (1 CN)
Can you smell this please (give piece of soap to smell)?

B. Optic nerve (2 CN)
- Visual acuity
Test each eye separately
Tell patient that you are going to check their eyesight

EXAMINATIONS

Ask them to close one eye and test distant vision using Snellen's chart at a distance of 10 feet
  • Visual fields

Sit directly opposite the patient at the same level with your right eye closed approximately one metre away. Ask the patient to cover left eye with left hand, not to move their head and to say yes when they see your finger. The finger should be equidistant from you and the patient. Bring the finger into the field of vision in a curved not a straight line. Repeat with other eye.
  • Fundoscopy

Given separately.
  • Accommodation

Ask the patient to look into the distance and then at the tip of their nose

C. Occulomotor nerve (3 CN), Trochlear (4CN), Abducent nerve (6CN)
Pupillary light reflex
Ask the patient to look into the distance and explain that you are going to shine a light into their eyes. Bring light from below and side. Observe for direct and consensual light reflex.
Repeat with other eye.
Extraocular movements
Tell the patient that you are going to check the movements of their eye muscles. Ask them to follow your finger with their eyes without moving their head and to tell you if they see double. You should again be at a distance of one metre from the patient. Make an H, pausing at the ends of each direction of gaze to observe for nystagmus.

D. Trigeminal nerve (5 CN)
Consists of 3 sensory and one motor divisions

a. Sensory
  • Light touch

Sensation is tested with cotton wisp, lightly touching (do not drag) both sides of forehead, cheek and chin. Avoid touching the angle of the jaw, which is innervated by upper cervical roots.

b. Motor
Supplies muscles of mastication. Palpate the temporalis and masseter muscles on each side. Ask the patient to clench their teeth tightly and palpate the muscles again. Ask the patient to open their mouth and then repeat against resistance from your hand under the patient's chin.
Jaw jerk
Place a finger in the midline, over patient's mandible, with patient's mouth slightly open. Tap your finger with a hammer.
Corneal reflex
Normally not checked

E. Facial nerve (7 CN)
a. Sensory
Ask the patient if they can taste their food as before

EXAMINATIONS

b. Motor Upper MN
Observe for narrowing of the palpebral fissure or loss of nasolabial fold.
Ask the patient to wrinkle their forehead. Ask the patient to close their eyes tightly and not let you open them.
Motor Lower MN
Smile or show their teeth
Ask them to blow out their cheeks.

F. Vestibulocochlear nerve (8 CN)
Hearing
Rub fingers close to the patient's ear and ask if they can hear the sound. Gradually move the fingers away and tell the patient to let you know when they can't hear the sound.
Rinne's test
Air conduction is better than bone conduction. Use tuning forks of 256 or 512 hertz frequency.

G. Glossopharyngeal nerve (9 CN) and Vagus nerve (10 CN)
Ask the patient to open their mouth and see if the uvula is central. Tell them to say "ah" and see if the fauces move.

H. Accessory nerve (11 CN)
Stand behind the patient and ask them to push their chin against your hand. Palpate sternocleidomastoid muscle while patient is doing this
Ask patient to shrug their shoulders against resistance. Check power by pushing down.

I. Hypoglossal nerve (12 CN)
Ask the patient to take out their tongue and move it from side to side.

Ask to press their tongue against the cheek and feel the muscle bulk. Repeat on the other side

Summarise
Thank you for cooperating with me and allowing me to examine you.
Comment on the positive or negative findings.

EXAMINATIONS

13. EXAMINATION OF UPPER LIMB MOTOR AND SENSORY SYSTEM

INSTRUCTIONS TO THE CANDIDATE
You have been asked to see this 34 yr. old man Jamie Brook.

TASK FOR THE CANDIDATE
- *Please do an examination of upper limb motor and sensory system.*

PAY PARTICULAR ATTENTION TO THE FOLLOWING (MENTAL CHECKLIST)
Upper and lower limb examination should include:
- *Inspection*
- *Tone*
- *Power*
- *Reflexes*
- *Sensations*
- *Vibration sense*
- *Co-ordination*

COMMUNICATION SKILLS
- *Obtain consent.*
- *Ask if a chaperone is required.*

Suggested approach
Introduction
C: Hello, I Dr ....I'm one of the psychiatrists. I understand your GP has asked me to see you. I have been asked to do a physical examination.
Is that all right with you?

Would you like a chaperone?

P: No thank you

(Use hand gel provided)

C: I will be commenting as I go along, please feel free to interrupt me if you do not understand me.
Ensure proper exposure
Explain what the examination involves

A. Inspection
Muscle bulk (wasting/hypertrophy)
Fasciculation
Abnormal movements (tremor, choreoform, tics, myoclonus)

B. Tone
Check for cogwheel and lead pipe rigidity

EXAMINATIONS

C. Power
Ask the patient to raise first the right arm and then the left one
Shoulder abduction: Ask the patient to hold arm outwards at their sides and keep them up. Explain that you will try to press down but they should not let you.
Shoulder adduction: Ask patient to push arms inwards against resistance from you.
Arm flexion: Stabilize elbow and ask patient to bend their elbow and pull you towards them. (Check both arms)
Arm extension: Ask patient to straighten flexed elbow against resistance and push you away. (Both arms)
Wrist extension: Stabilize the wrist. Ask patient to clench fist and bend wrist up and not let you stop them. (Both wrists)
Wrist flexion: Ask patient to push the other way against resistance from you.
Thumb abduction: Ask patient to hold hand with palm facing the ceiling and point thumb towards the ceiling against resistance applied by your finger.
Finger adduction: Tell patient to hold a piece of paper between their fingers and not let you take the paper out.
Finger abduction: Ask patient to spread fingers wide apart and not let you push them together.

D. Reflexes (both sides)
Supinator
Biceps

E. Sensations
Compare sensations on both sides for symmetry
Tell patient to say yes every time they feel you touch with cotton wool. Do not stroke as this tests tickle which travels in the spinothalamic tract.
Touch: outer border of arm, lateral border of forearm, thumb, middle finger, little finger and medial border of forearm.
Joint position sense
Hold the distal interphalangeal joint of one finger. Explain to the patient that you will move the finger up and down. Show them both
positions. Ask them to close their eyes and say if the finger is up or down.

F. Vibration sense
Make a fork vibrate silently. Place it on the patient's sternum and ask them if they can feel it. Now check on the distal interphalangeal joint of a finger with patients eyes closed.

G. C-ordination
Ask patient to touch your finger with their index finger and then touch their nose. Move patient's hand once to show how it's done so that it is clear. Tell them to do it quickly.

Summarise
Thank you for cooperating with me and allowing me to examine you.
Comment on the positive or negative findings.

EXAMINATIONS

14. PHYSICAL EXAMINATION IN ANOREXIA NERVOSA

INSTRUCTIONS TO THE CANDIDATE
You have been asked to see this 16yr old young lady Eva Smith who has been admitted with Anorexia Nervosa.

TASK FOR THE CANDIDATE
- Please do a physical examination in anorexia nervosa.

PAY PARTICULAR ATTENTION TO THE FOLLOWING (MENTAL CHECKLIST)
- General examination
- Examination of the hands/arm
- Examination of the face
- Cardiovascular examination
- Abdominal examination
- Neurological examination
- Medical complications

COMMUNICATION SKILLS
- Obtain consent.
- Ask if a chaperone is required.

Suggested approach
Introduction
C: Hello, I Dr ....I'm one of the psychiatrists. I understand your GP has asked me to see I have been asked to do a physical examination.
Is that all right with you?
Would you like a chaperone?

P: No thank you

(Use hand gel provided)
C: I will be commenting as I go along, please feel free to interrupt me if you do not understand me.

A. General examination
- Thin/emaciated
- Dry skin/yellow discolouration
- Weigh patient and check height. Calculate BMI
- Ask when was your last normal period?

B. Examination of hands/arm
- Brittle nails
- Calluses/laceration on knuckles (Russell's sign)
- Pallor
- Bradycardia/Low blood pressure
- Swollen joints/healed fractures

EXAMINATIONS

- *Lanugo hair (arms and chest)*
- *Look for signs of self-harm*

C. Examination of the face
- *Swollen parotid glands*
- *Dental caries*
- *Conjunctival haemorrhages from vomiting*

D. Cardiovascular examination
- *Apex beat*
- *Auscultation*
- *Sacral and pedal oedema*

E. Abdominal examination
- *Scratch marks (hyperbilirubinaemia)*
- *Liver palpation*
- *Ascites*

F. Neurological examination
- *Proximal myopathy (ask the patient to rise from squatting position)*
- *Rule out peripheral neuropathy.*

Associated medical complications
G. Medical complications –electrolyte imbalances to consider
- *Elevated growth hormone*
- *Low T3/high T4/suppressed TSH*
- *Decreased gonadotrophin hormones*
- *Bradycardia, hypotension and dehydration*
- *Normochromic normocytic anaemia, leucopoenia and thrombocytopenia*
- *Hypokalaemia and hypernatremia*
- *Low calcium, phosphate and magnesium*
- *Deranged LFT(Liver function tests)s*
- *Low foliate and vitamin B levels*

Summarise
Thank you for cooperating with me and allowing me to examine you. I am concerned about your recent weight loss and would like to arrange with your GP to have these tests done. I will arrange to see you with these results.

EXAMINATIONS

15. OPIATE WITHDRAWAL HISTORY AND PHYSICAL EXAMINATION

INSTRUCTIONS TO THE CANDIDATE
You have been asked to see this man 34 yr. old man, Colin Balliram, with a history of heroin dependence.

TASK FOR THE CANDIDATE
- *Do a physical examination in a heroin dependant person.*

PAY PARTICULAR ATTENTION TO THE FOLLOWING (MENTAL CHECKLIST)
- *Perform a general examination.*
- *Check for withdrawal signs and symptoms.*
- *Check for intravenous drug use -paranerphalia sites.*
- *Suggest further investigations and treatment.*
- *Discuss harm reduction techniques if using intravenous. substances*

COMMUNICATION SKIILLS
- *Obtain consent.*
- *Ask if a chaperone is required.*

Suggested approach
Introduction
C: Hello, I Dr ....I'm one of the psychiatrists. I understand your GP has asked me to see I have been asked to do a physical examination.
Is that all right with you?

Would you like a chaperone?

P: No thank you

(Use hand gel provided)

C: I will be commenting as I go along, please feel free to interrupt me if you do not understand me.

A. Brief history of withdrawal symptoms
1. Can you tell me what substances you are using?
2. When was it last taken?
3. Do you have any cravings?
4. Have you had any joint pains, muscle aches, twitching or headaches? (Withdrawal symptoms)
5. Have you had any abdominal cramps, nausea, vomiting and diarrhoea?
6. Have you had any hot and cold flushes?
7. Have you been sneezing?
8. How have you been sleeping? (Restless sleep)
9. Have you been feeling anxious? (Agitation or Anxiety)

EXAMINATIONS

(Opiate withdrawal symptoms peak between 36-72 hours. Symptoms run their course in 5-7 days though craving continues for some time.)

B. Physical examination
1. Check B.P., pulse, temperature and respiratory rate (all raised in withdrawal)
2. Check patient's palms and hands. (Wet sweaty palms and piloerection commonly seen.)
3. Check for intravenous drug use –paranerphalia sites
4. Comment if the patient is shaking or yawning
5. Check for lacrimation, rhinorrhoea and dilated pupils
6. CVS examination concentrating on the presence or absence of murmurs.
7. Examine for signs of liver failure

C. Tests
1. Full blood count, LFT (Liver function tests)s, U&Es
2. Hepatitis screen and HIV test after counselling the patients
3. Urine drug screen for opioids.
4. ECG and chest X-Ray. Echo if any cardiac murmurs.
5. Tests for sexually transmitted disease if patient has been promiscuous and has not been taking precautions.

D. Treatment
1. Supportive treatment
2. Clonidine to help with physical symptoms
3. Buprenorphine
4. Methadone detoxification

Summarise
Thank you Colin for allowing me to examine you. If you wish I would like to make an appointment with you to discuss the treatment options available.

EXAMINATIONS

16. RECORD A 12 LEAD ECG

INSTRUCTIONS TO THE CANDIDATE
You have been asked to see this 40 yr. old man.

TASK FOR THE CANDIDATE
- *Please record an ECG.*

PAY PARTICULAR ATTENTION TO THE FOLLOWING (MENTAL CHECKLIST)
- *Explain procedure.*
- *Clean the area aseptically.*
- *Please position the leads according to the anatomic diagram V1-V6.*
- *Get electronic printed copy of ECG.*

COMMUNICATION SKILLS
- *Obtain consent.*
- *Ask if a chaperone is required.*

Suggested approach
Introduction
Hello I'm Dr.... I'm one of the psychiatrists. I have been asked to do a tracing of the heart. I will explain the procedure more in detail with you. Is it all right with you? Would you like a chaperone?

P: Yes that is all right.

C: Explain the procedure to the patient. Patient will have to remove the shirt to expose the chest. Reassure that it will be painless and will only take a few minutes. Patient should then be helped on the couch and asked to lie with legs and arms uncrossed.
A. Clean areas of electrode placement with alcohol wipes.

B. Place pads for limb and chest electrodes.
- Limb leads are colour coded. Start with the red lead and attach it to the right wrist. Yellow is attached to the left wrist, green to the left leg and black to the right leg.

C. Position of chest leads
- V1: Fourth intercostal space at the right sternal border. (First palpable intercostal space, below the clavicle is the 2nd intercostal space.
- V2: Fourth intercostal space at the left sternal border
- V3: Midway between V2 and V4
- V4: Fifth intercostal space in the midclavicular line
- V5: Anterior axillary line at the same horizontal level as V4
- V6: Mid-axillary line at the same horizontal plane as V4 and V5.

EXAMINATIONS

Switch on the machine, if it has a filter button press it to erase previously recorded ECG. Record ECG.

Summarise
Thank you for cooperating with me and allowing me to examine you.
Interpret the ECG.

EXAMINATIONS

17. EXAMINATION OF HOW TO INTERPRET ECG

INSTRUCTIONS TO THE CANDIDATE
You have been asked to see the psychiatric consultant.

TASK FOR THE CANDIDATE
- *Please explain your interpretation of the ECG.*

PAY PARTICULAR ATTENTION TO THE FOLLOWING (MENTAL CHECKLIST)
- *Interpret the axis of the leads.*
- *Interpret whether normal sinus rhythm.*
- *Interpret the values of the ECG.*
- *Calculate the rate.*

COMMUNICATION SKILLS
- *Obtain consent.*
- *Ask if a chaperone is required.*

Suggested approach
Introduction
C: Hello, I Dr ....I'm one of the psychiatrists on call.

A. Background to ECG
ECG machines pick up electrical activity through 4 limb electrodes and 6 chest electrodes and convert it into 6 limb leads (I, II, III, aVR, aVL and aVF) and 6 chest leads (V1-V6)
- Leads I and aVL look at the left side of the heart.
- Leads II, III and aVF look at the inferior surface of the heart.
- A VR is always negative as it looks at the heart from the position of the right shoulder and electrical current moves away from it. The negative waves confirm that the electrodes have been connected correctly.

The 6 chest leads look at the heart in the horizontal plane, from the front and around.
- V1 and V2 give information about the right heart.
- V3 and V4 about the interventricular septum.
- V5 and V6 give information about the left side of the heart.

B. Interpretation of the waves

- P wave: represent atrial systole.
- QRS complex: ventricular systole.
- T wave: ventricular relaxation or diastole.
- Atrial systole gets buried in the ventricular systole and therefore does not produce a wave form.

EXAMINATIONS

- *Q waves: When heart muscles are damaged the electrical current does not pass through them and instead of upright R waves, downwards Q waves are produced.*

C. Intervals
When ECG is recorded the paper speed is 25 millimetres/second so in 1 second ECG tracing covers 5 large squares or 1 large square is equal to 0.2 seconds and one small square is equal to 0.04 seconds.

- *PR interval is measured from the start of the P wave to the beginning of the QRS complex. The normal PR interval is 0.12 to 0.2 seconds or 3-5 small squares.*
- *Duration of QRS complex is normally 0.12 seconds or 3 small squares.*
- *QT interval is the time between the onset of depolarization to repolarization. It is affected by diet, gender, alcohol, time of the day, menstrual cycle and heart rate. QTc is the QT interval which has been corrected for the heart rate.*
- *QTc = QT msec/square root of RR.*

It can be challenging to calculate QTc with the above formula. An easier way is to calculate the RR interval (number of large squares) and if QT interval is longer than 50% of the RR interval (again check the number of large squares between beginning of Q and end of T) it is an indication that it is prolonged. You can then take out your calculator and do it properly.
*Potential consequences of QT prolongation include torsade de pointes (syncope), ventricular fibrillation and sudden death. **If QTc prolongation is associated with T wave changes refer to the cardiologist.***

D. Calculation of heart rate
Hear rate can be easily determined by counting the number of large squares between 2 consecutive QRS complexes (R-R interval). Normally the heart rate is between 60 and 100/min.

- *1 large square: rate is 300/m*
- *2 large squares: rate is 150*
- *3 large squares: rate is 100*
- *4 large squares: rate is 75*
- *5 large squares: rate is 60 (1 QRS per second)*
- *6 large squares: rate is 50*

Patient is said to be bradycardic if under 60 and tachycardic if heart rate is more than 100.

E. How to determine axis
Axis can be checked by looking at the direction of wave forms in leads I, II and III. A normal (11'o clock to 5 o' clock axis means that current is flowing towards leads I, II and III and results in upward deflections in all 3.

- *In right axis deviation the deflections in I will become negative with positive waves in II and III.*
- *In left axis deviation waves are negative in II and III.*
  If deflections are negative in all 3 it is extreme left axis deviation.

Summarise
Thank you

18. EXAMINATION OF HOW TO INTERPRET ECG

INSTRUCTIONS TO THE CANDIDATE
You have been asked to see this on call consultant to discuss the findings
of the abnormal ECG

TASK FOR THE CANDIDATE
- Explain your findings of ECG to the consultant

PAY PARTICULAR ATTENTION TO THE FOLLOWING (MENTAL CHECKLIST)
- Explain the findings of the ECG rhythm strip.
- Explain rhythm abnormalities.
- Comment on myocardial infarction and Acute coronary syndrome.
- Explain hyperkalemia.

COMMUNICATION SKILLS
- Obtain consent.
- Ask if a chaperone is required.

Suggested approach
Introduction
C: Hello, I Dr ....I'm one of the psychiatrists on call. I would like to discuss this ECG with you.

Explain findings from the rhythm strip
1. Is electrical activity present? (Does the tracing have any wave forms?)
2. What is the heart rate?
3. Is atrial activity present? (Are p waves present?)
4. Is the ventricular rhythm regular or irregular? (QRS complexes equally spaced or not)
5. Is QRS complex width normal or prolonged? (3 small squares or more)
6. How is atrial activity related to ventricular activity? (Every p wave should be followed by a QRS complex)

A. Important rhythm abnormalities Atrial flutter (I.H.D/Digitalis toxicity): Saw tooth appearance of p waves. It is due to re-entry within the atria. As compared to atrial fibrillation is relatively regular. Often presents with 2:1 or 4:1 AV blocks.
- Atrial fibrillation: A chaotic rhythm, which originates from multiple sites in atria. Only some impulses get through to the ventricles. Atria contract rapidly and ventricular response is generally variable so every p wave will not be followed by QRS complex.
- Ventricular tachycardia: H.R > 100, QRS complexes wide (> 3 small squares). P waves may or may not be present.

- *Ventricular fibrillation: Irregularly irregular heart rate. No p waves. Wide QRS complexes. Medical emergency treated with cardioversion.*

B. Myocardial infarction and Acute coronary syndrome
- *Acute MI is characterised by ST elevation of 2 mm (2 small squares) in the chest leads or 1 small square in the limb leads.*
- *T wave inversion denotes ischaemic changes (acute and chronic).*
- *ST Depression signifies acute coronary syndrome or unstable angina.*
- *Elevation/Depression in a single lead is insignificant.*

C. Hyperkalaemia
- *Tall T waves or tenting of T waves.*
- *If associated with QRS prolongation it can lead to life threatening ventricular arrhythmias.*

Summarise
Thank you.

19. MANAGEMENT OF NEUROLEPTIC MALIGNANT SYNDROME

INSTRUCTIONS TO THE CANDIDATE
A 25 yr. old male, David Williams, have suffered a NMS reaction.

TASK FOR THE CANDIDATE
Speak to the ward manager and explain NMS-Neuroleptic Malignant Syndrome.

PAY PARTICULAR ATTENTION TO THE FOLLOWING (MENTAL CHECK LIST)
- *Explain Diagnosis.*
- *Explain investigations.*
- *Explain emergency management.*
- *Explain management in terms of medical management.*
- *Explain future risks.*

COMMUNICATION SKILLS
- *Obtain consent.*
- *Ask if a chaperone is required.*

Suggested approach
Introduction
C: Hello, I Dr ....I'm one of the psychiatrists. I understand that your son suffered this reaction NMS. I have come to tell you more about this.

WM: What is NMS-Neuroleptic Malignant syndrome?

C: It is a rare, but potentially life threatening condition. It is known as an idiosyncratic reaction and occurs in a minority of the cases treated with antipsychotics.

WM: What are the causes of NMS?

C: It can develop at any time but usually occurs on initiation or increase in the dose of antipsychotics. The causes are thought to be the inhibition of central dopamine receptors in hypothalamus (part of the brain which regulates temperature) which results in increase heat generation and decreased loss. We do know that there are certain people who are more susceptible to get NMS. It is more common in patients with dehydration, organic brain pathology and in young males.

WM: How common is it?

C: as I have mentioned before it is a very rare condition and it occurs in 2in100 of the population.

WM: What is the mortality rate?

EXAMINATIONS

C: The mortality rate varies between 5-20% but if picked up early and managed appropriately it has a good prognosis.

WM: what are the signs and symptoms of NMS?

C: Muscle rigidity, increased salivation, dyskinesia (difficulty in performing vol. movements), orbiculogyric crisis (uncontrollable upward movement of eyes) and dysphagia.
Hyperthermia (can be as high as 108 degree F but rarely goes this high), fluctuating blood pressure, increased heart rate, rapid breathing and confusion.

Explain management of NMS
1. Medical investigations-Blood/urine tests
- Metabolic acidosis
- Increased CPK
- Increased transaminases
- Increased WBC count
- Hyponatremia, hyperkalaemia and hypocalcaemia
- Myoglobinuria

2. Treatment and management
- Stop the offending drug
- Monitors vitals
- Serial CPK to note the trend
- Cooling blankets
- Medical opinion and transfer to ICU
- Oral bromocriptine/sub cutaneous apomorphine or dantrolene for muscular rigidity
- I/V hydration and correction of electrolyte abnormalities
- DIC prophylaxis/intubation and artificial ventilation if required
- Sedation with benzodiazepines

To note
3. Restarting antipsychotics
- Do not give antipsychotics for 2 weeks · Use different antipsychotic, preferably atypical. Best not to use depots.
- Start with a low dose and gradually increase
- Benzodiazepines for agitation and ECT can be used to treat Psychosis

4. Complications
- Rhabdomyolysis
- Renal failure
- Respiratory failure/PE

EXAMINATIONS

20. MANAGEMENT OF SEROTONERGIC SYNDROME

> **INSTRUCTIONS TO THE CANDIDATE**
> You have been asked to review the medication for a 29 yr. old lady who
> has been on an SSRI and started on Lithium. She is now experiencing
> tachycardia and sweating.
>
> ---
>
> **TASK FOR THE CANDIDATE**
> * Please explain the management of serotonergic syndrome to the
>   nurse on the ward.
>
> **PAY PARTICULAR ATTENTION TO THE FOLLOWING (MENTAL
> CHECKLIST)**
> * Explain symptoms and signs of Serotonergic syndrome.
> * Explain how the diagnosis is made.
> * Explain the immediate management.
>
> **COMMUNICATION SKILLS**
> * Obtain consent.
> * Ask if a chaperone is required.

Suggested approach
Introduction
C: Hello, I Dr ….I'm one of the psychiatrists. I understand this lady has now
had an addition of lithium to her antidepressant medication. From the history
you have given me, it appears that she has suffered a reaction to the lithium.
A. Sign and symptoms of serotonergic syndrome
* Restlessness, confusion, agitation and lethargy.

* Hyperthermia, tachycardia, sweating, abdominal pain, nausea,
  vomiting, diarrhoea and dilated pupils.

* Myoclonus and hyperreflexia (symmetrical and commonly in lower
  limbs), hypertonia, tremor and ataxia.

B. Diagnosis
It is caused by excess of serotonin in the central nervous system. It occurs
soon after starting or changing the dose of certain drugs. Most cases are
self-limiting. It can be serious if two or more serotonergic drugs are used.

B. Treatment and management of serotonergic syndrome
* Stop the medicine.
* Monitoring of vital signs.
* Benzodiazepines for rigidity and seizures.
* Rapid cooling.
* Involve medics.
* Transfer to ICU.

EXAMINATIONS

- *Serotonin agonist: Cypraheptadine. Other drugs like propranolol and methysergide can also be used.*

Summarise
Thank you for cooperating with me and allowing me to examine you.
Comment on the positive or negative findings.

Drugs that causes serotonergic syndrome
Drugs that have been implicated include SSRIs (fluoxetine has the longest half-life), MAOIs, TCAs, Lithium, Buspirone, St. John's wort, Tramadol, Selegiline, Pethidine and OD of amphetamines, cocaine, ecstasy, LSD.
Differential diagnosis: NMS, dystonia, encephalitis and thyroid storm.
Diagnosis is made on clinical grounds. On investigations WBC count can be mildly increased and a rise in CPK may occur because of rhabdomyolisis. Complications include Rhabdomyolysis, DIC, adult respiratory distress syndrome, coma and death.

EXAMINATIONS

21 PARIETAL LOBE TESTS

Parietal Lobe Tests to include the following

Test for dominant lesion
Finger Agnosia
Astereoagnosia-inability to recognise objects by palpation-e.g. coins in hand
Dysgraphaethesia –inability to recognise letters or numbers written on the hand

Test for non-dominant lesion
Constructional dyspraxia- inability or draw shapes or construct patterns
Asomatognosia- inability to recognise parts of the body

Test for visual fields

Speech
Alexia
Receptive Dysphasia
Conduction Asphasia-person can't repeat what is said to them

Other tests of reading and writing
Also ask if how they would brush teeth, comb hair etc

EXAMINATIONS

22 TEMPORAL LOBE TESTS

Temporal Lobe Tests to include the following :

Language function
Repetition-word and sentence repetition

Memory
Semantic memory
Aspects of objects
Recall and knowledge of famous people e.g. Marilyn Monroe
Recall and knowledge of famous landmarks e.g. Eiffel Tower

Temporal lobe personality
Pedantic-teacher like speech
Egocentric
Perseveration –Stickiness
Pay attention to trivial detail

Auditory functions
Ability to recognise melodies

Visual function
Name 10 objects
Prosopagnosia- inability to recognise familiar faces

Visual fields
Colour recognition
Test of visual fields

©smartsesh

INDEX

INDEX

INDEX

INDEX

INDEX

INDEX

INDEX

INDEX

INDEX